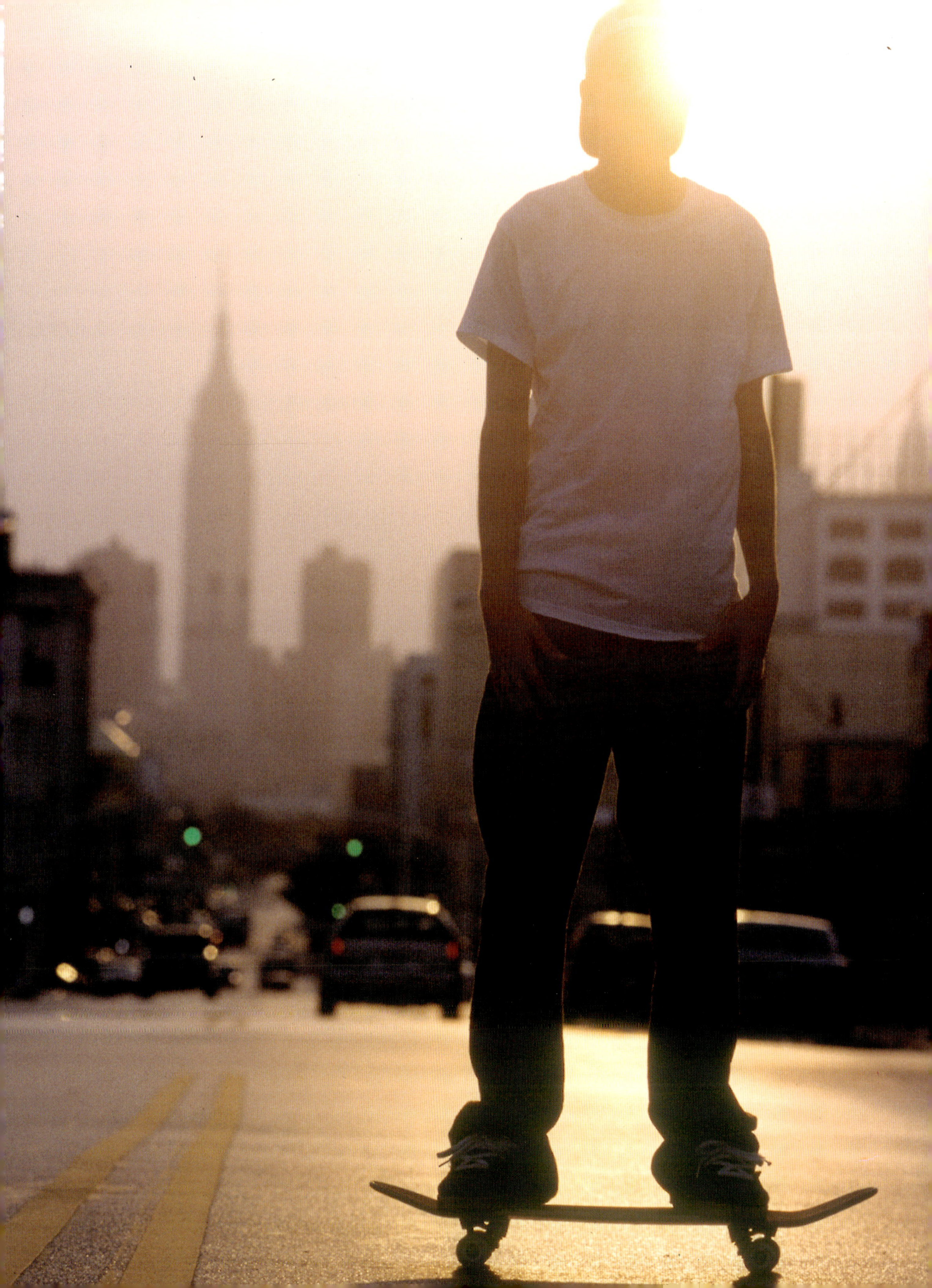

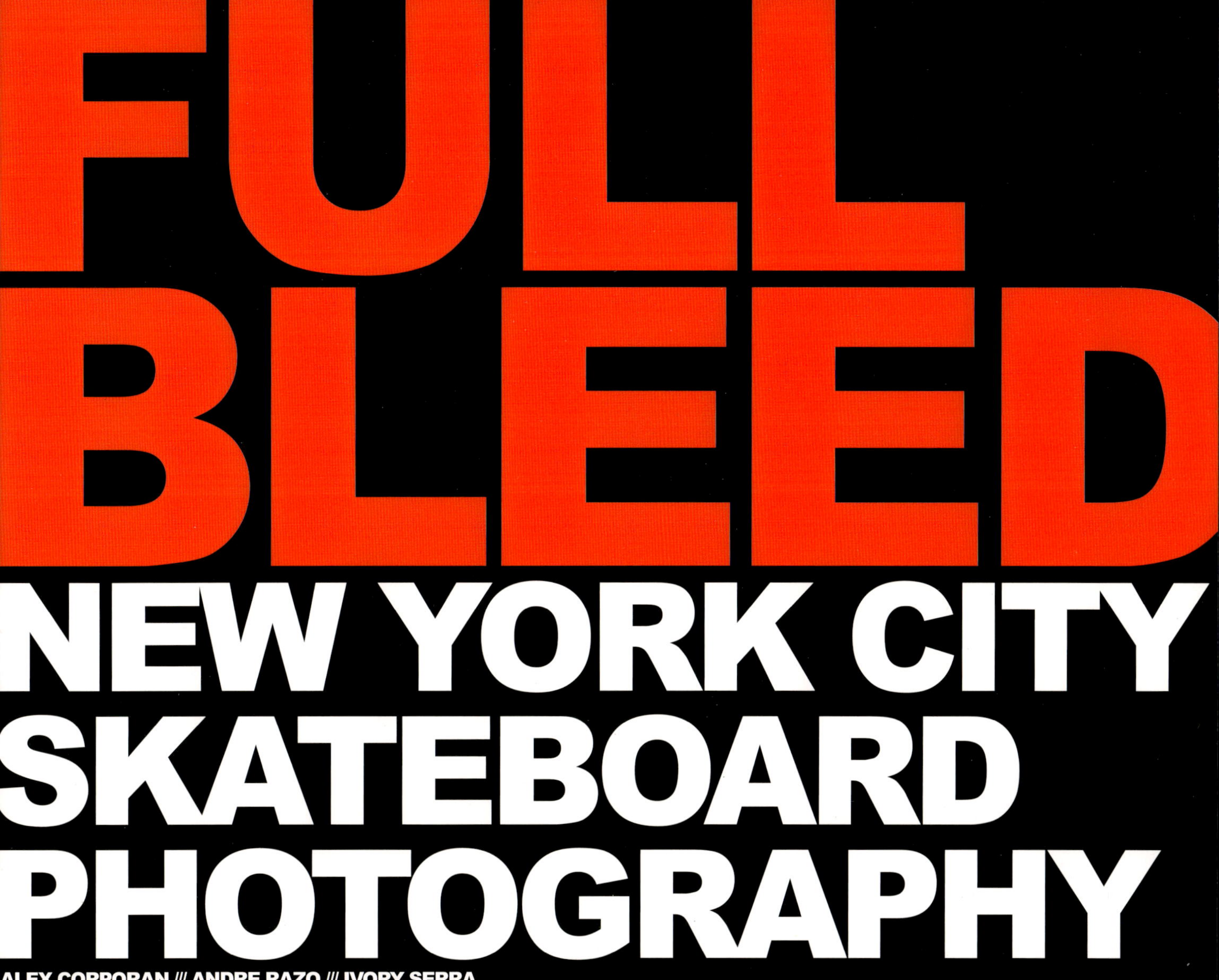
FULL
BLEED
NEW YORK CITY
SKATEBOARD
PHOTOGRAPHY
ALEX CORPORAN /// ANDRE RAZO /// IVORY SERRA

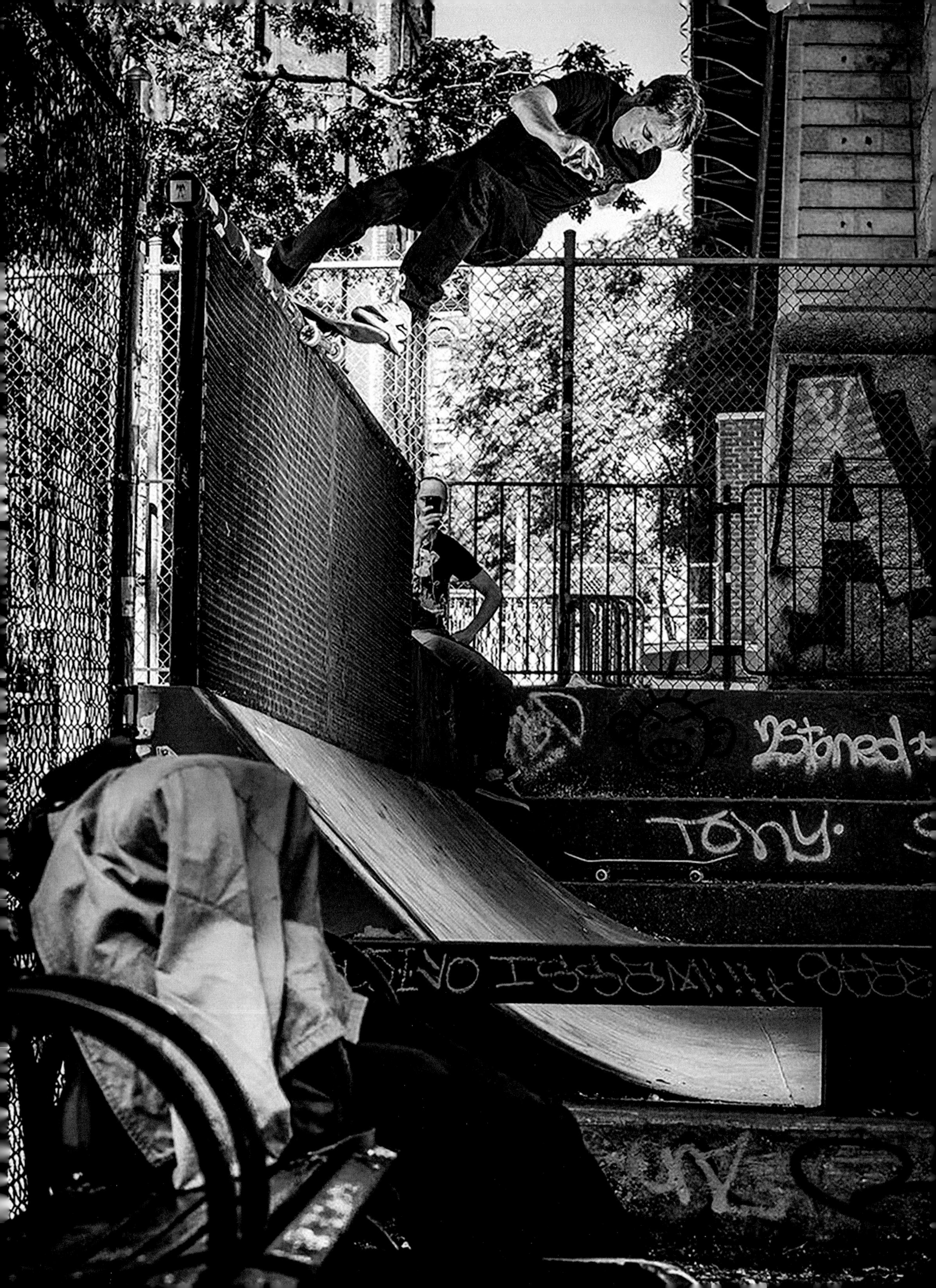
Stoned
Tony.

Skating in NYC has always been a challenge. The city is not welcoming to a crew that just wants to grind a ledge, session a handrail, or just skate as transportation. Cars, pedestrians, shop owners and police are constant barriers for skaters, among other dangers that can lurk in the shadows. That's why it was nearly impossible to grow up skating in and around the city, especially in the early days. I have great respect for those that endured, and I believe street skating in general emerged much faster because of those that did. And thanks to the diversity of the five boroughs, street culture emerged with it.

My first visit to NYC was during a Bones Brigade Tour in 1987. We parked our beat up tour van in the Lower East Side and made our way to CBGB to buy some shirts. It was frightening, especially to a kid like me who grew up in suburban San Diego where surfing and skating thrived. It was obvious that natives were assessing us as we made our way through the streets, and when we returned to the van we got a stern warning from some nearby NYPD that we were lucky it was still there at all. Through that culture shock, I got a sense that there was a burgeoning scene underneath the scary exterior; of skating, of music, of fashion, and of art, and I wished I could participate in some way. But I didn't come from there and I didn't understand the scene in a meaningful way.

These days I love visiting NYC, especially the LES area. The city is vibrant and gritty, and it celebrates skateboarding. It is immersed in the city: billboards highlight skate imagery, the skate shops are among the busiest retail outlets, and there are finally skateparks in the area!

This book is dedicated to those that kept skating alive through the hard times. It is a testament to the perseverance and talents of a rare breed, the ones that kept at it against all odds and paved the way for generations to come.

Tony Hawk

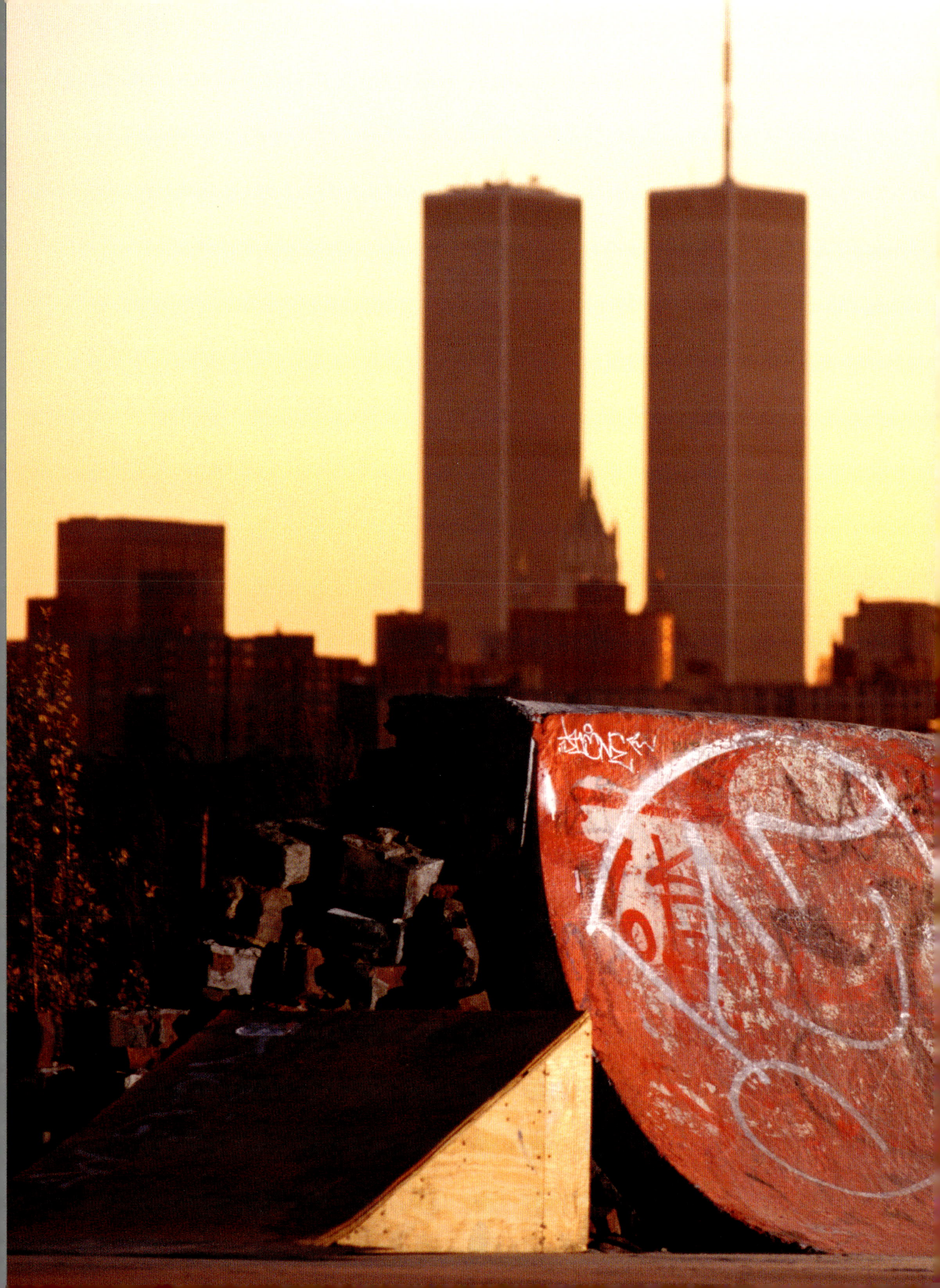

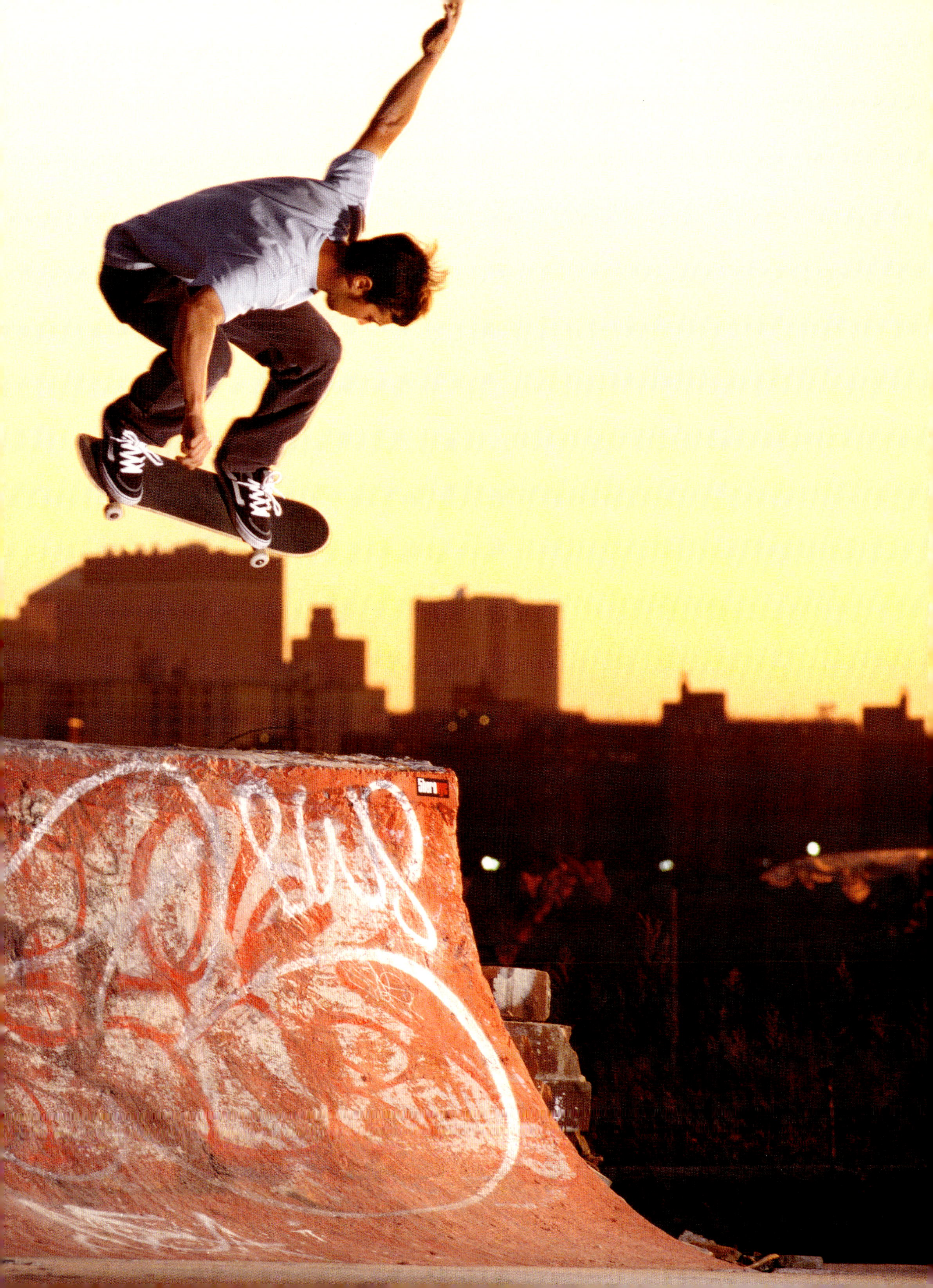

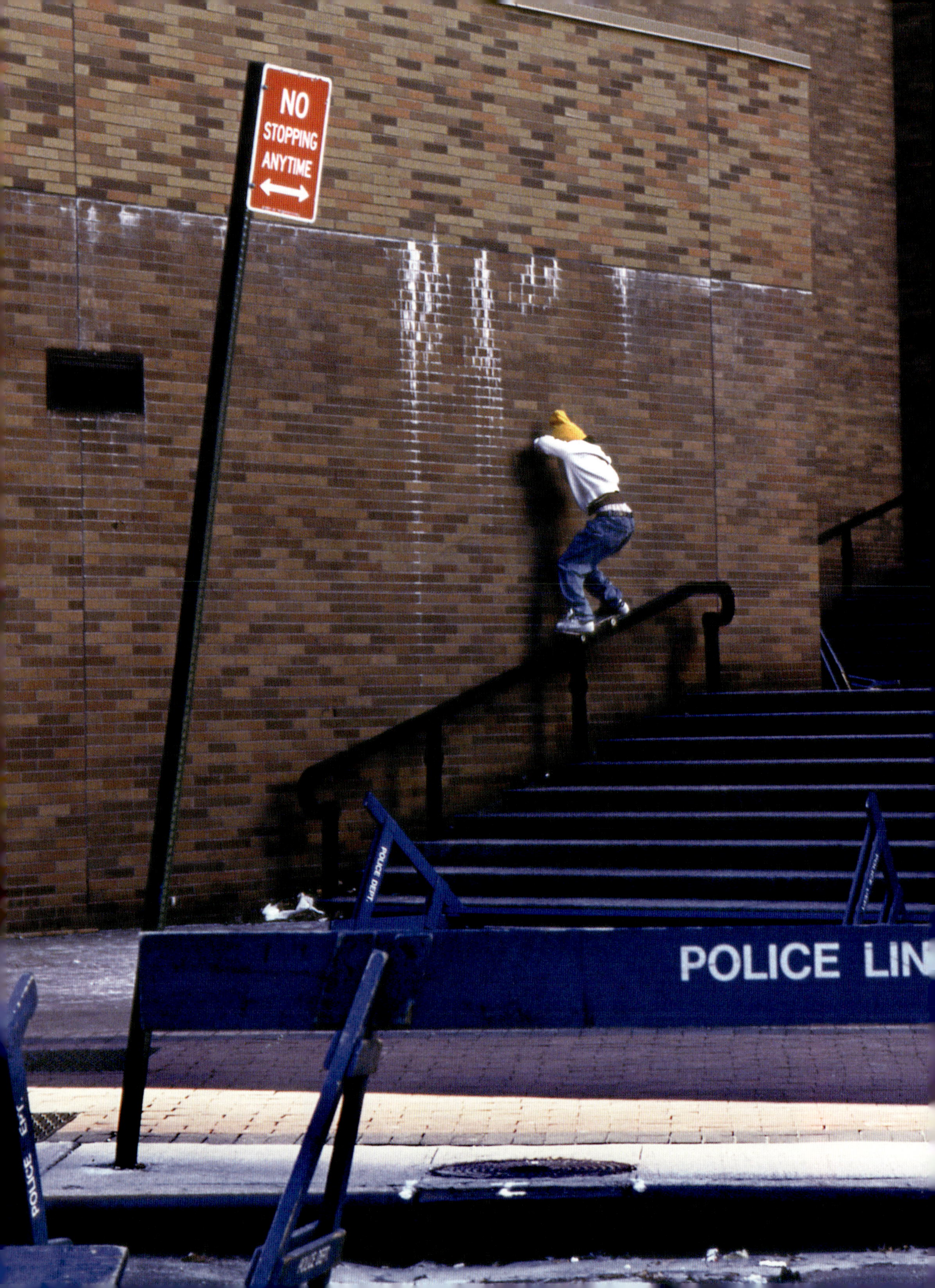
NO
STOPPING
ANYTIME
POLICE LIN

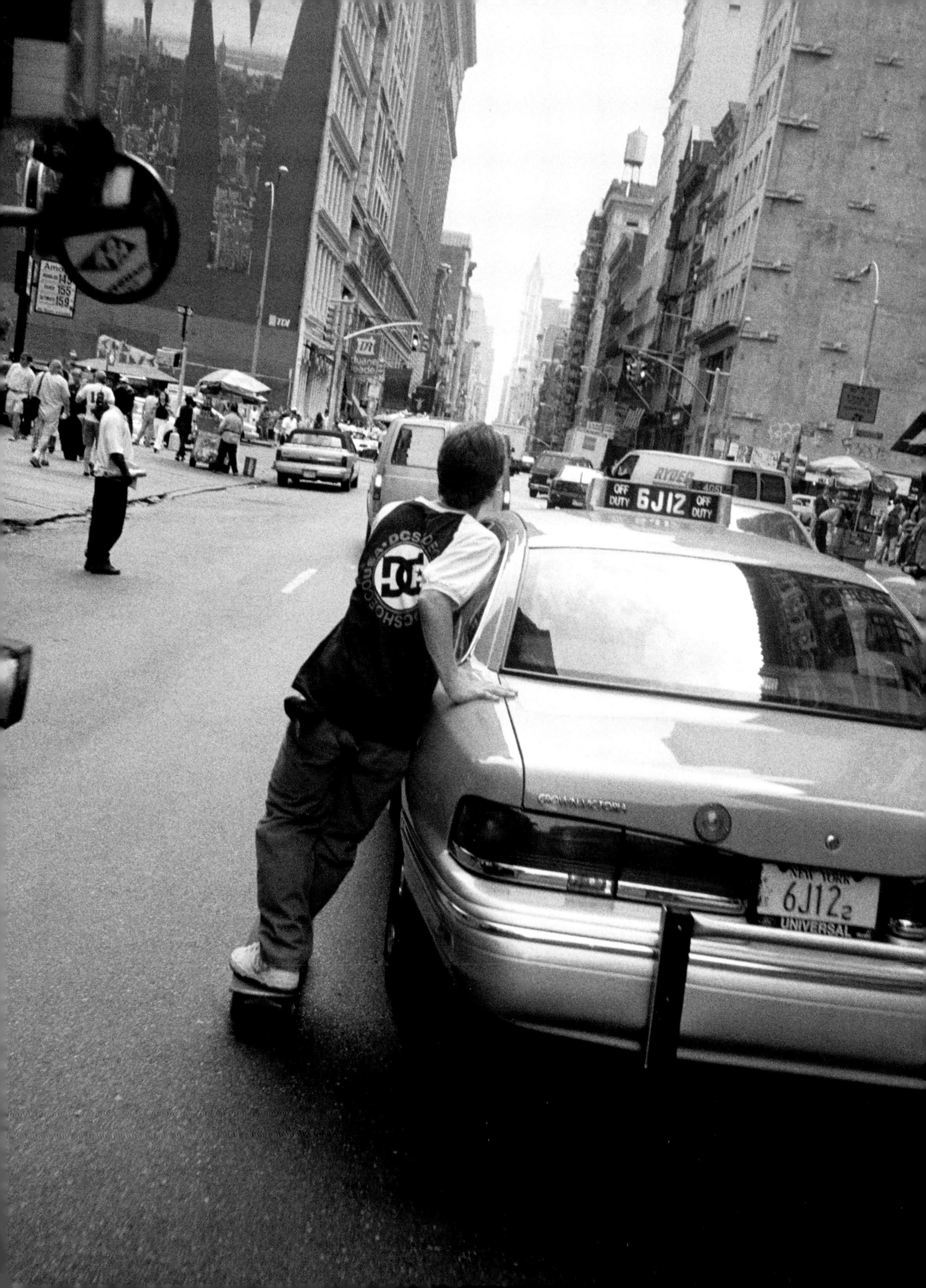
OFF DUTY
6J12
OFF DUTY
RYDER
NEW YORK
6J12
UNIVERSAL

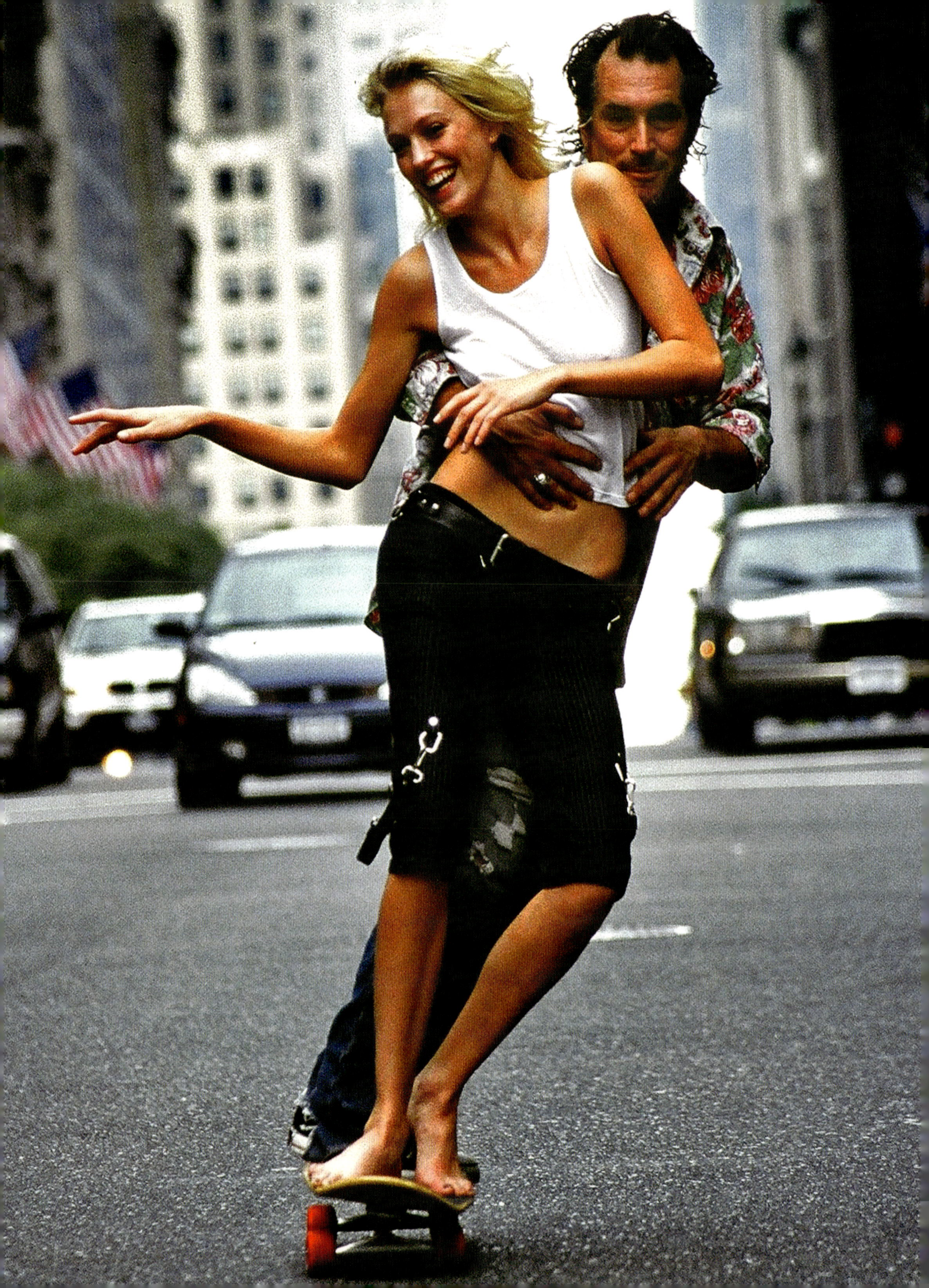

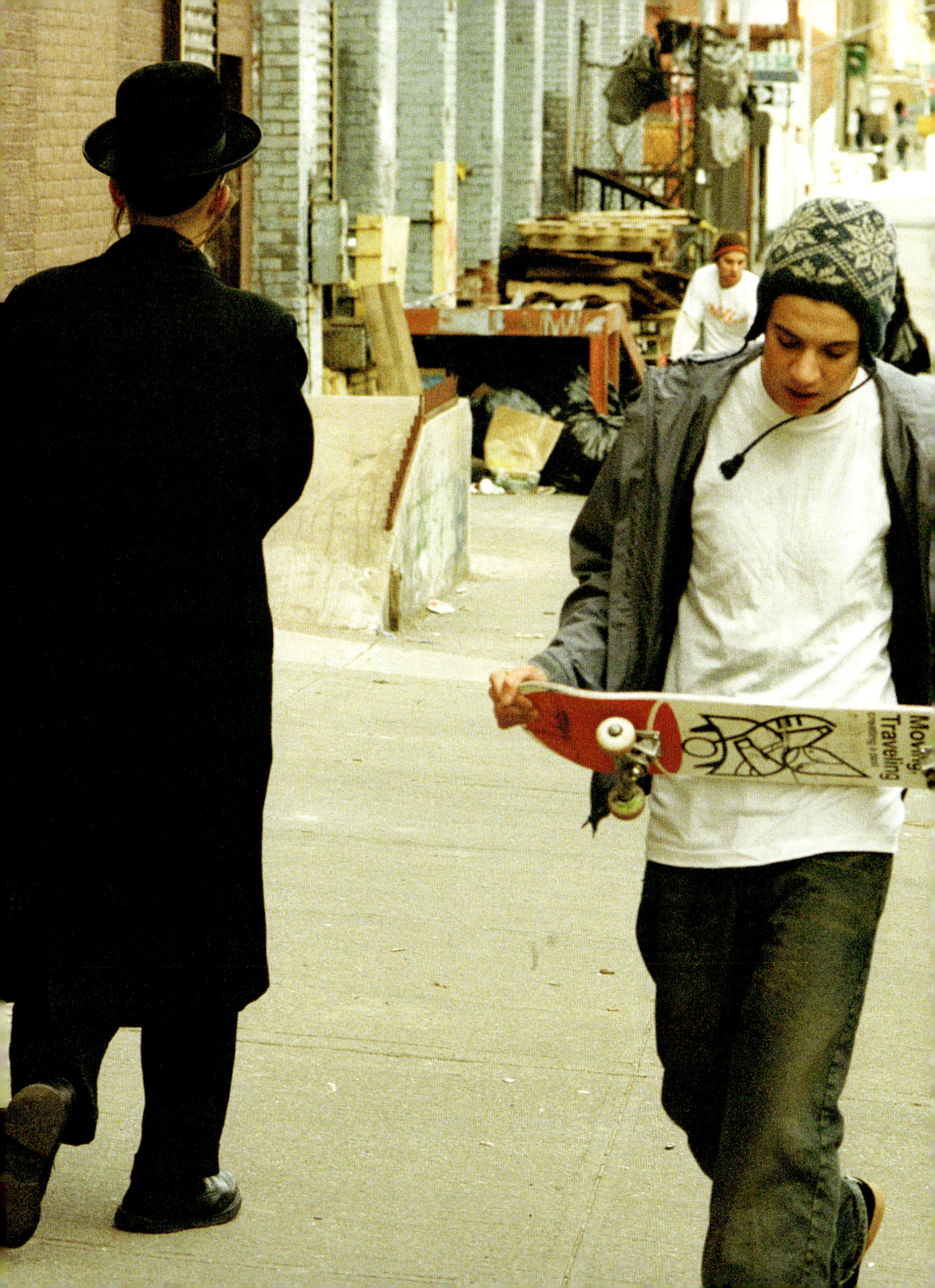
Moving
Traveling

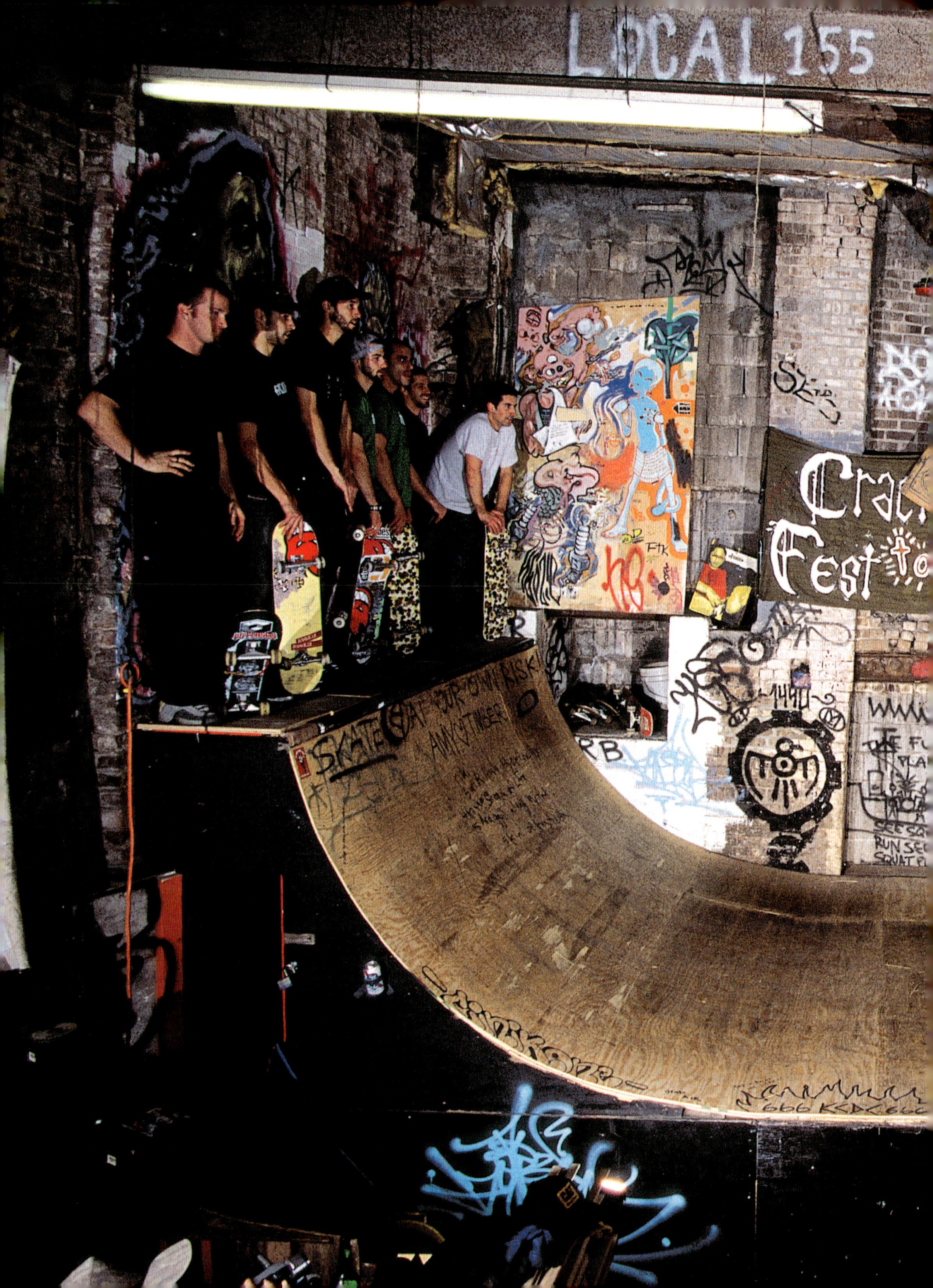
LOCAL 155
SKATE
Fest

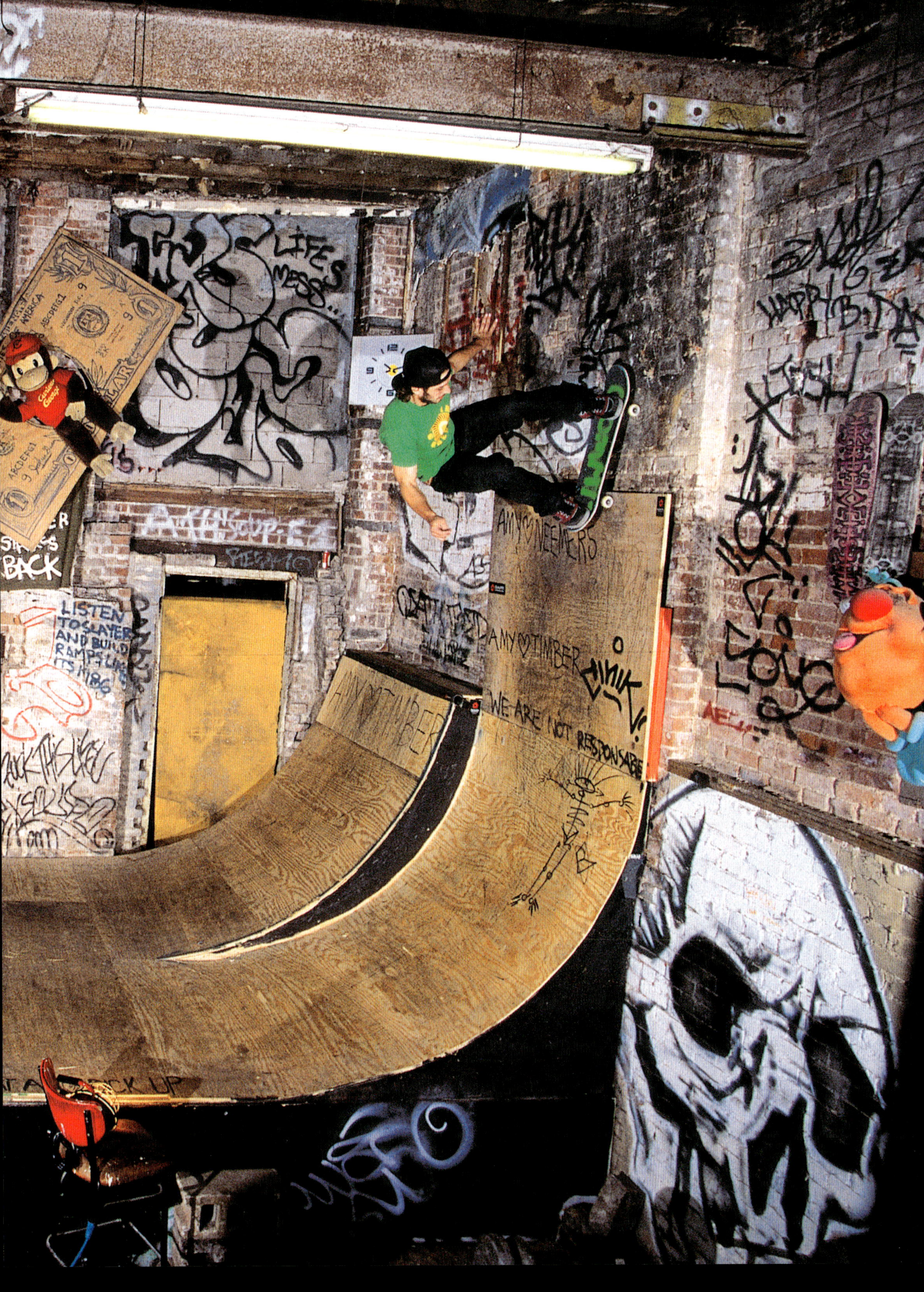
LIFES MESS...
LISTEN TO SLAYER AND BUILD RAMPS LIKE ITS 1986
AMY ♡ TIMBER
WE ARE NOT RESPONSABLE
BACK

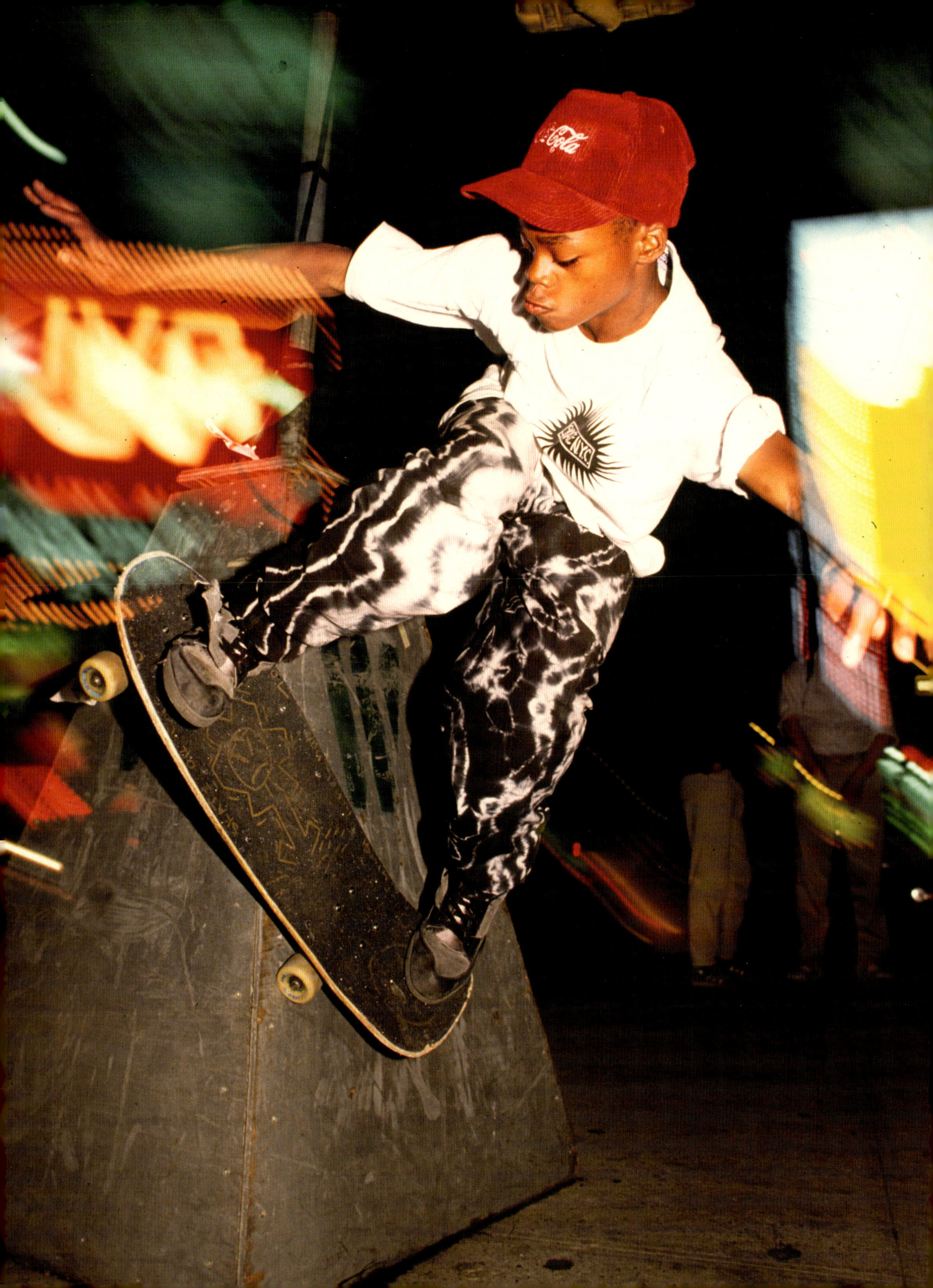

Cola
N.Y.C.

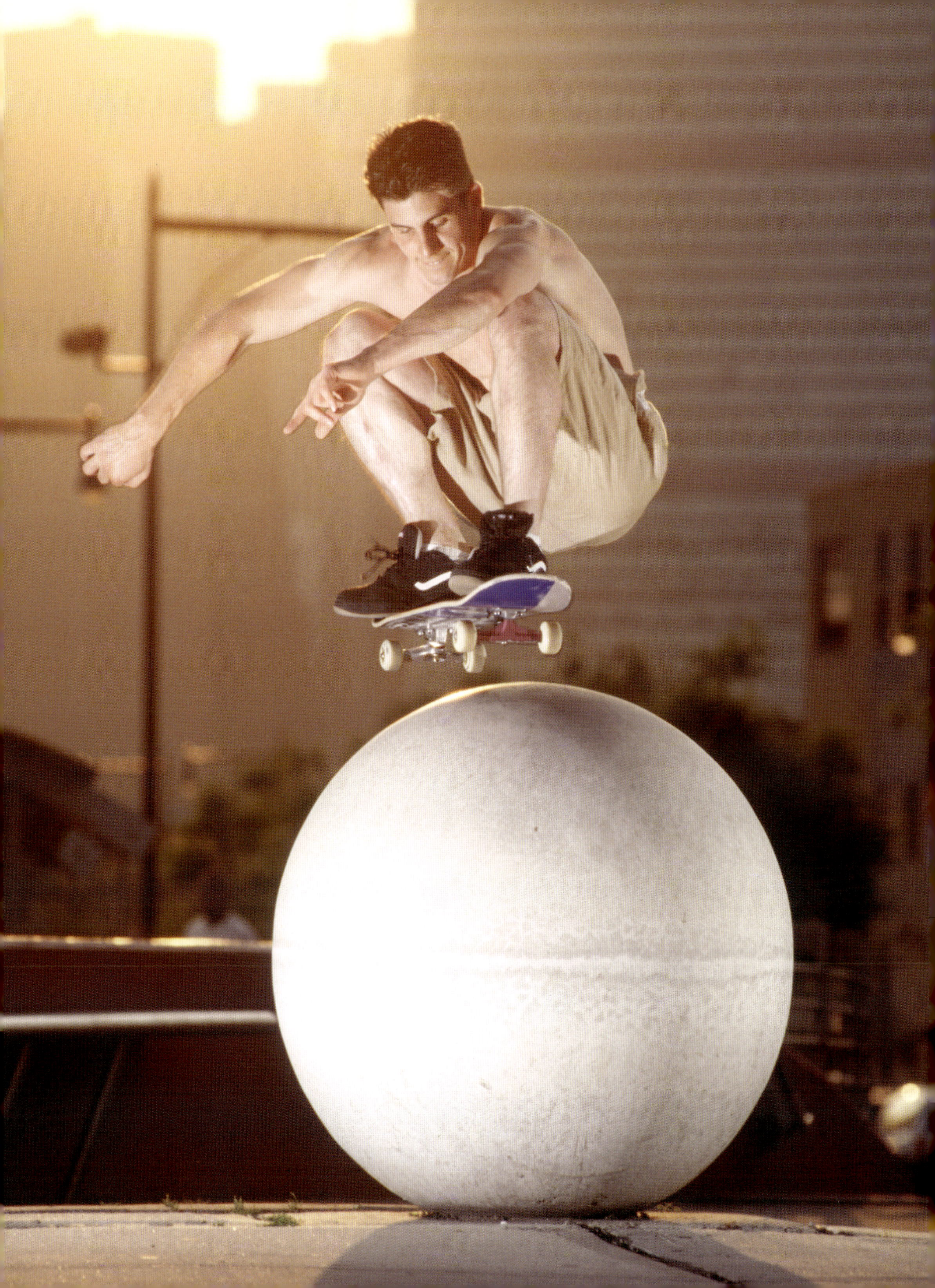

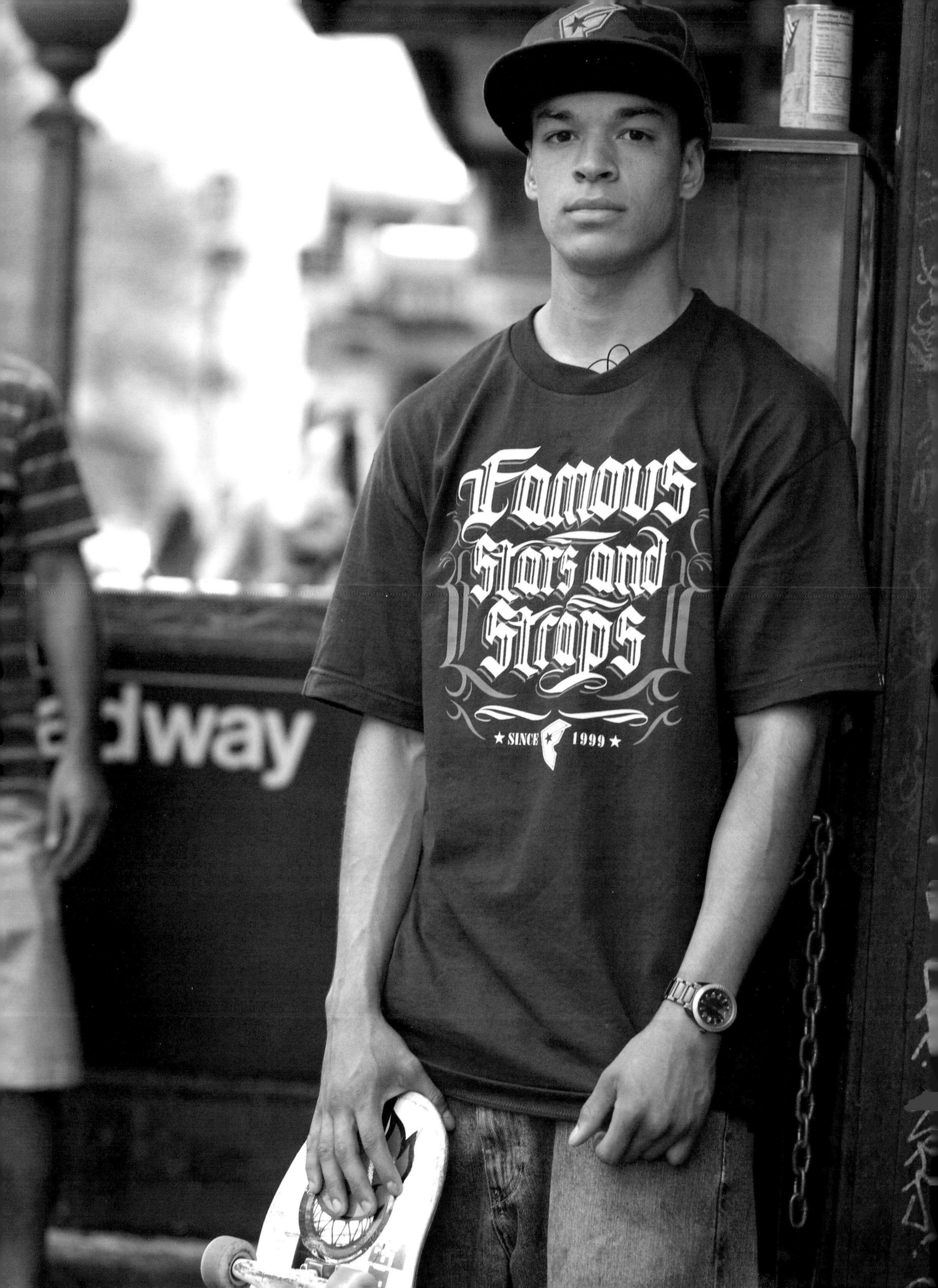
dway
Famous
Stars and
Straps
★ SINCE 1999 ★

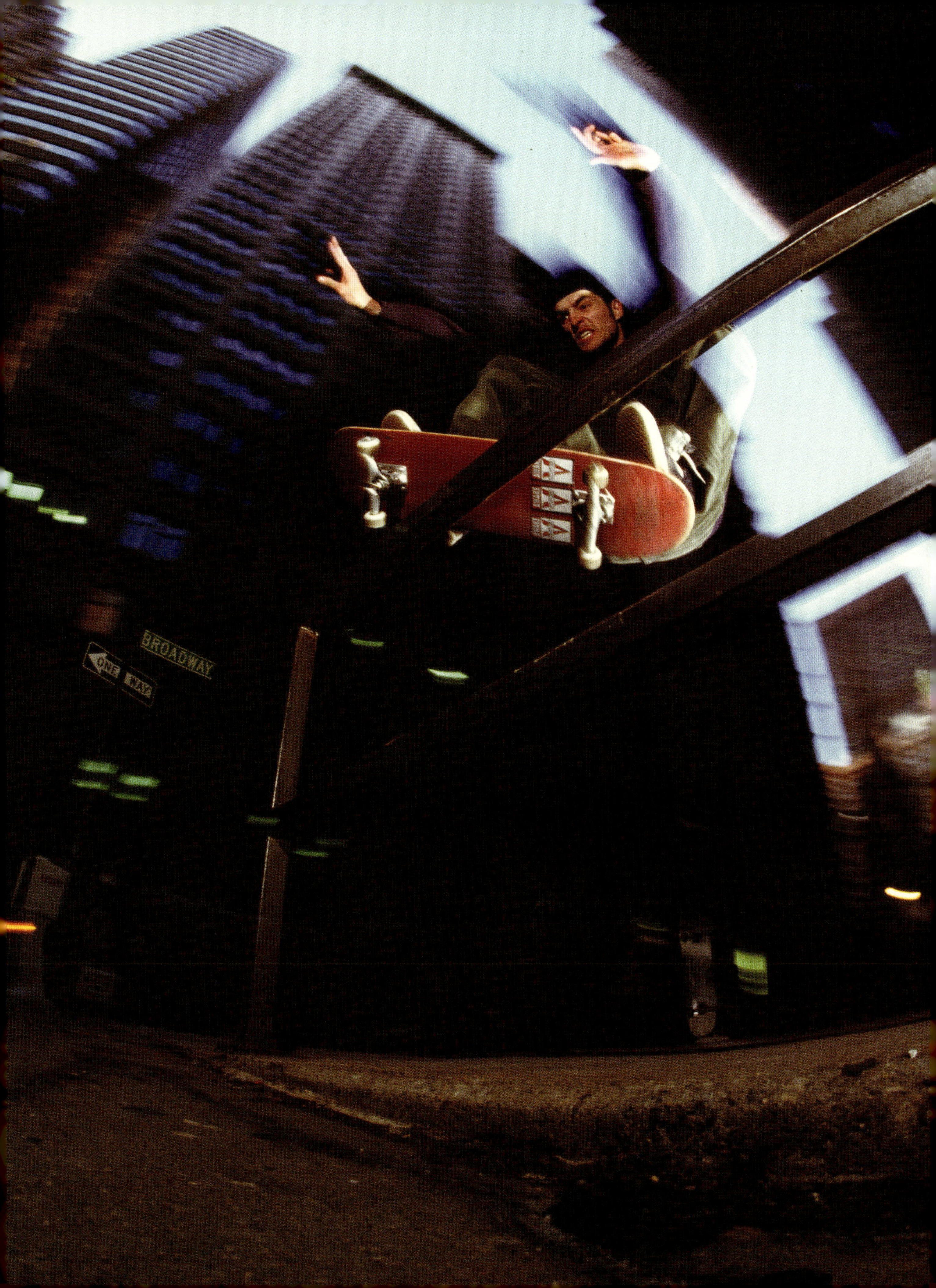
BROADWAY
ONE WAY

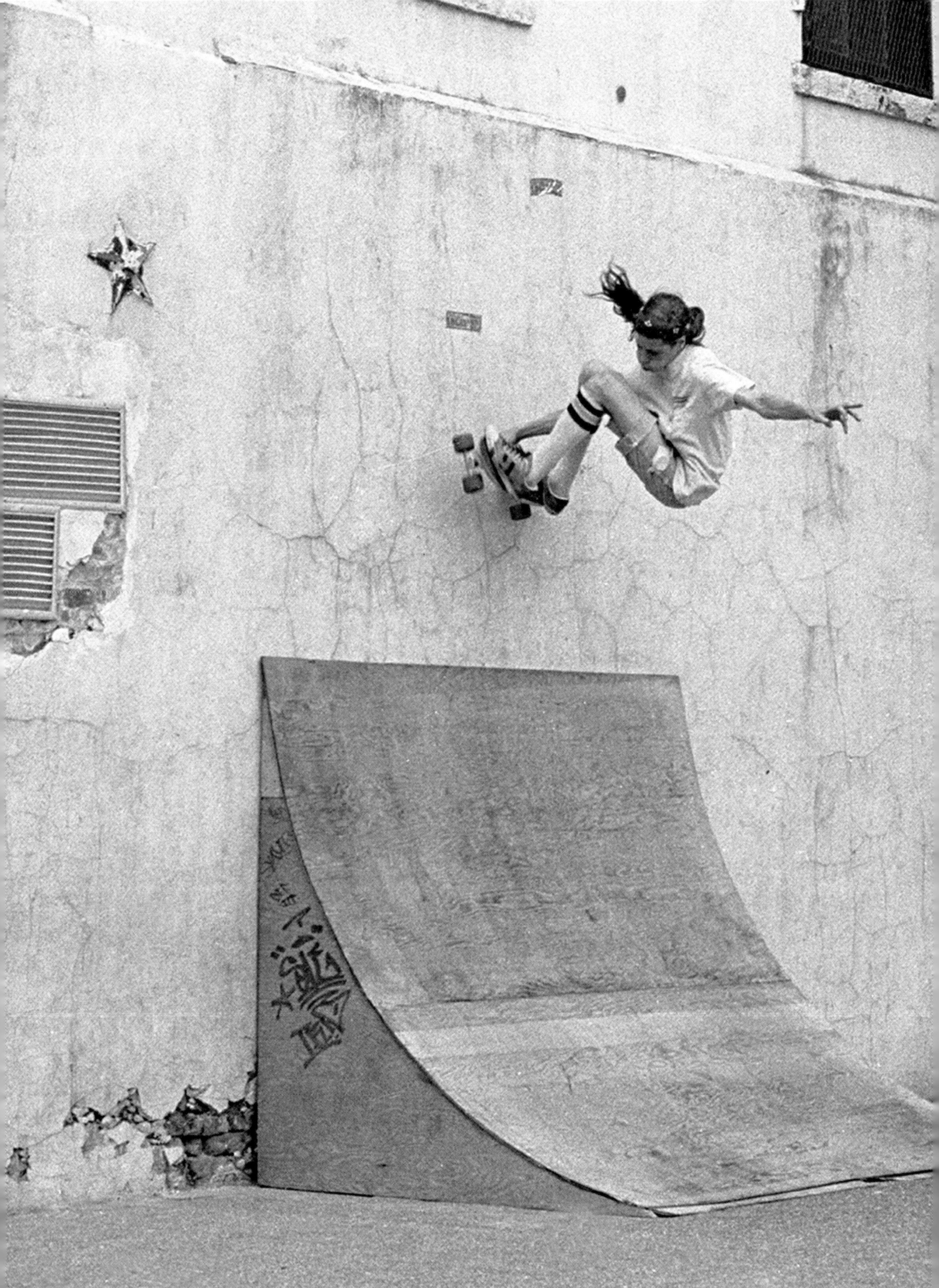

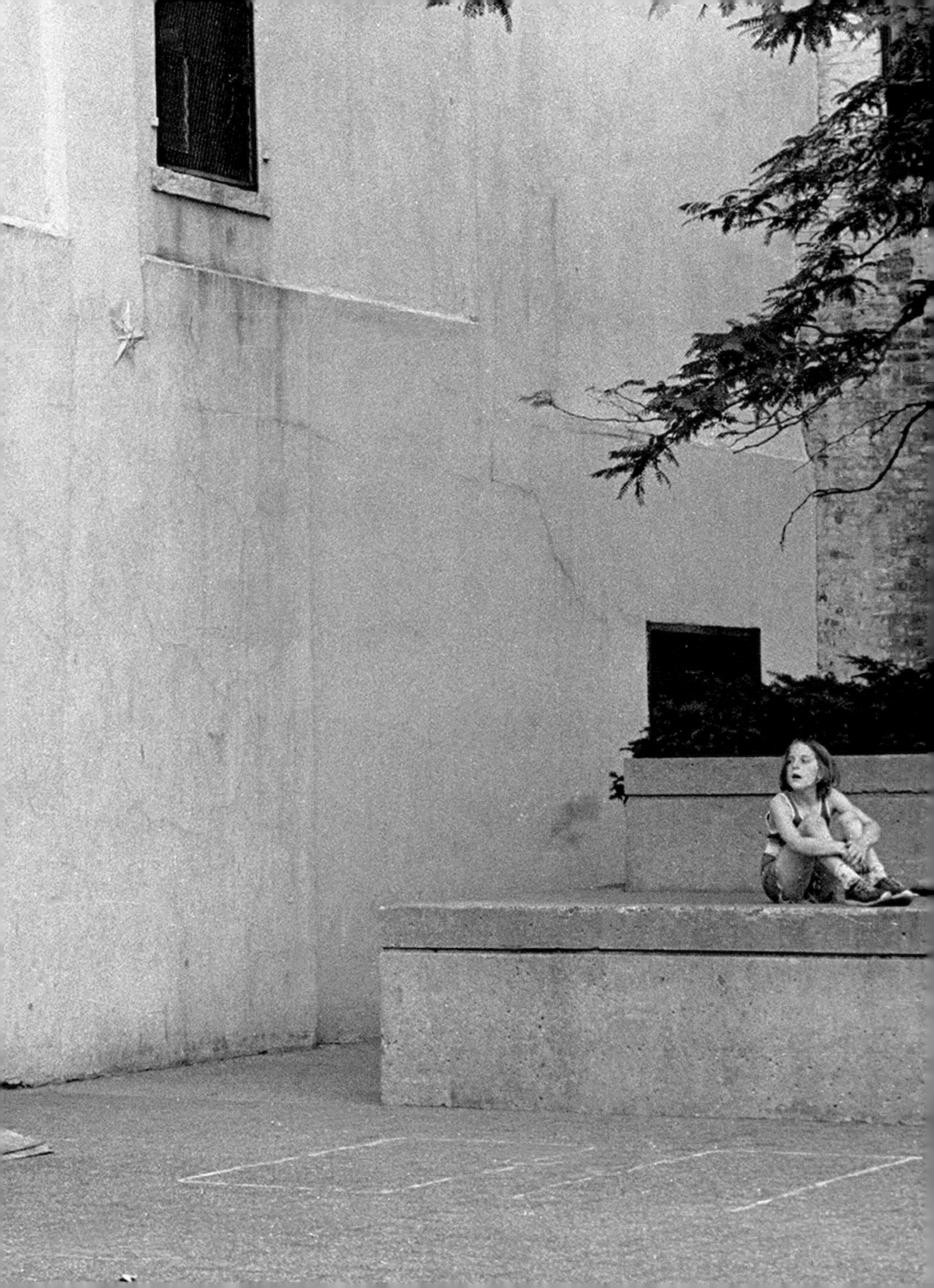

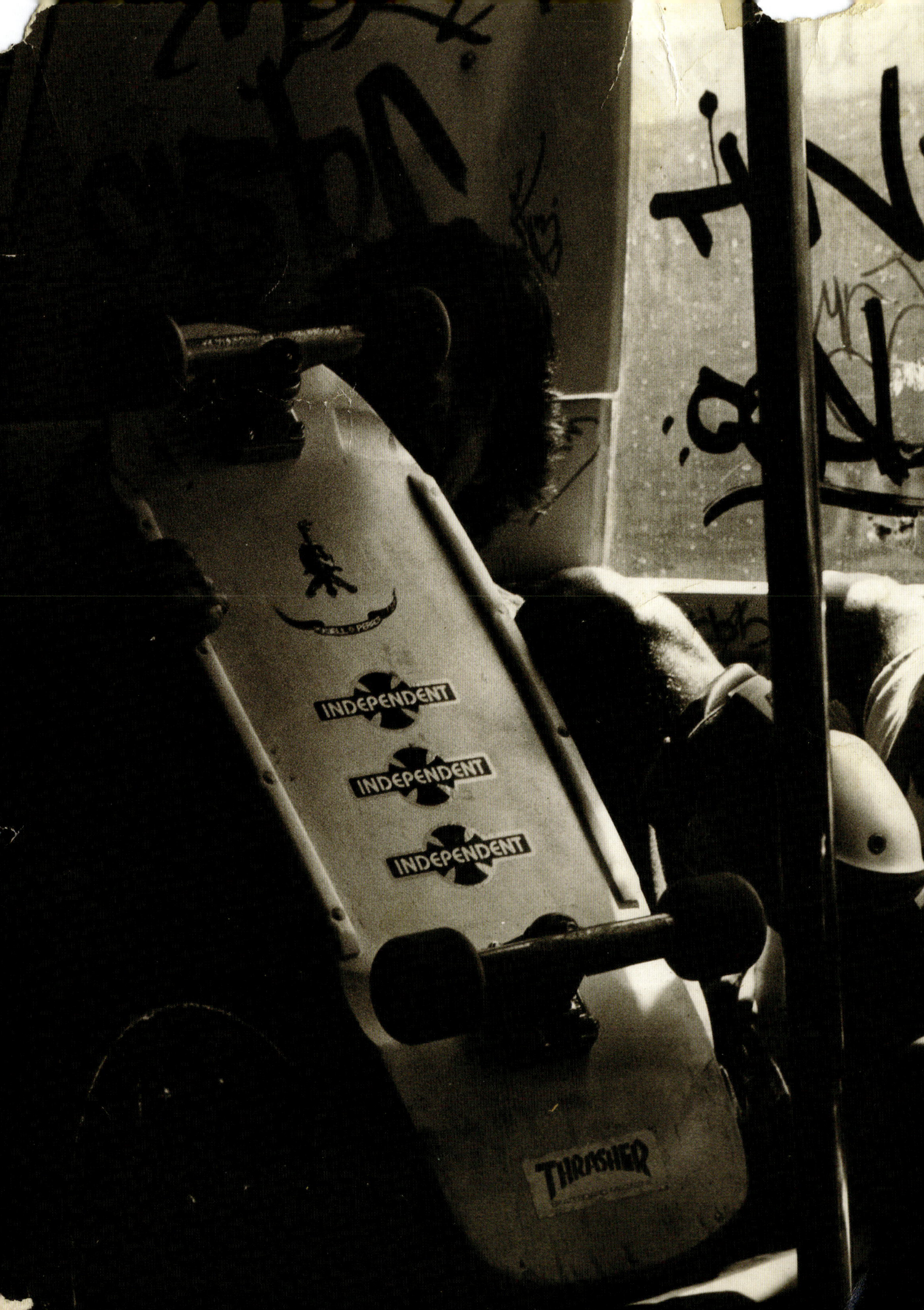
INDEPENDENT
INDEPENDENT
INDEPENDENT
THRASHER

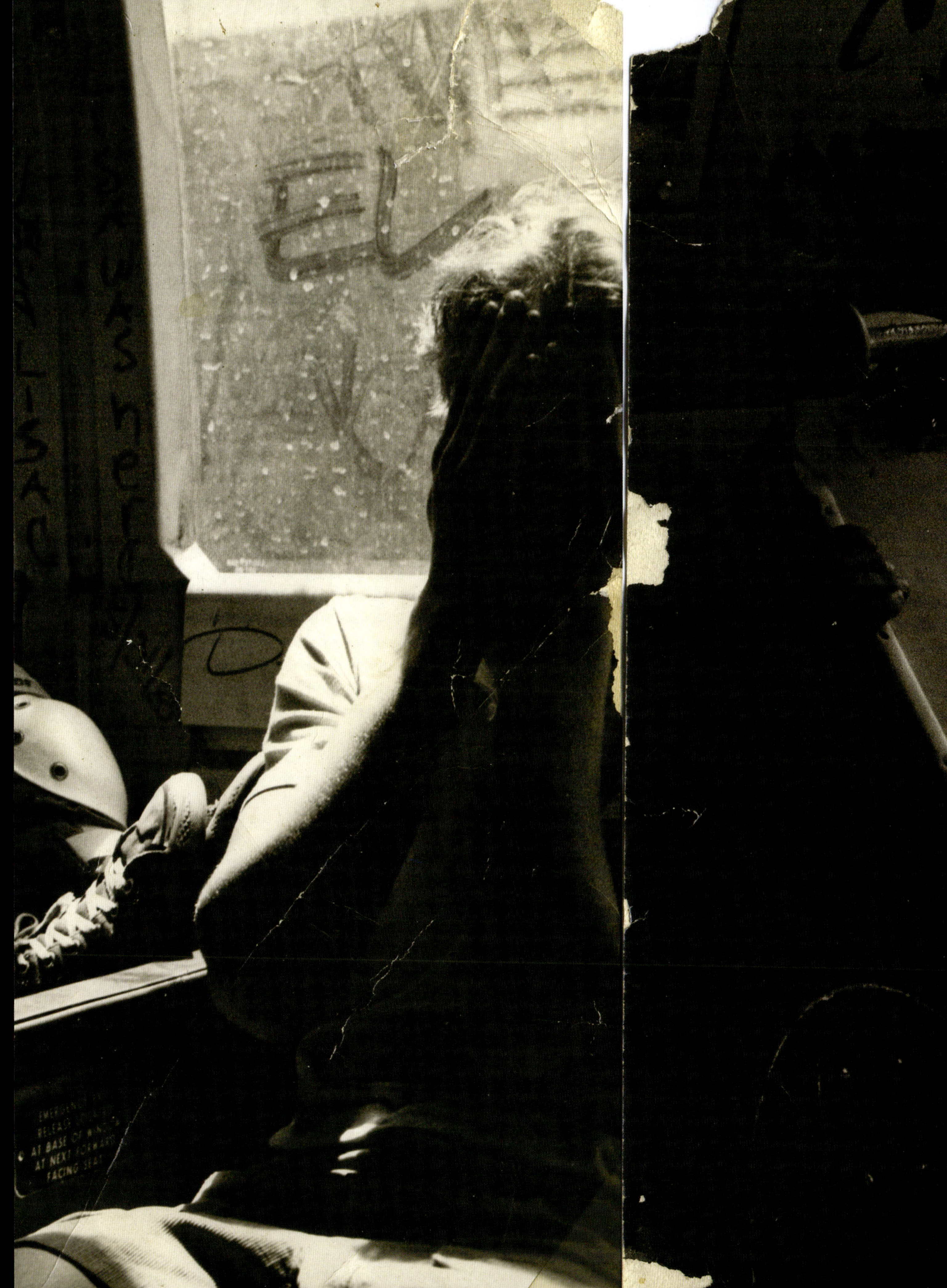

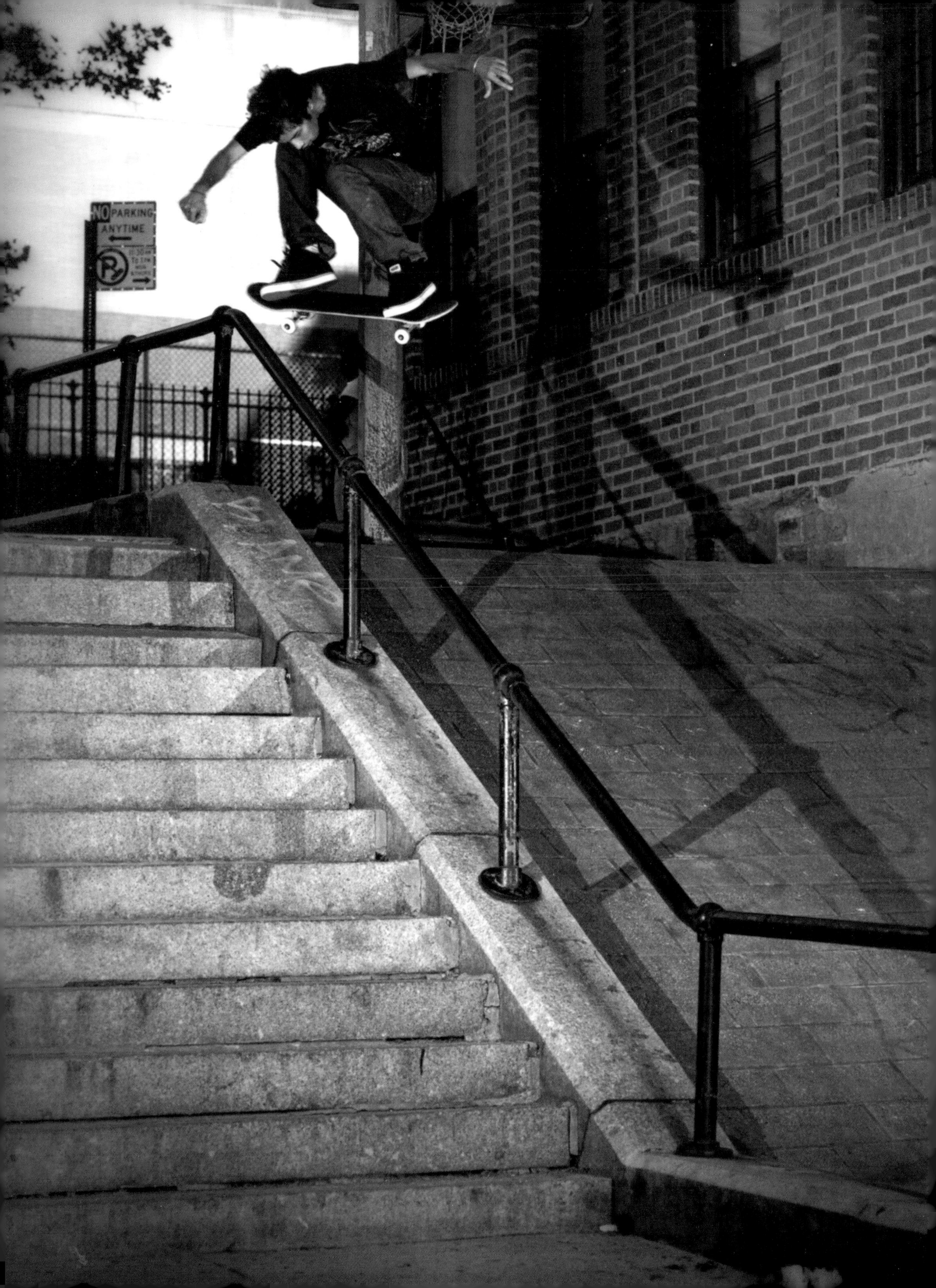
NO PARKING
ANYTIME

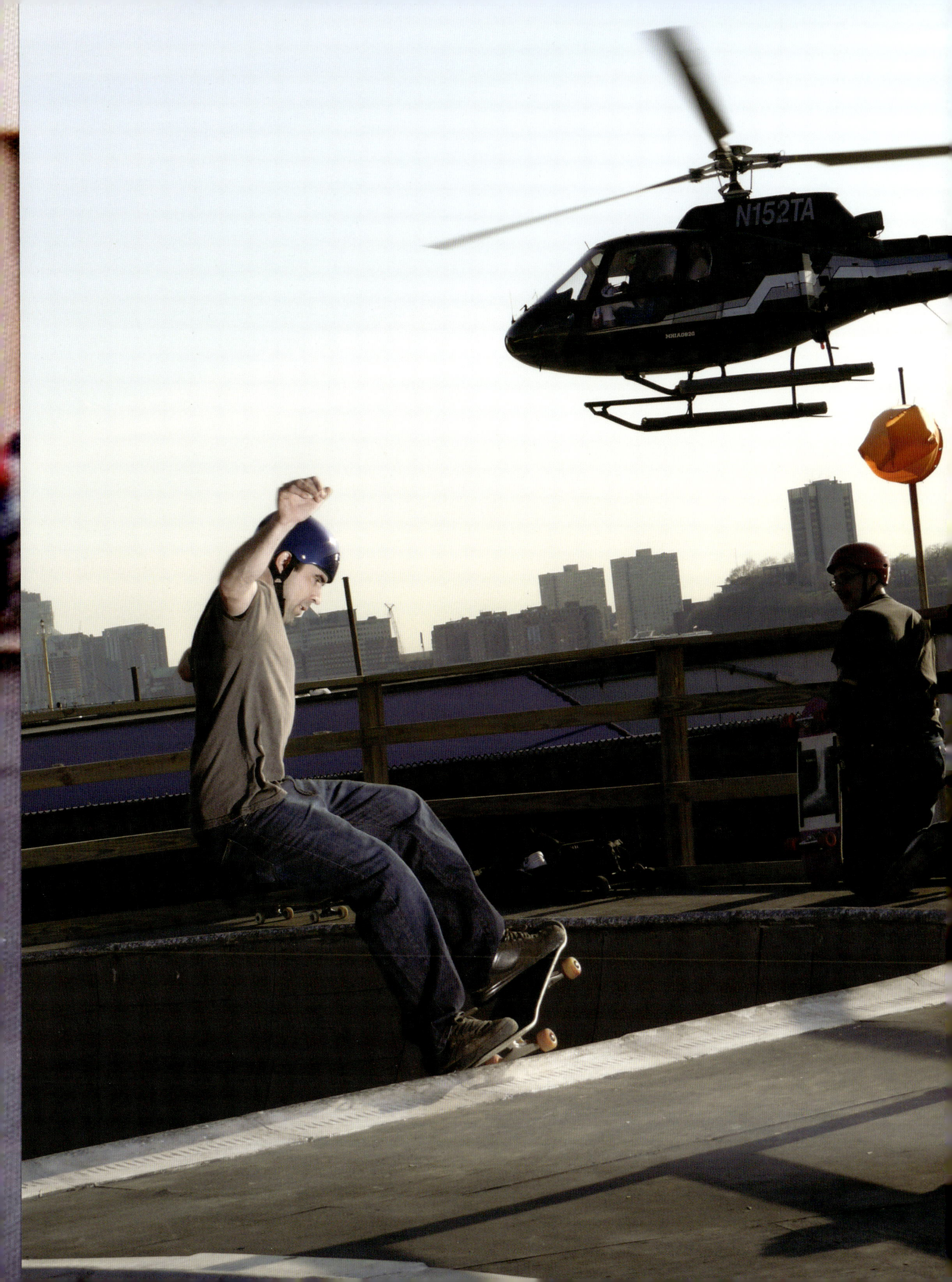
N152TA

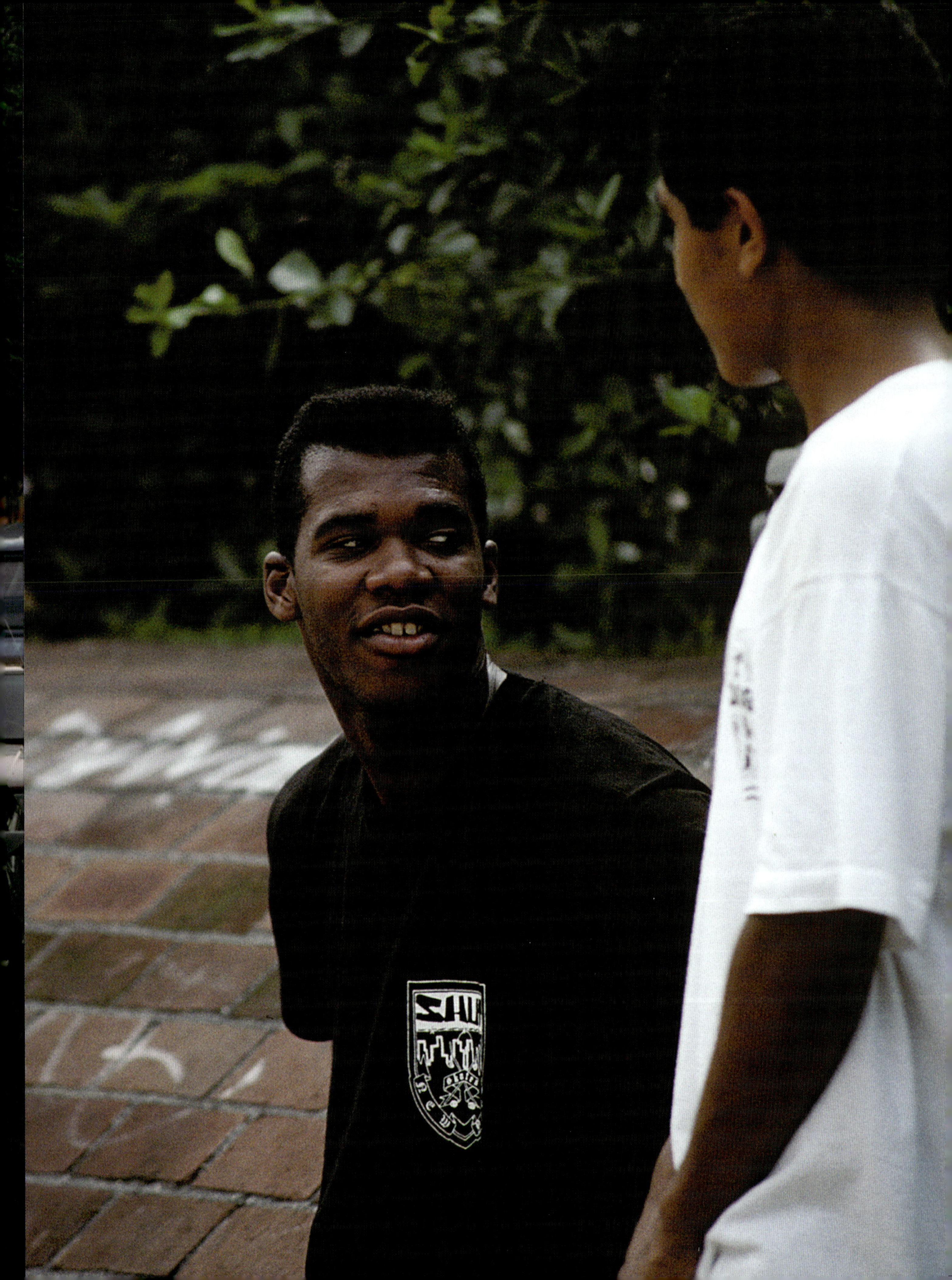

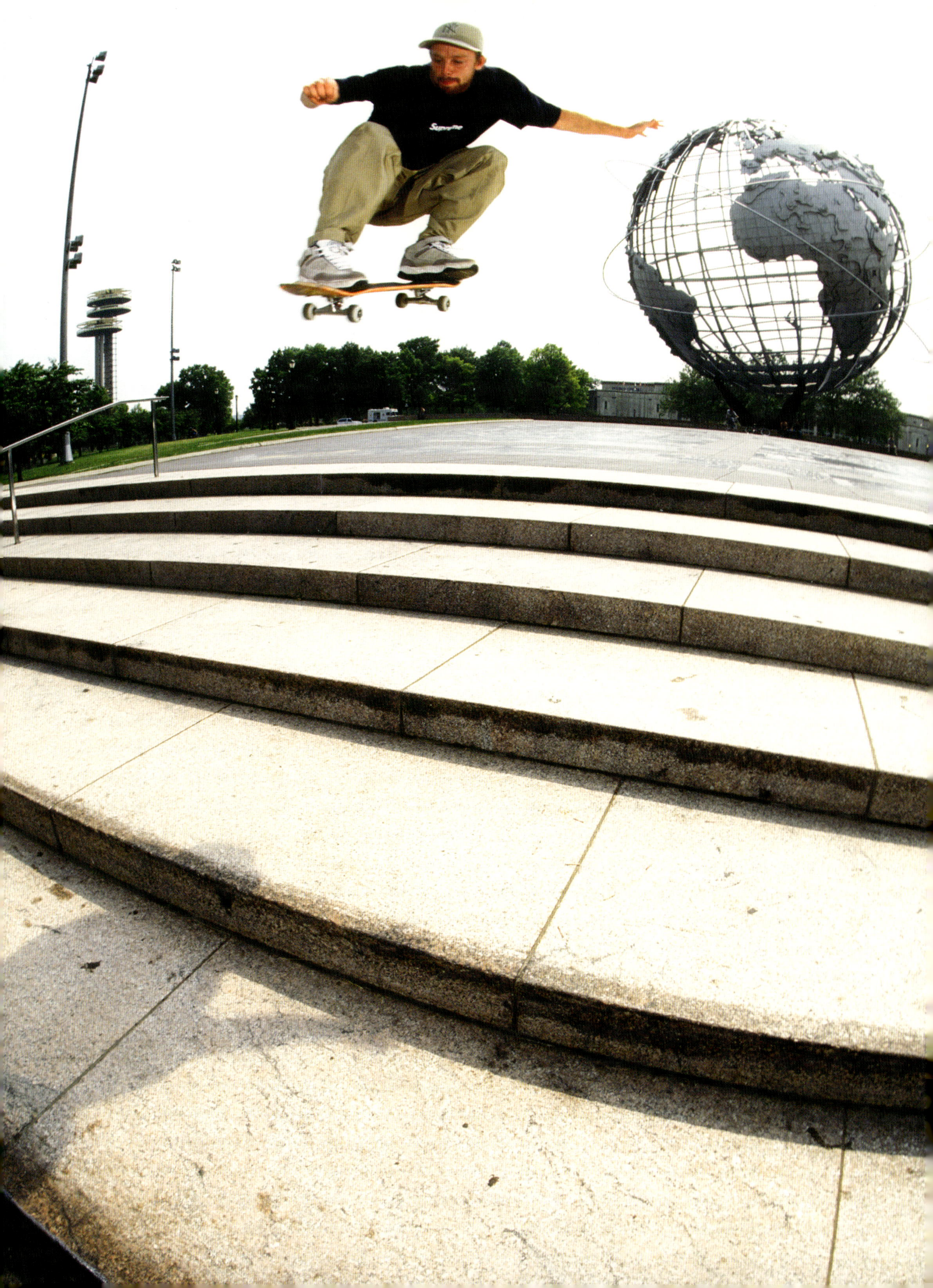

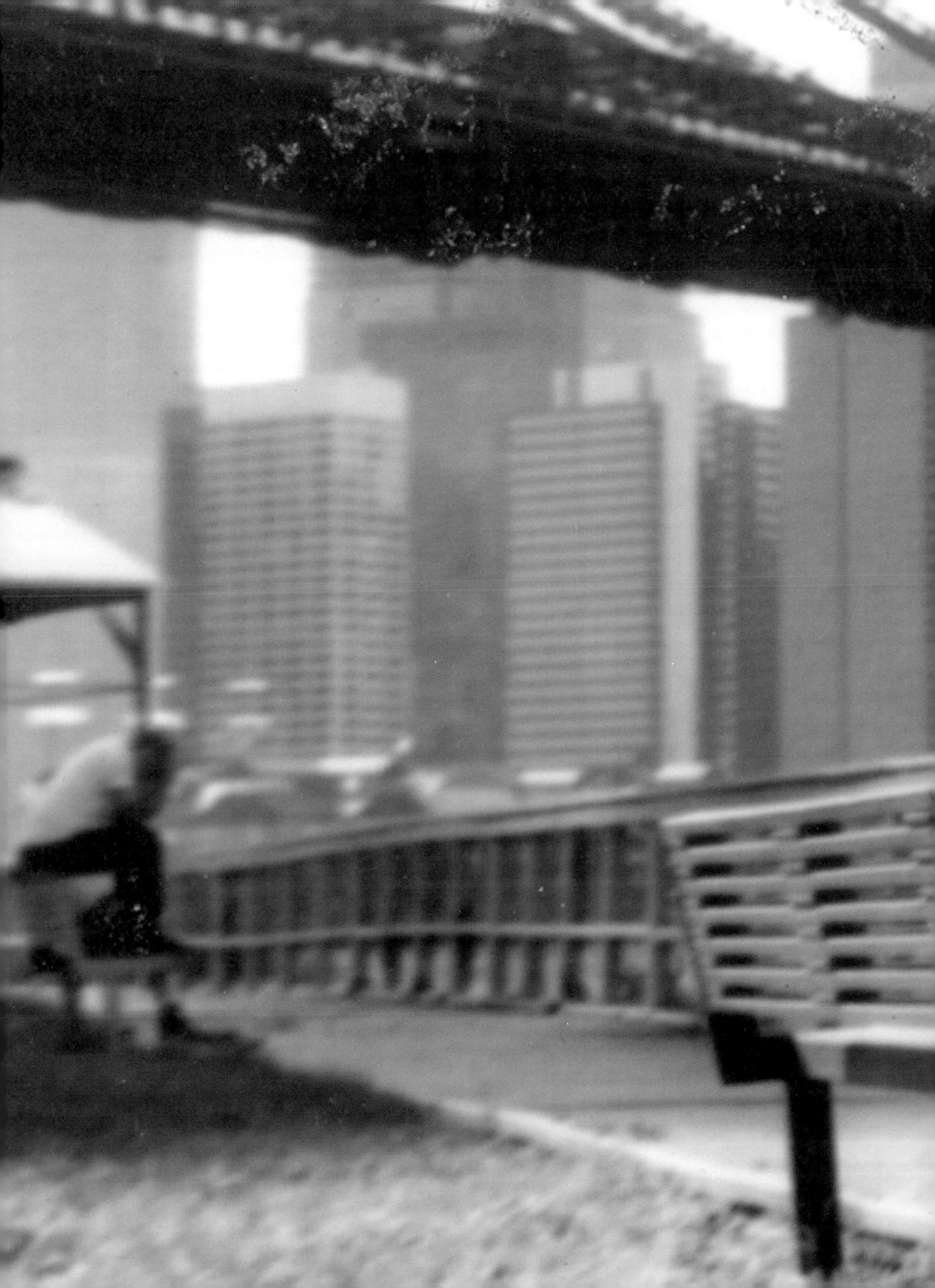

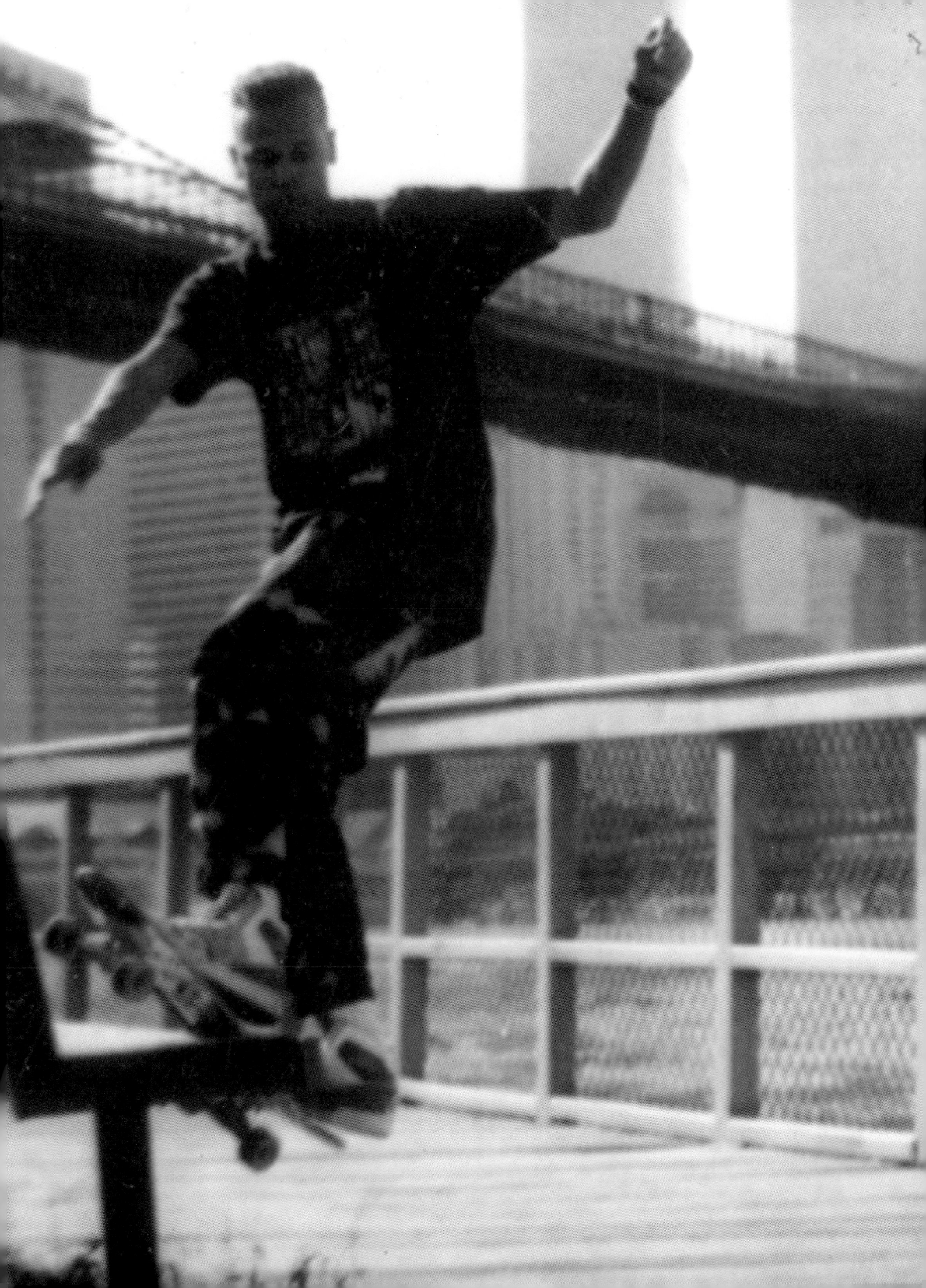

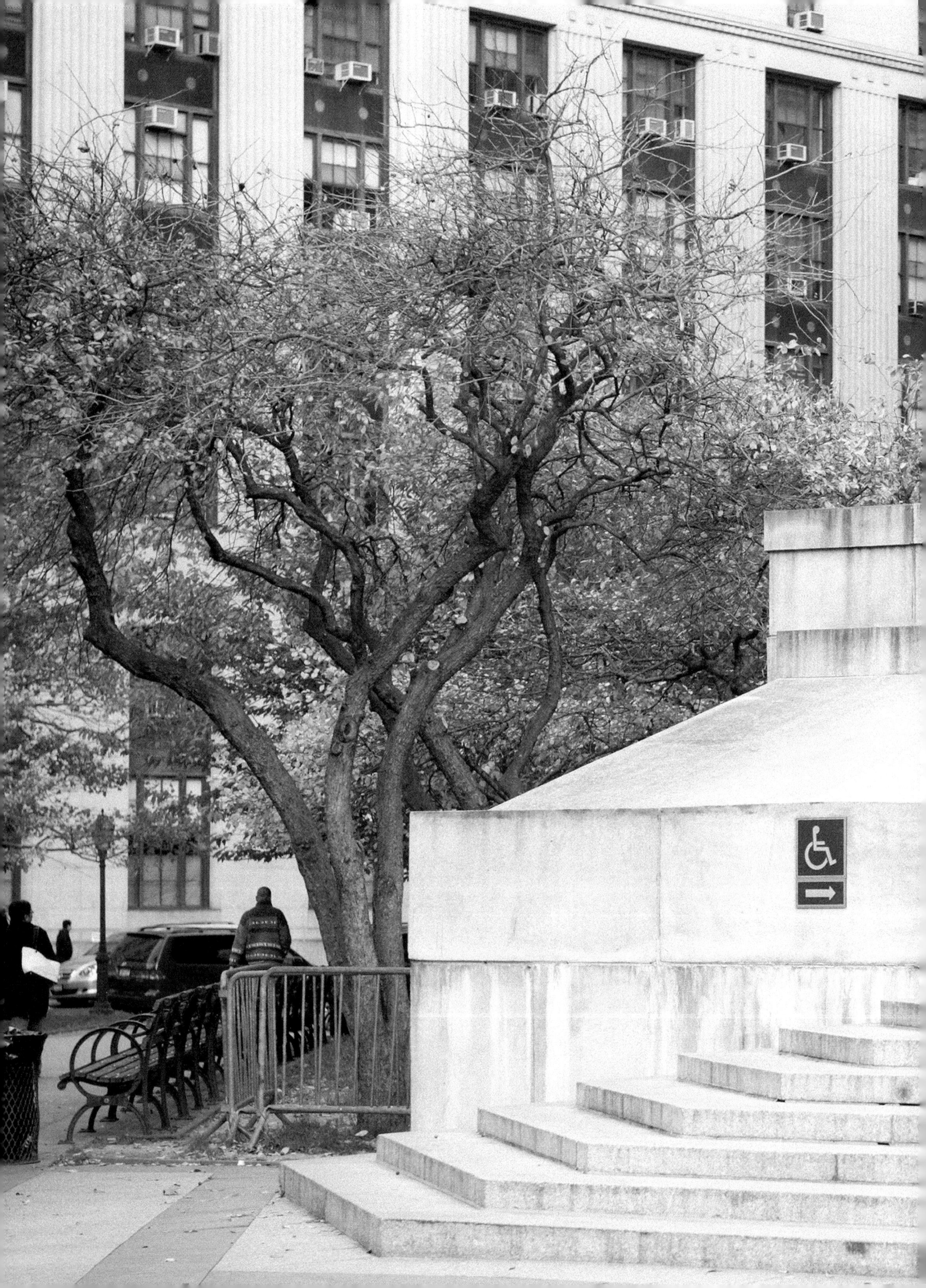

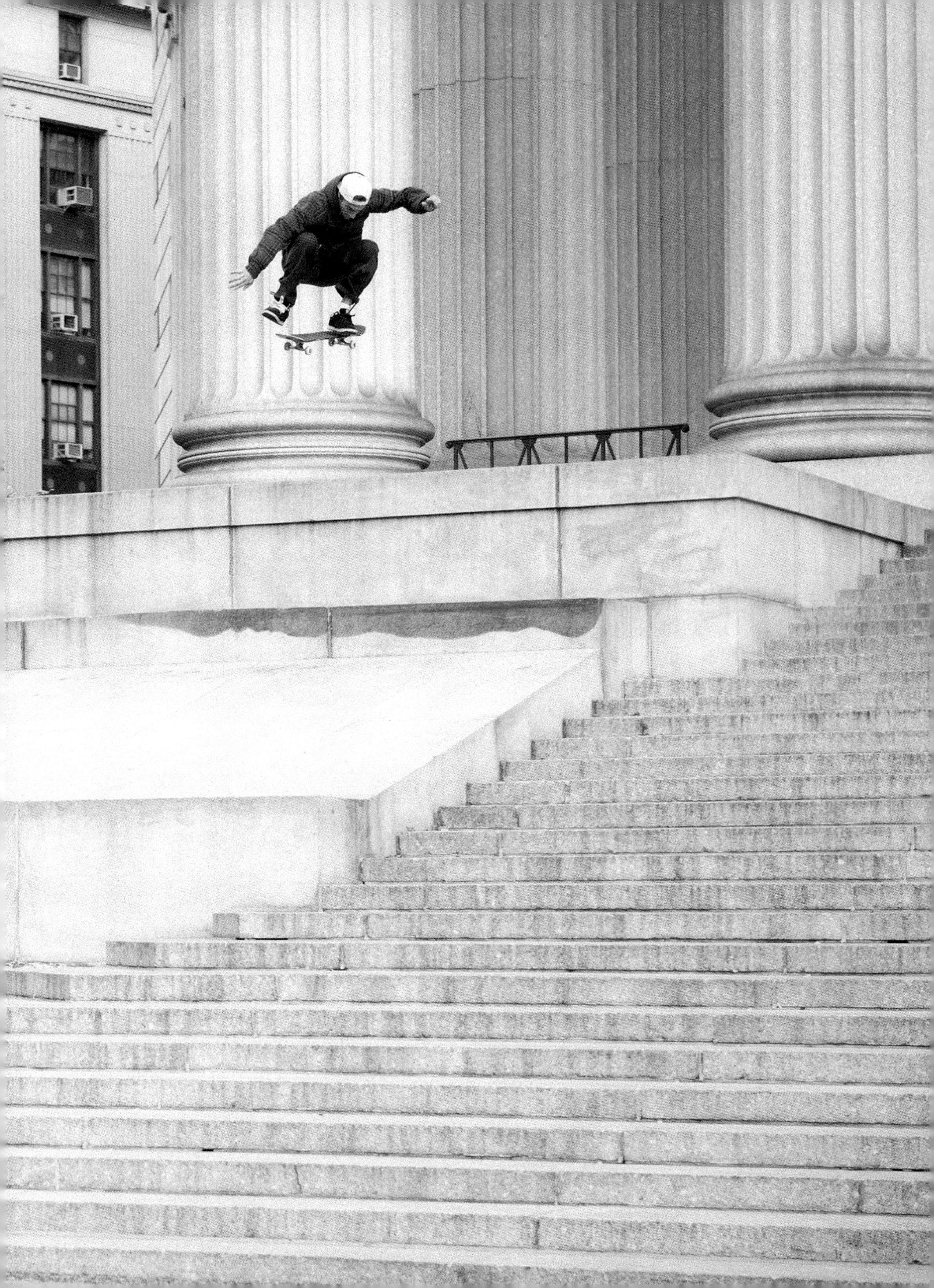

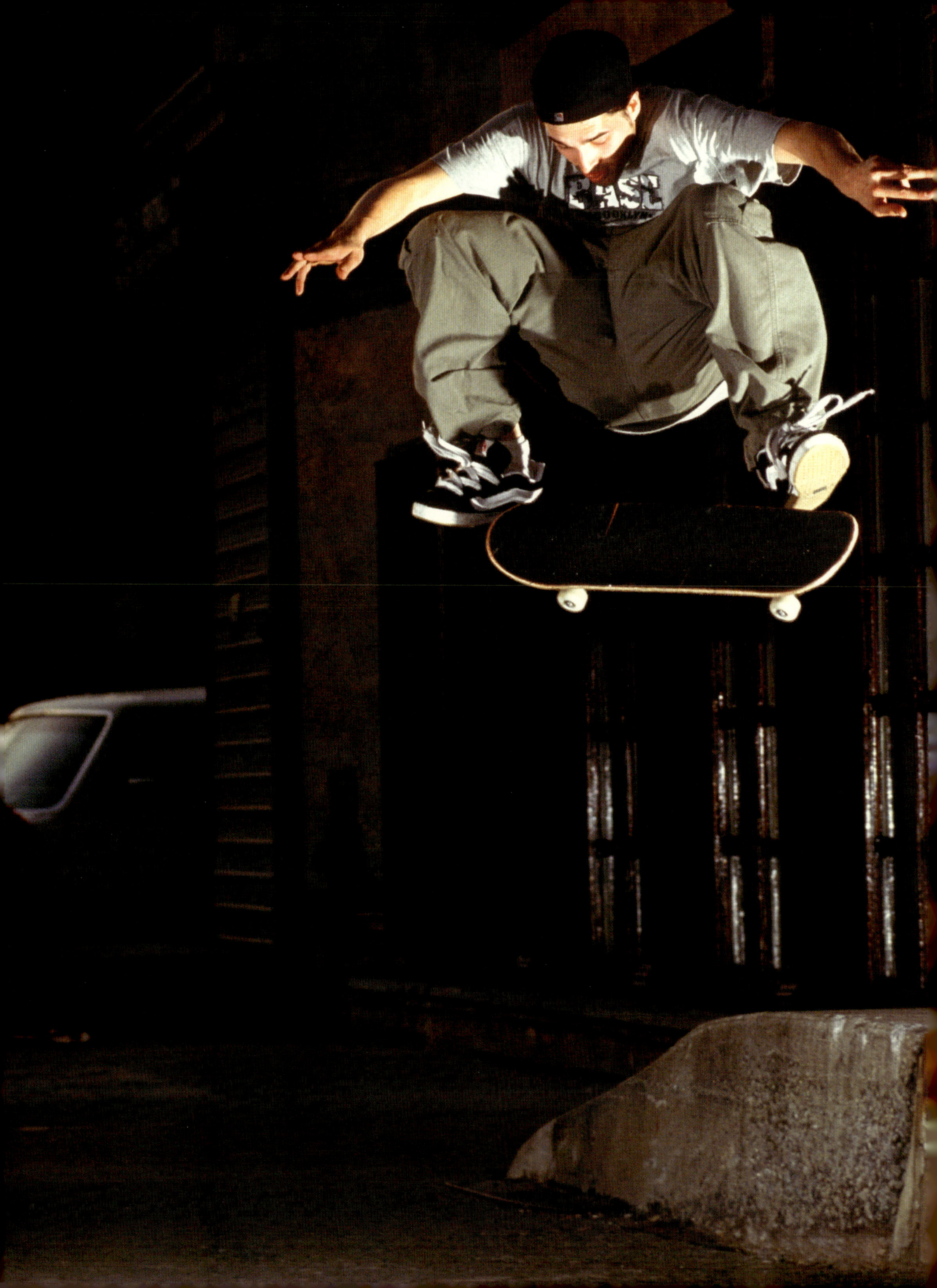

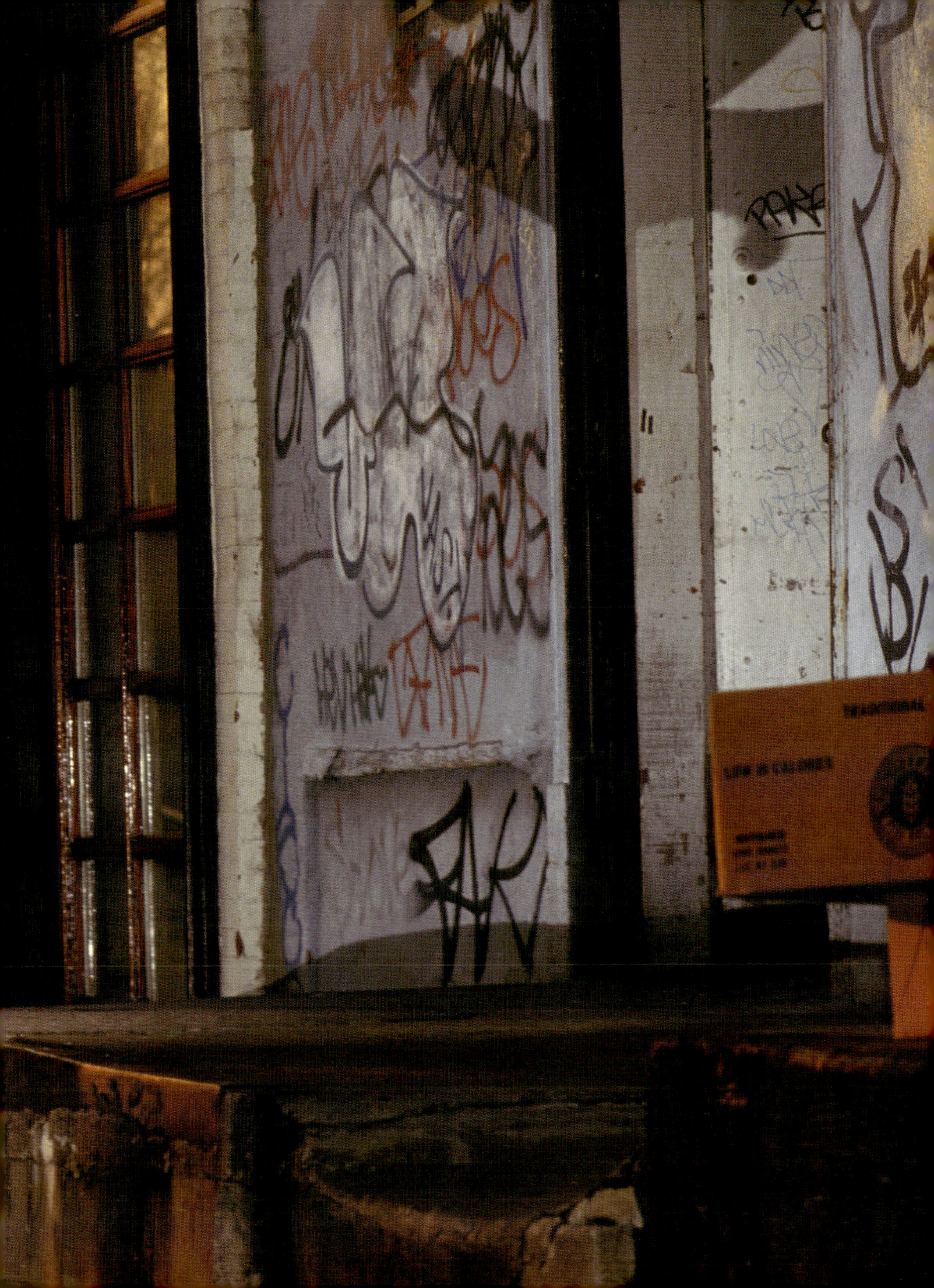
TRADITIONAL
LOW IN CALORIES

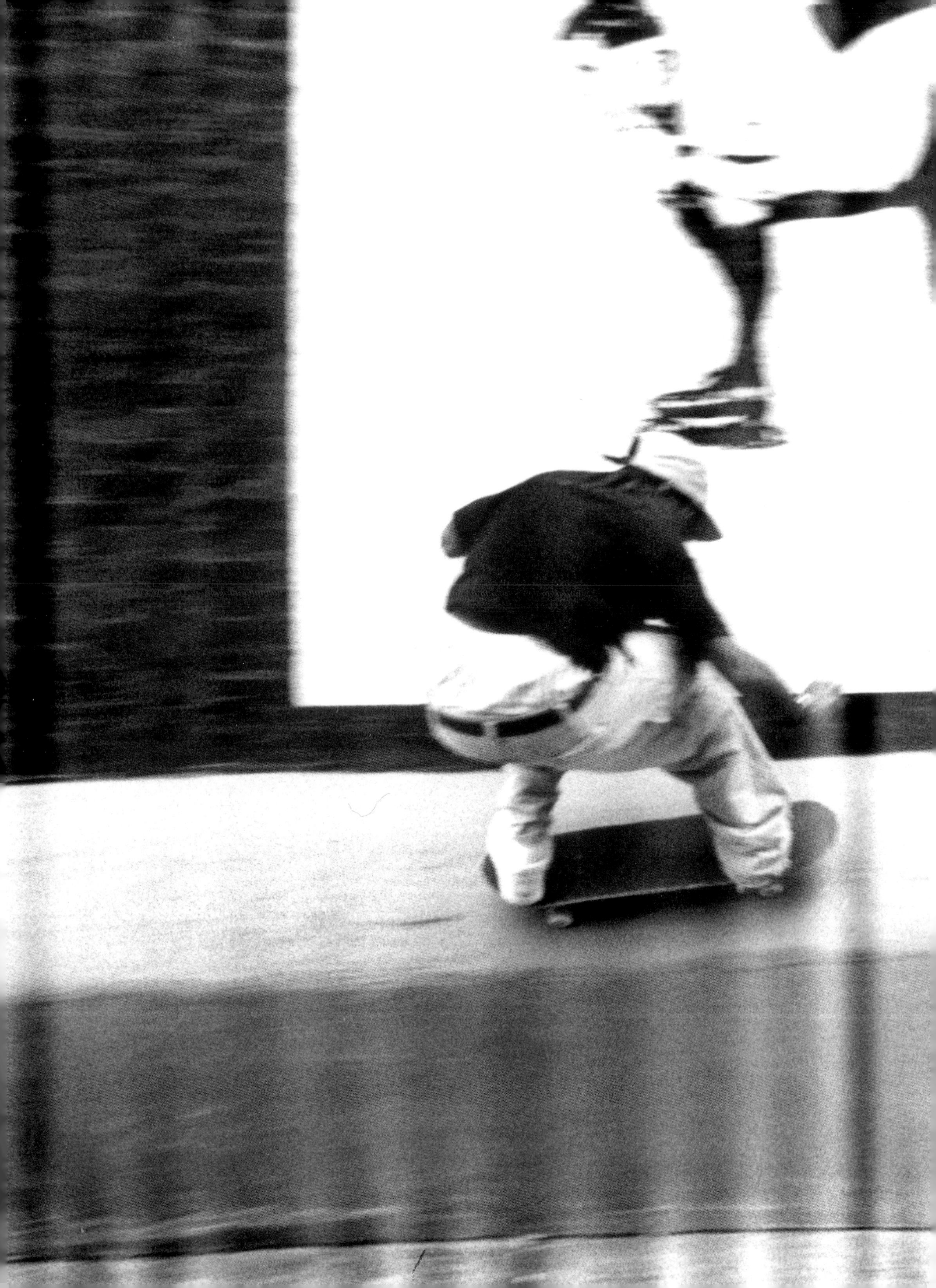

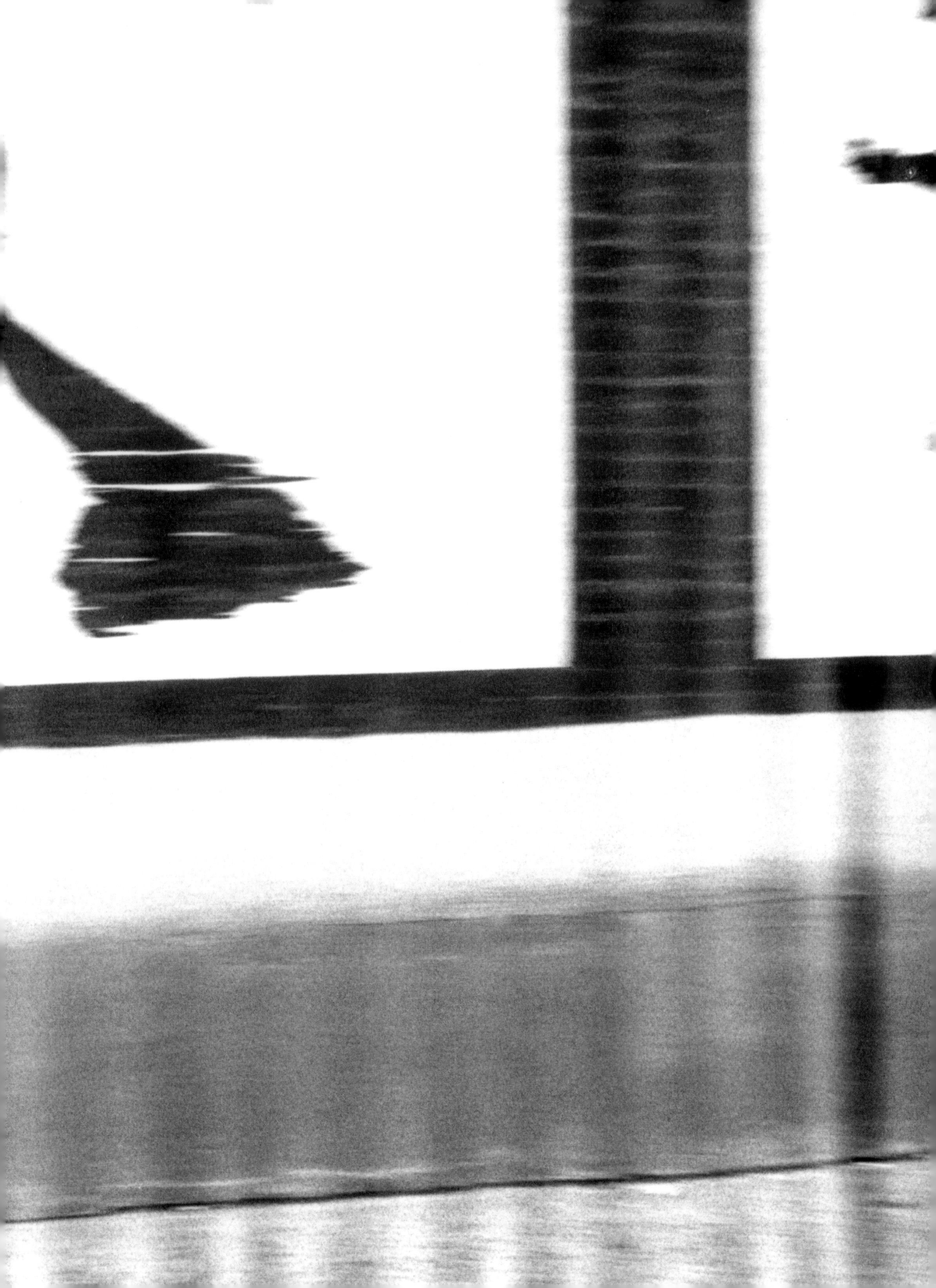

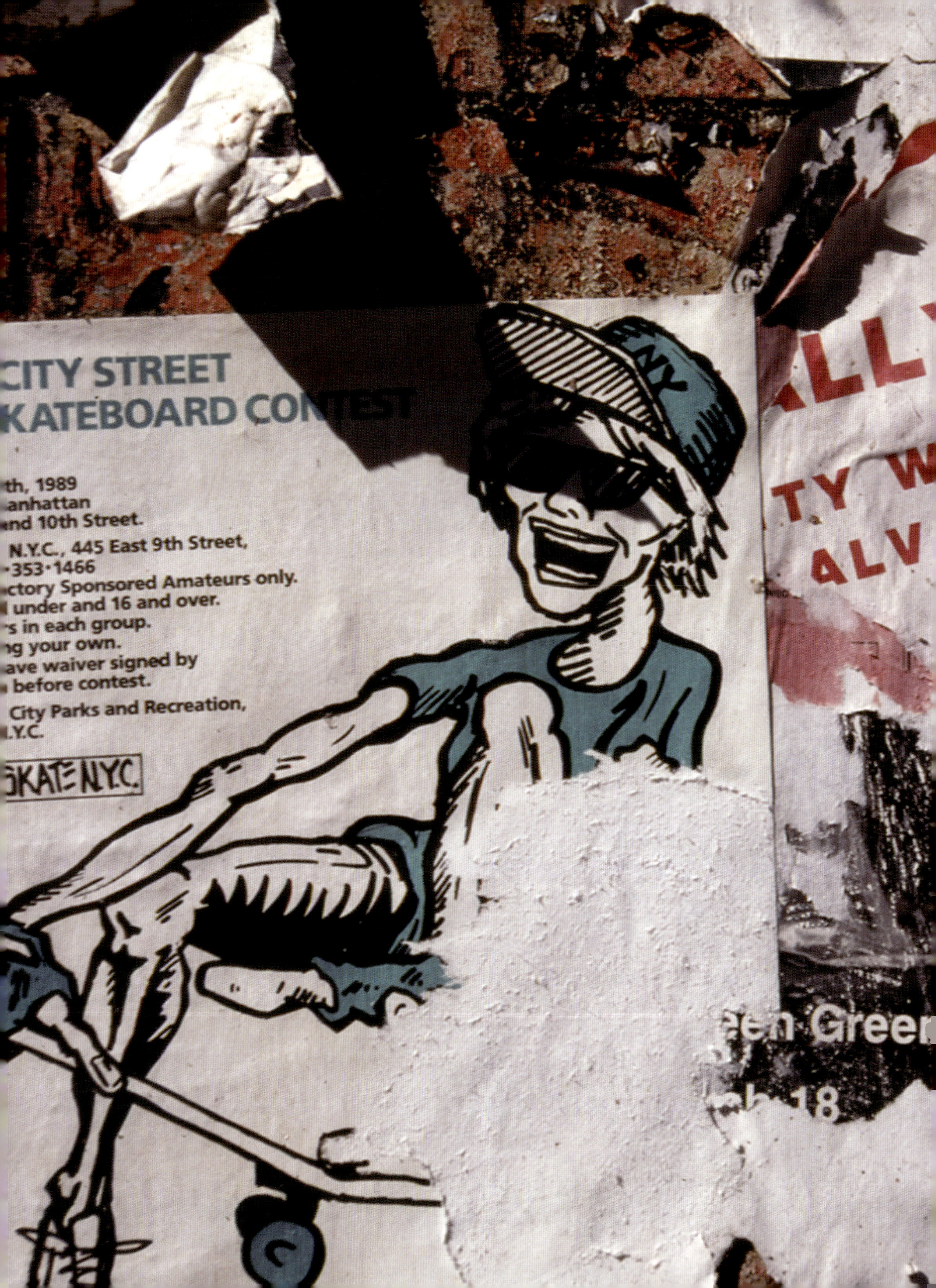
CITY STREET
KATEBOARD CONTEST
th, 1989
anhattan
nd 10th Street.
N.Y.C., 445 East 9th Street,
353-1466
ctory Sponsored Amateurs only.
under and 16 and over.
s in each group.
ng your own.
ave waiver signed by
before contest.
City Parks and Recreation,
.Y.C.
SKATE N.Y.C.
NY
ALL
TY W
ALV
een Green
18

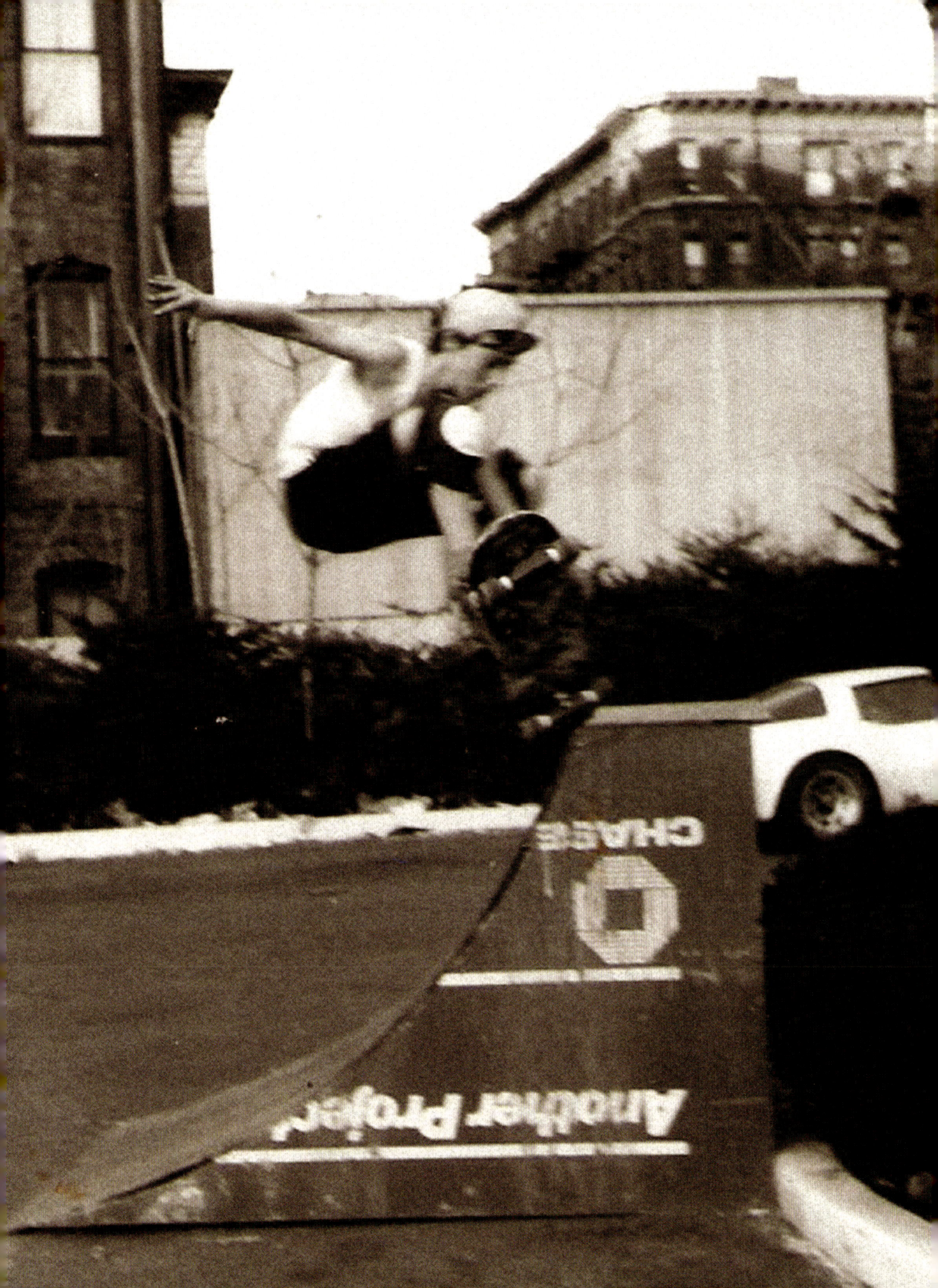
Another

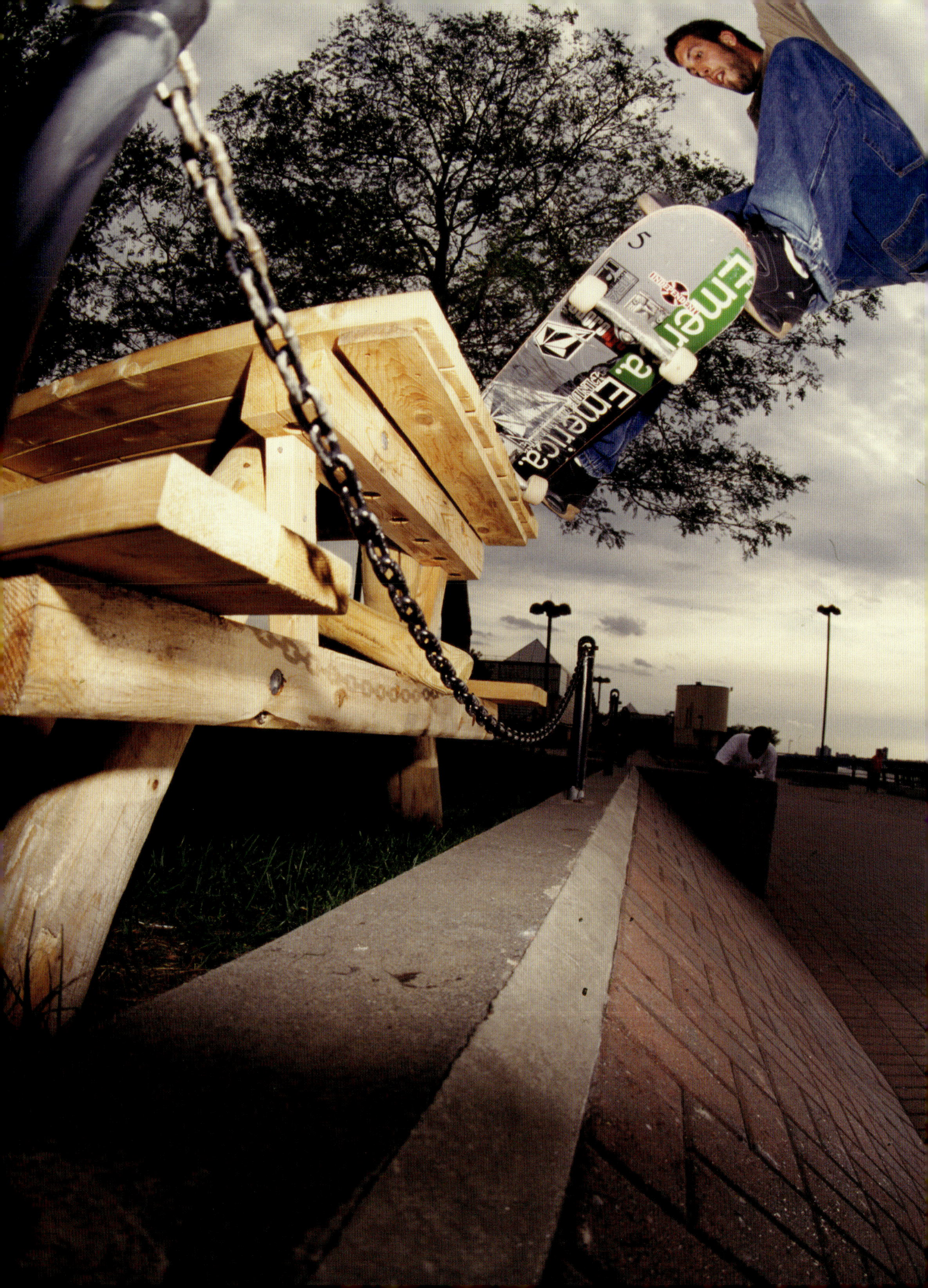
5
Emerica.
Emerica.

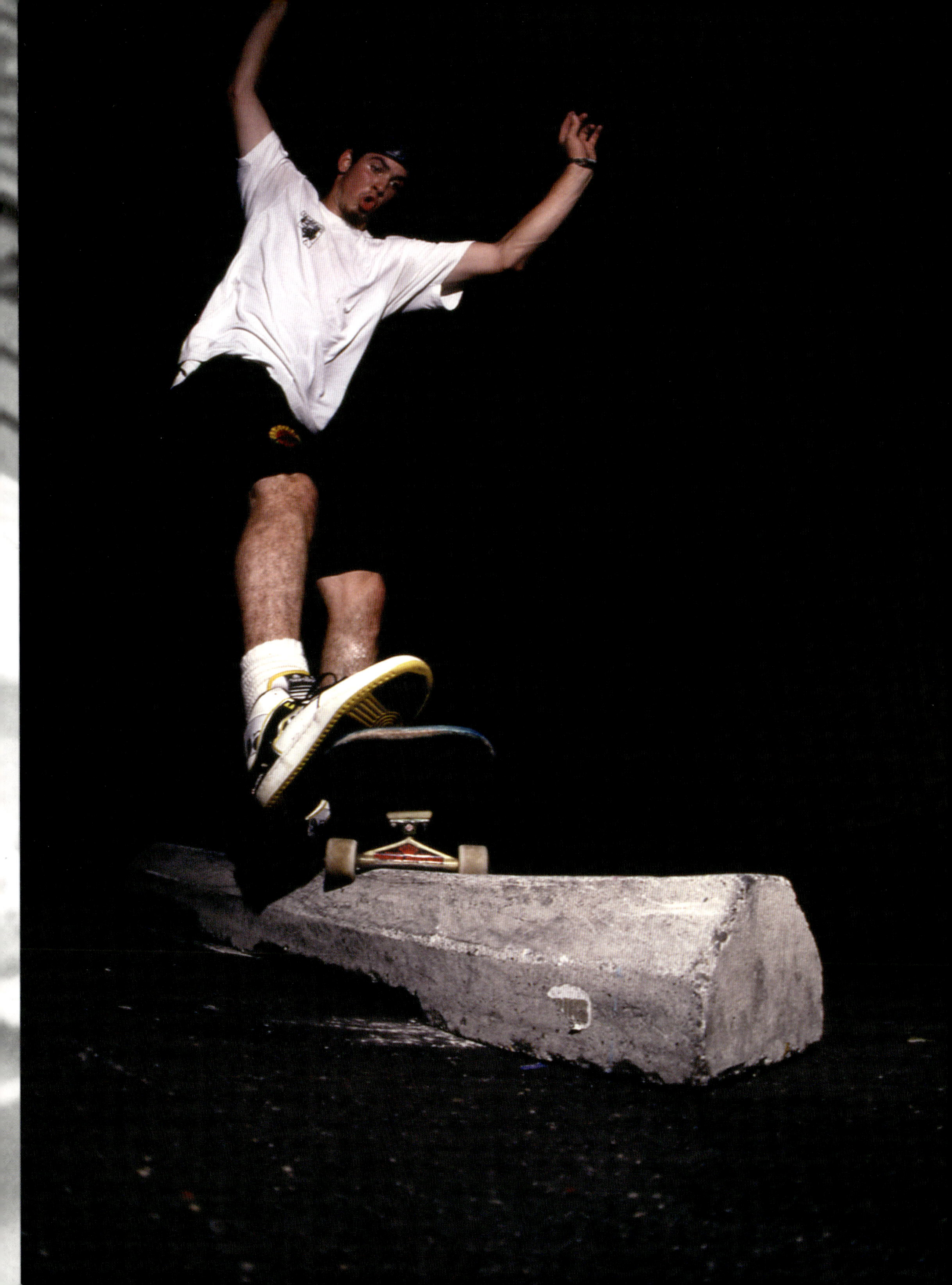

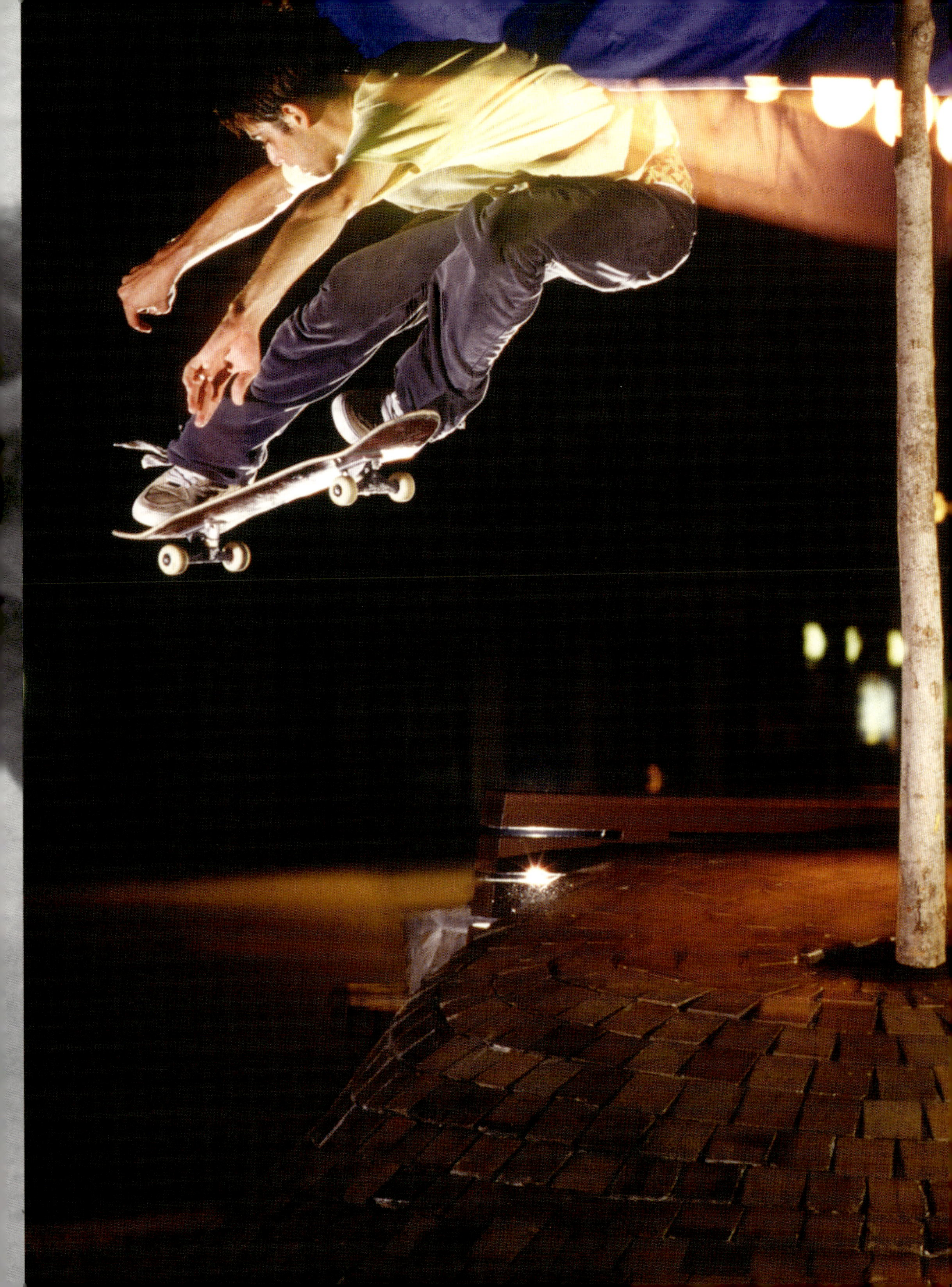

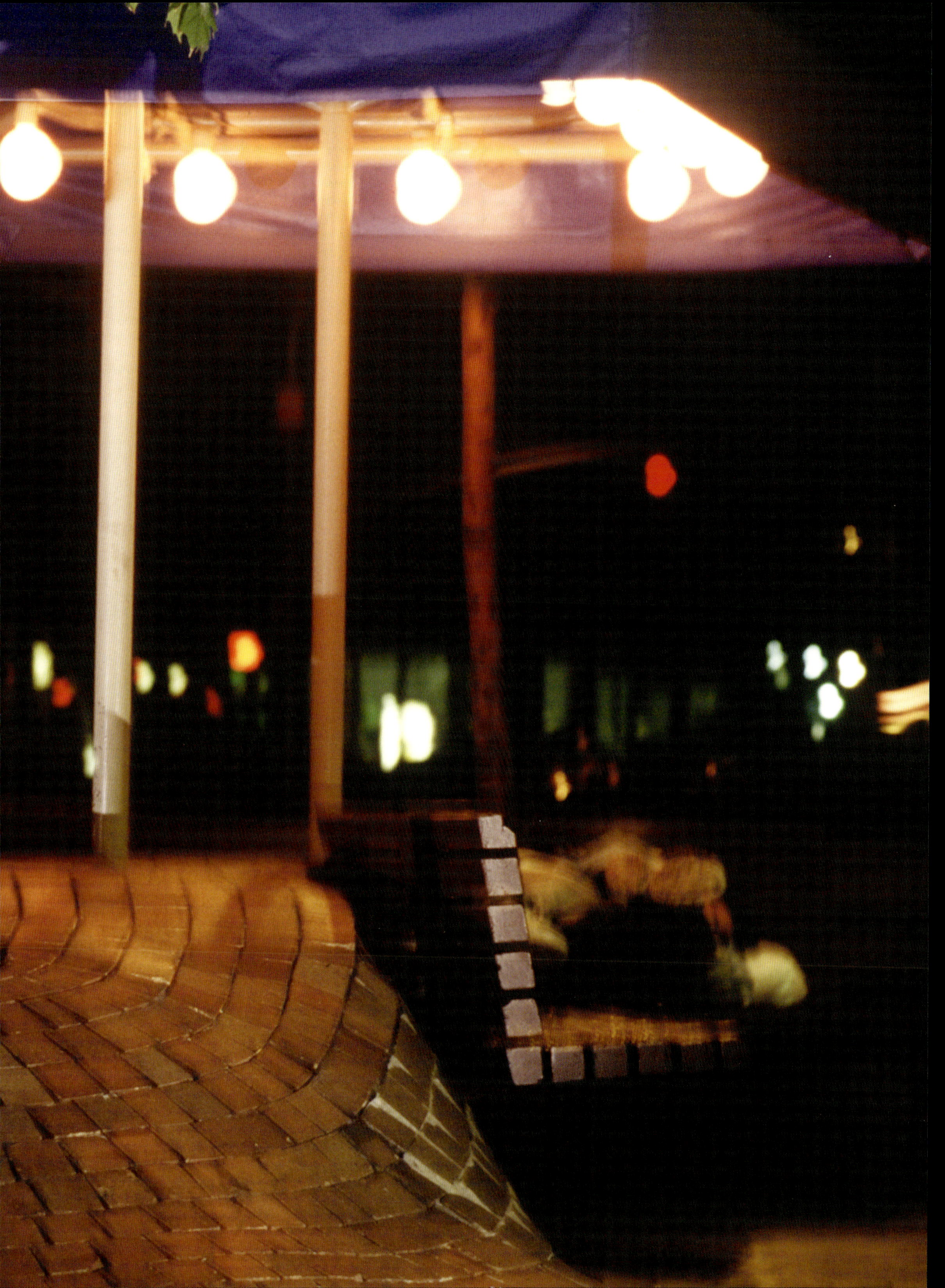

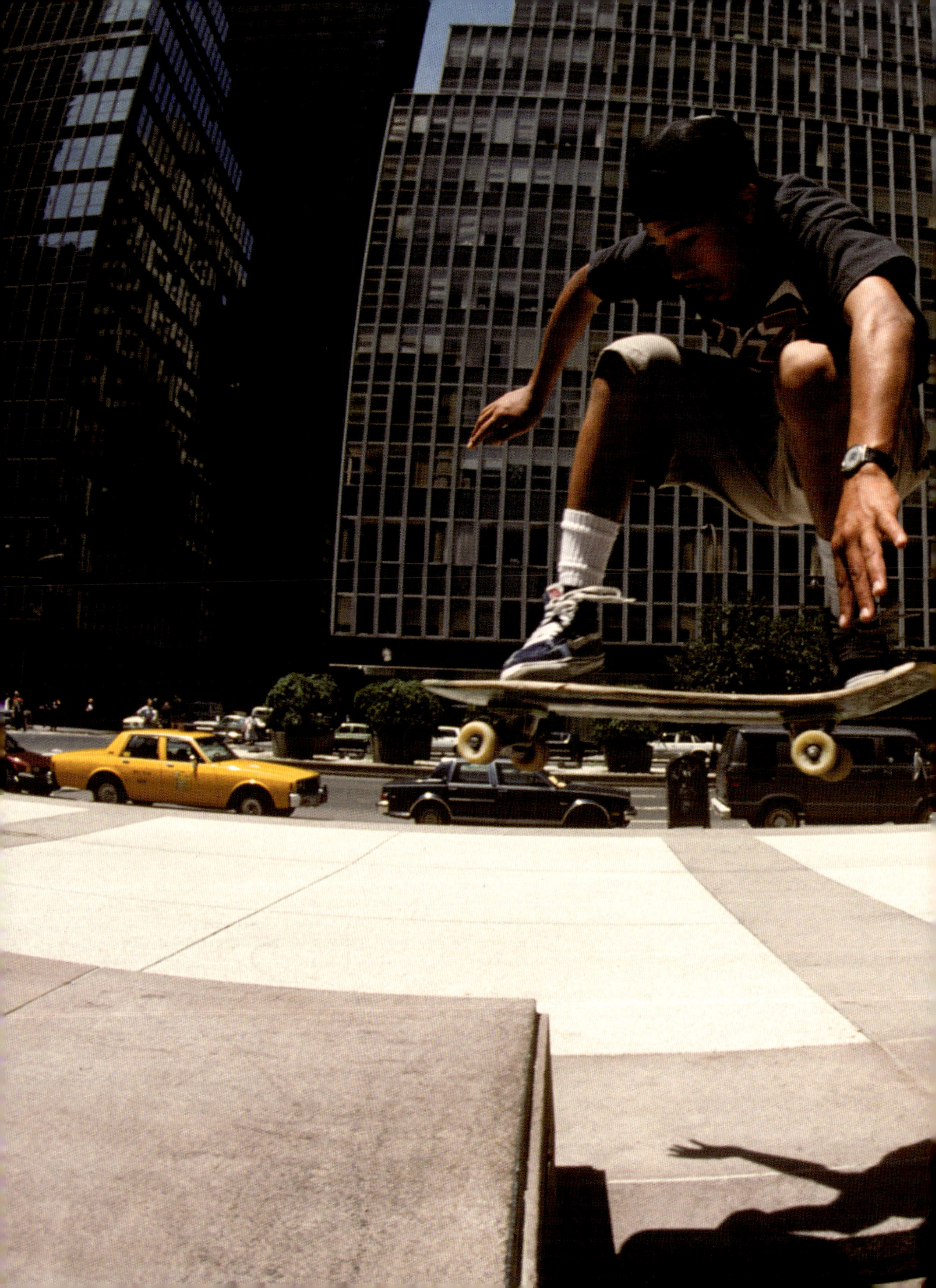

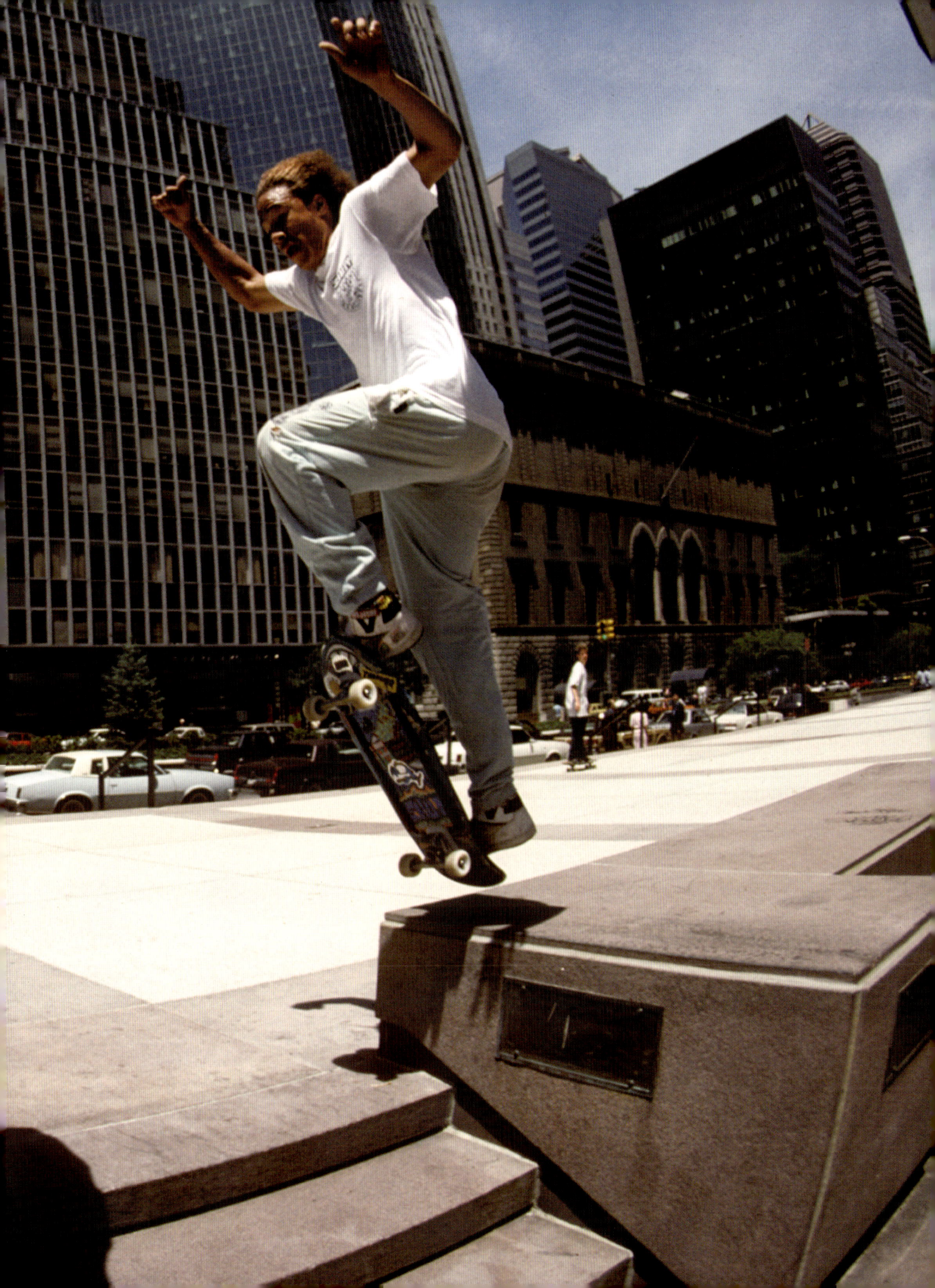

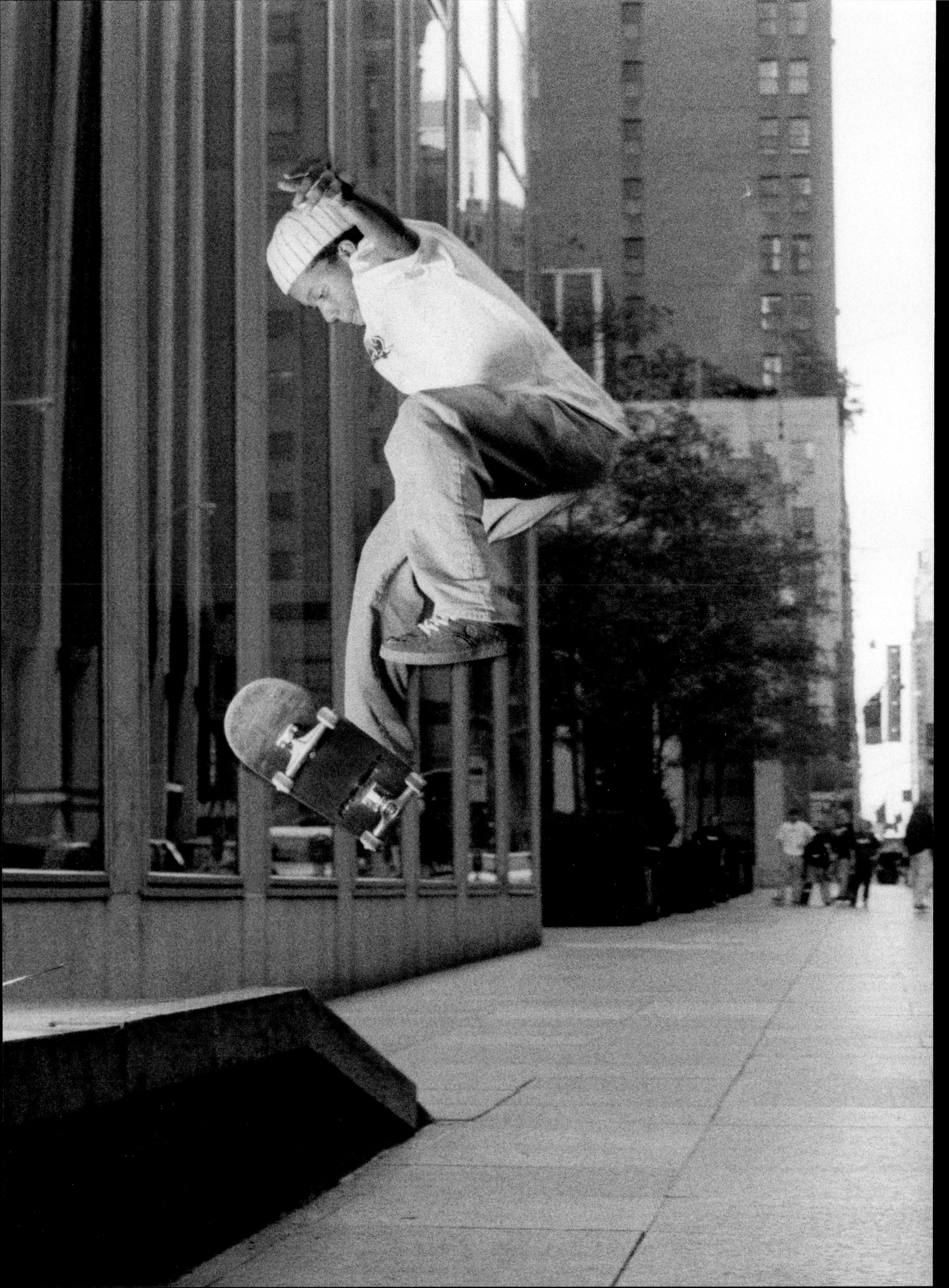

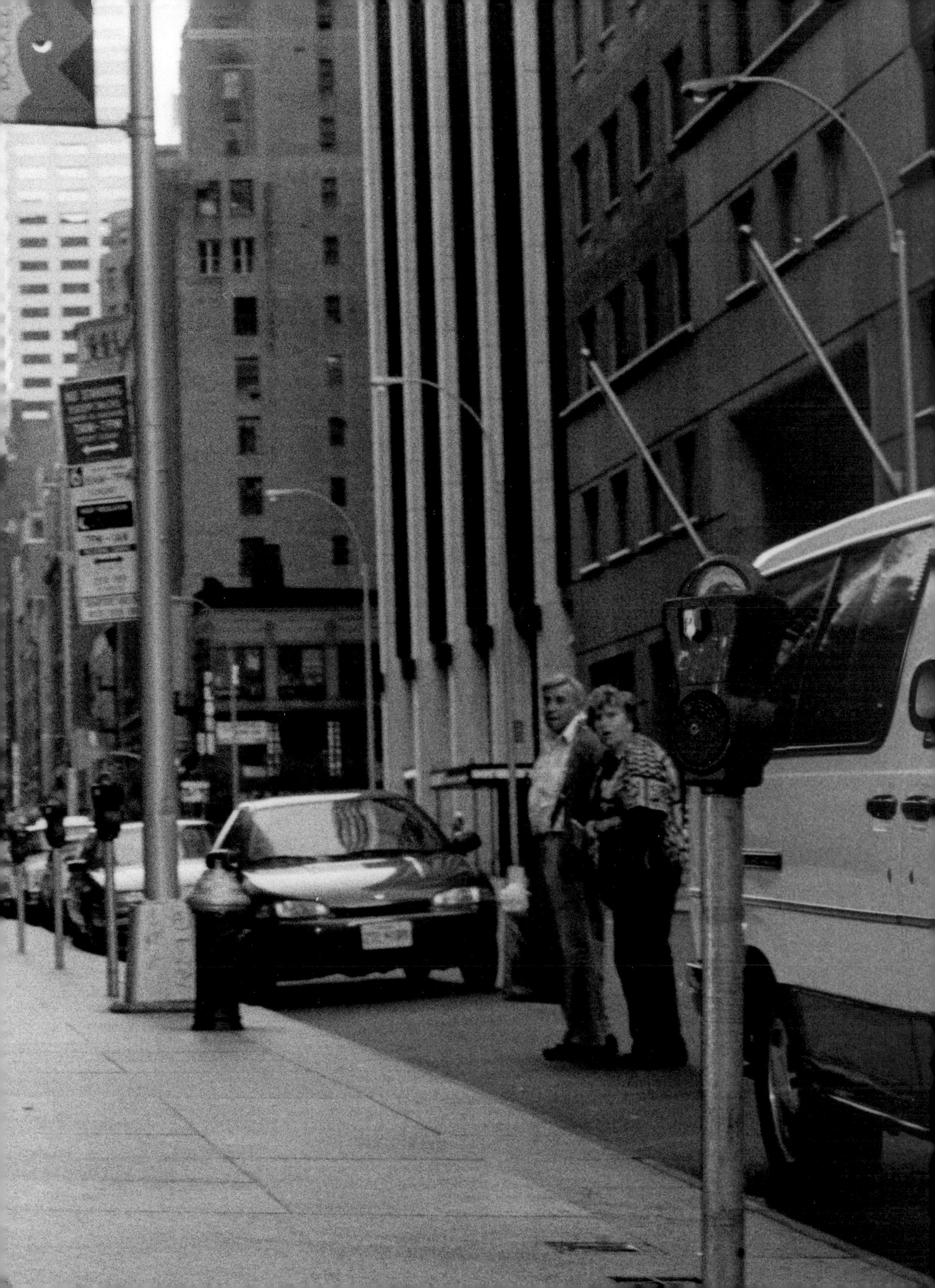

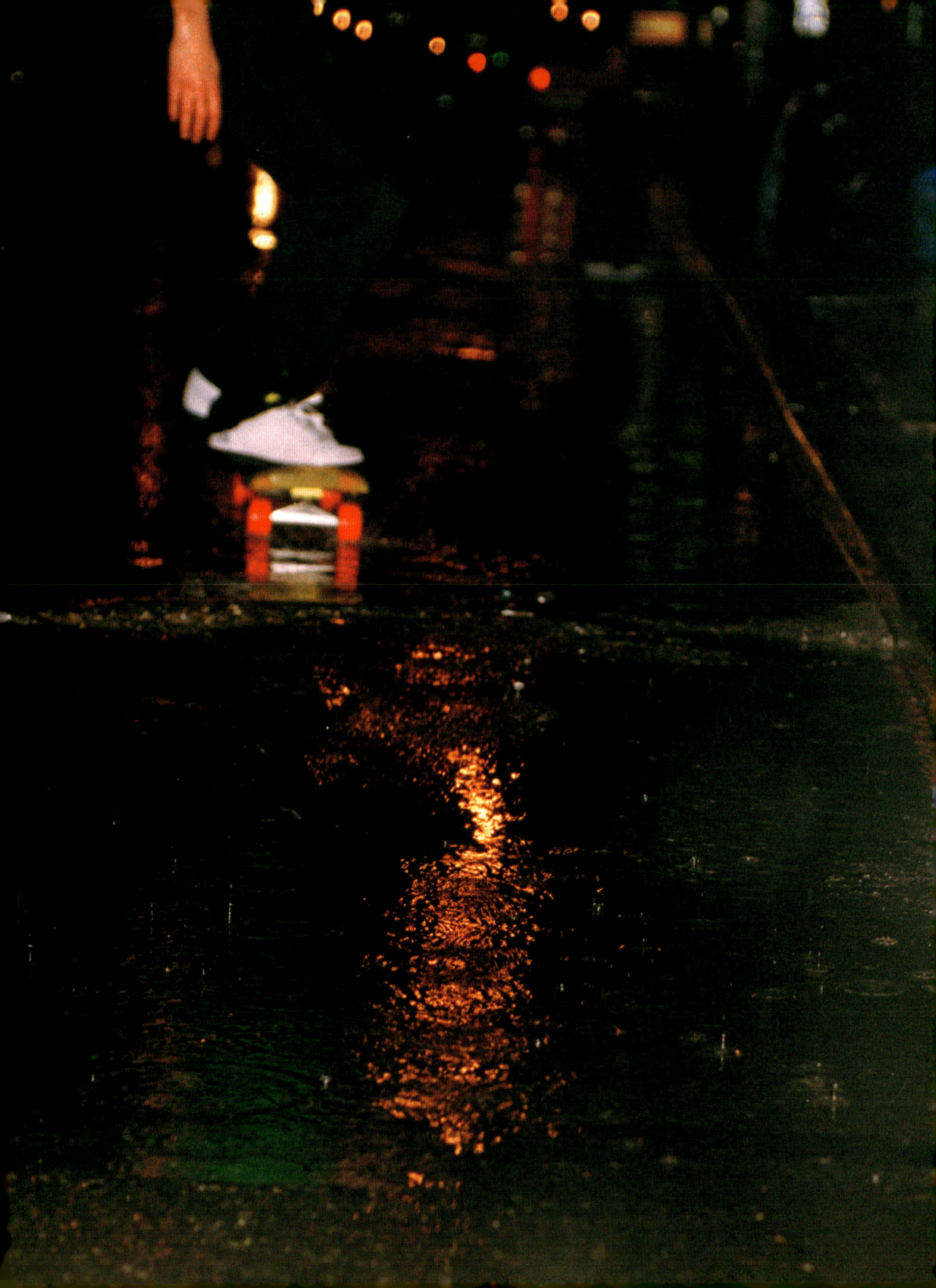

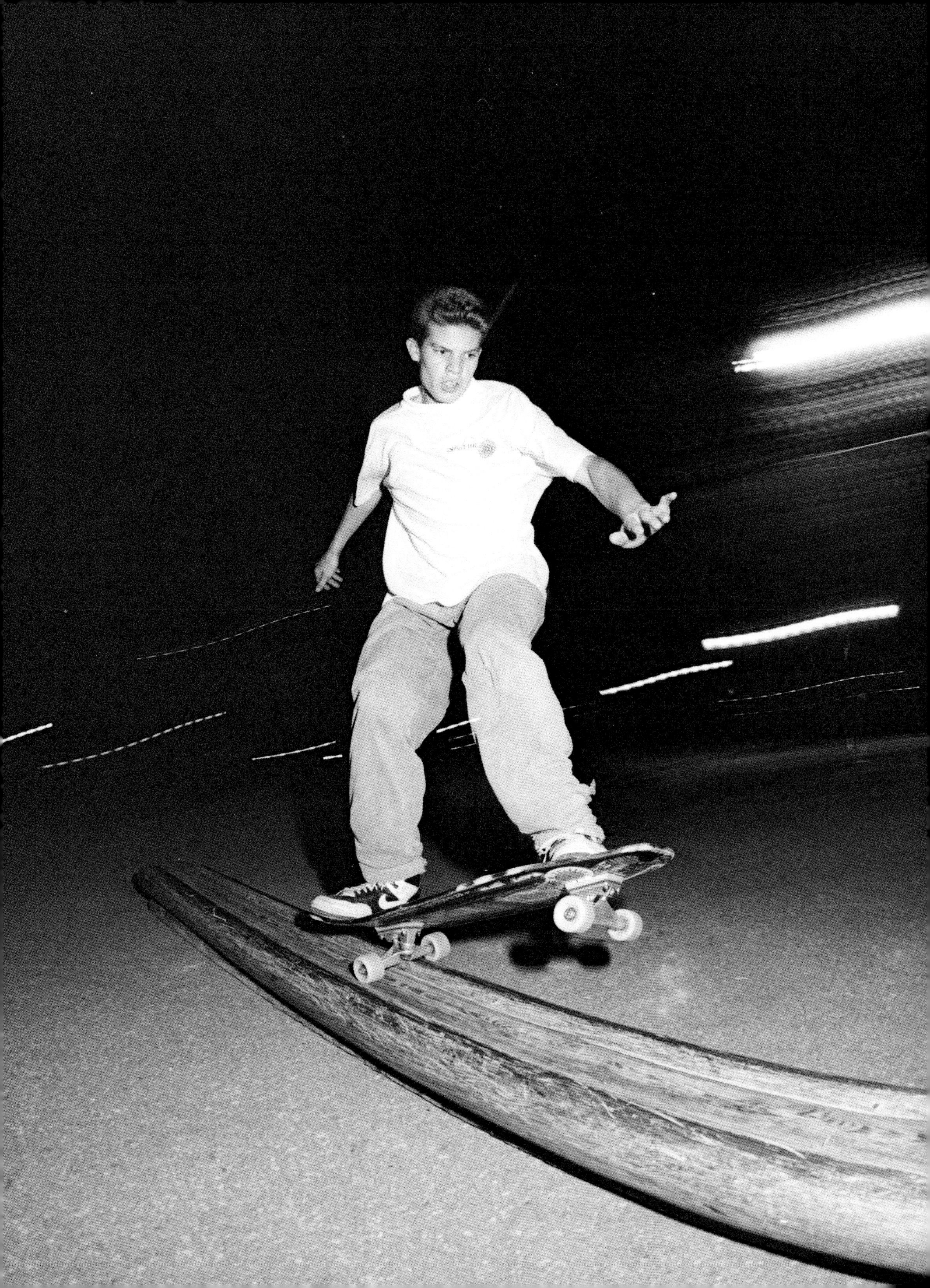

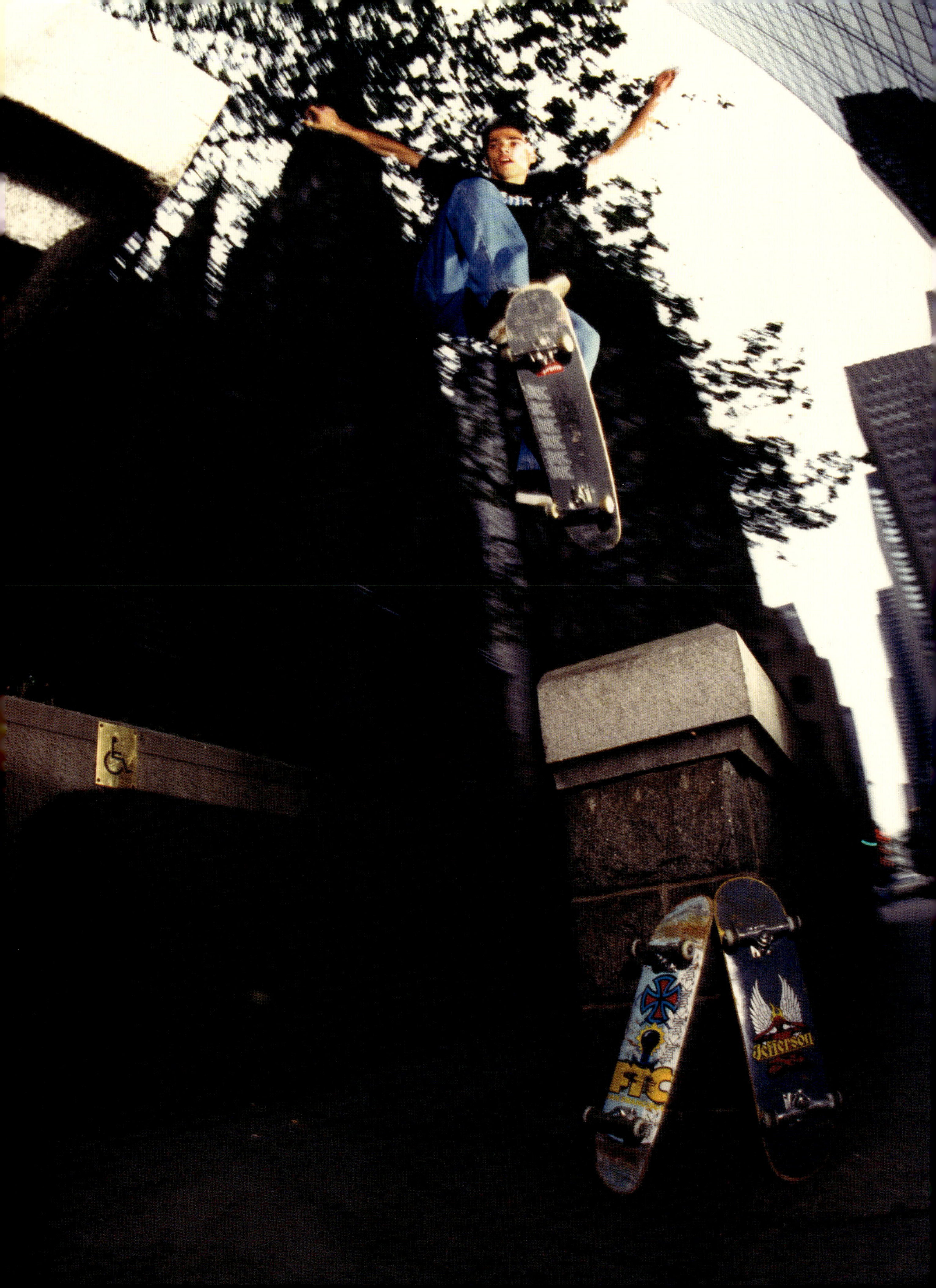
FTC
Jefferson

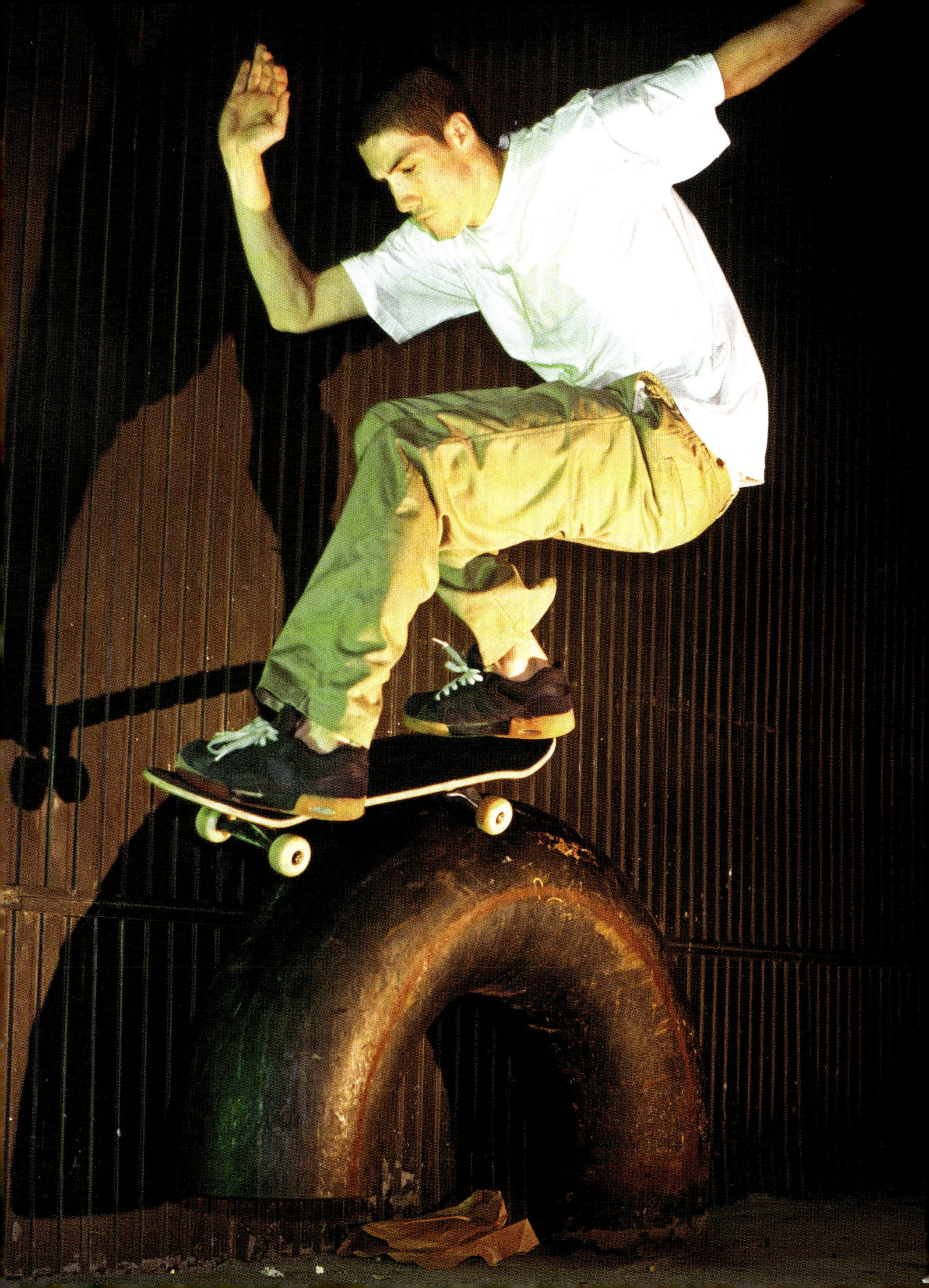

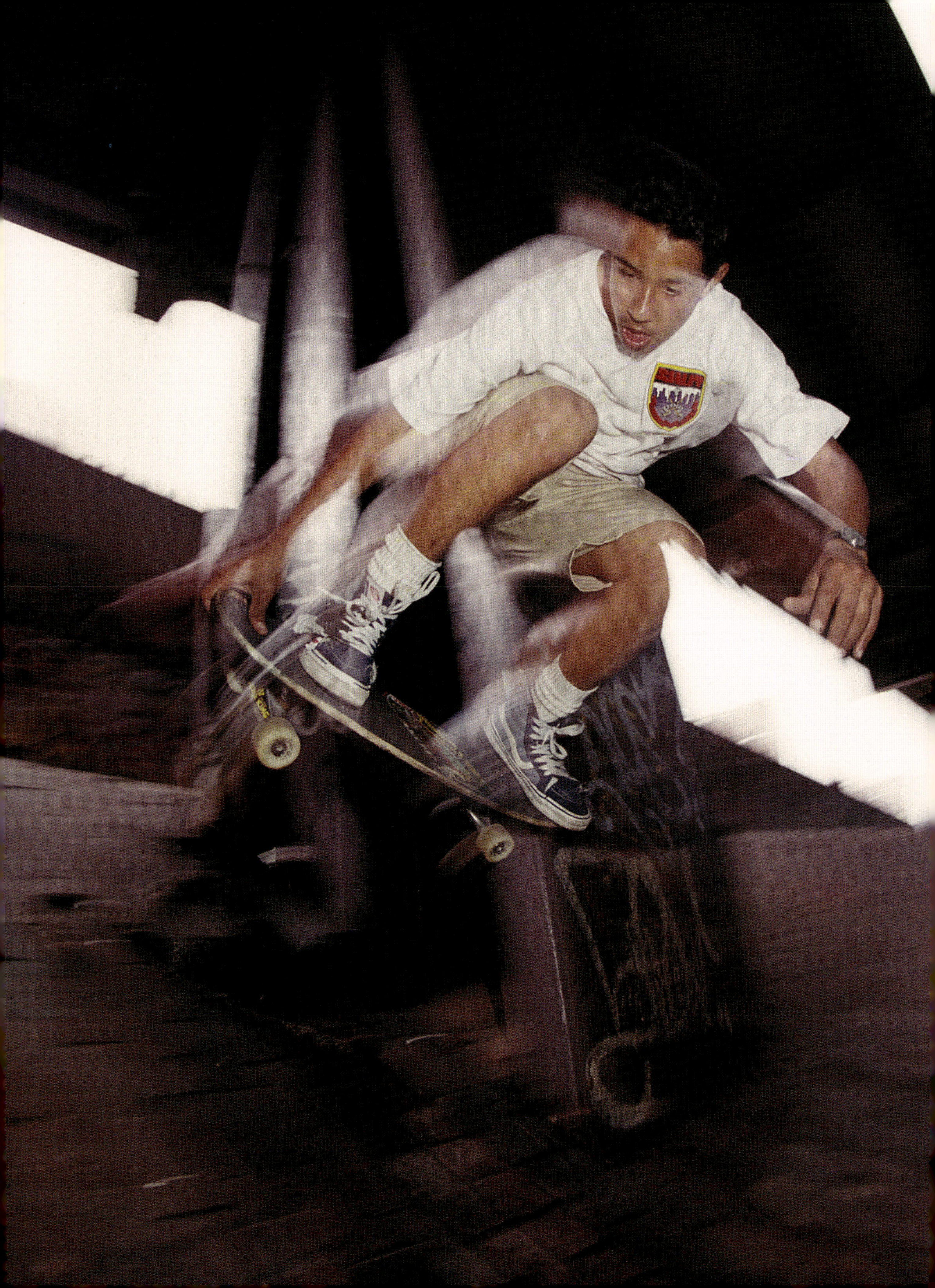

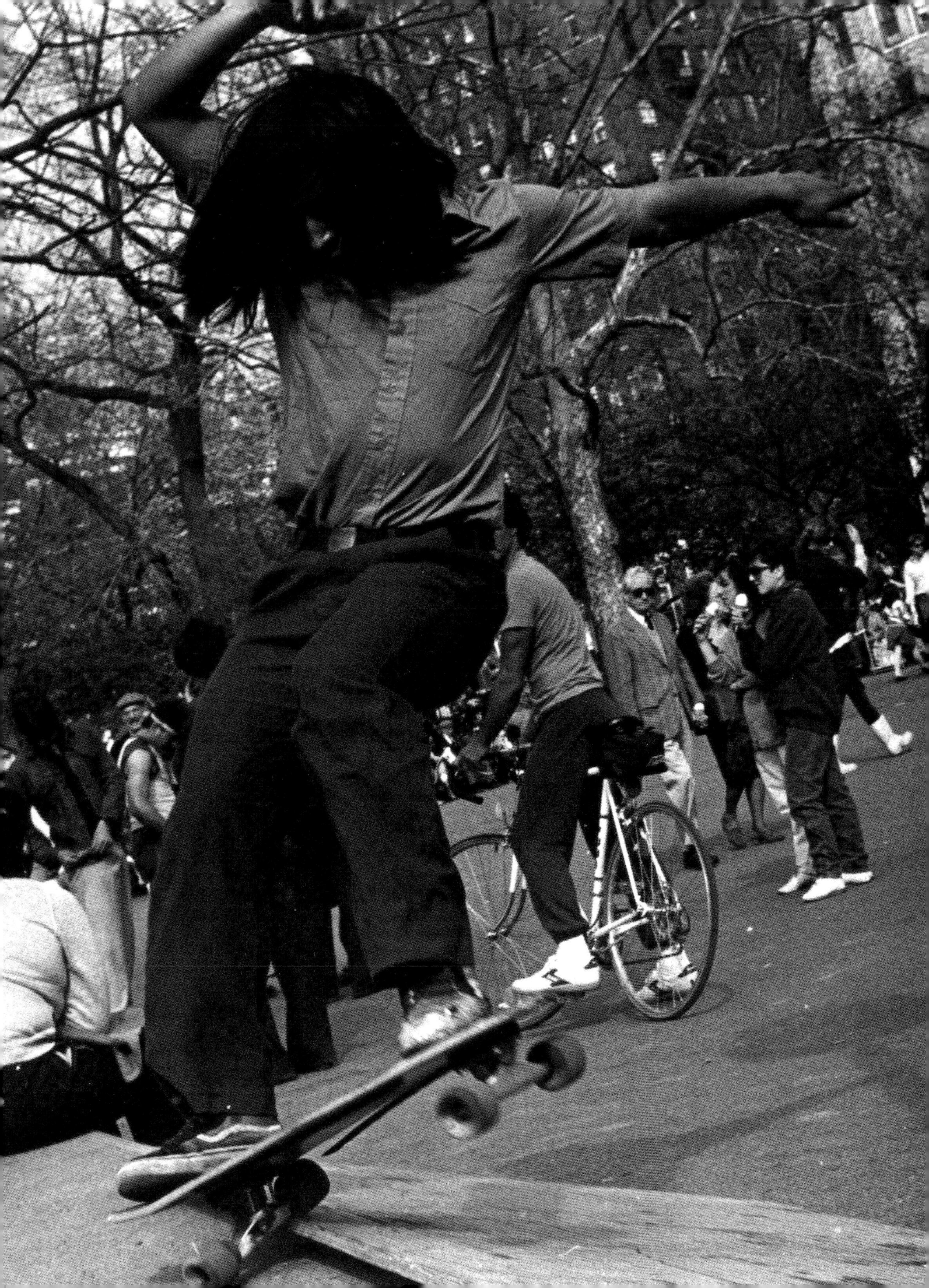

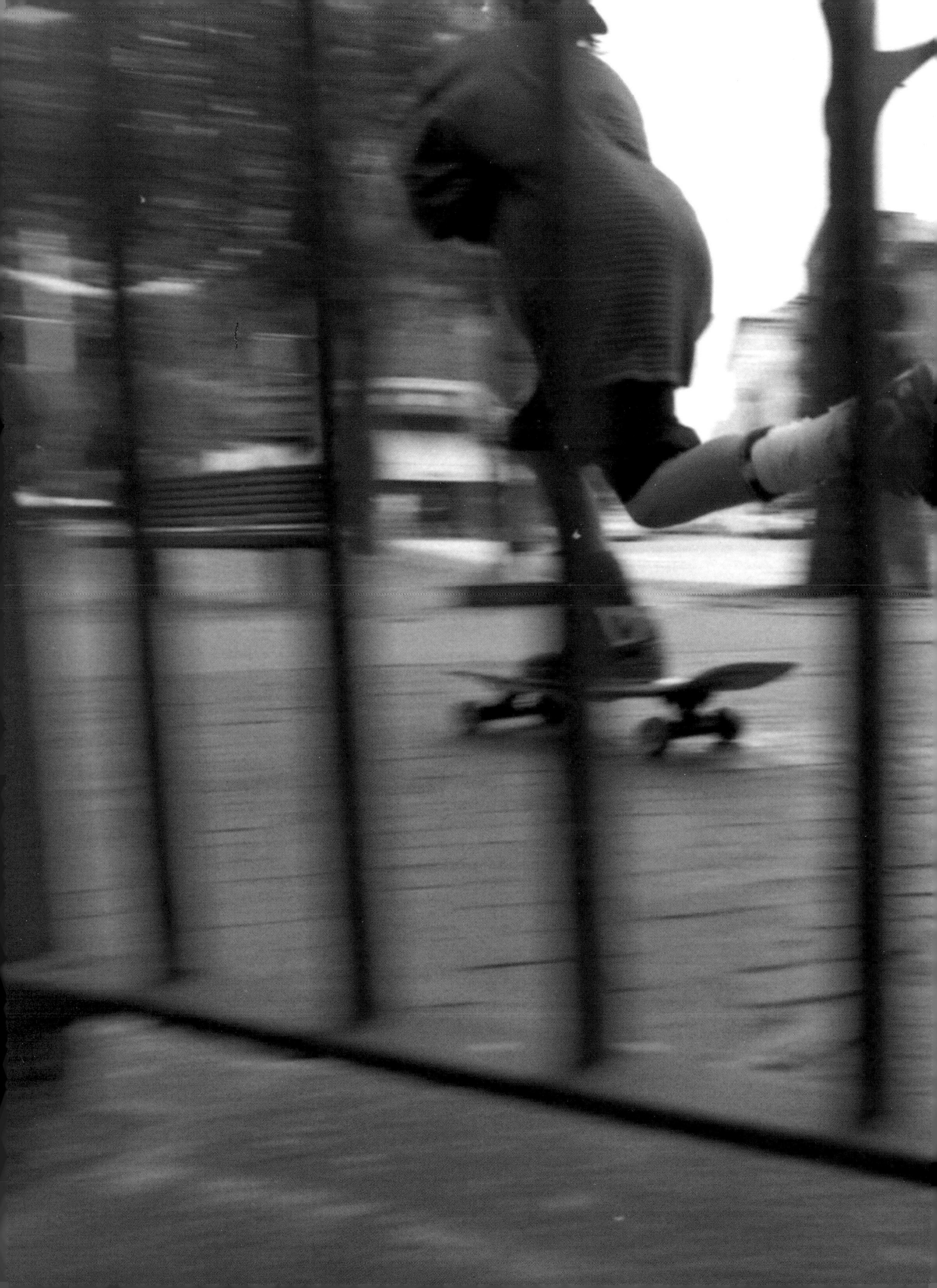

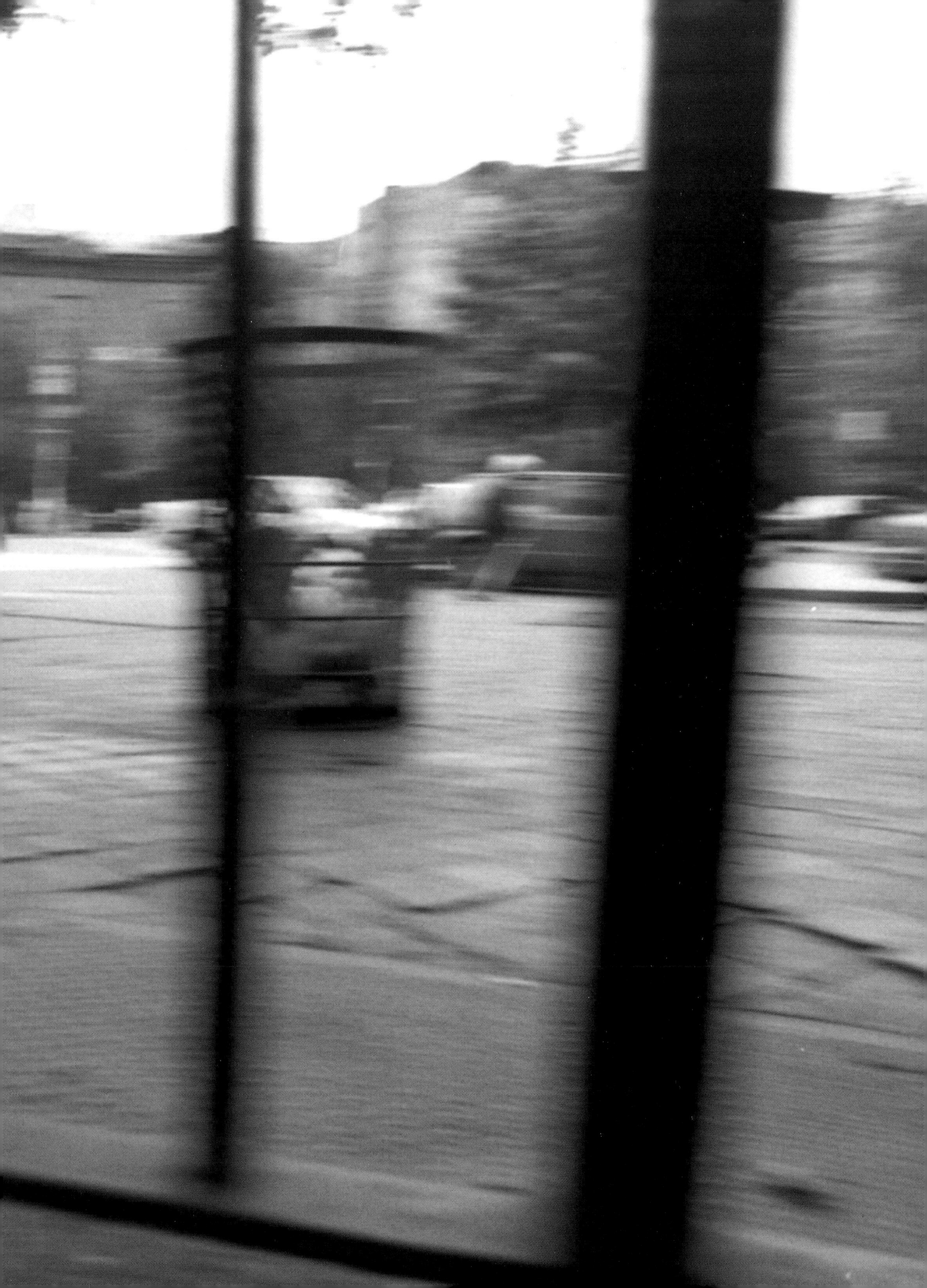

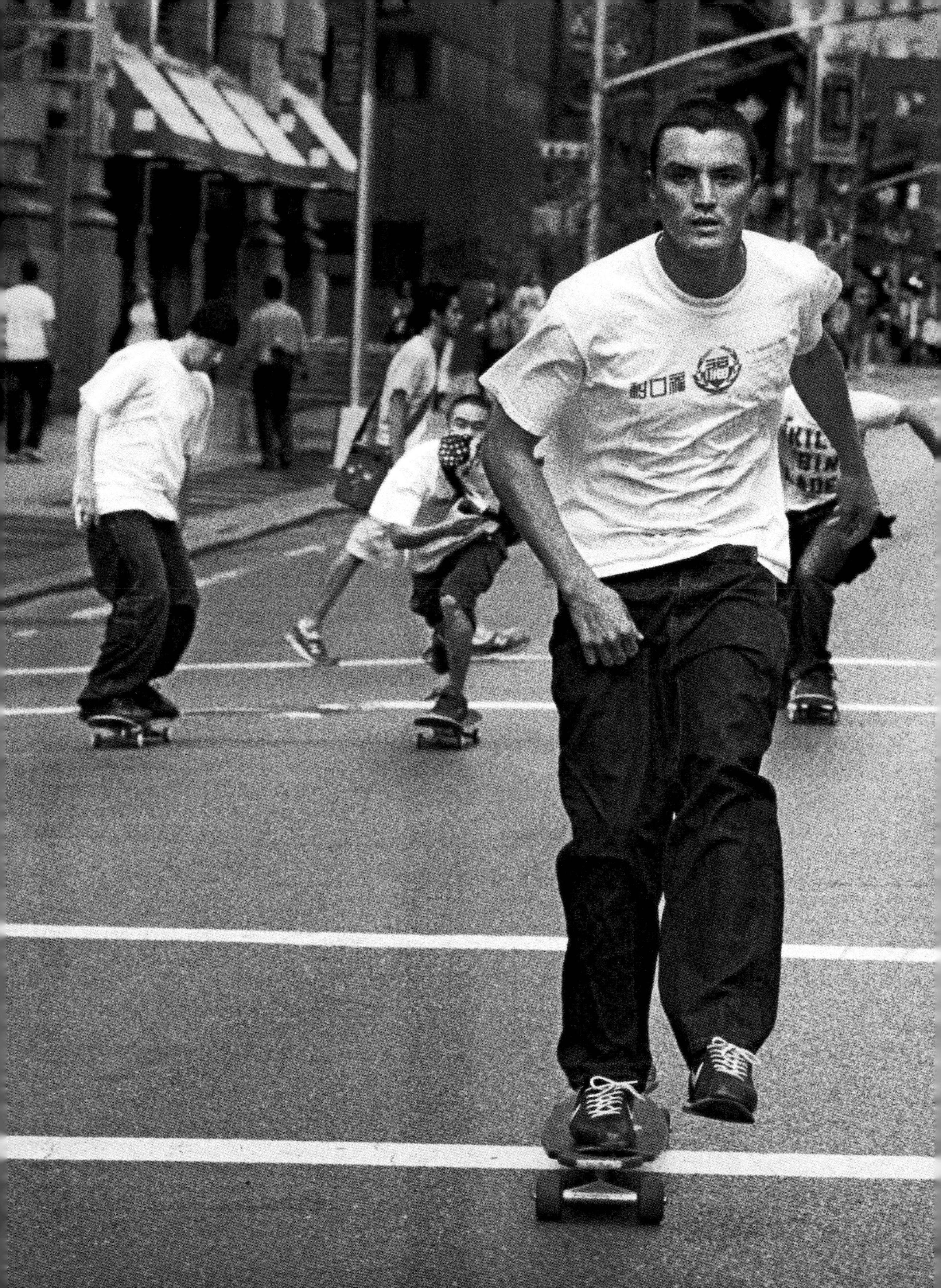

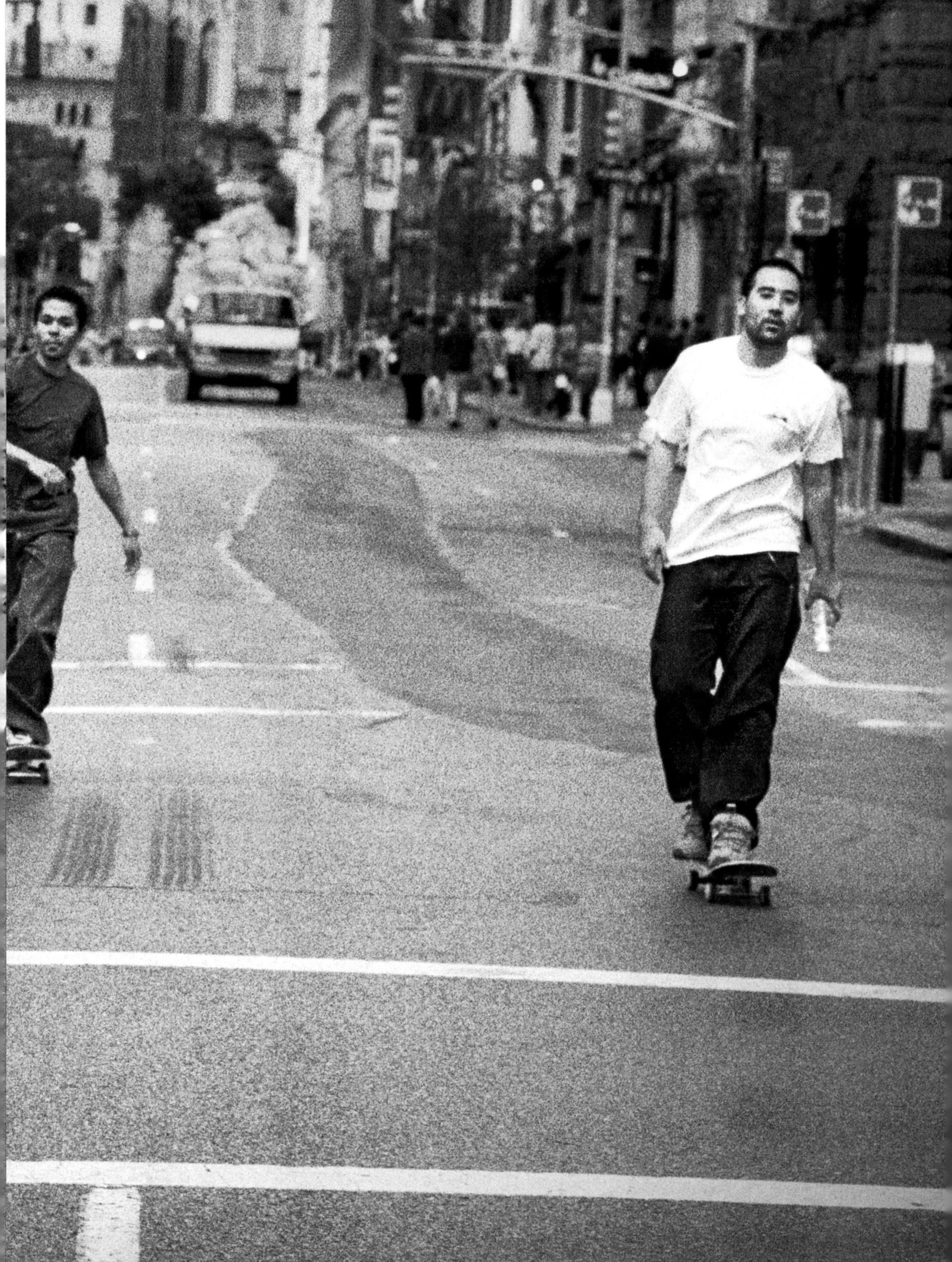

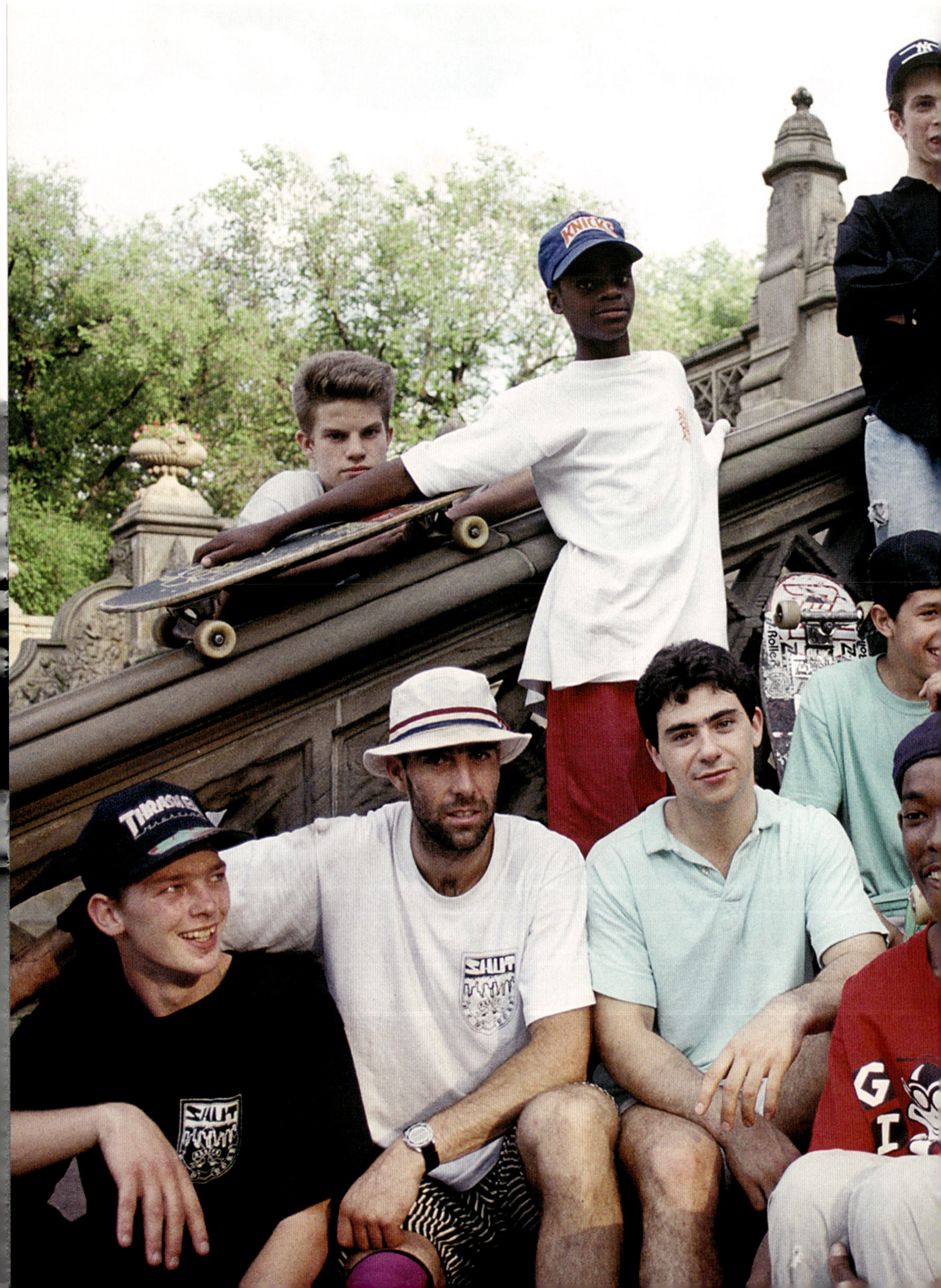
THRASHER
SHUT
SHUT

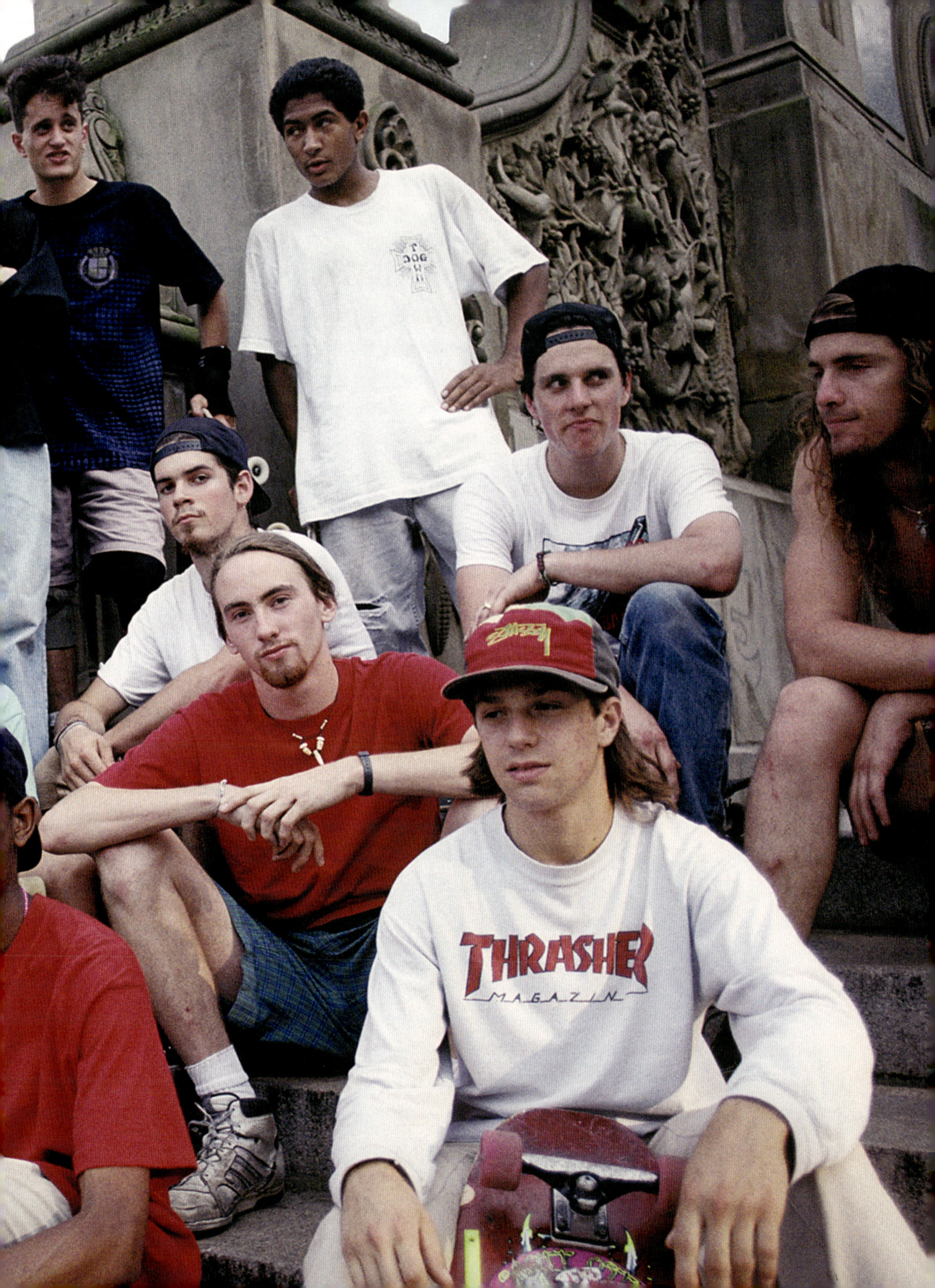
THRASHER
MAGAZIN

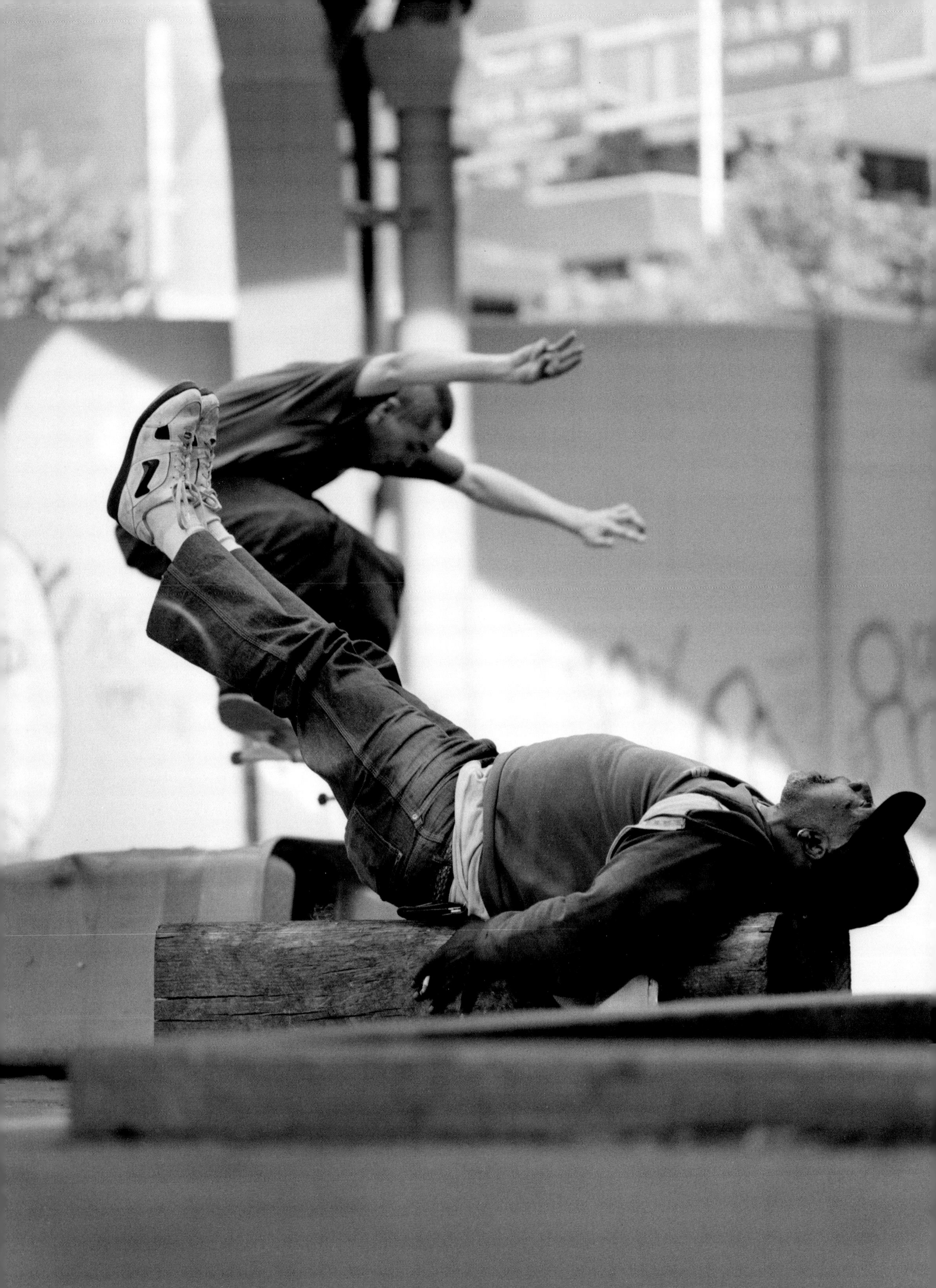

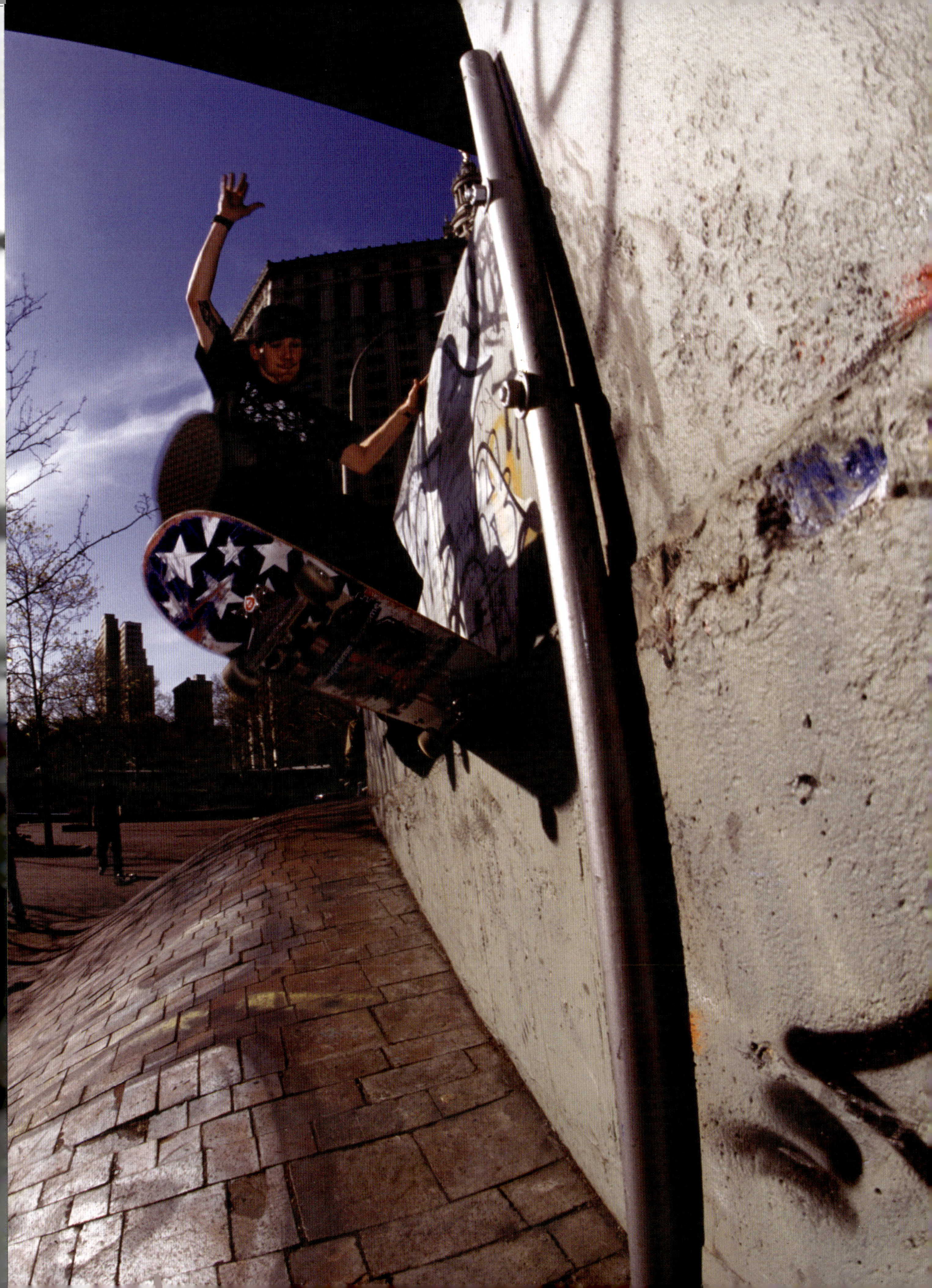

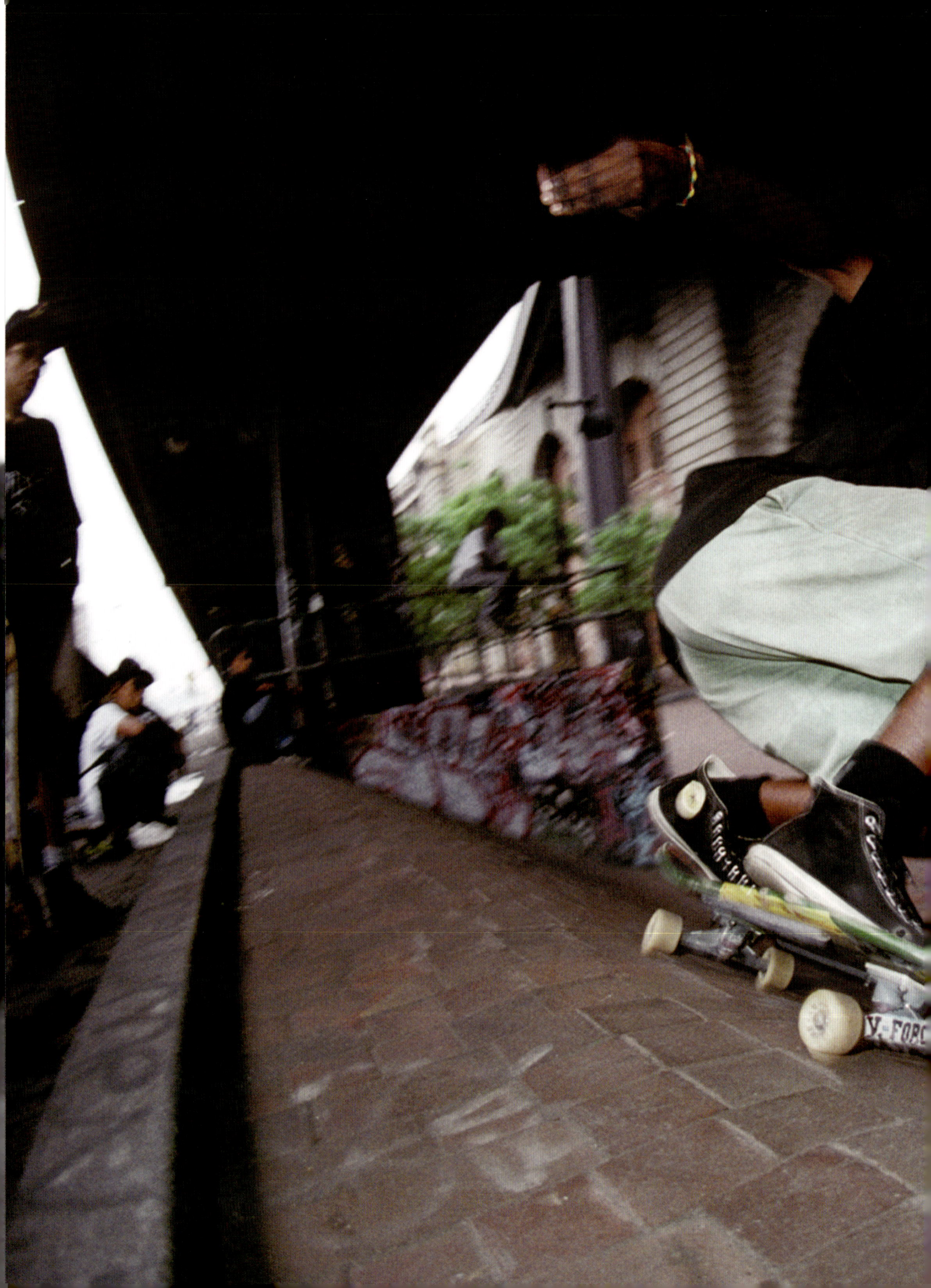

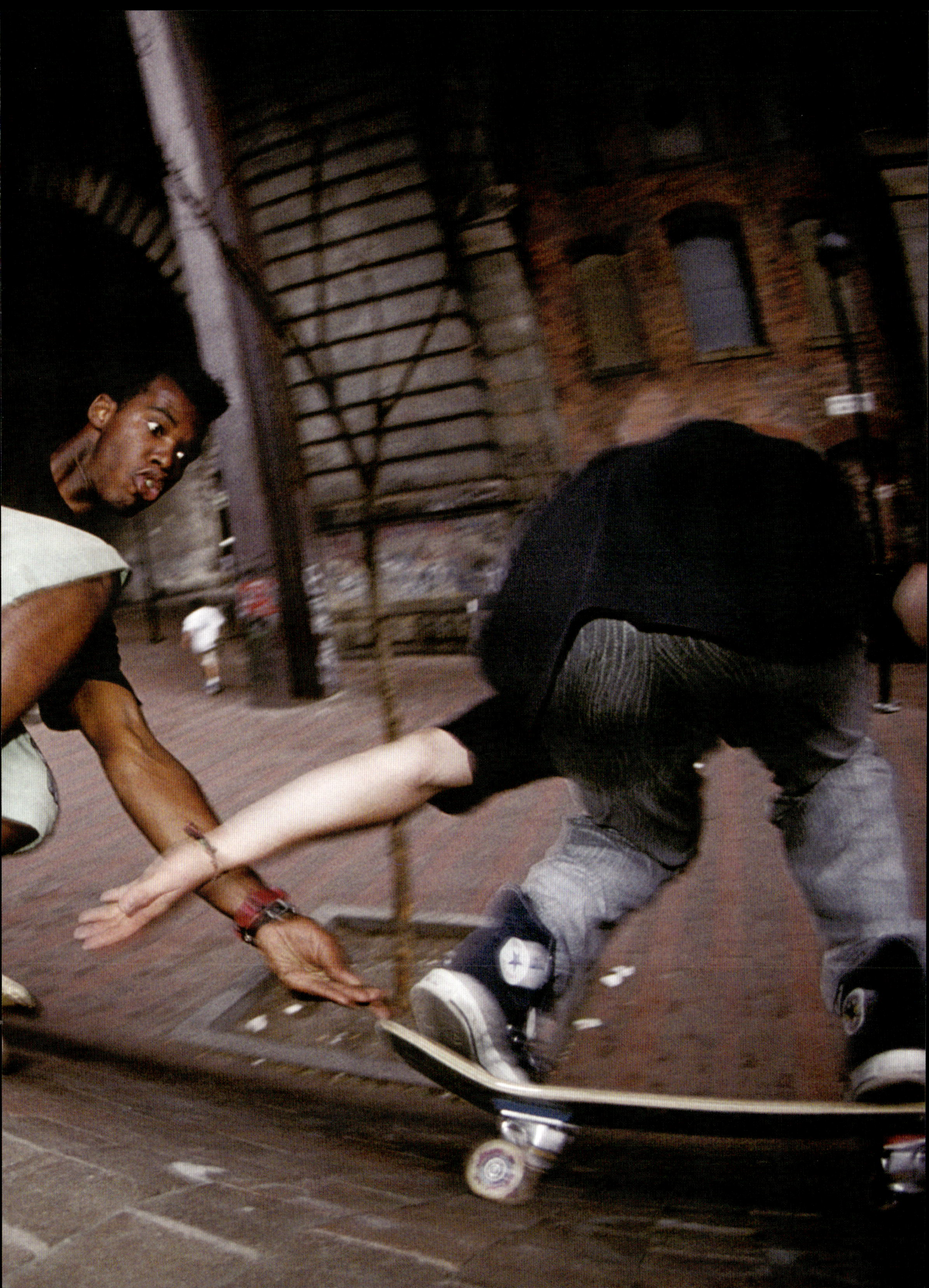

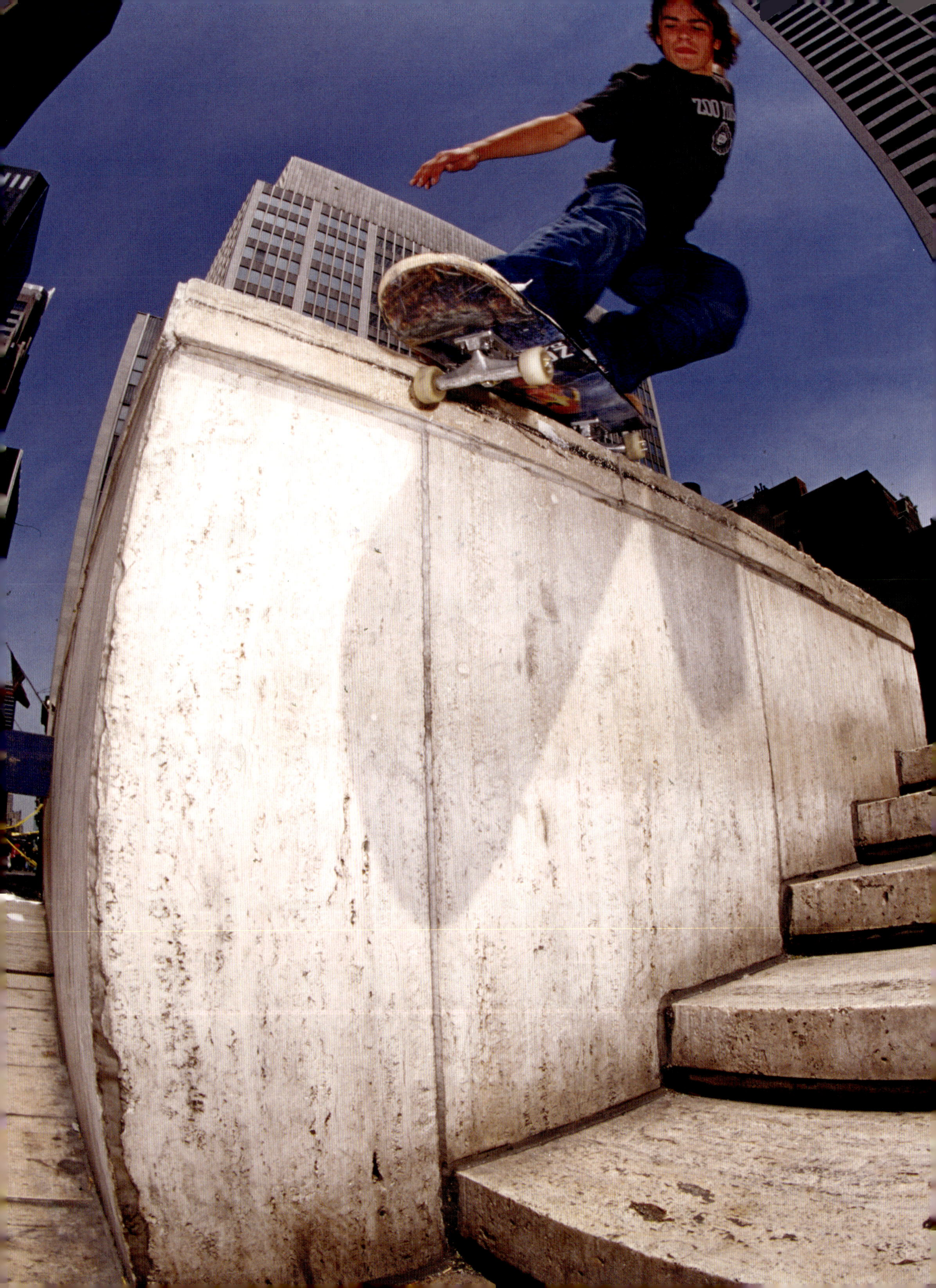

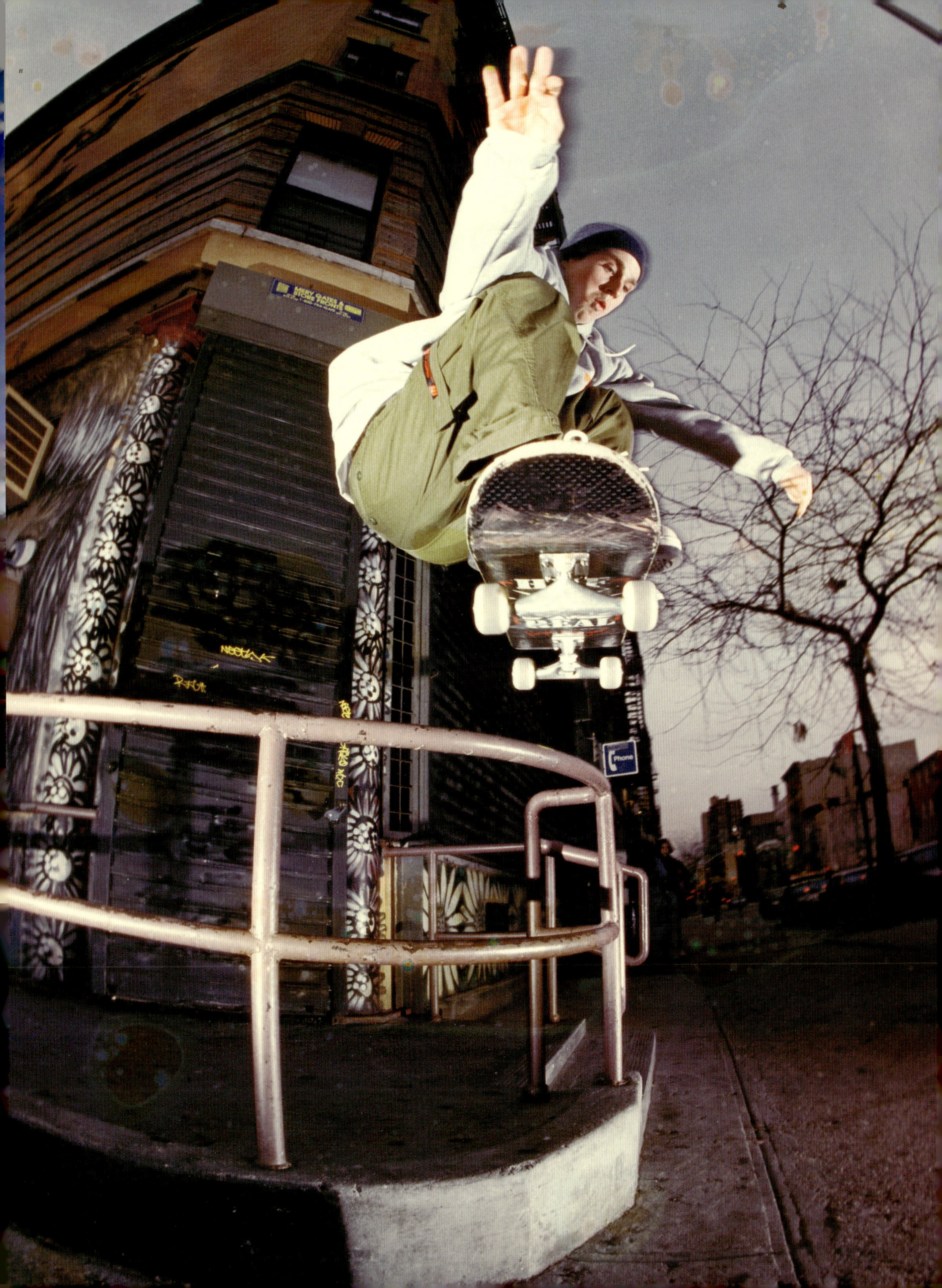
REAL
Phone

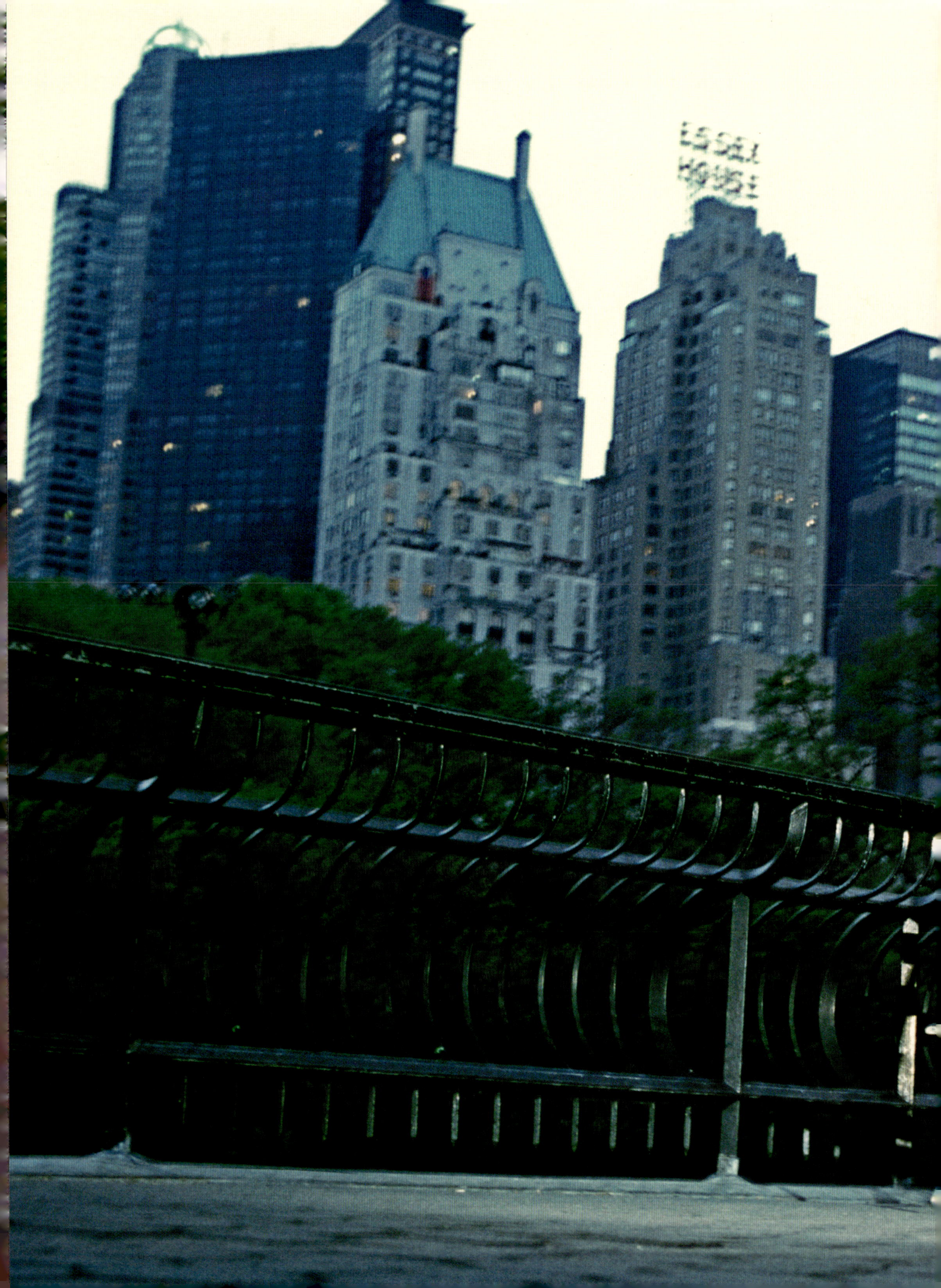

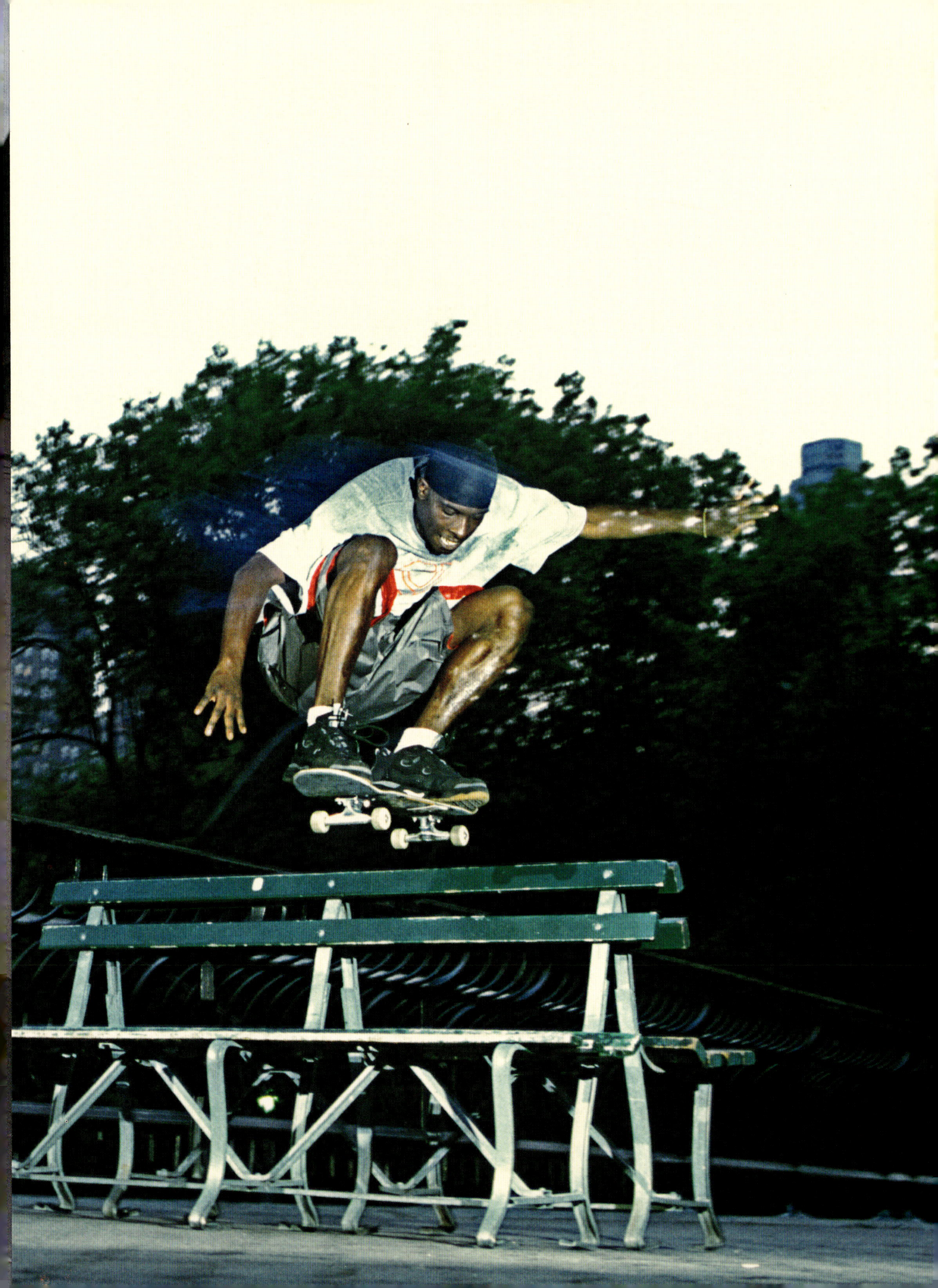

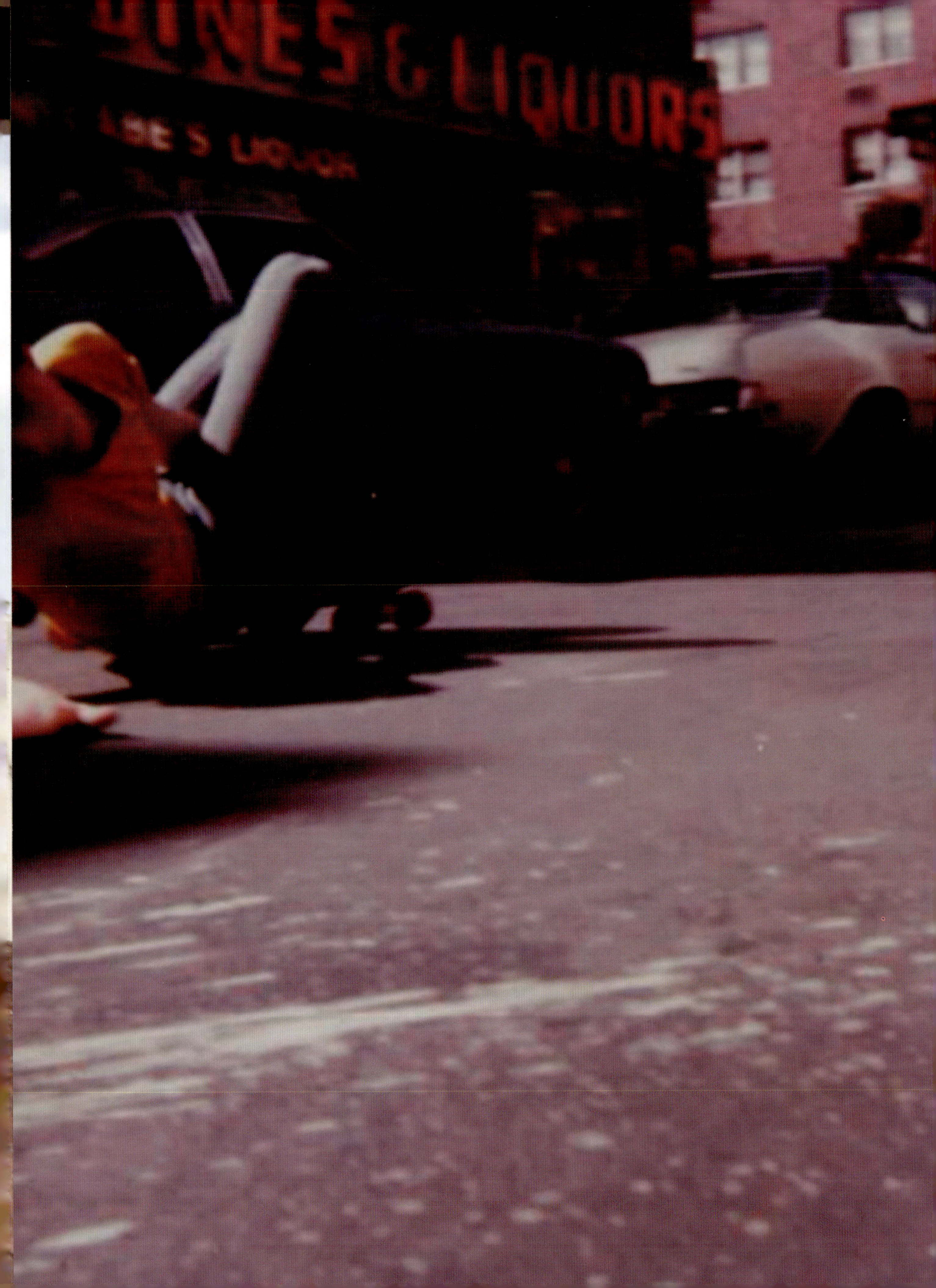
LIQUORS

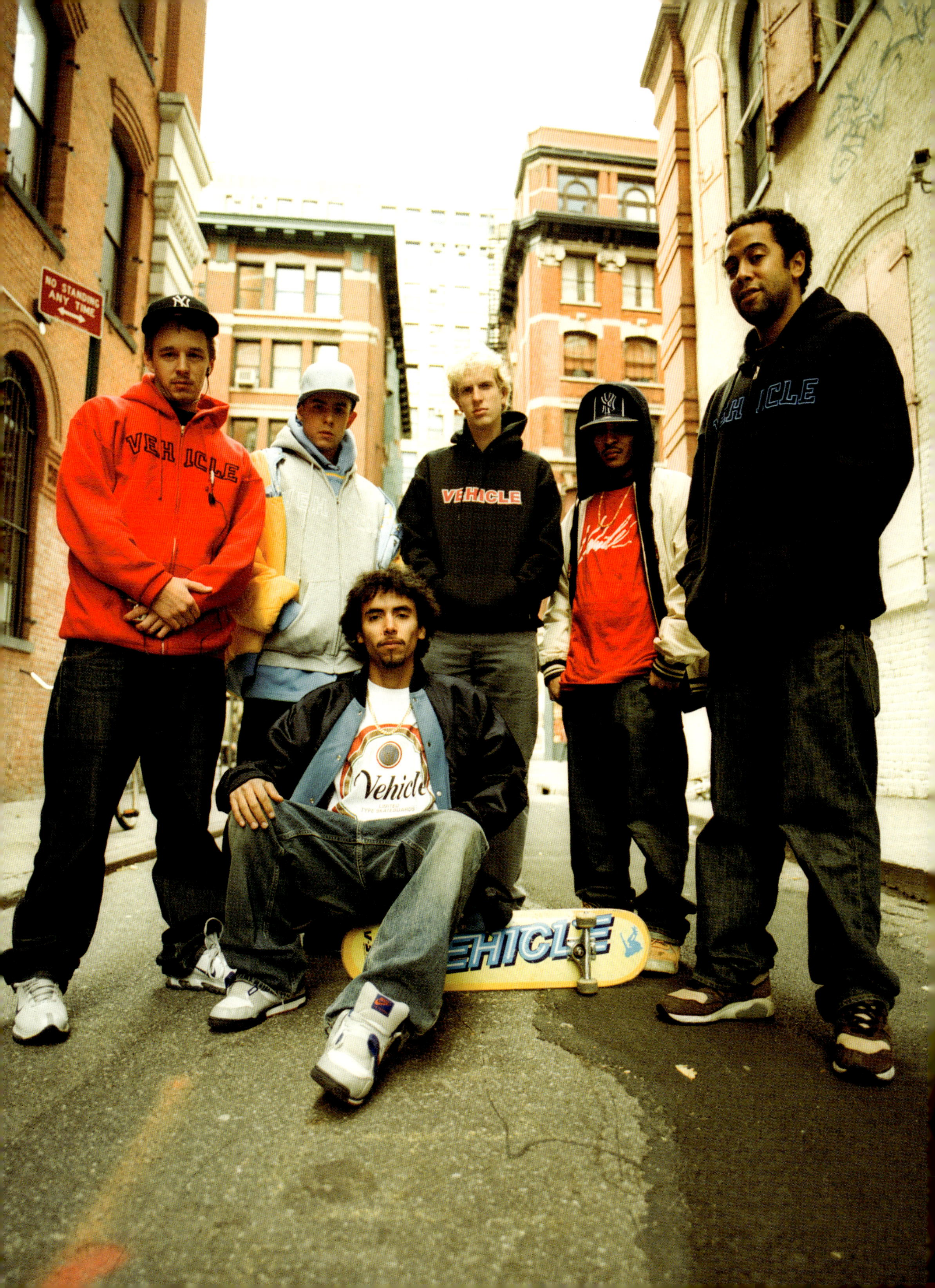
NO STANDING
ANY TIME
VEHICLE
VEHICLE
VEHICLE
Vehicle
VEHICLE

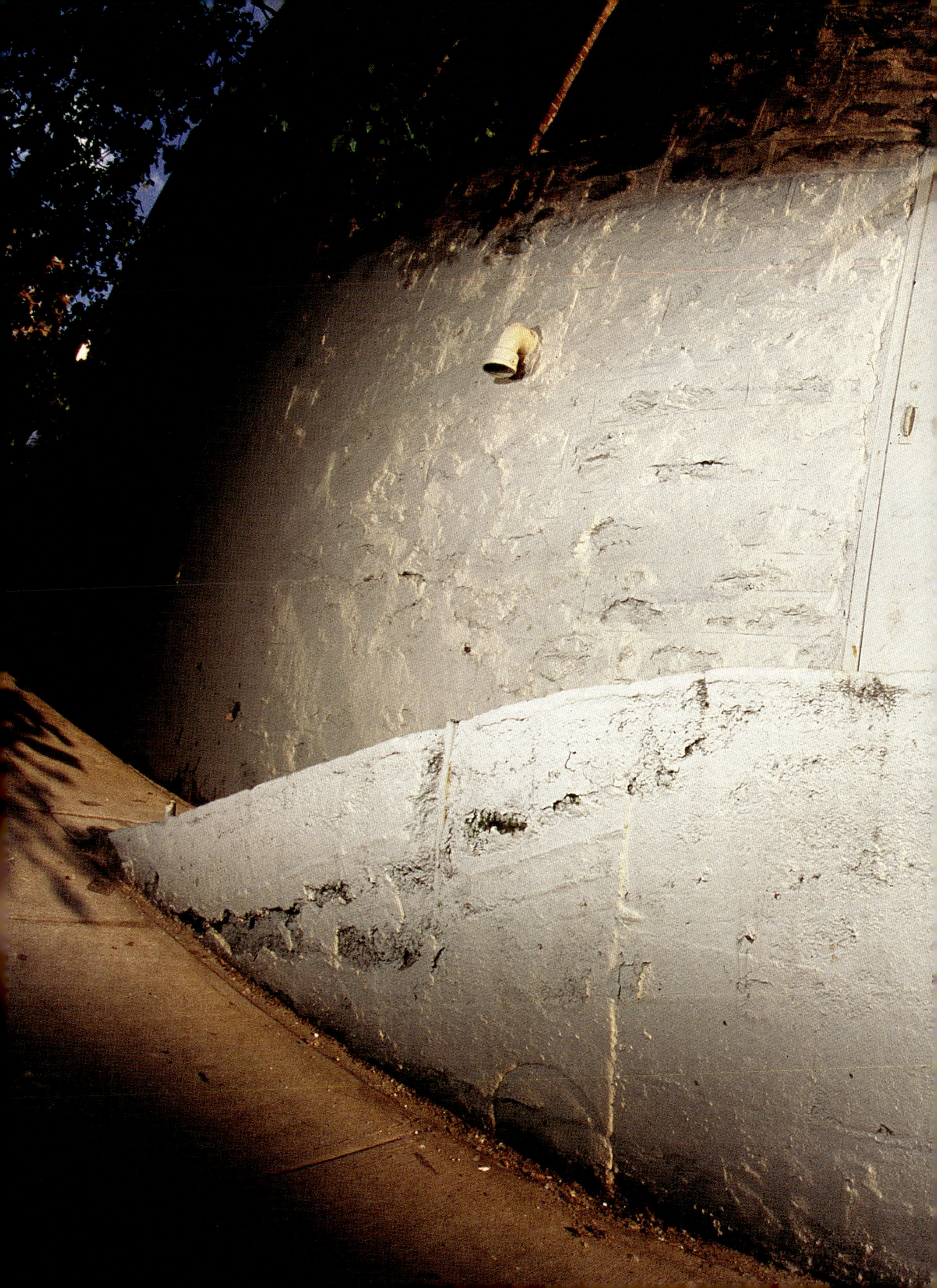

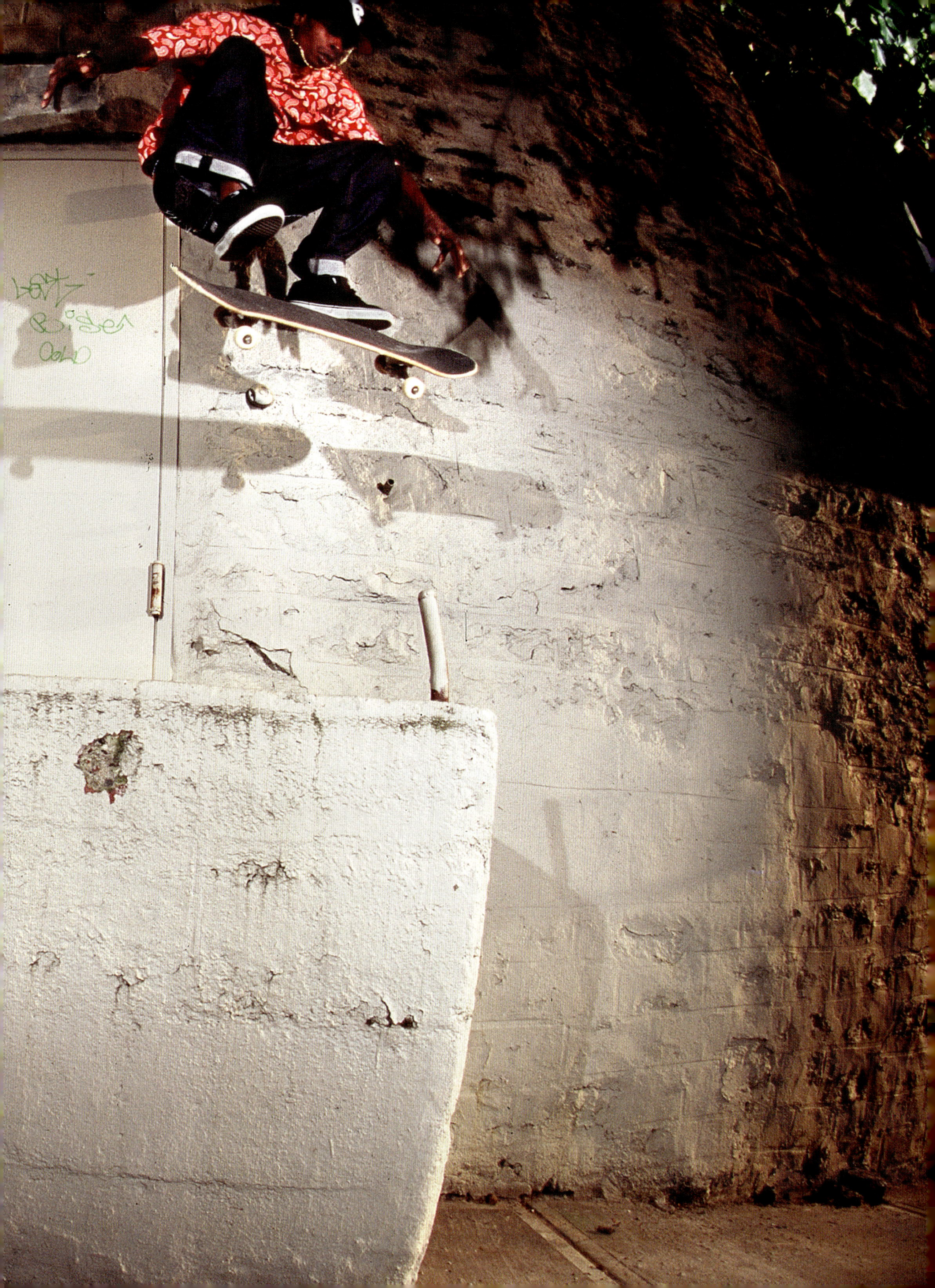

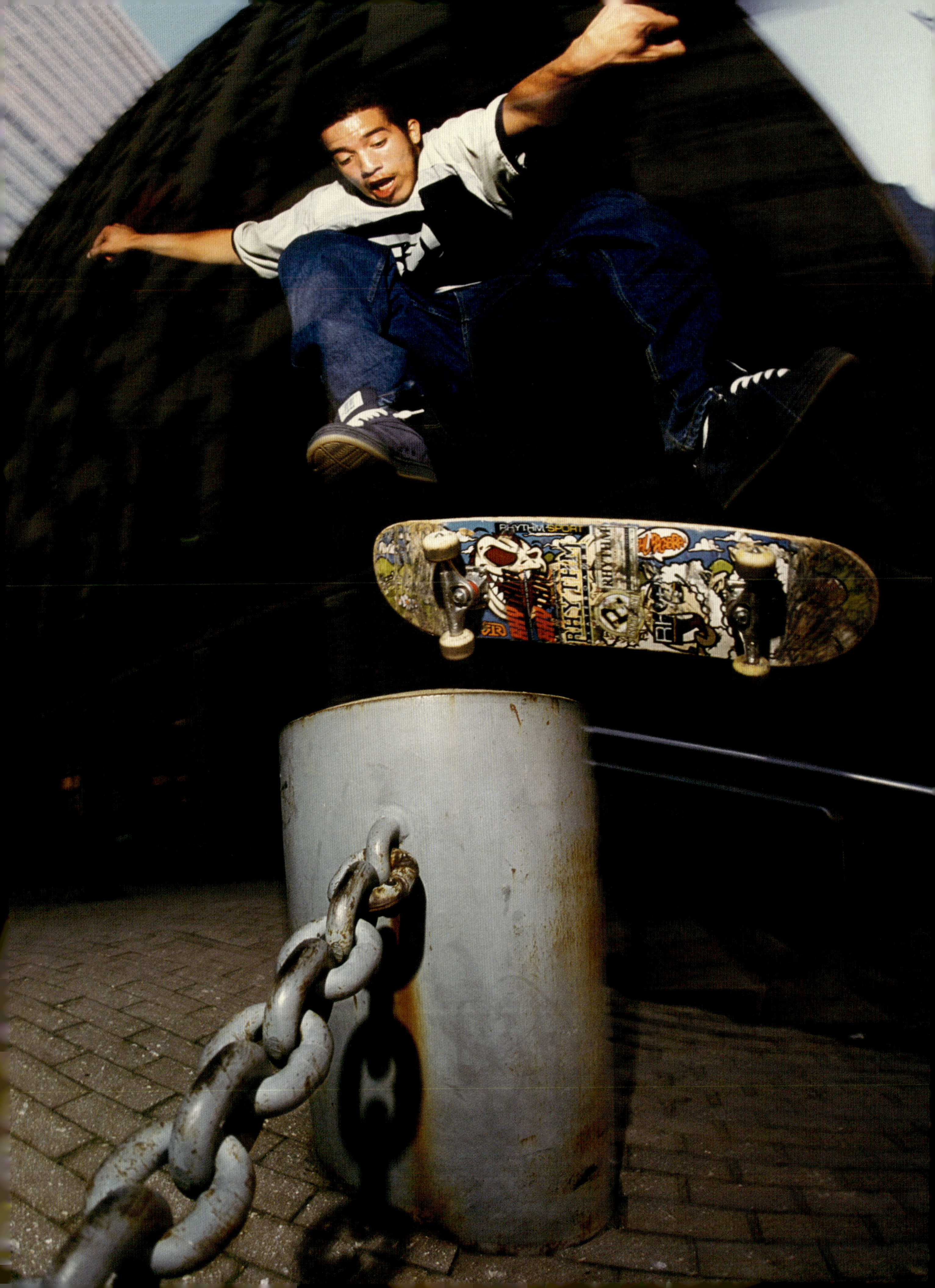
RHYTHM SPORT
RHYTHM

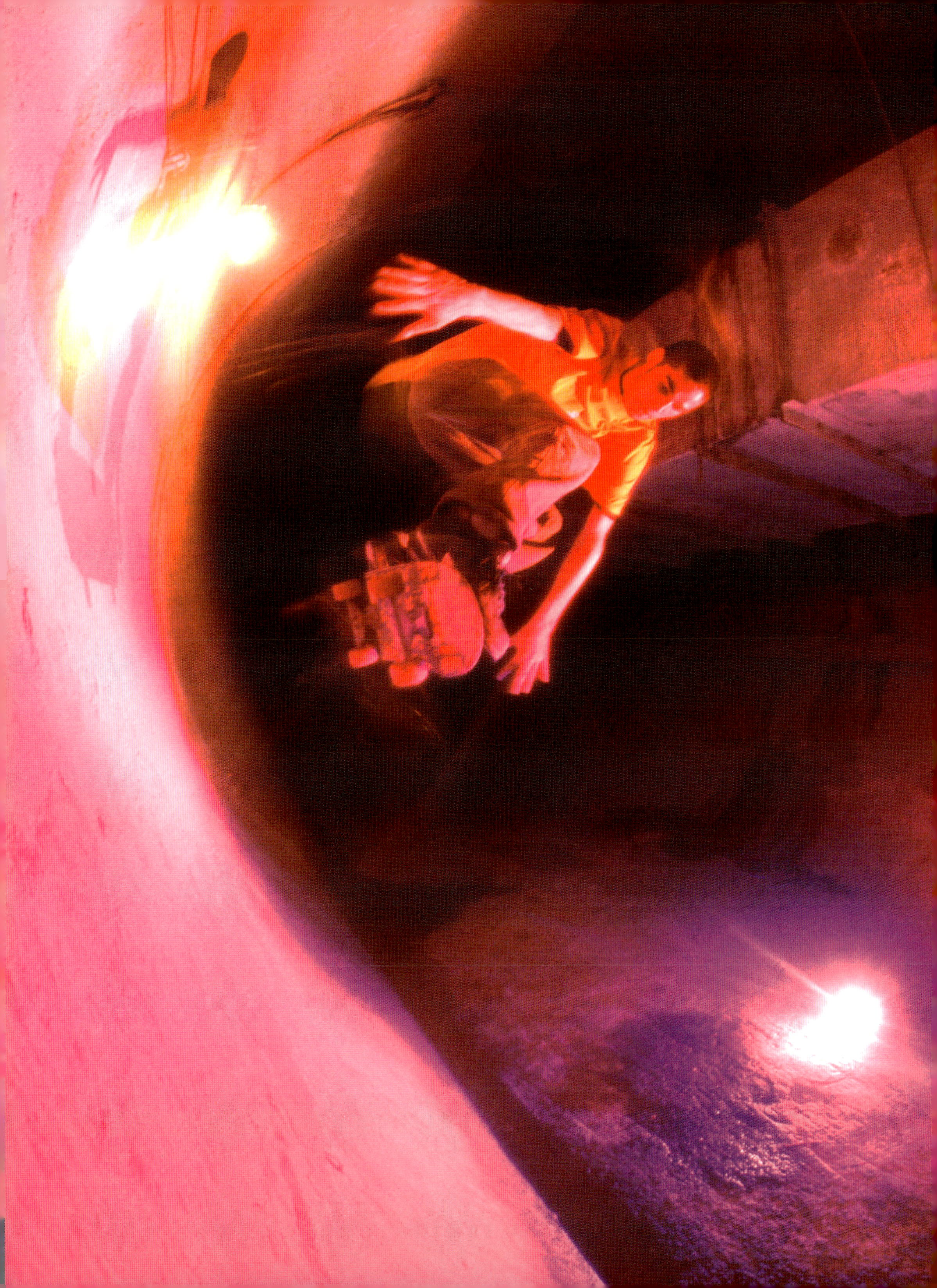

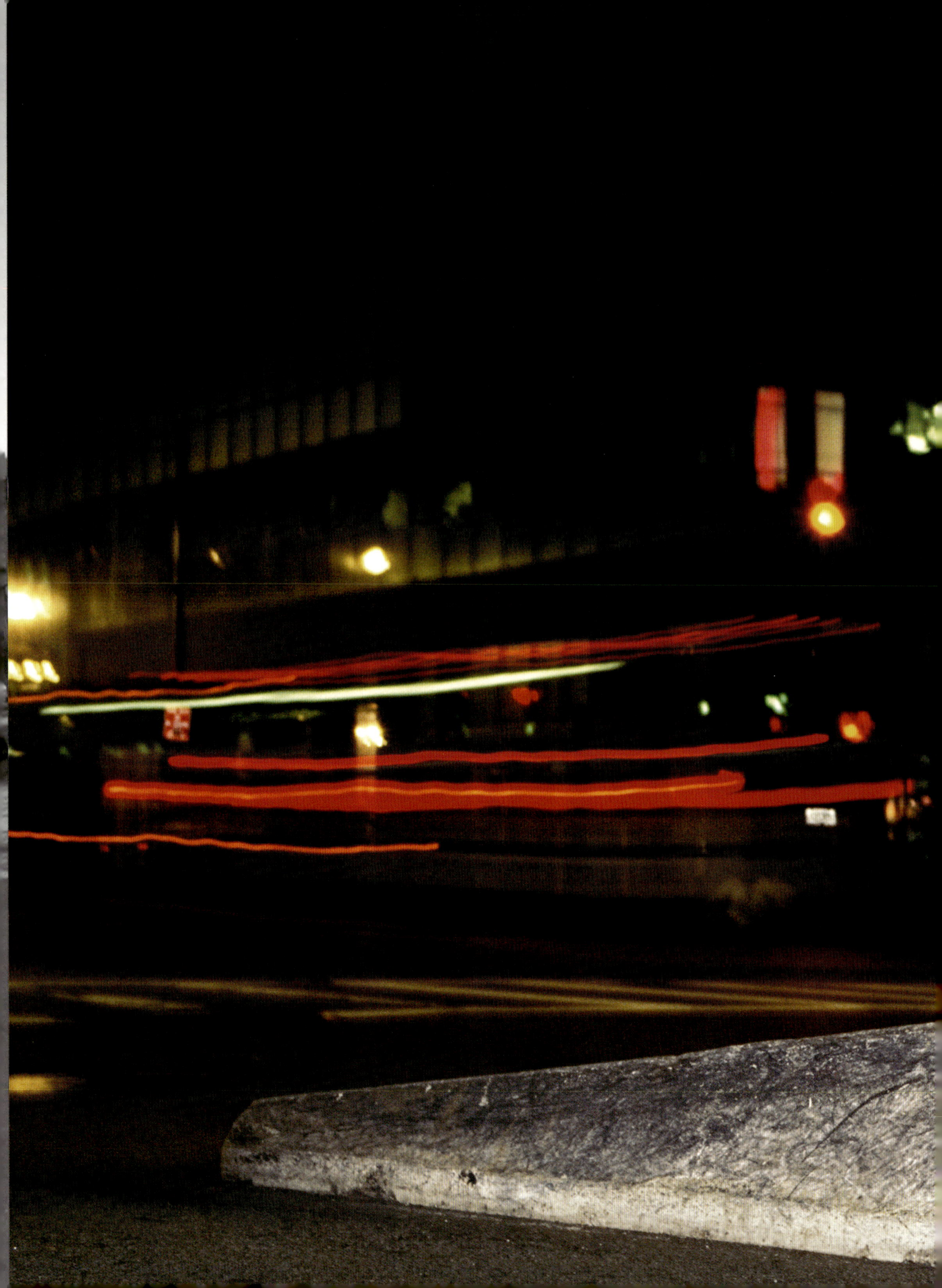

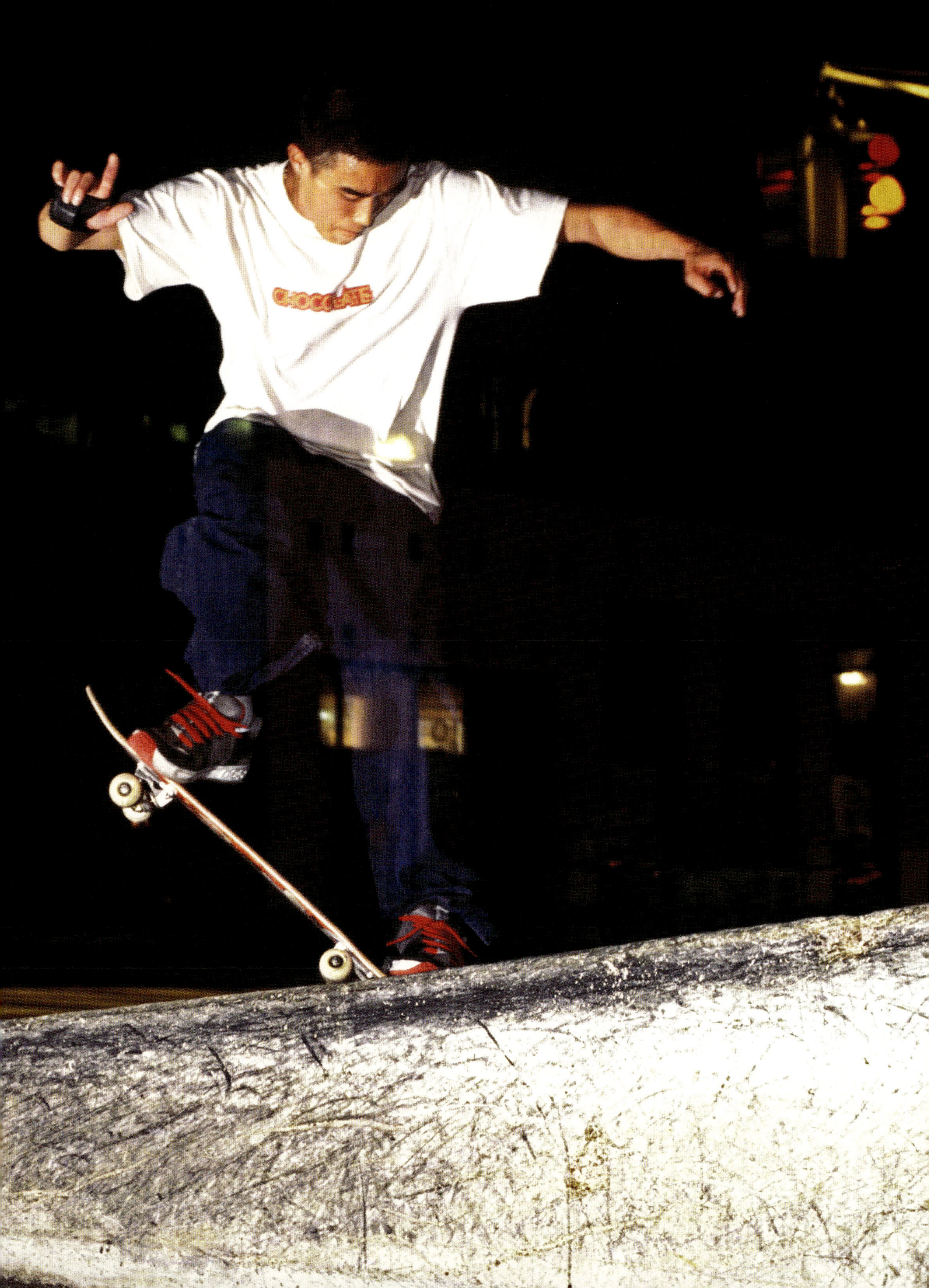
CHOCOLATE

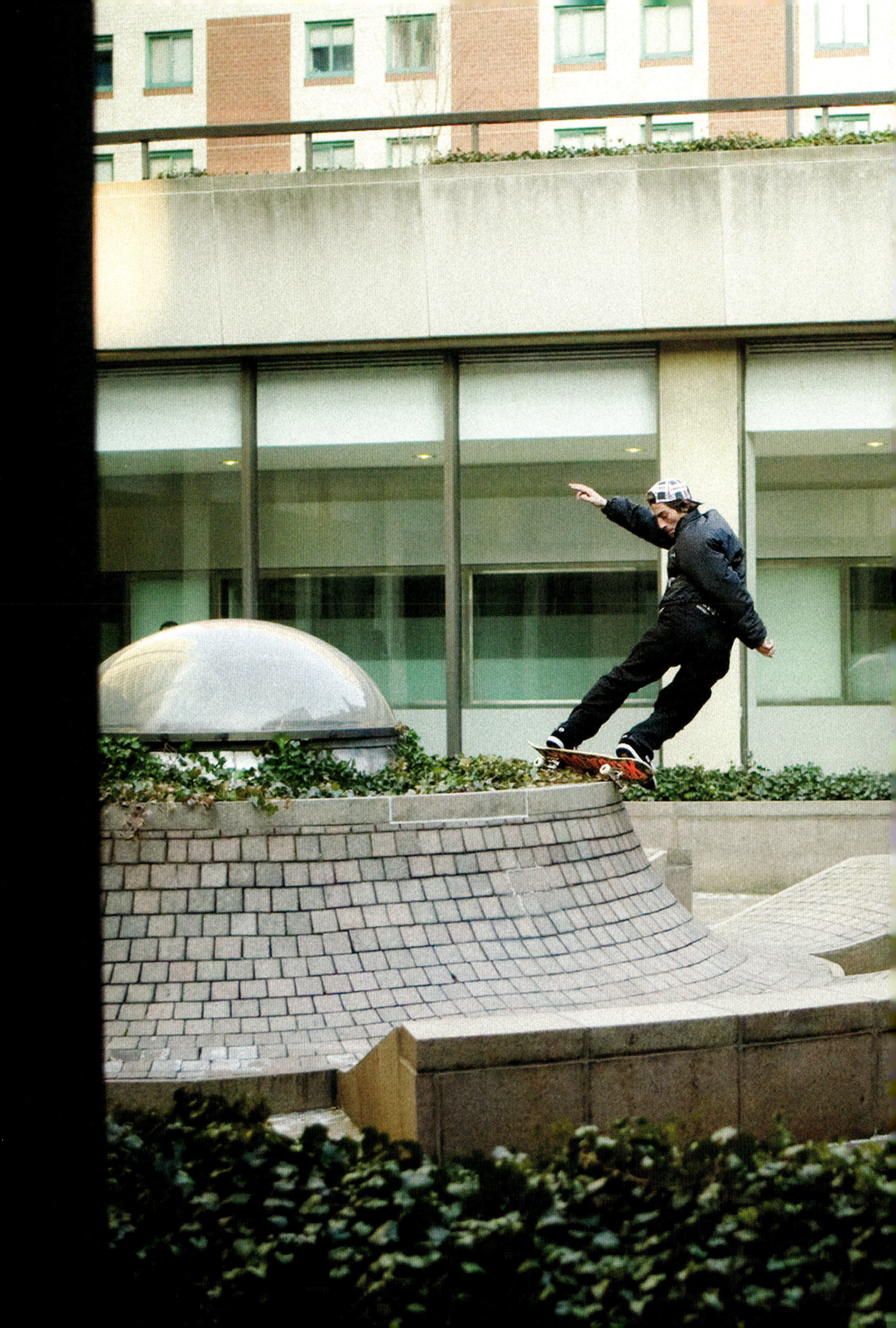

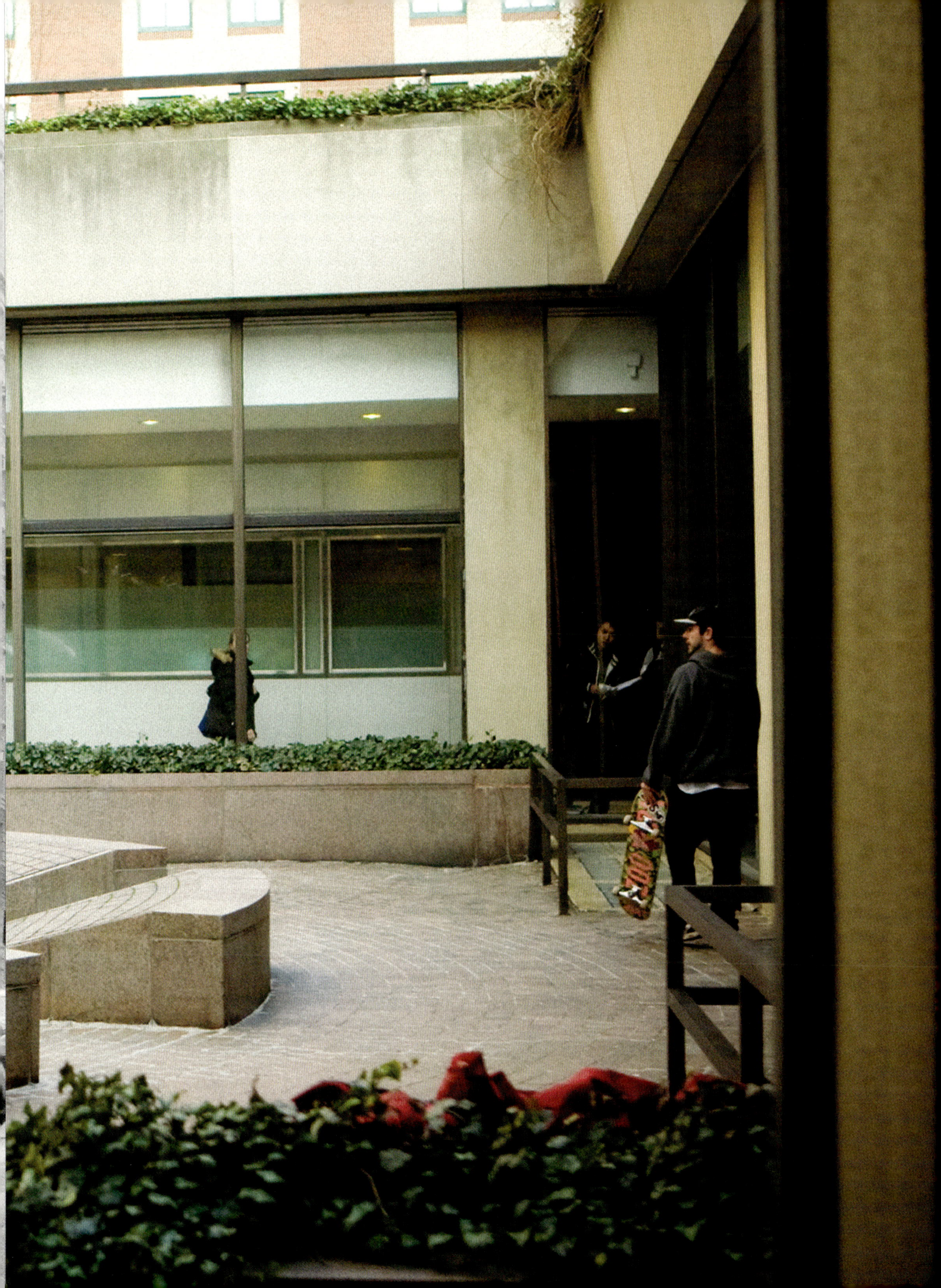

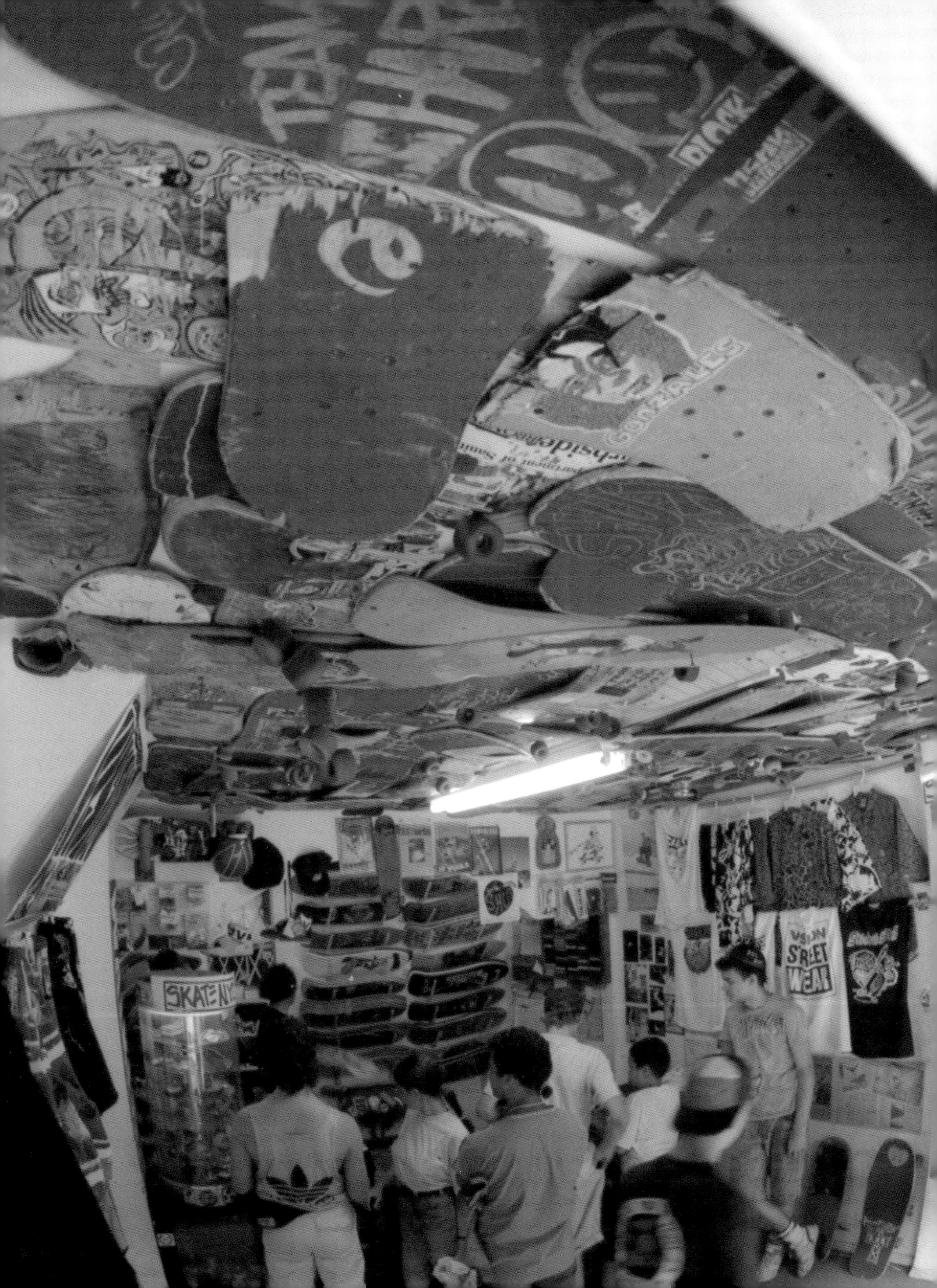
GONZALES
VISION
STREET
WEAR

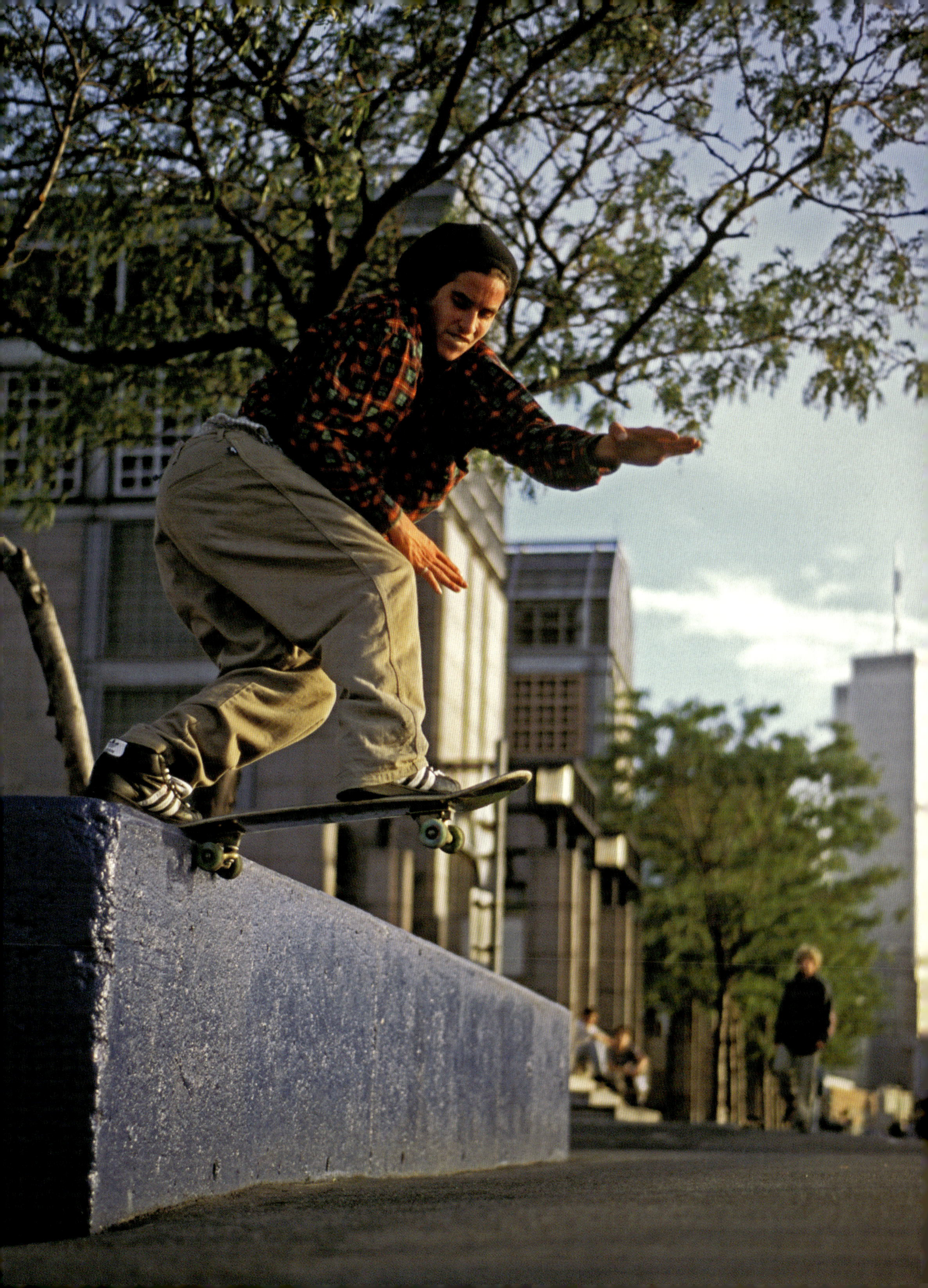

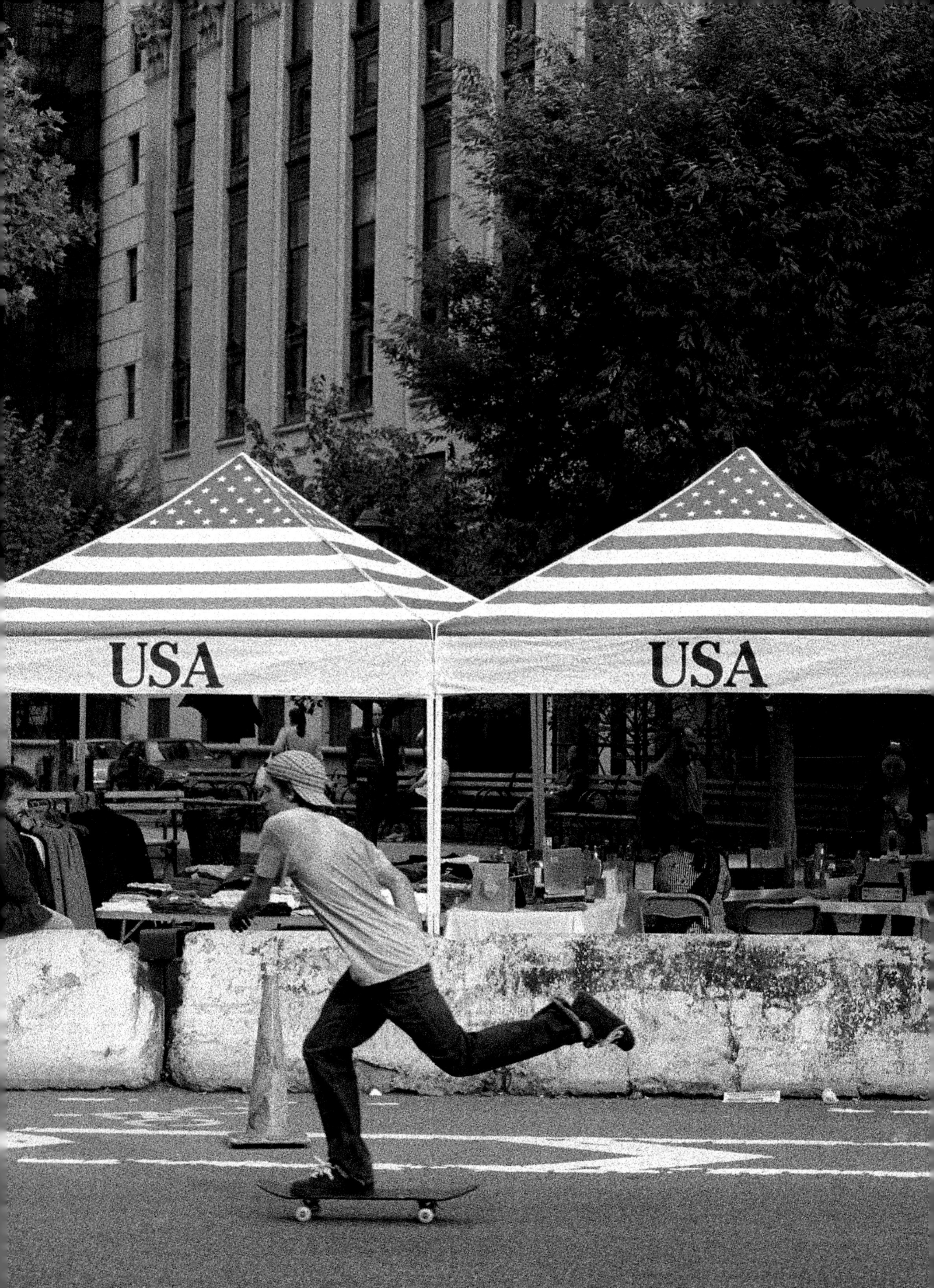
USA
USA

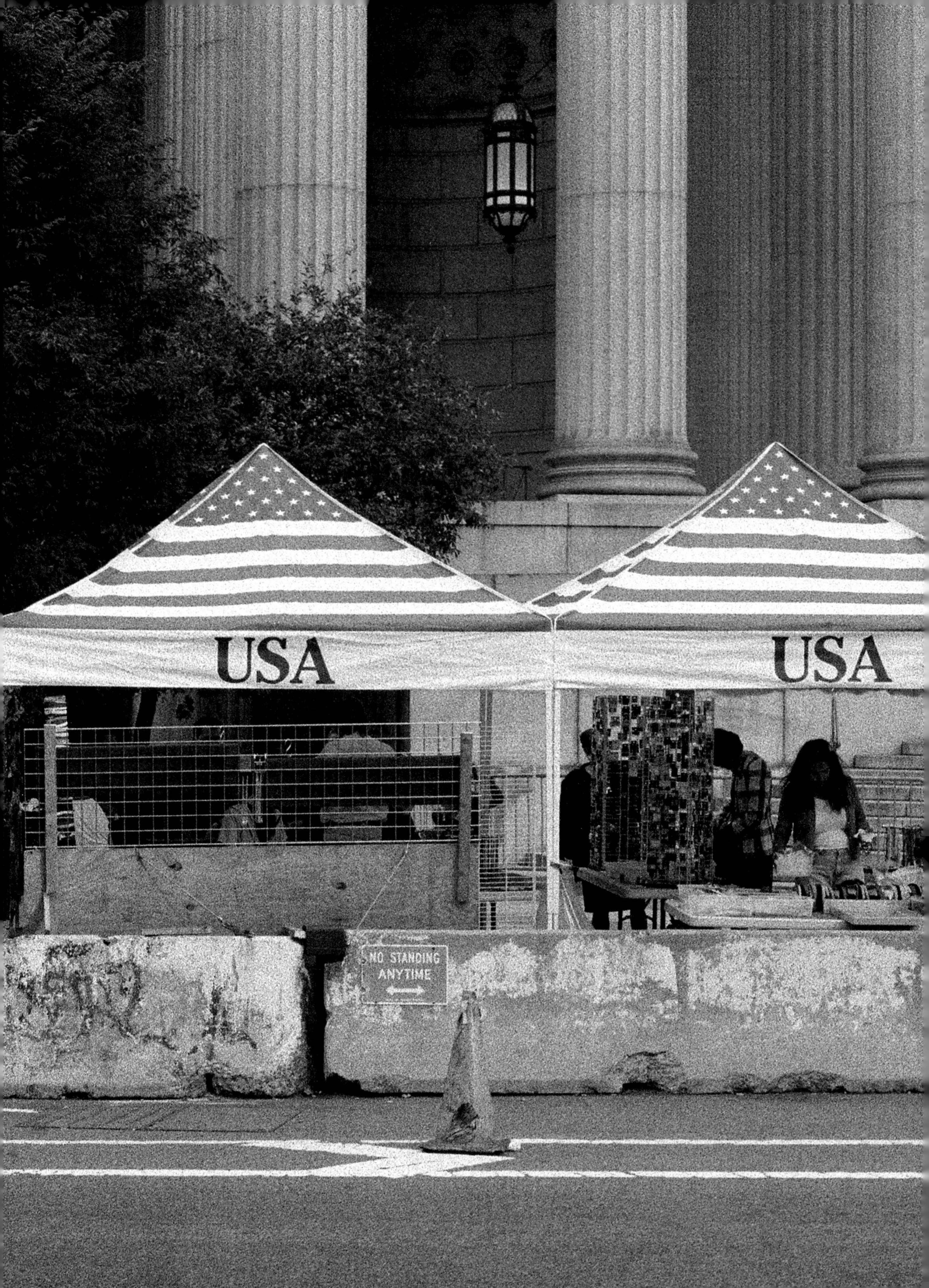
USA
USA
NO STANDING
ANYTIME

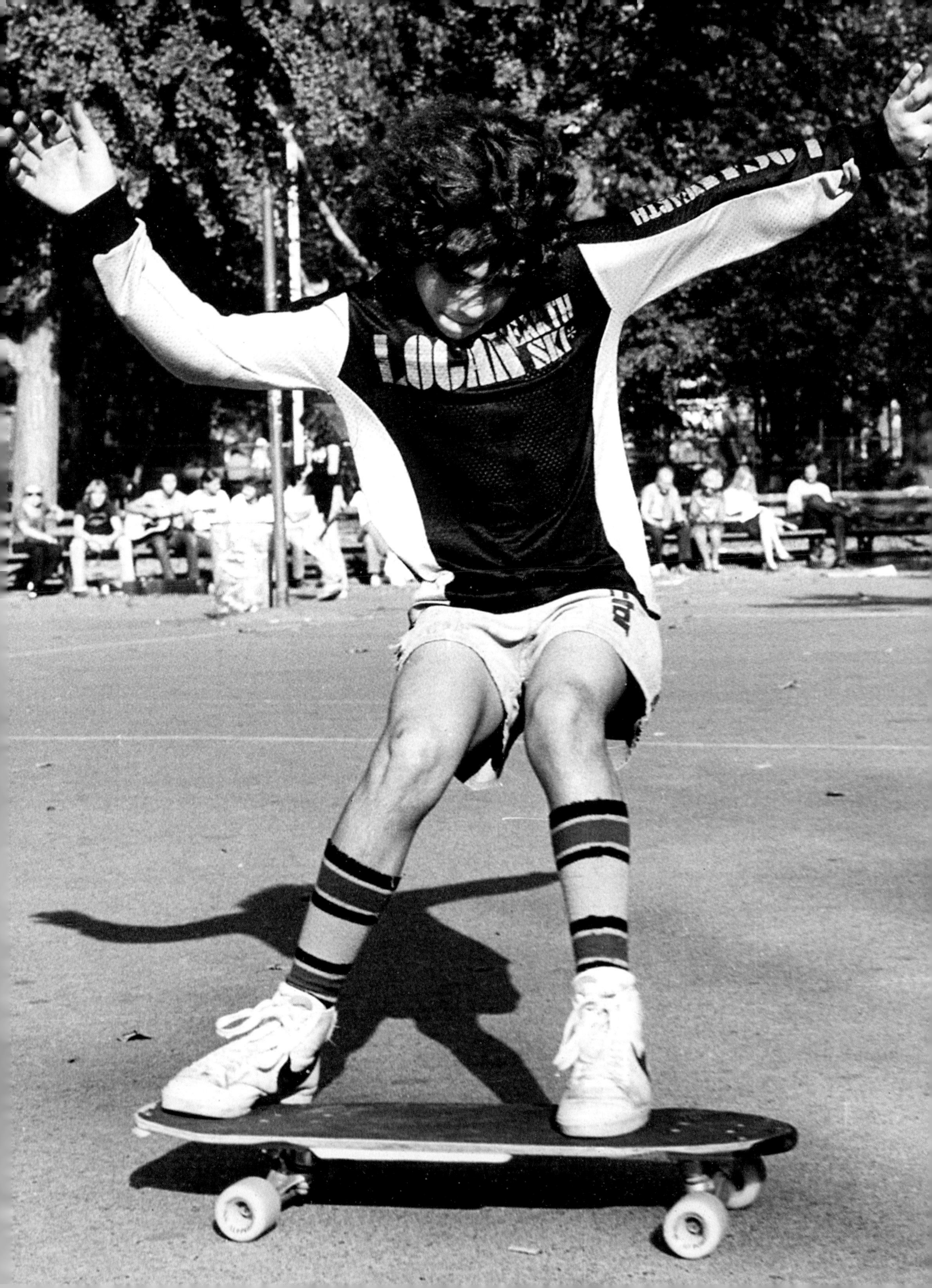
LOGAN
SKI

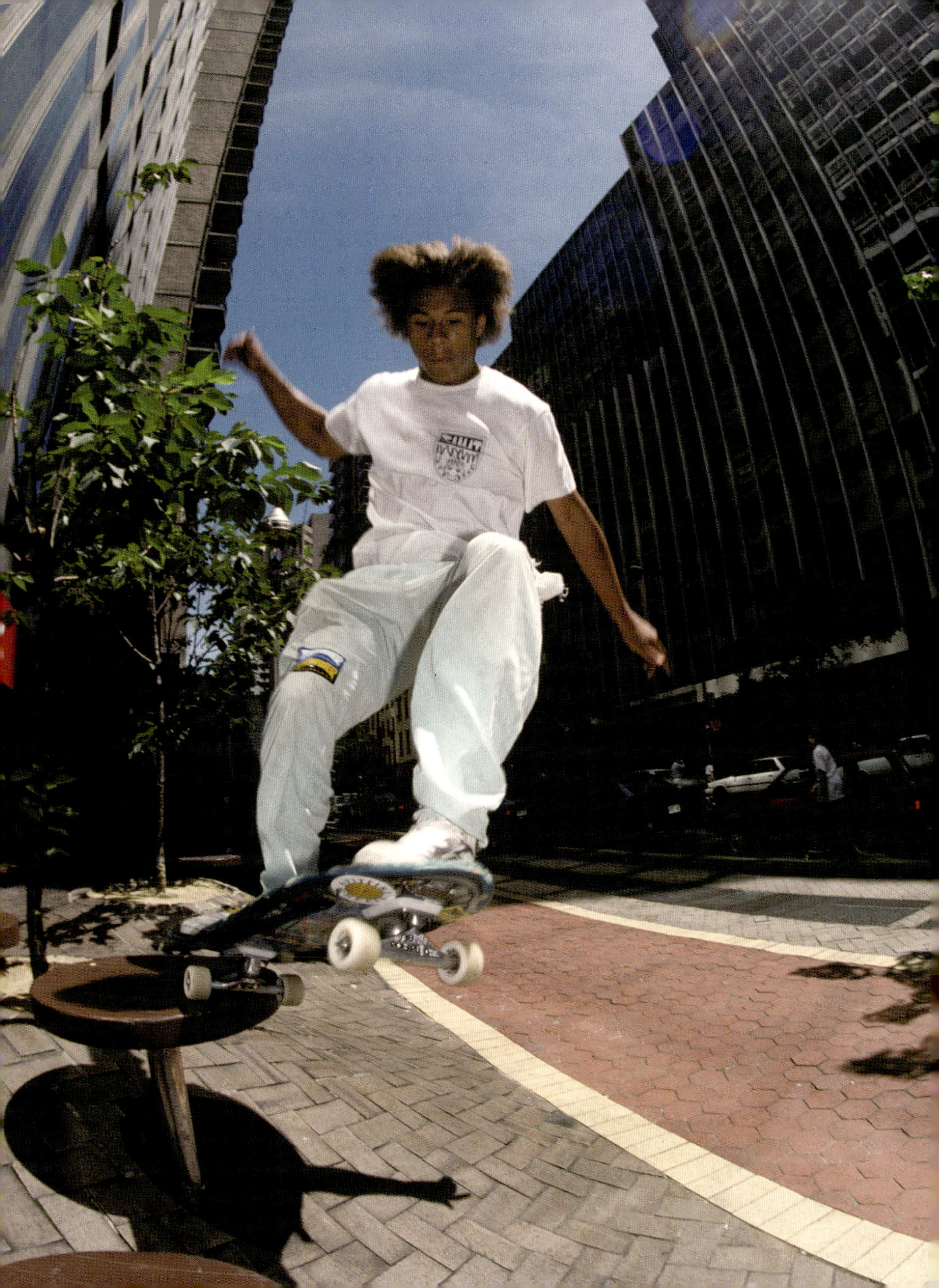

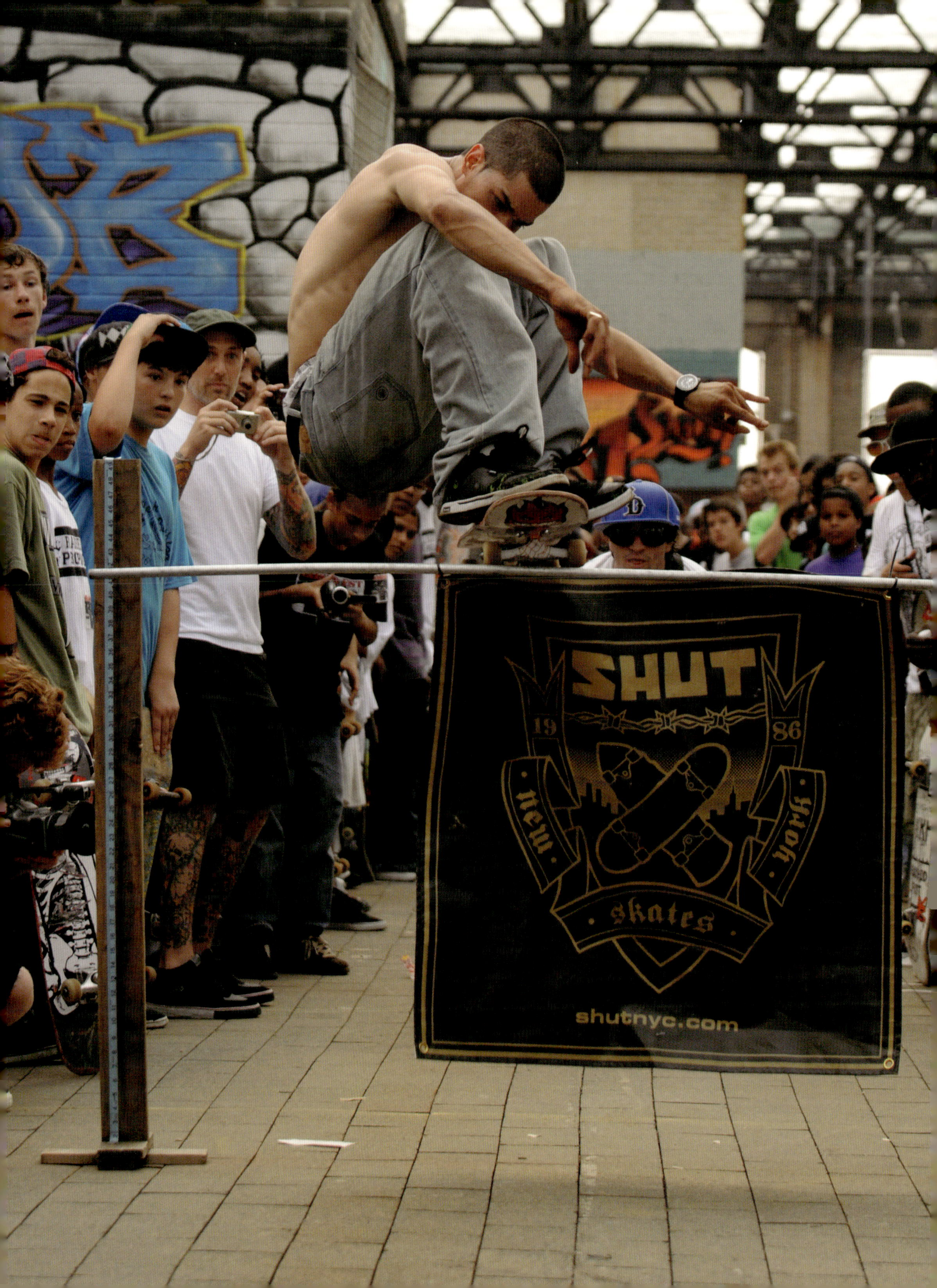
SHUT
19
86
new york
skates
shutnyc.com

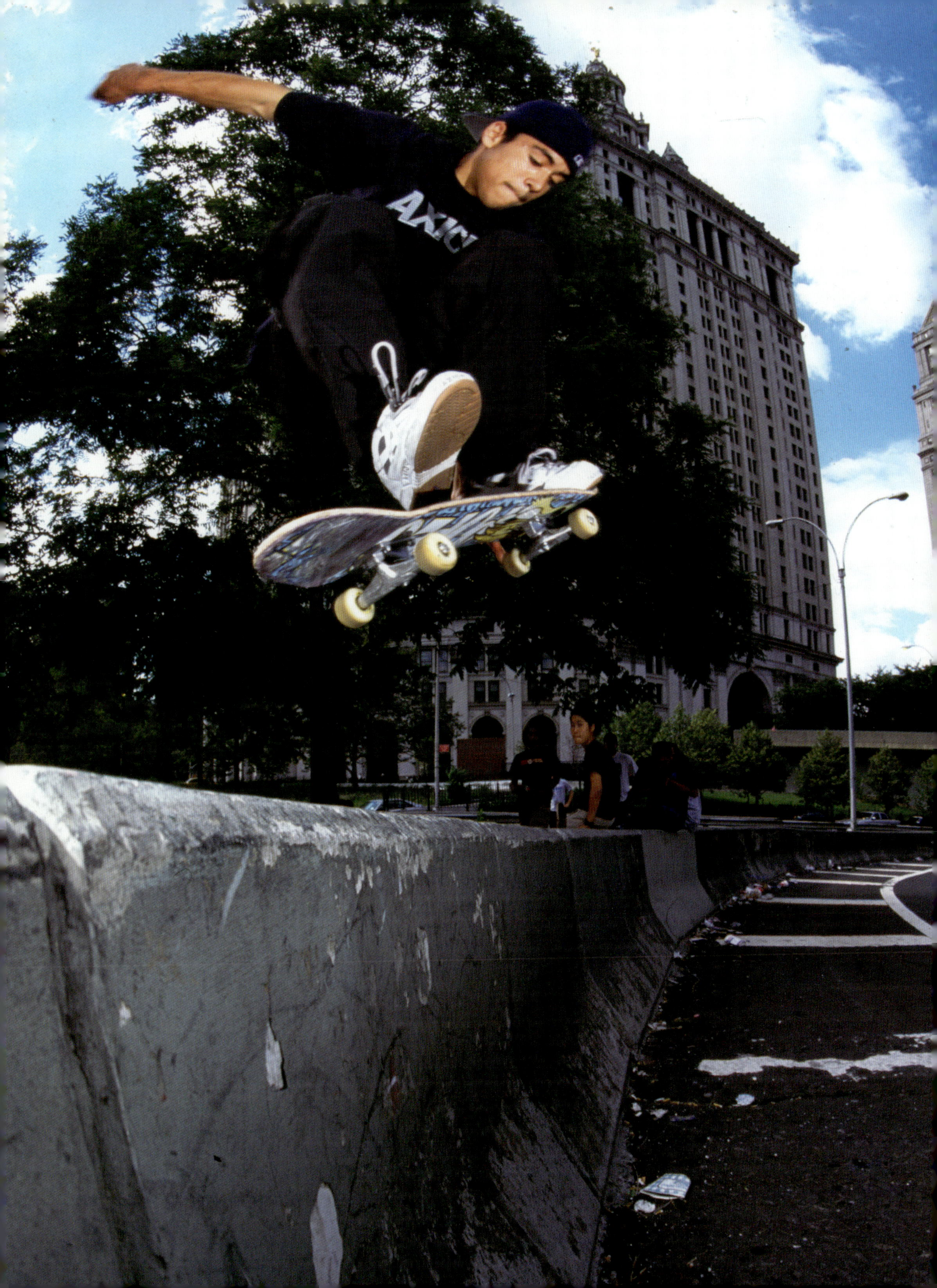

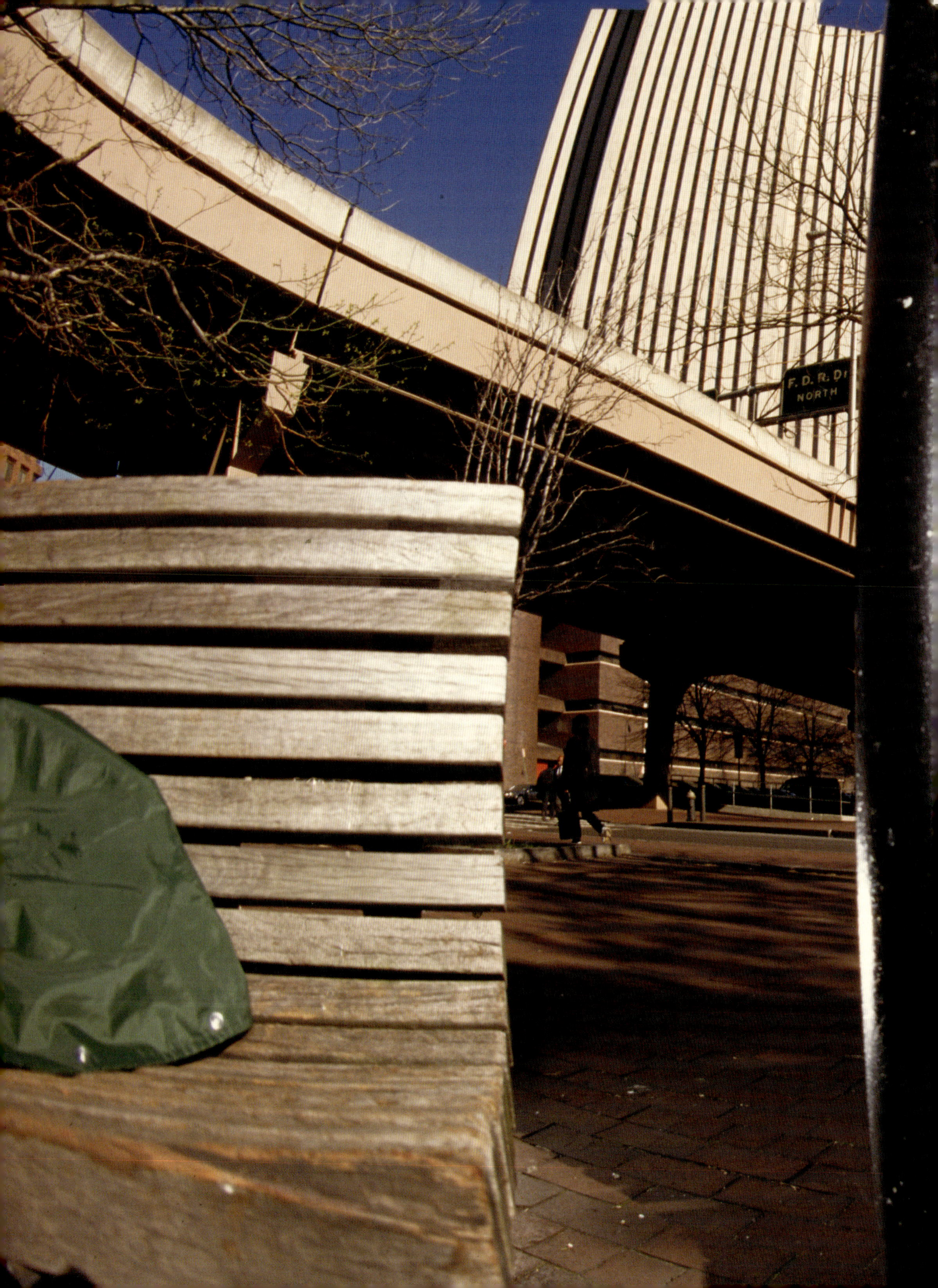
F.D.R. Dr
NORTH

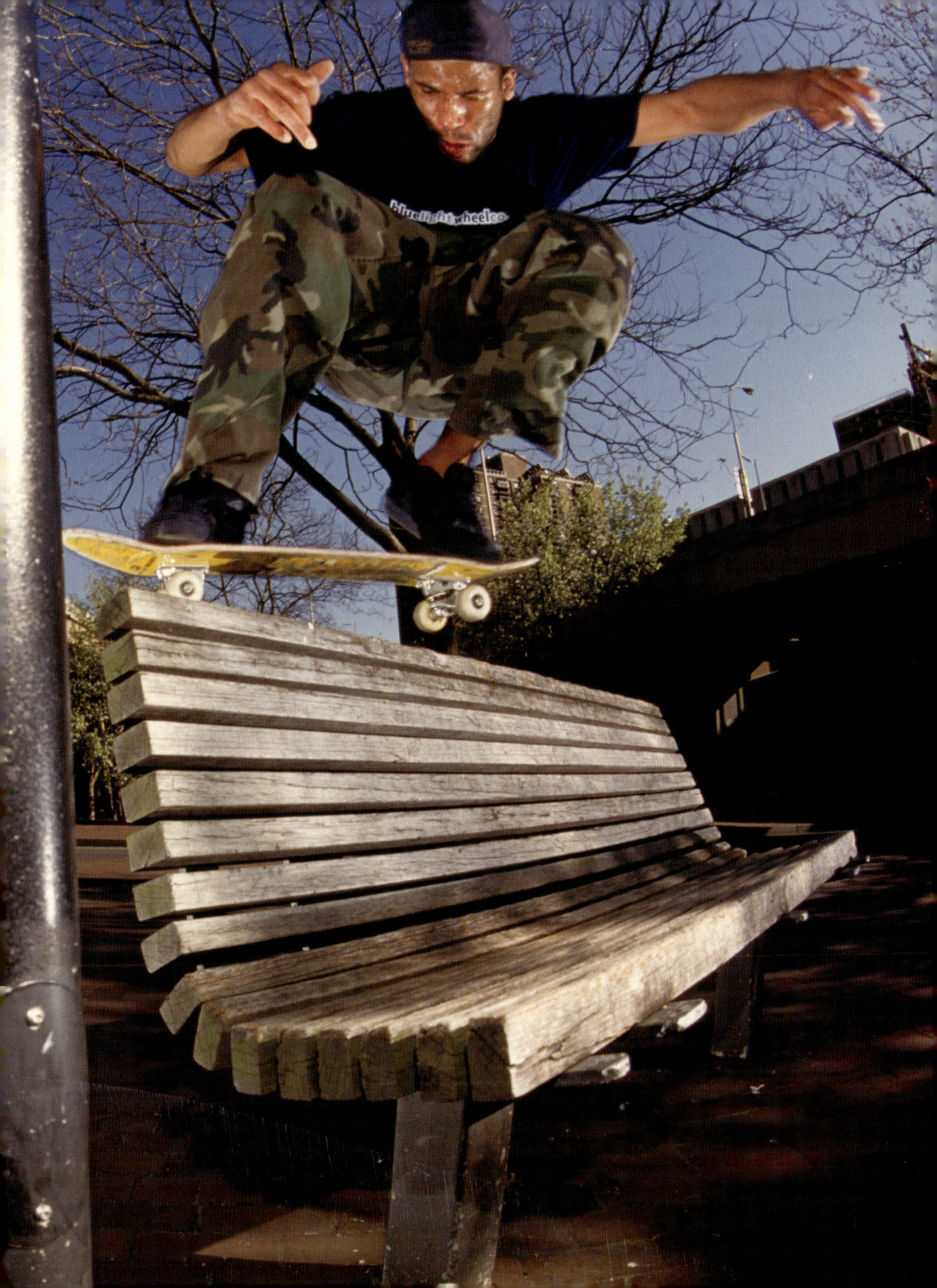
bluelightwheelco.

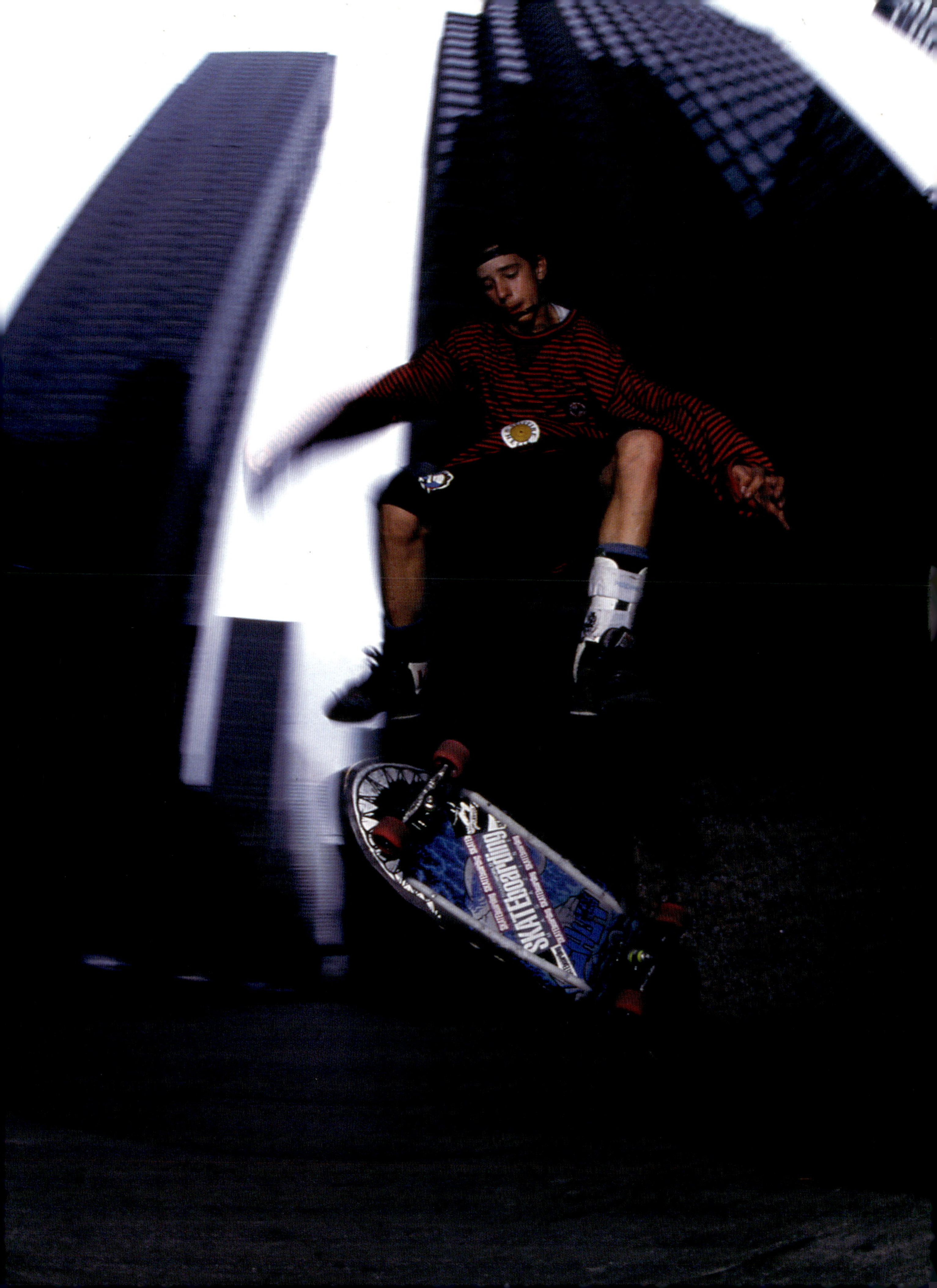
SKATEboarding

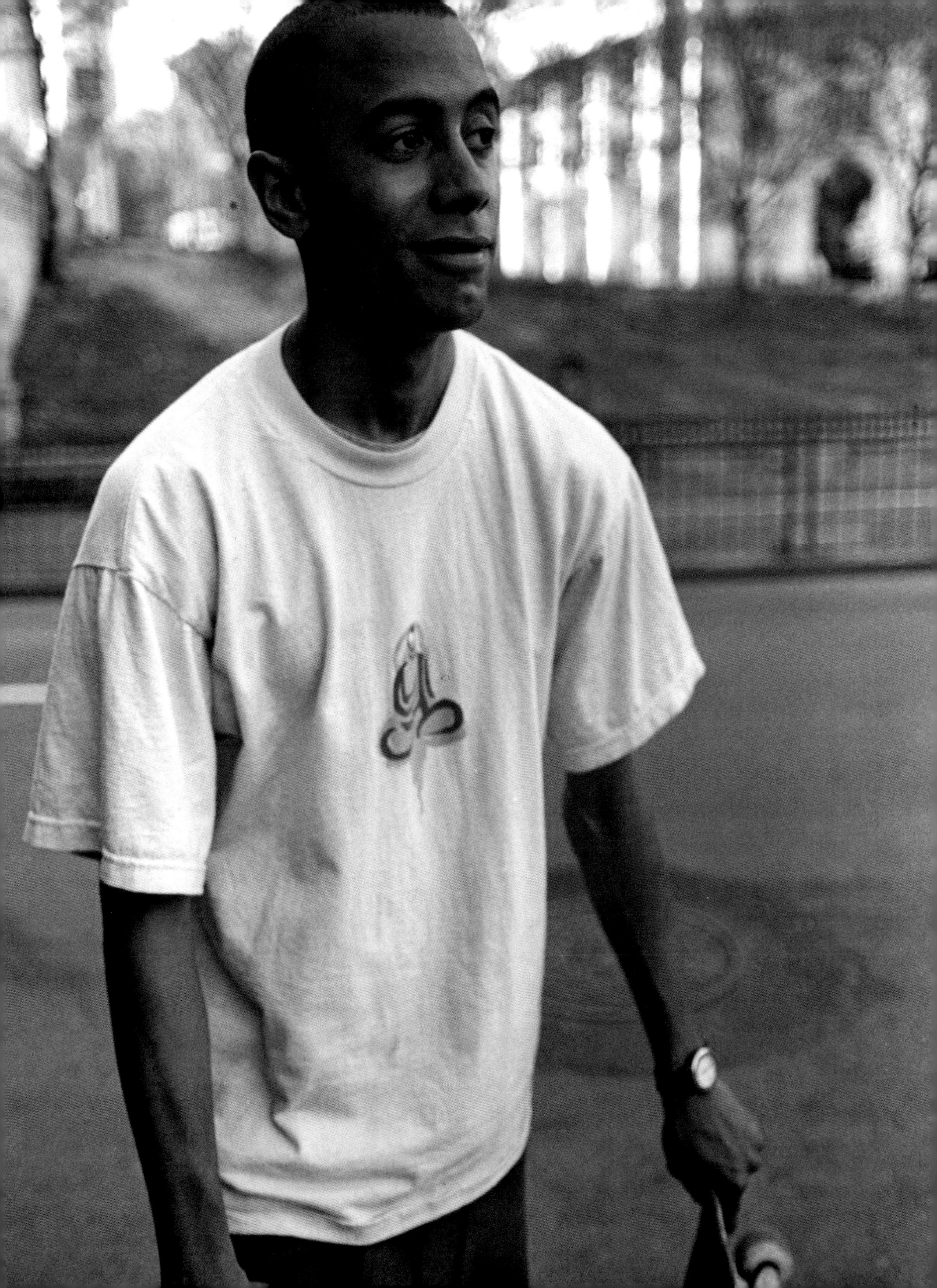

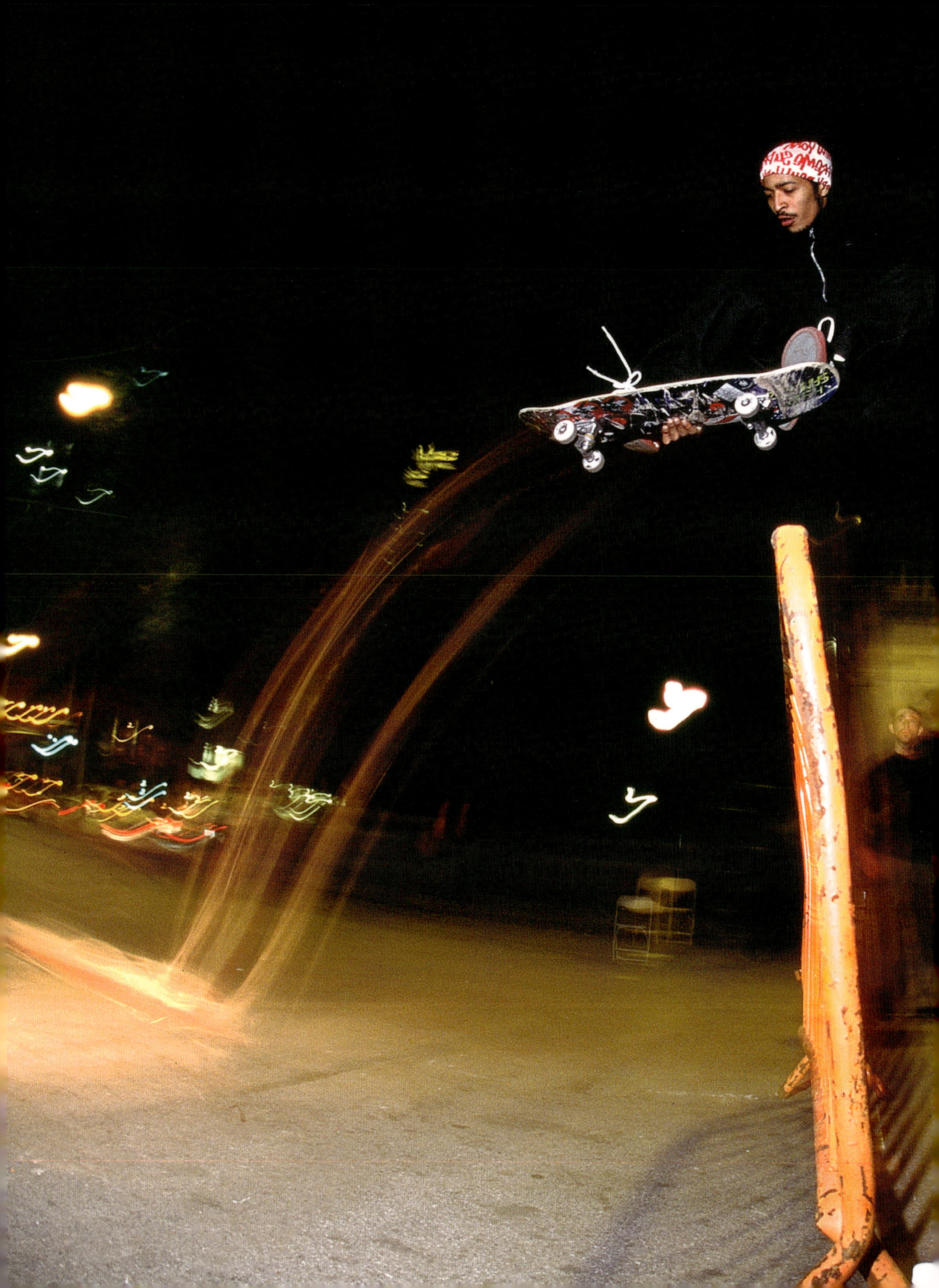

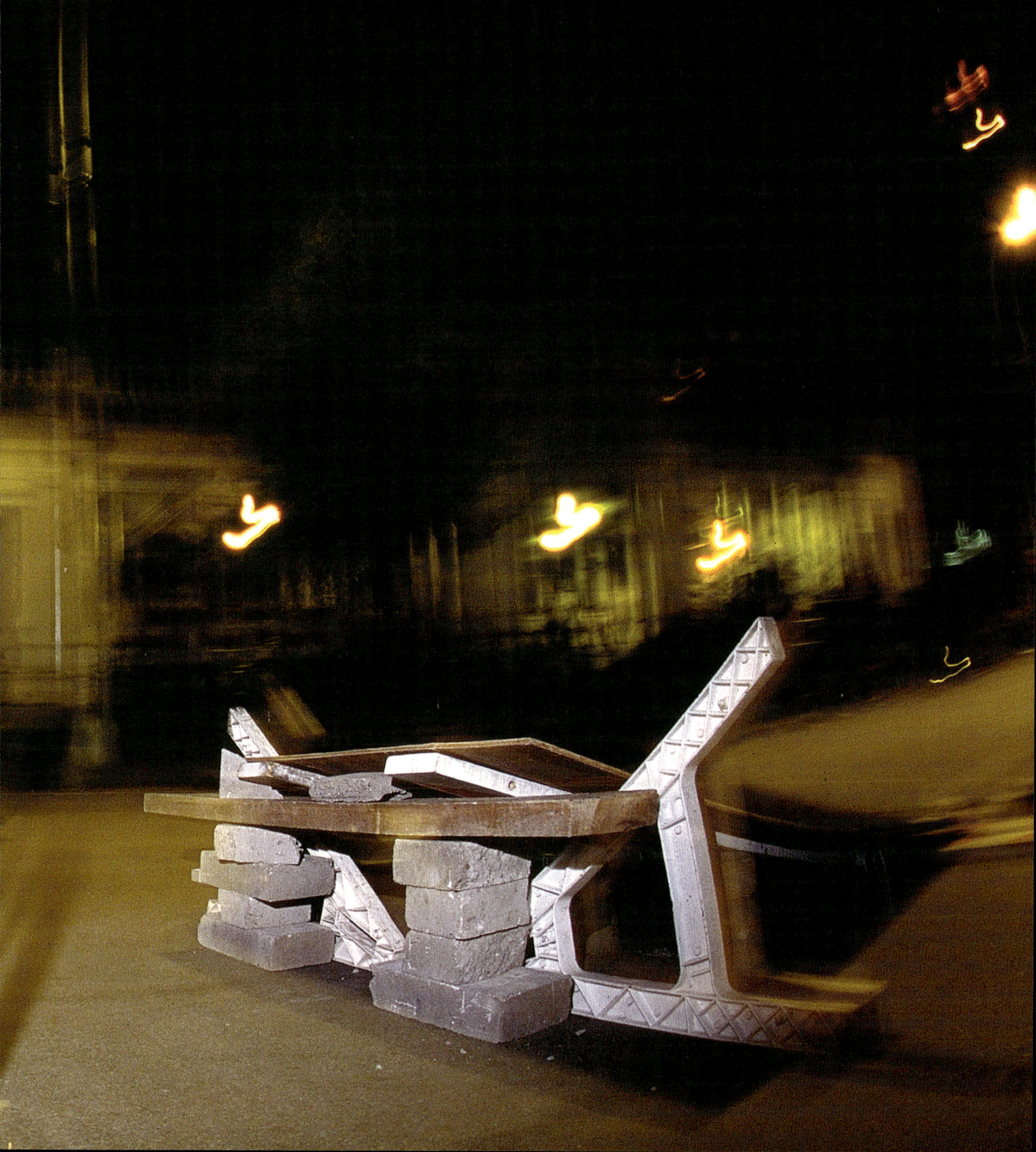

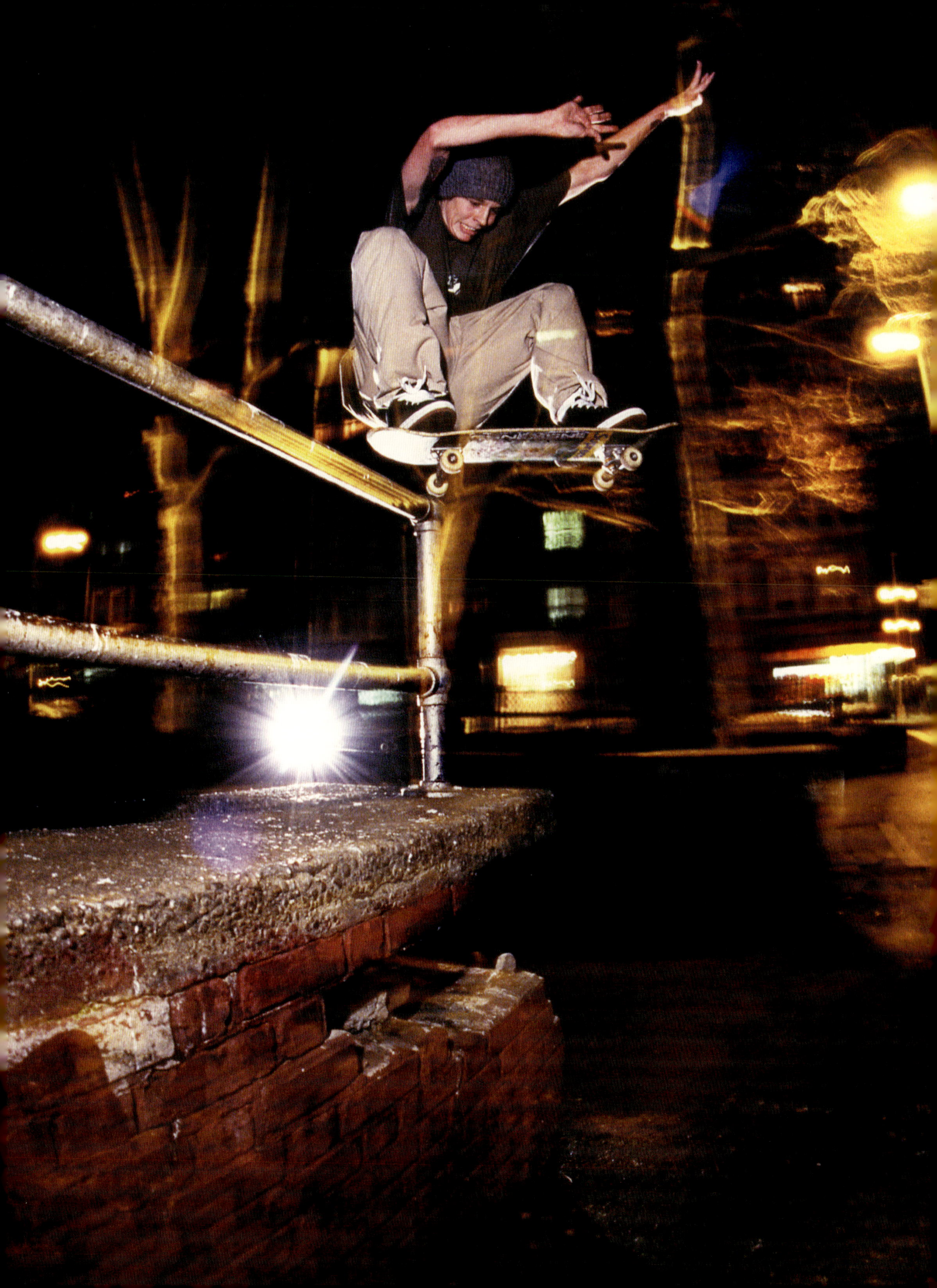

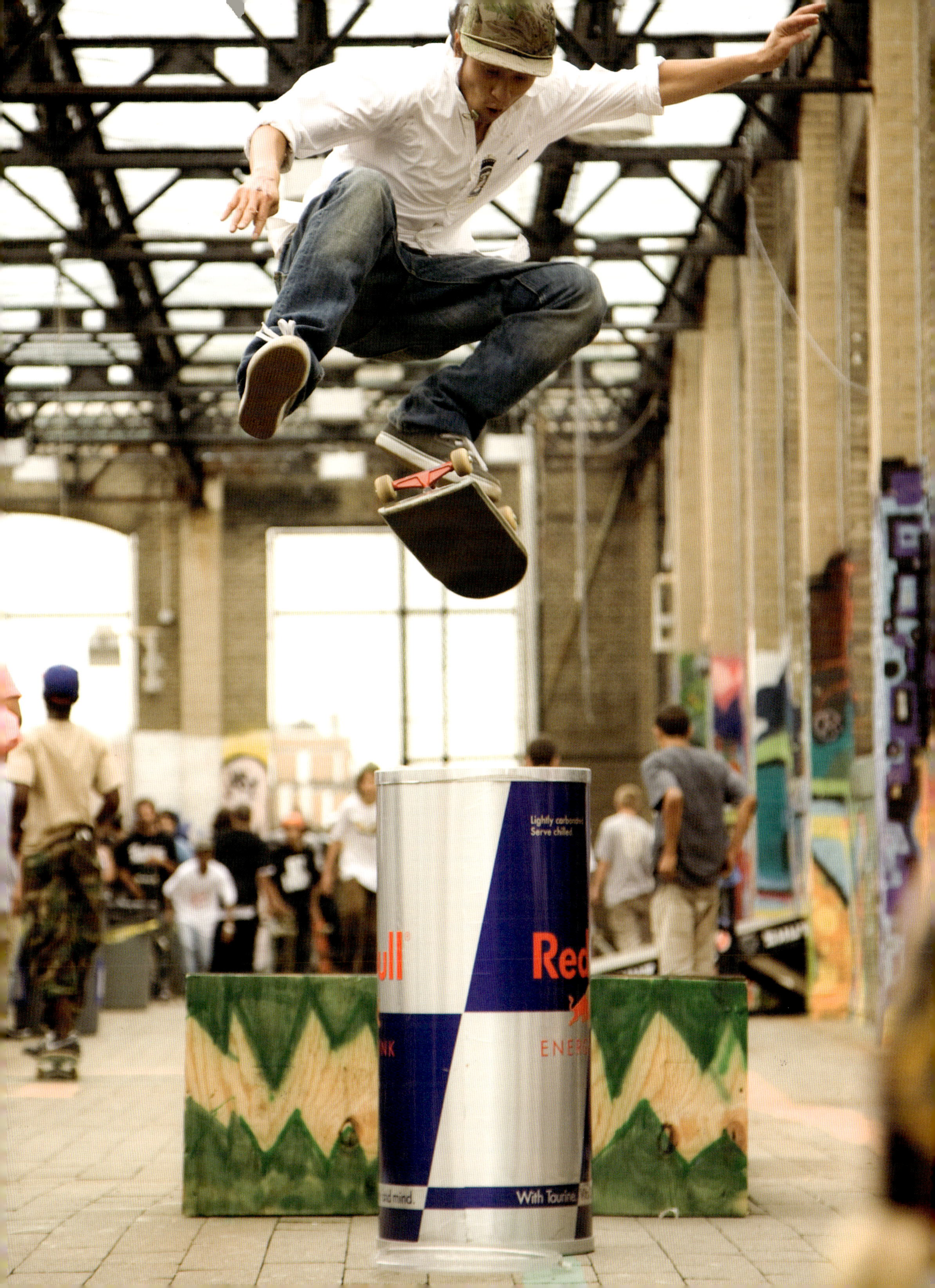
Serve chilled
Red
With Taurine.

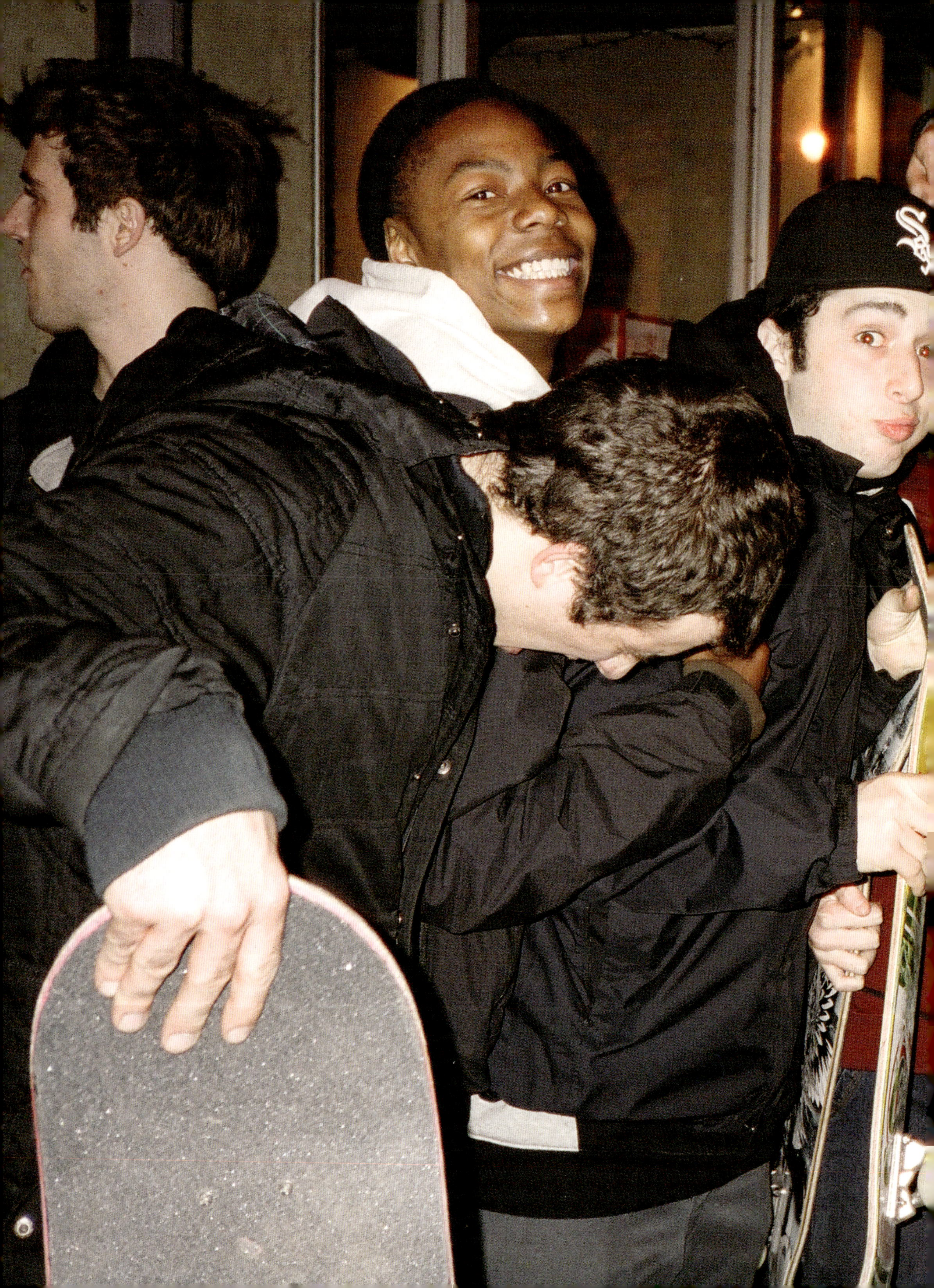

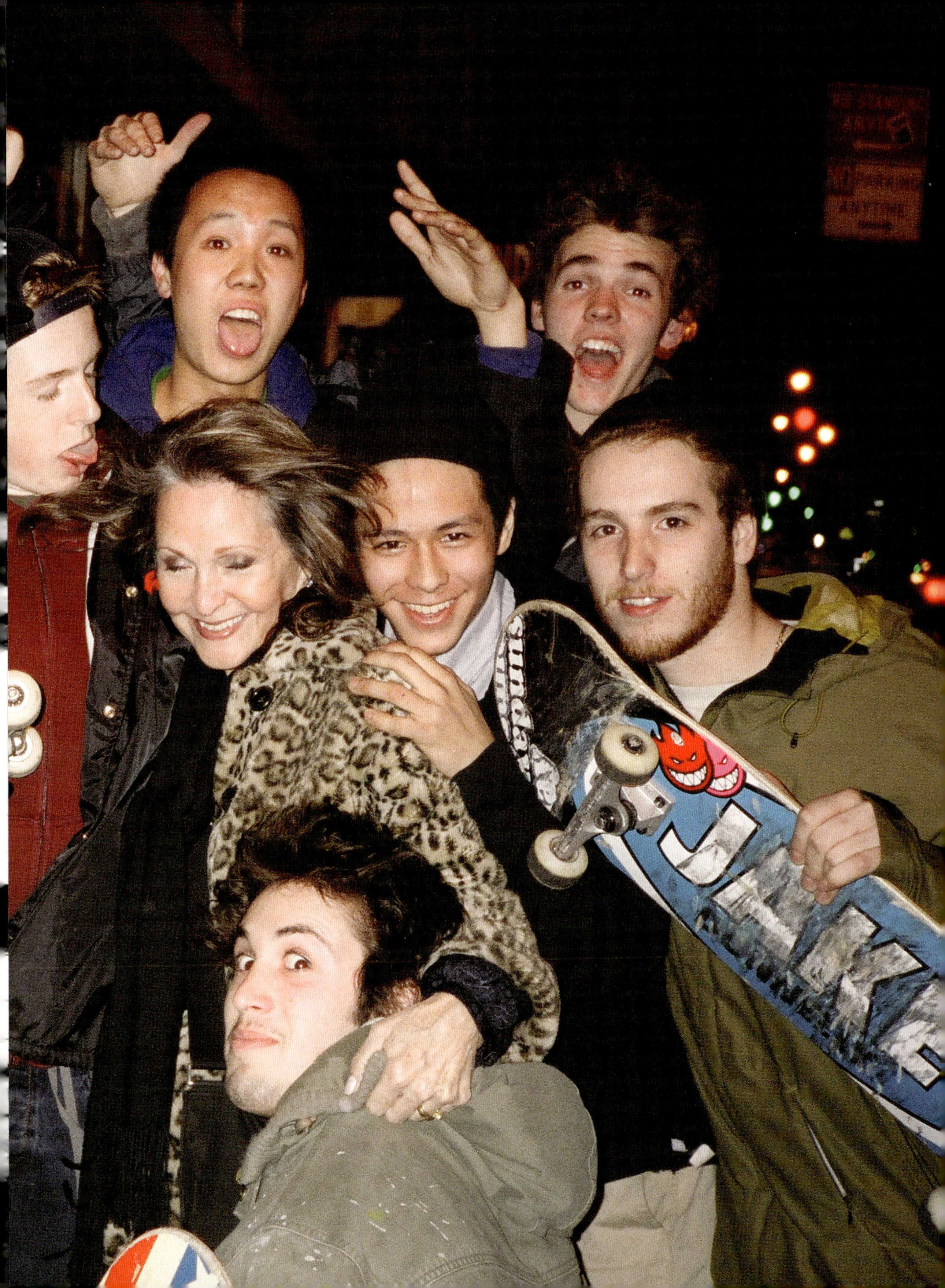

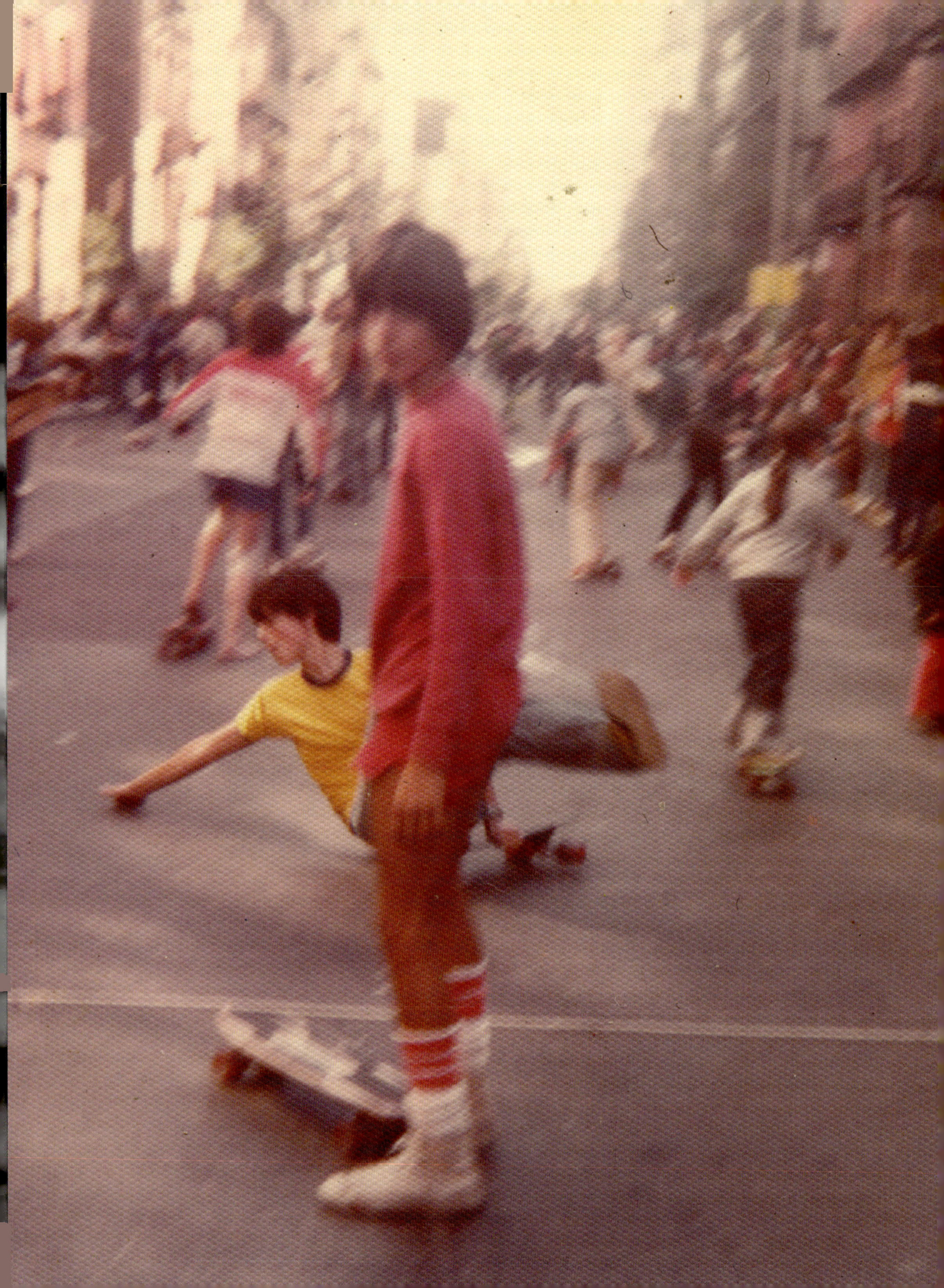

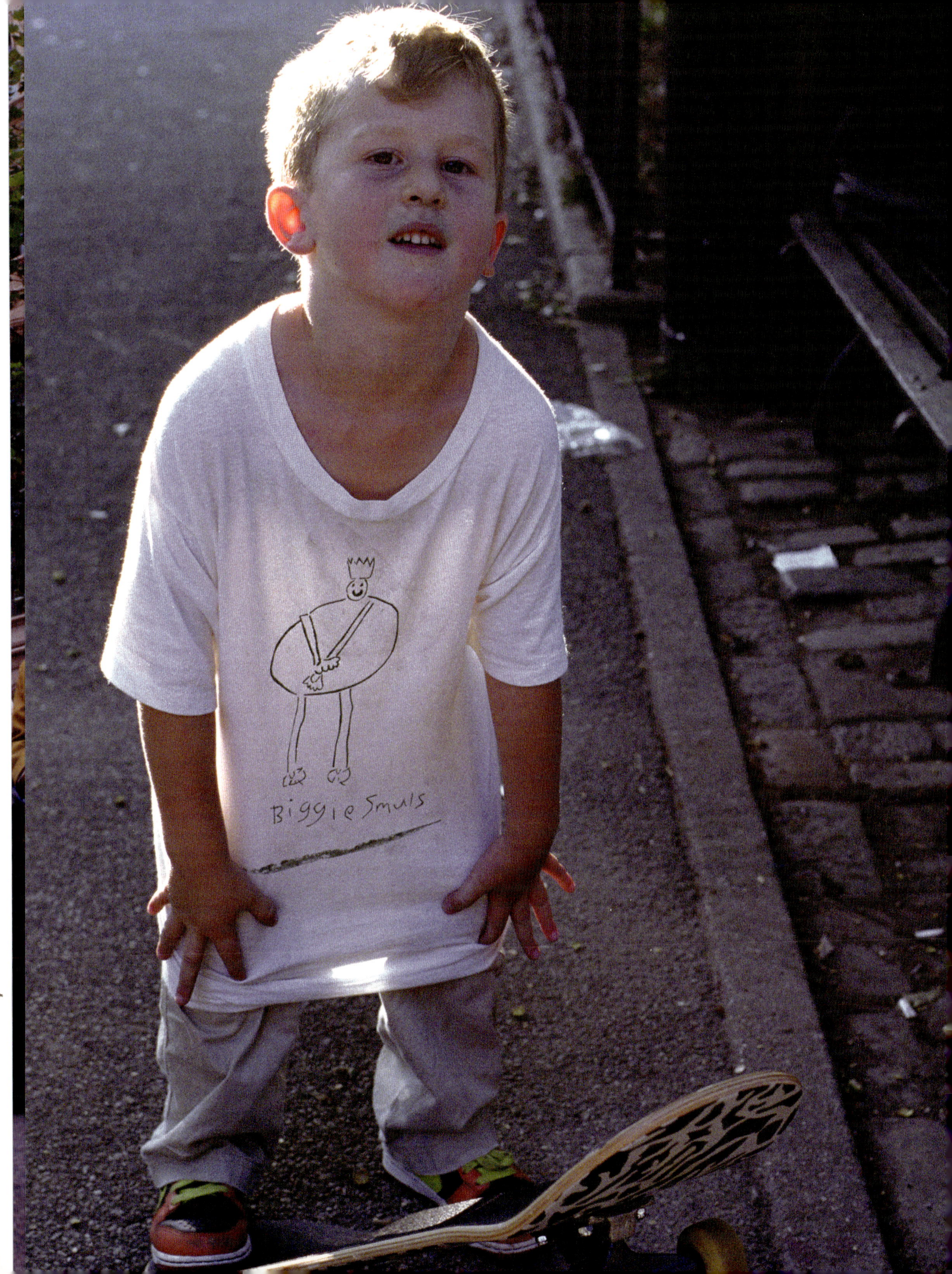
Biggie Smuls

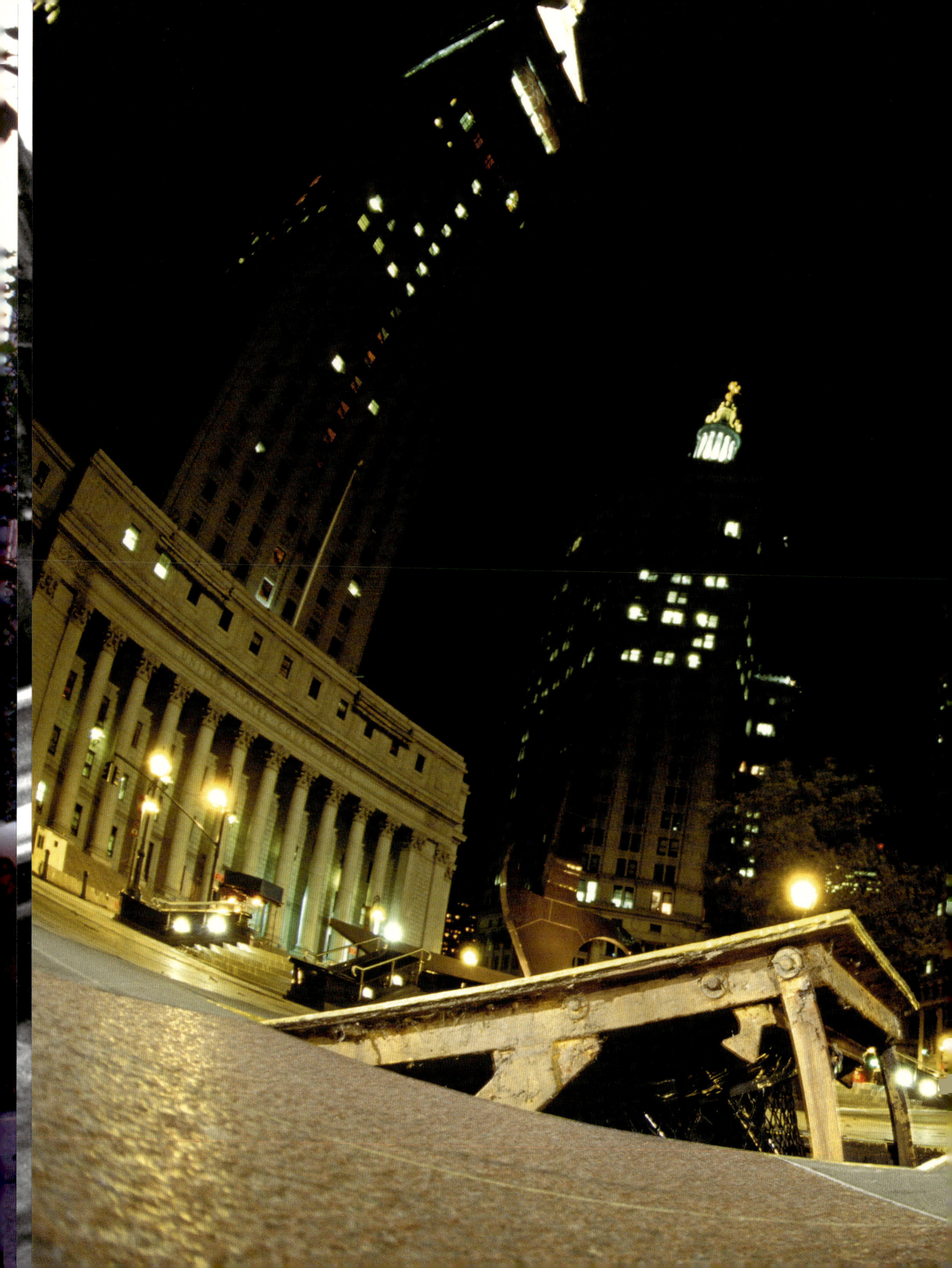

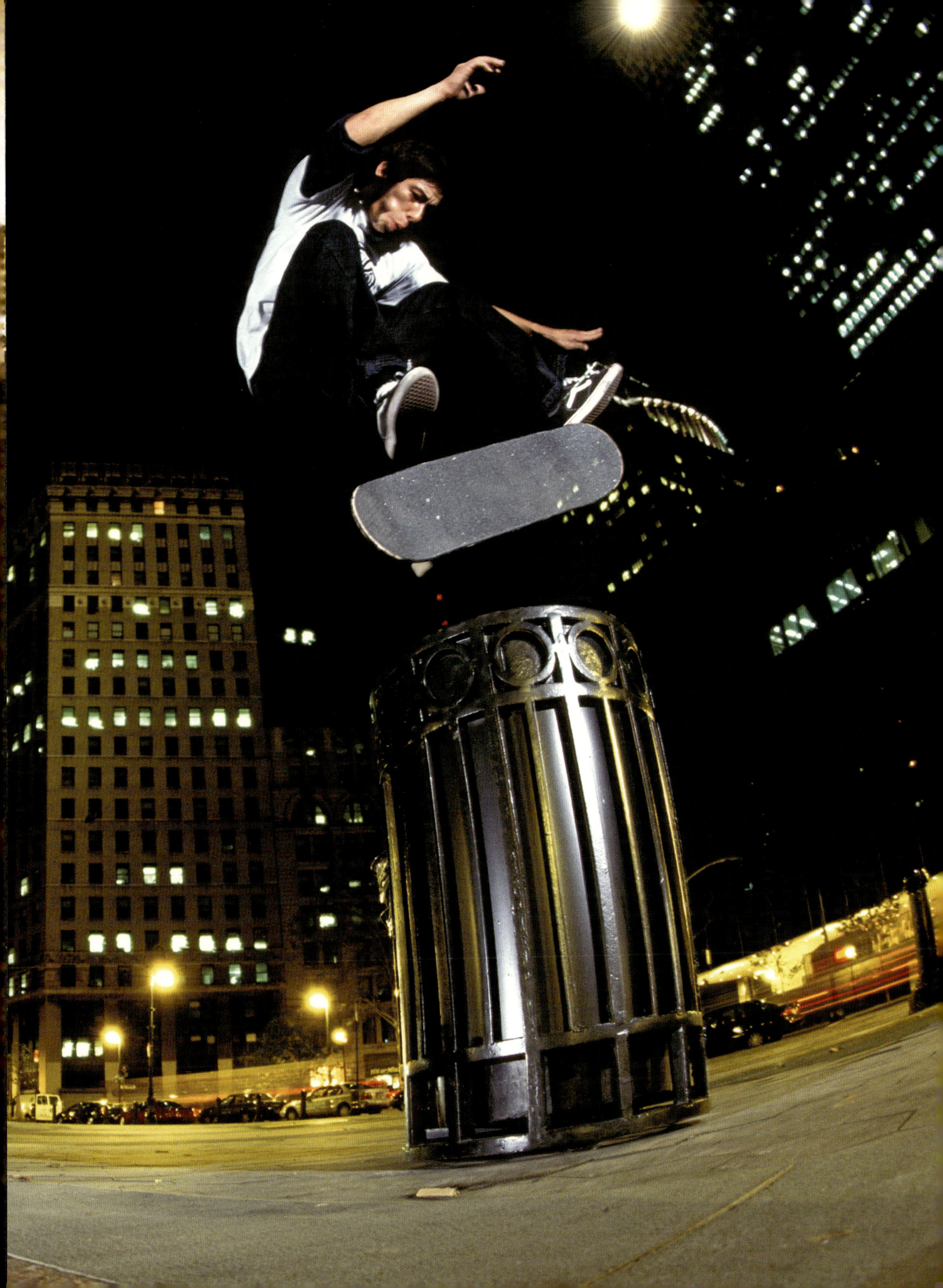

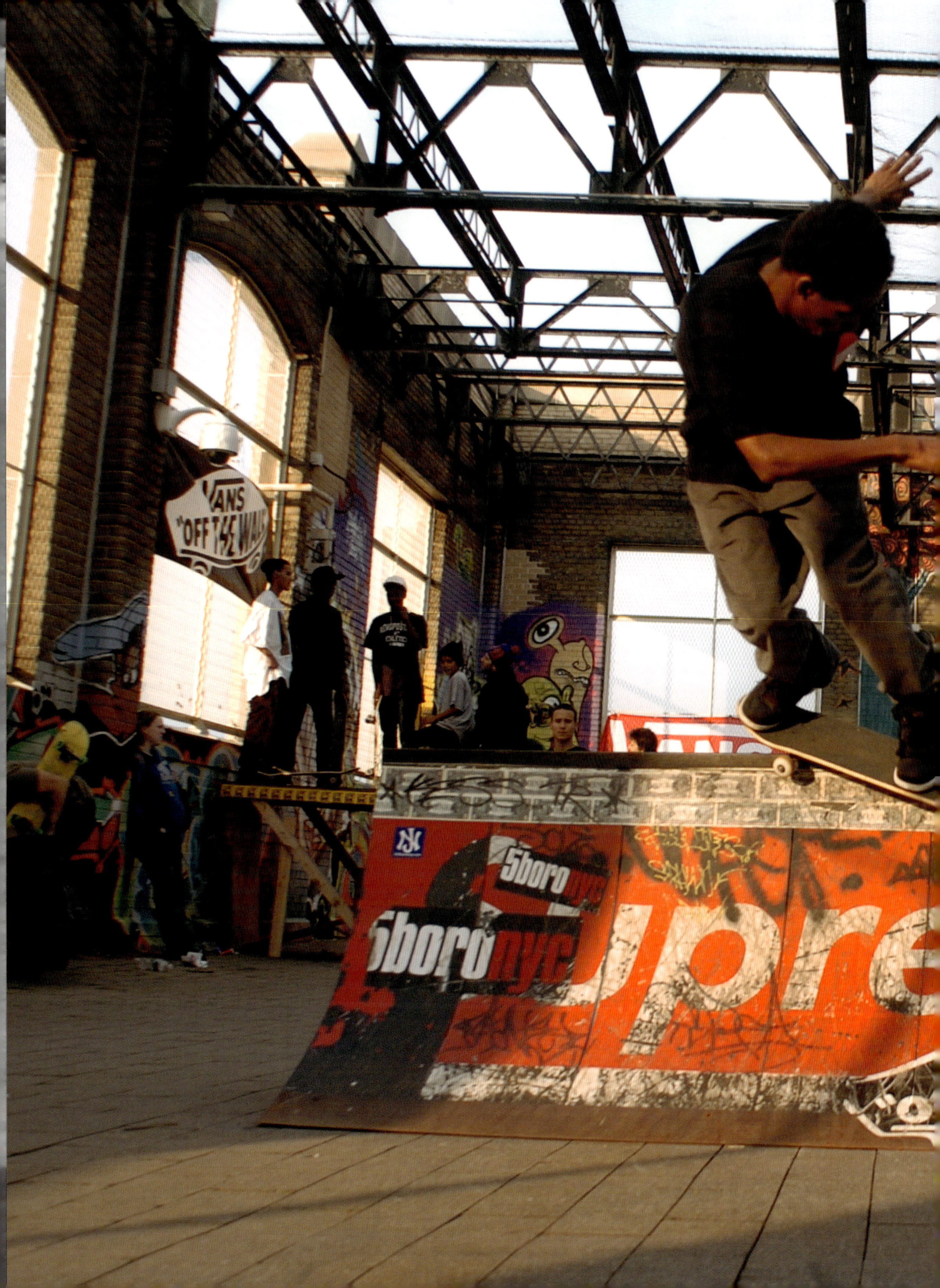
VANS "OFF THE WALL"
5boronyc
5boronyc

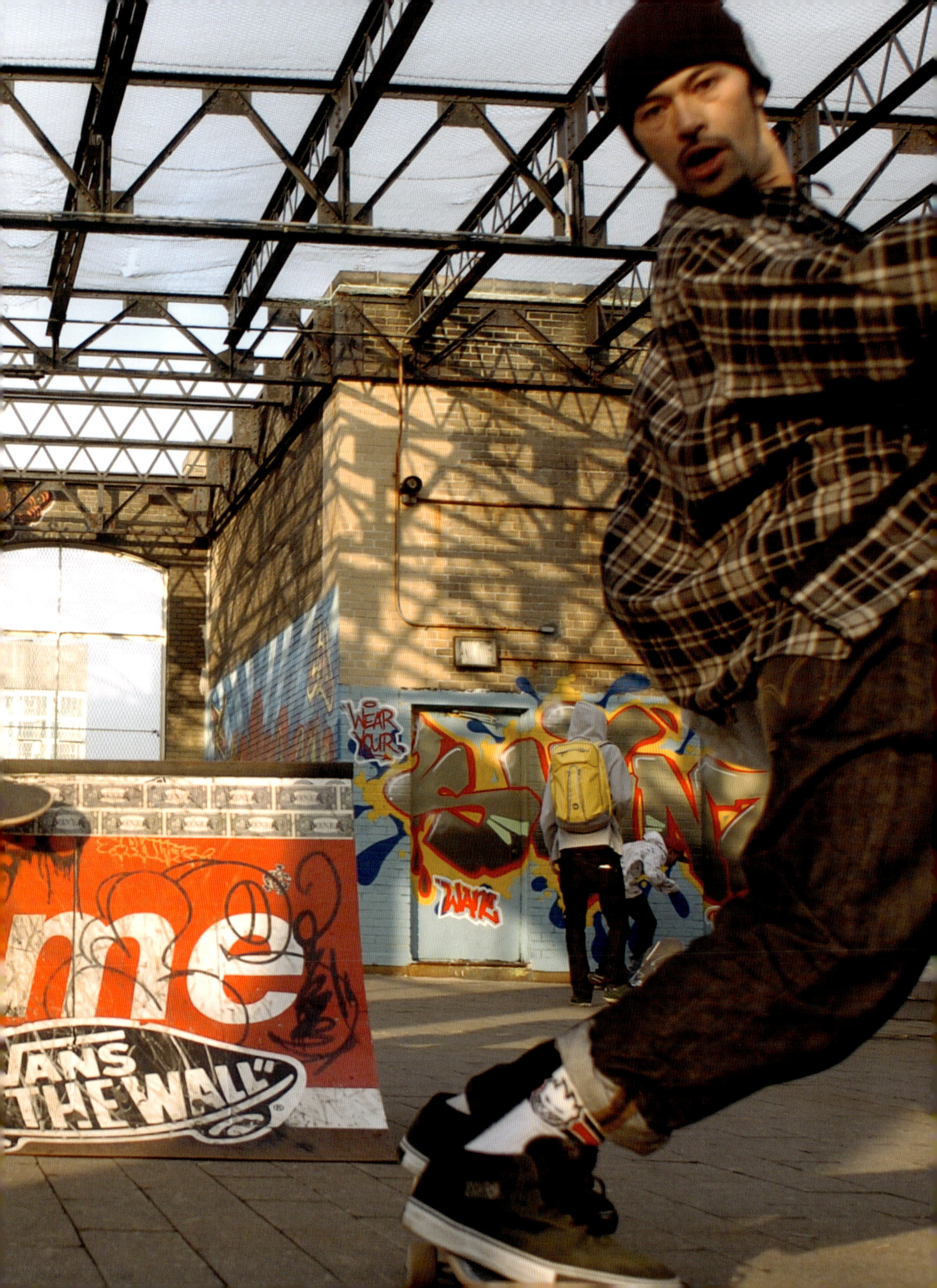
WEAR YOUR
me
ANS
THE WALL"

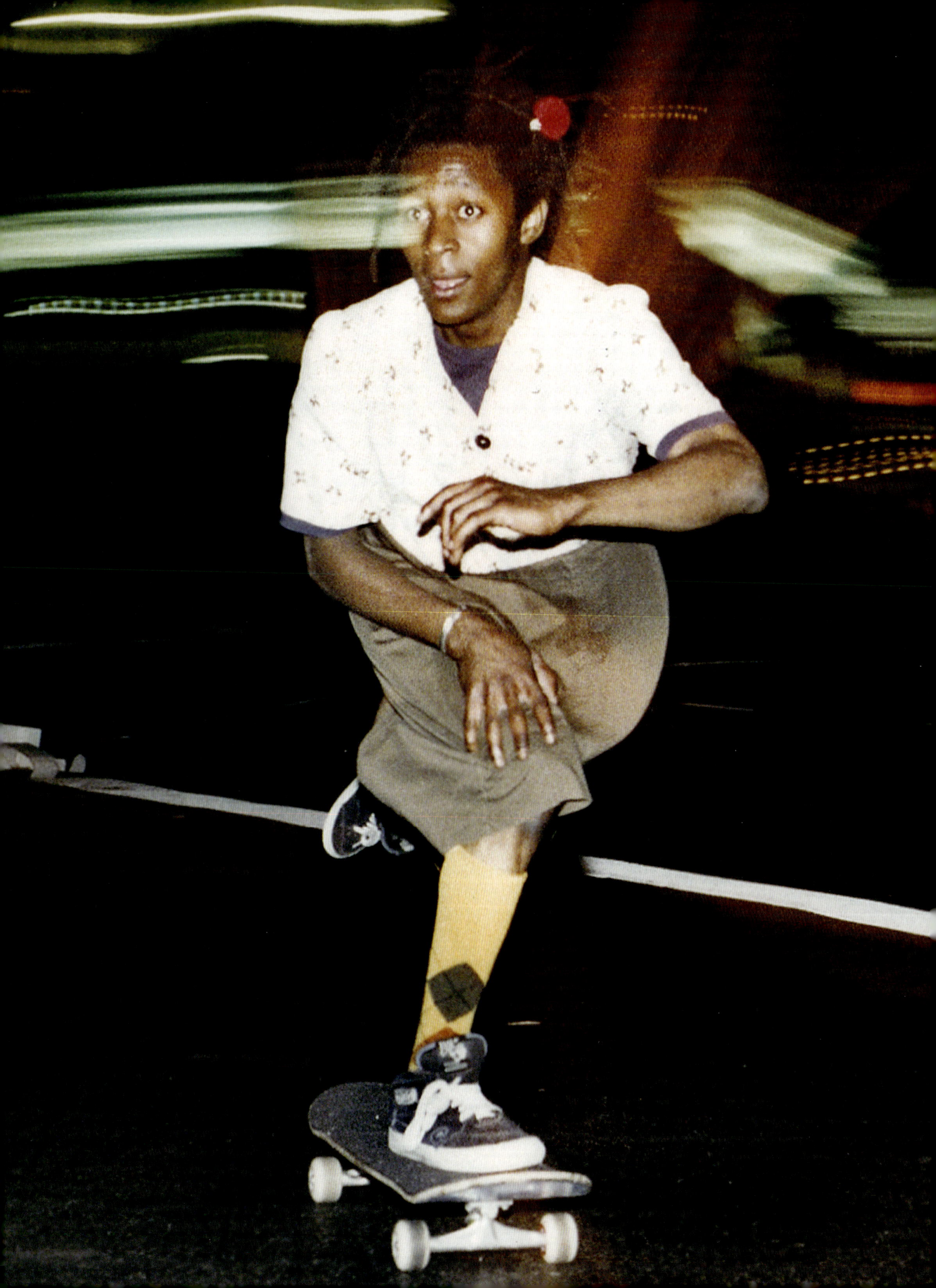

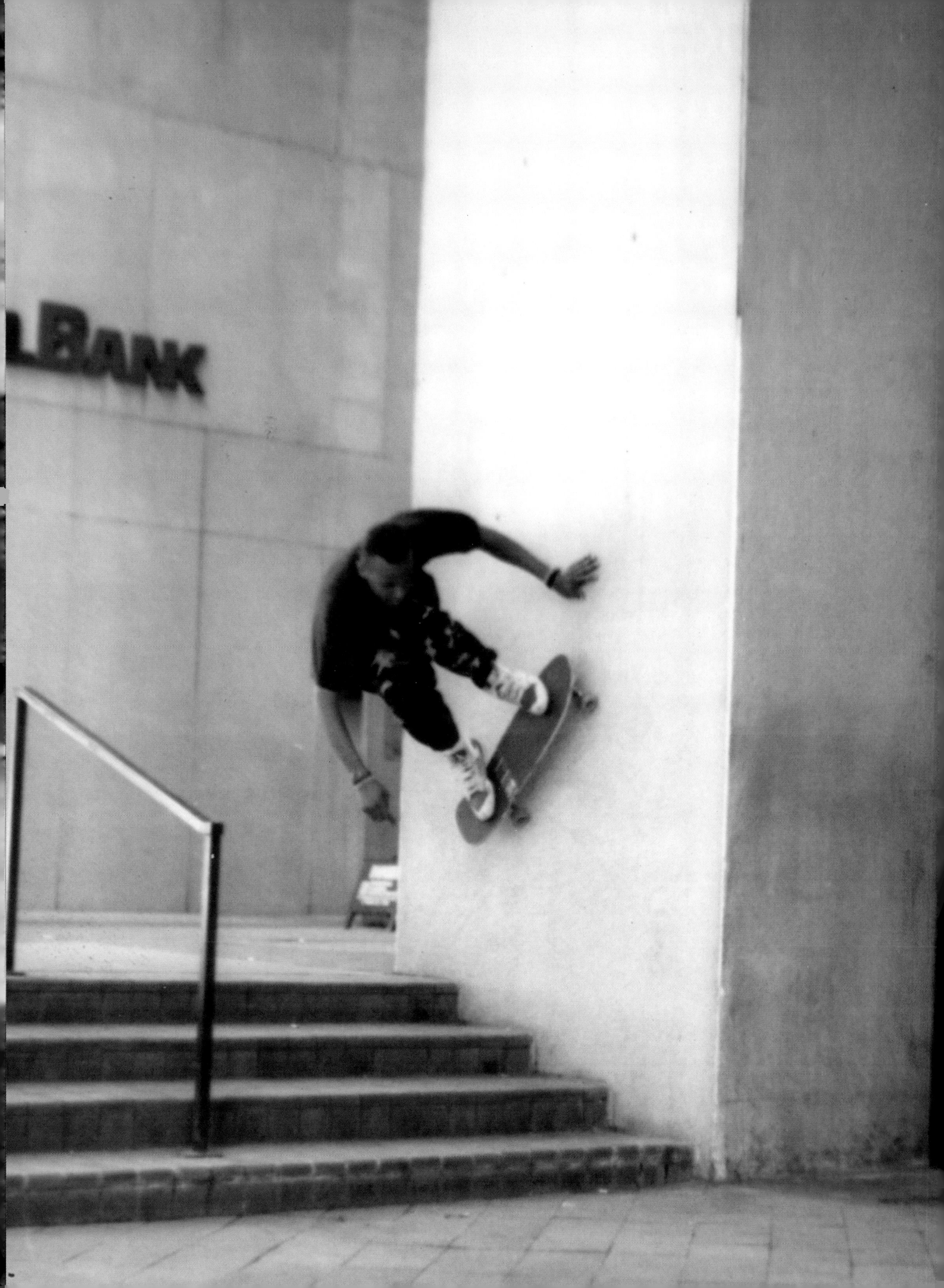

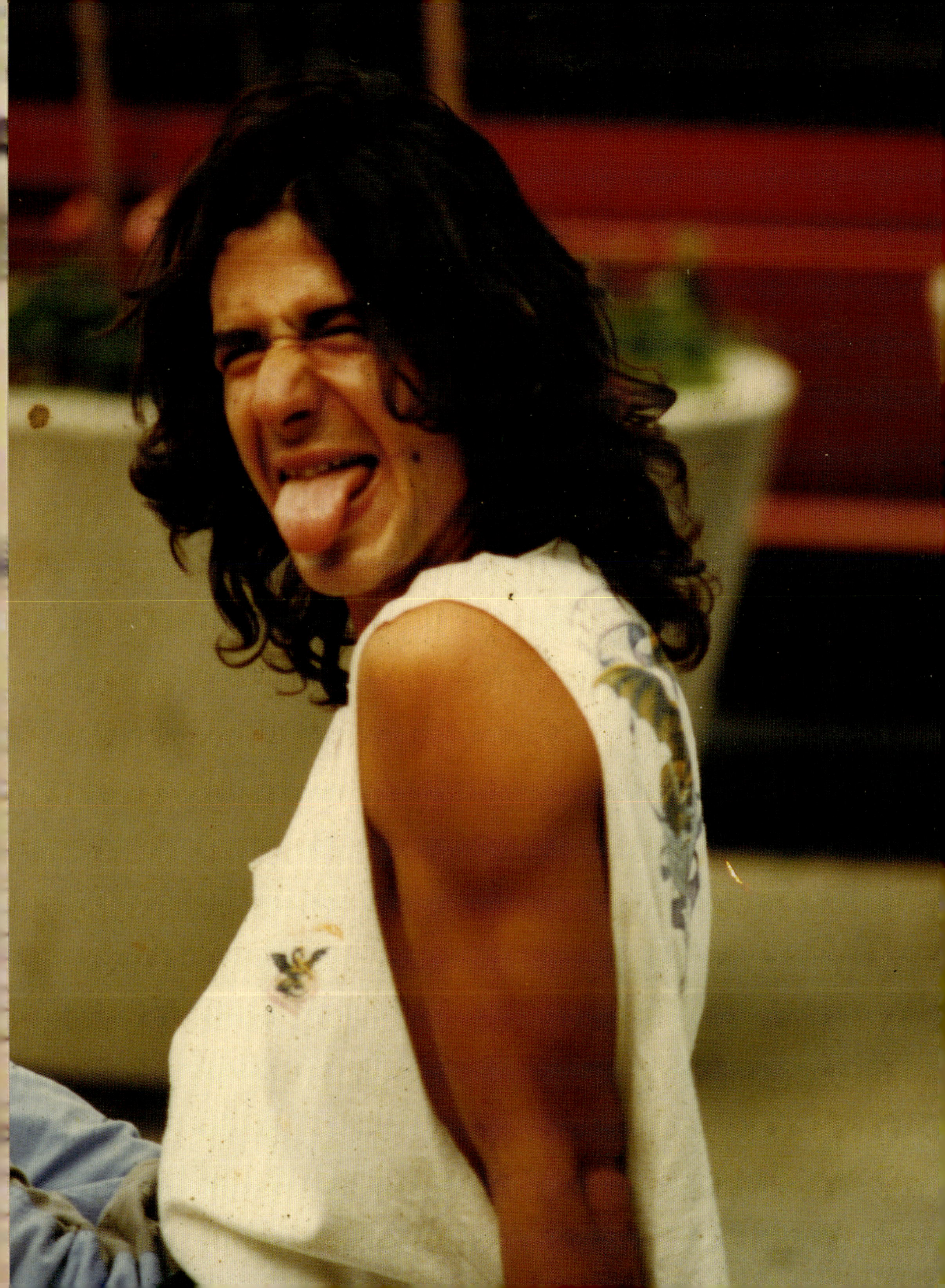

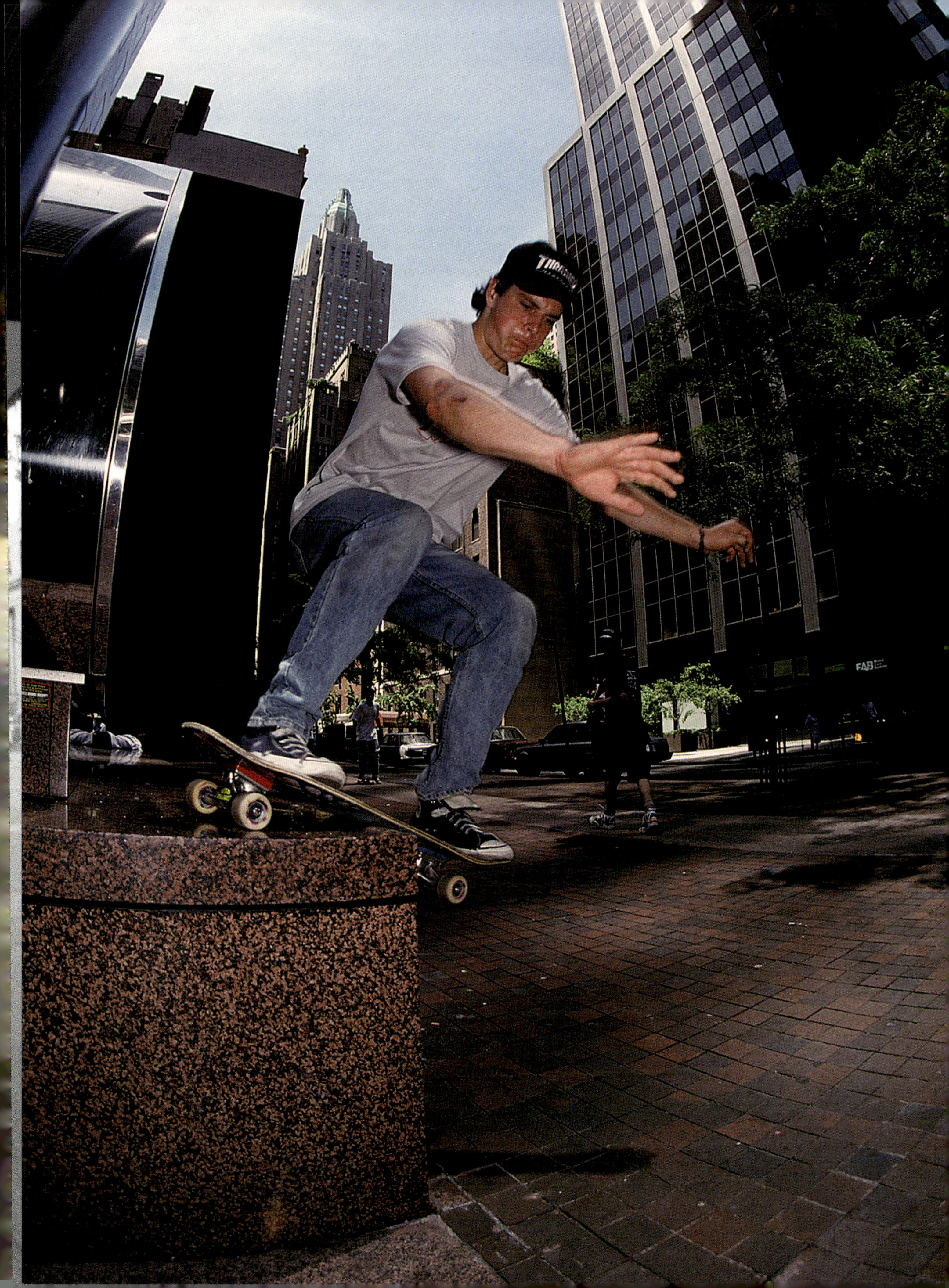
FAB

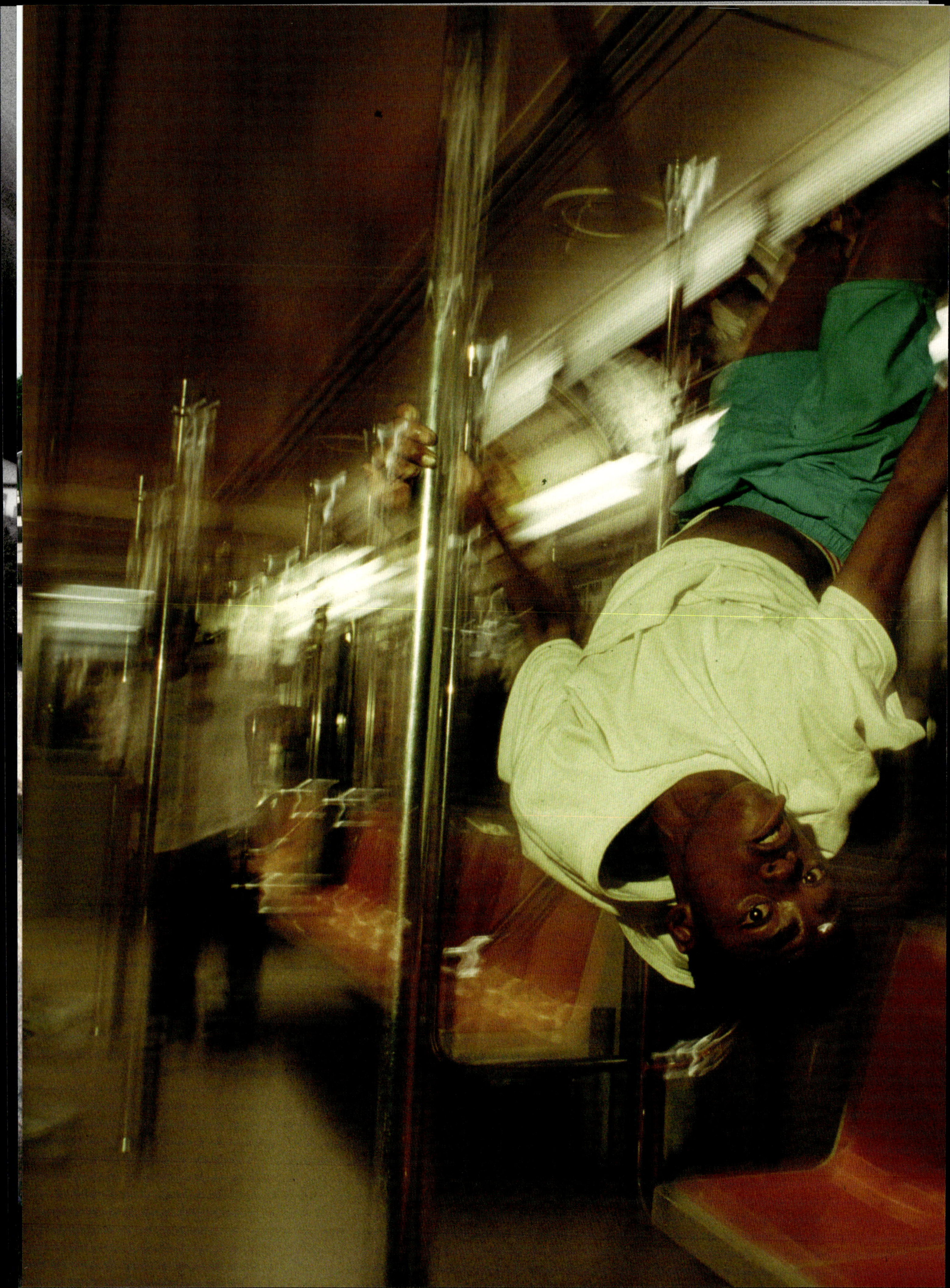

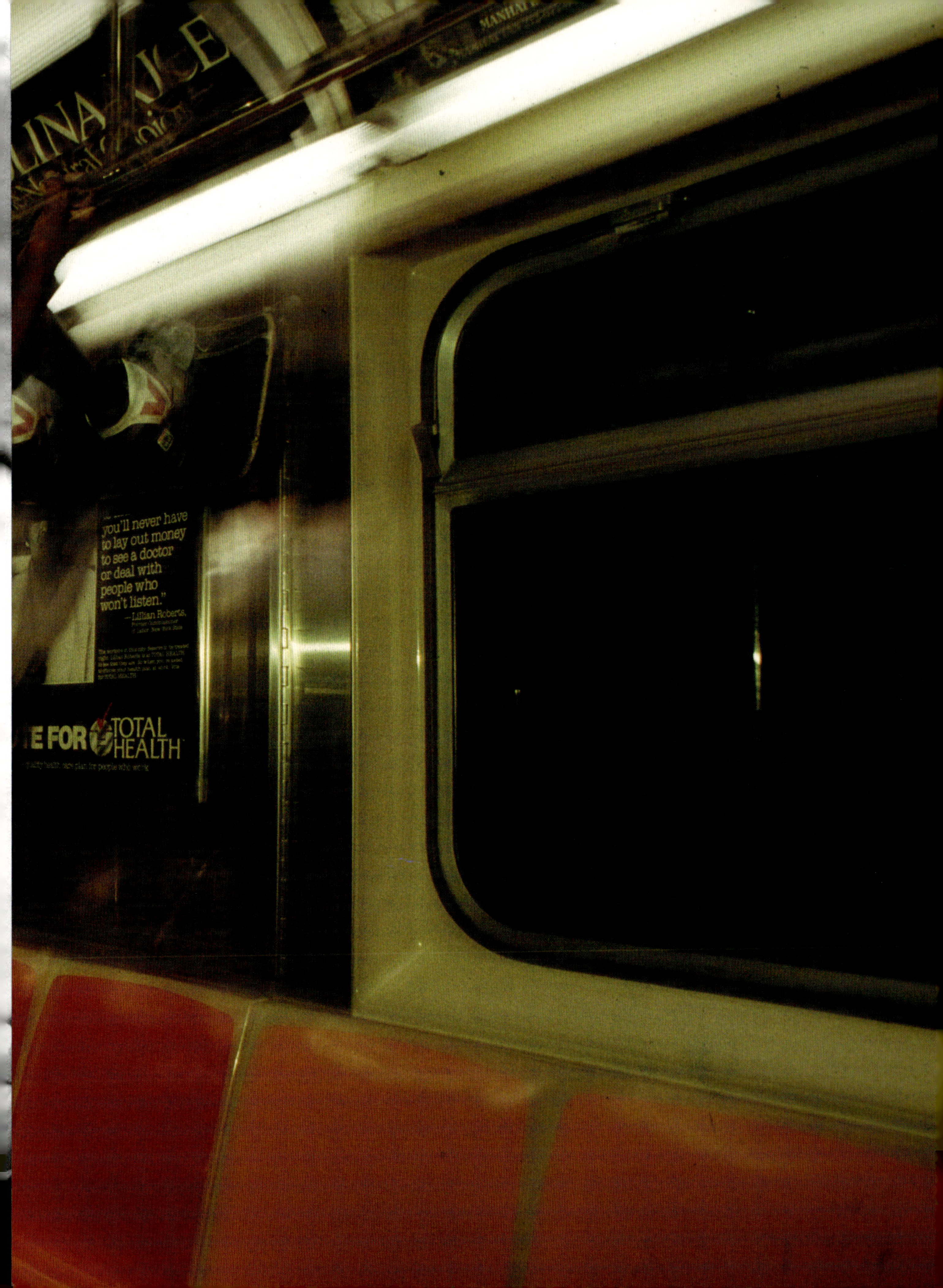
you'll never have to lay out money to see a doctor or deal with people who won't listen."
—Lillian Roberts,
TOTAL HEALTH

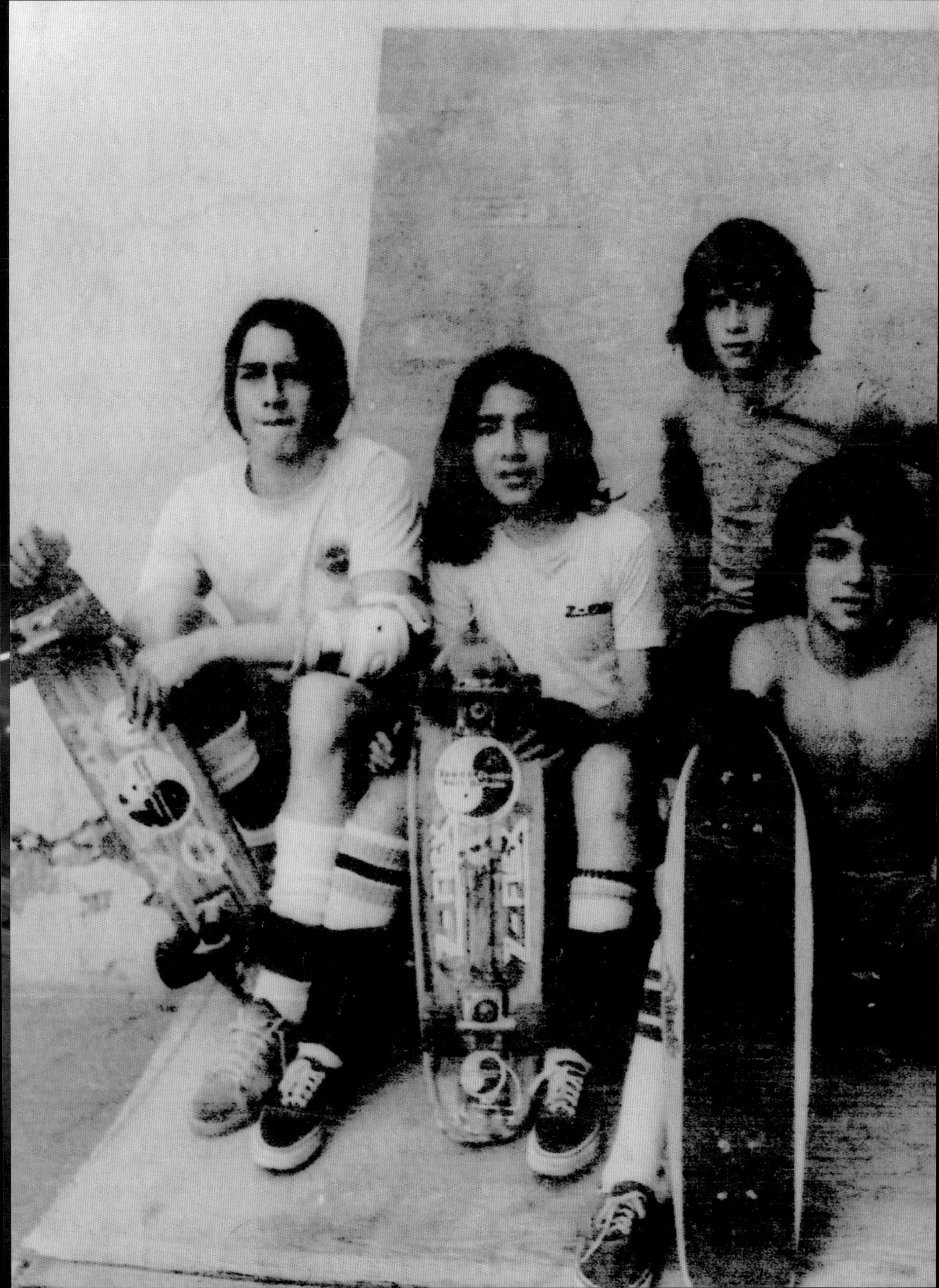

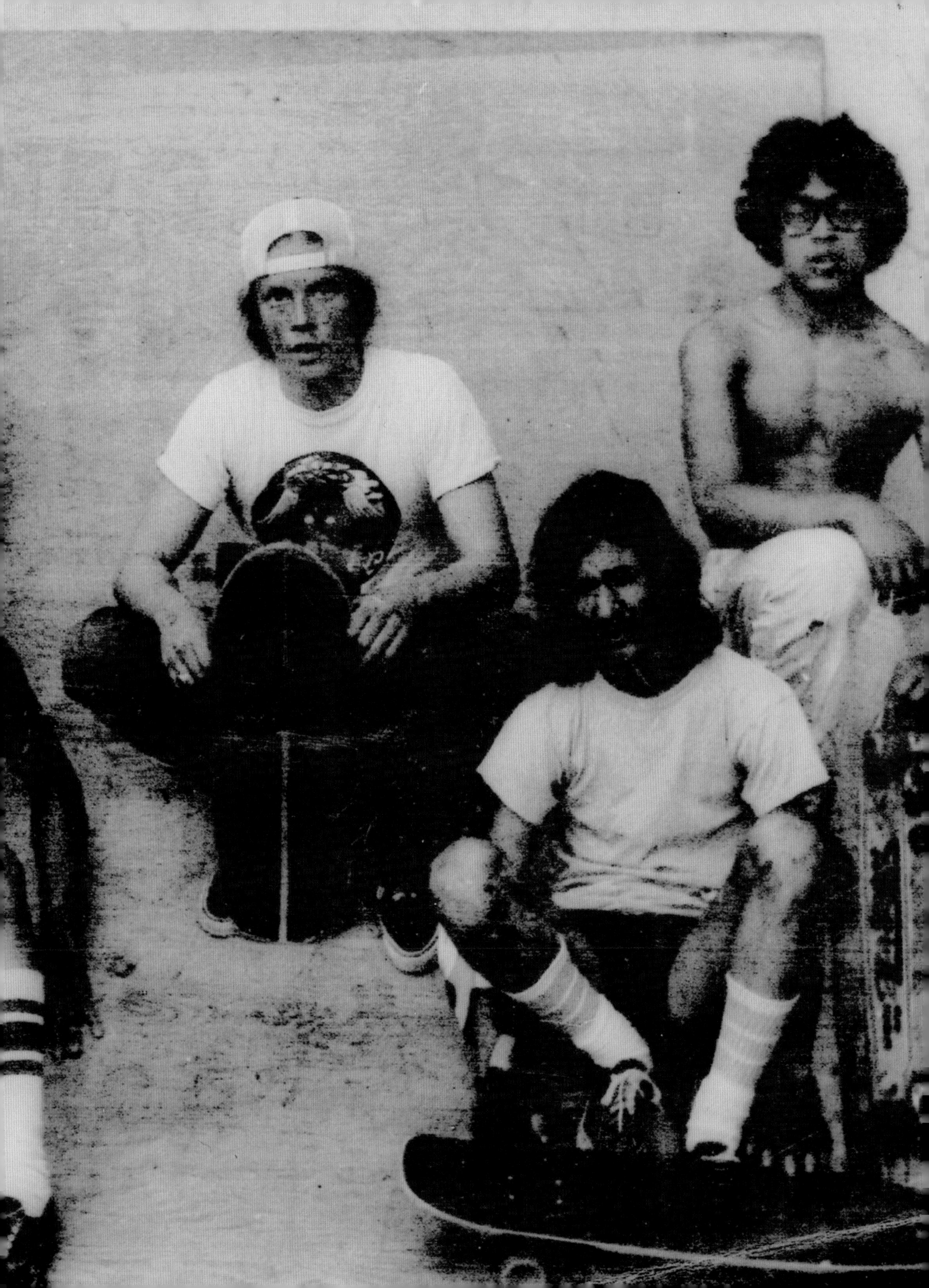

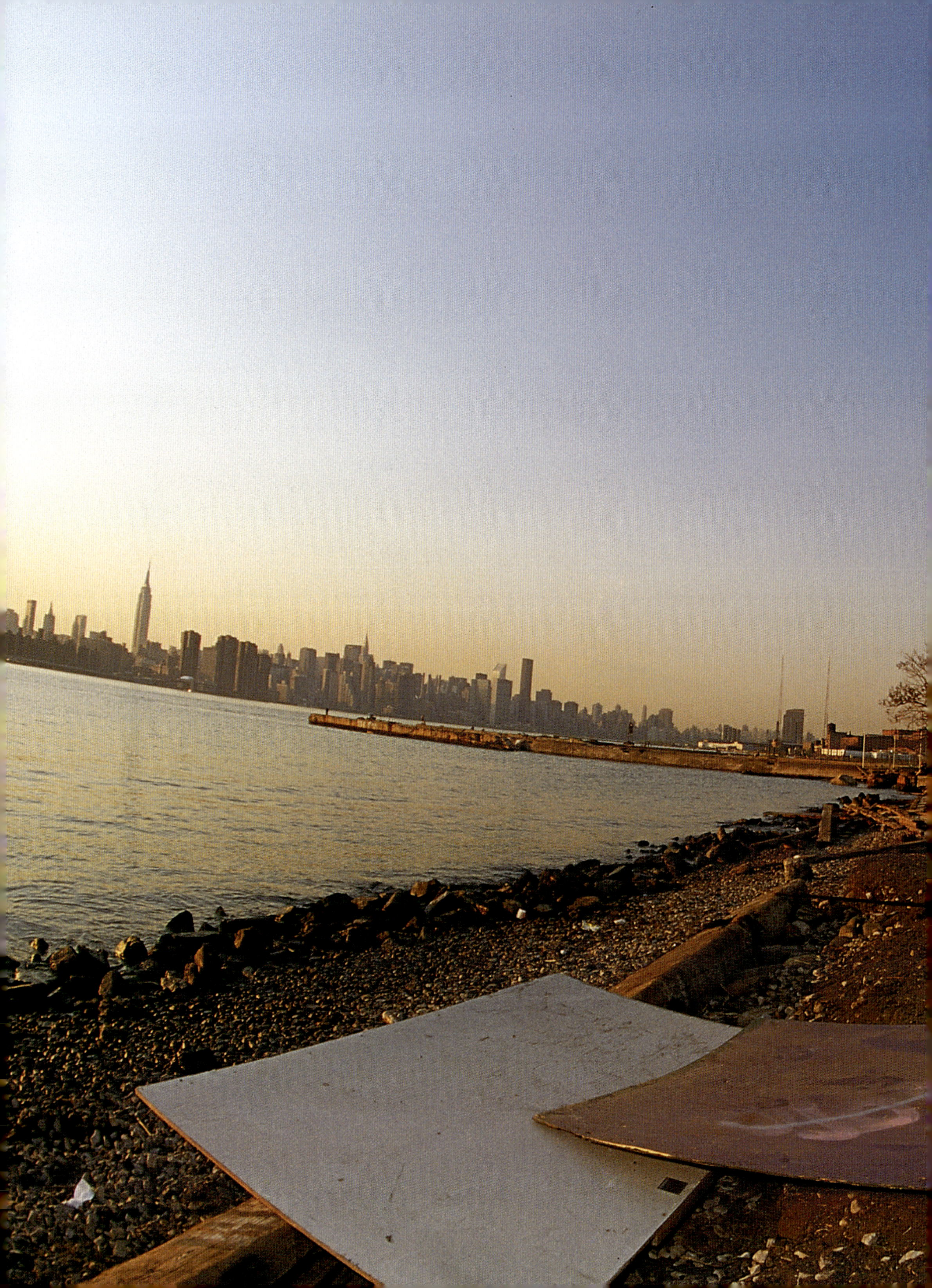

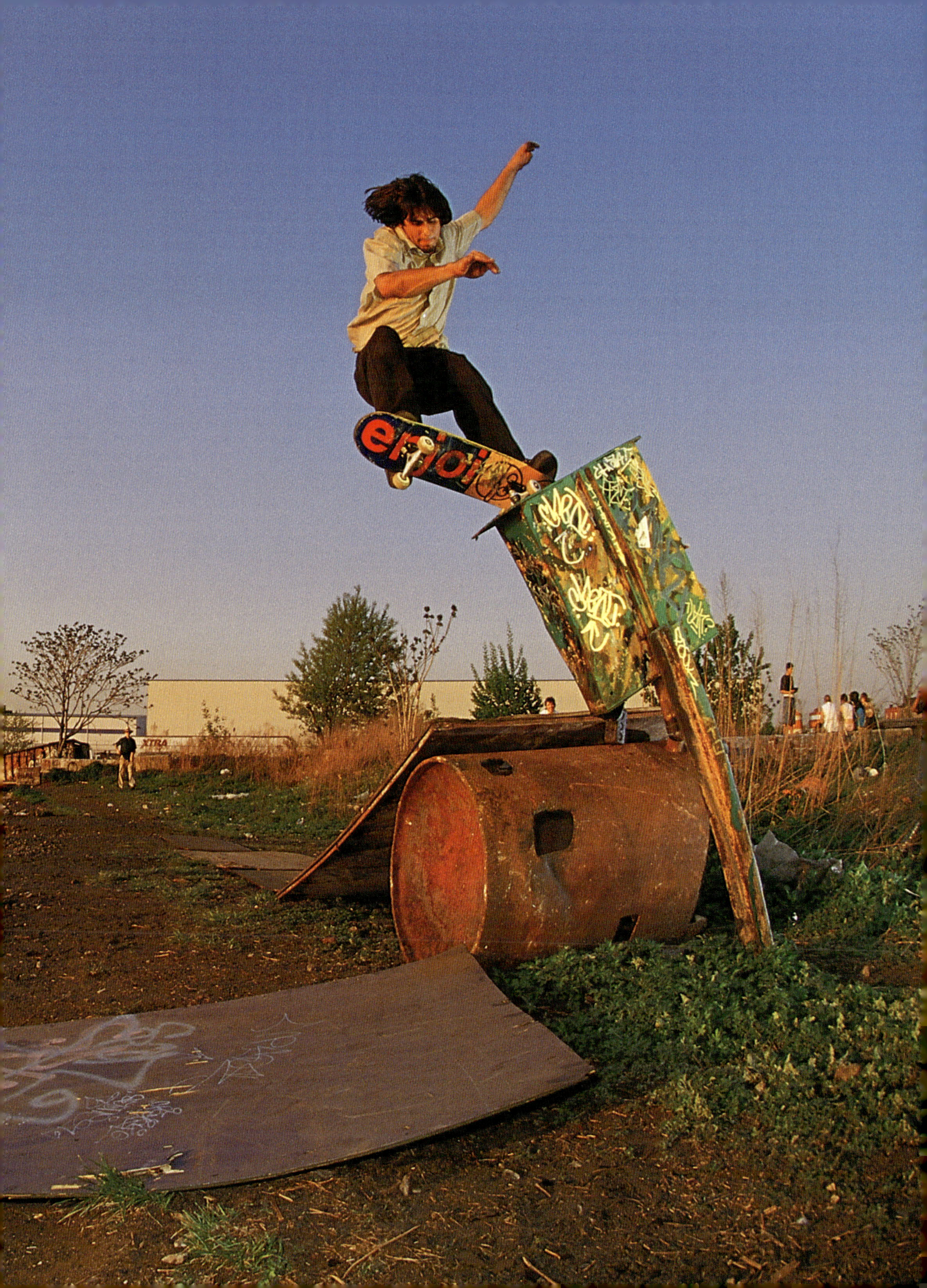
enjoi
XTRA

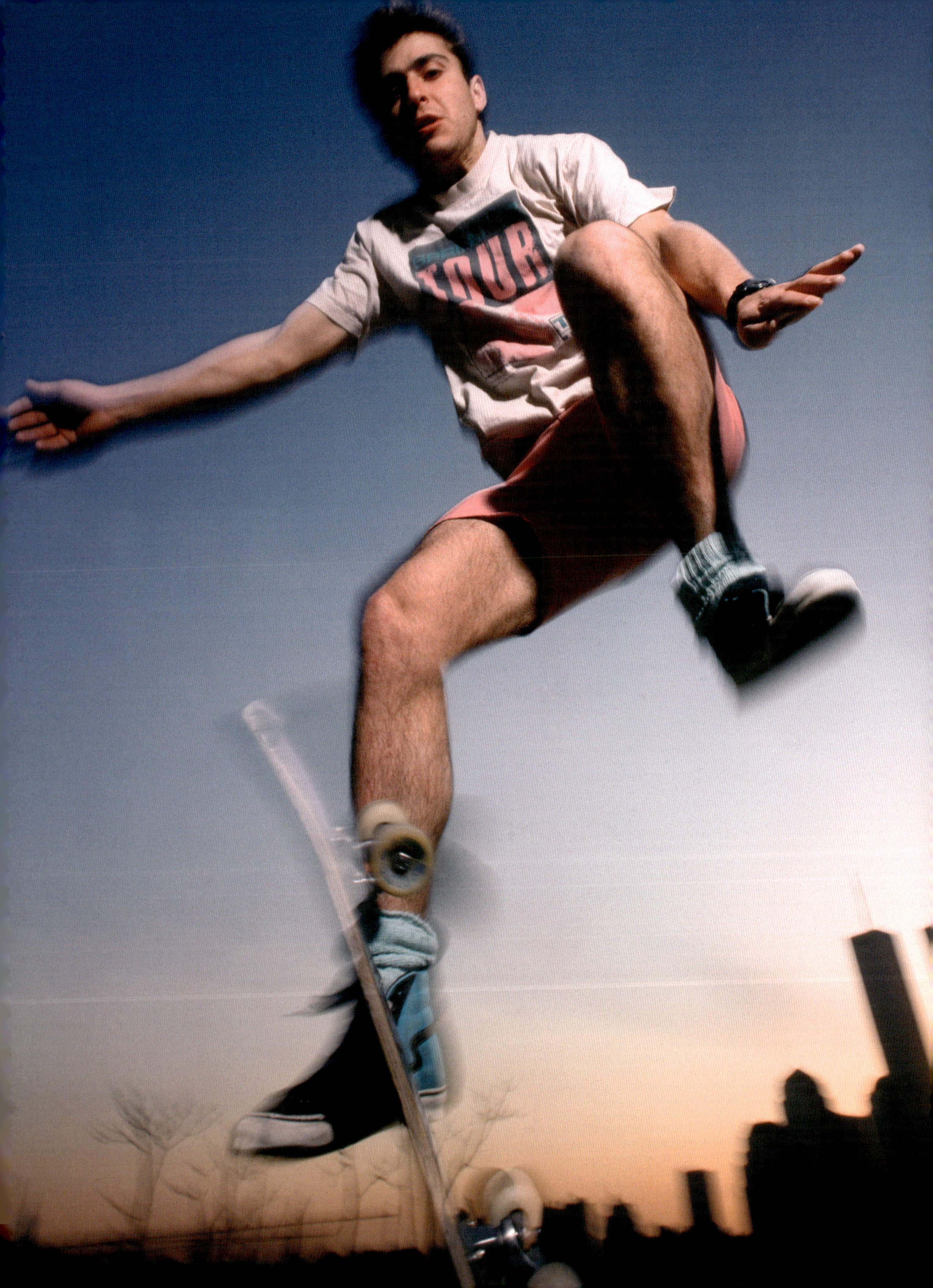
TOUR

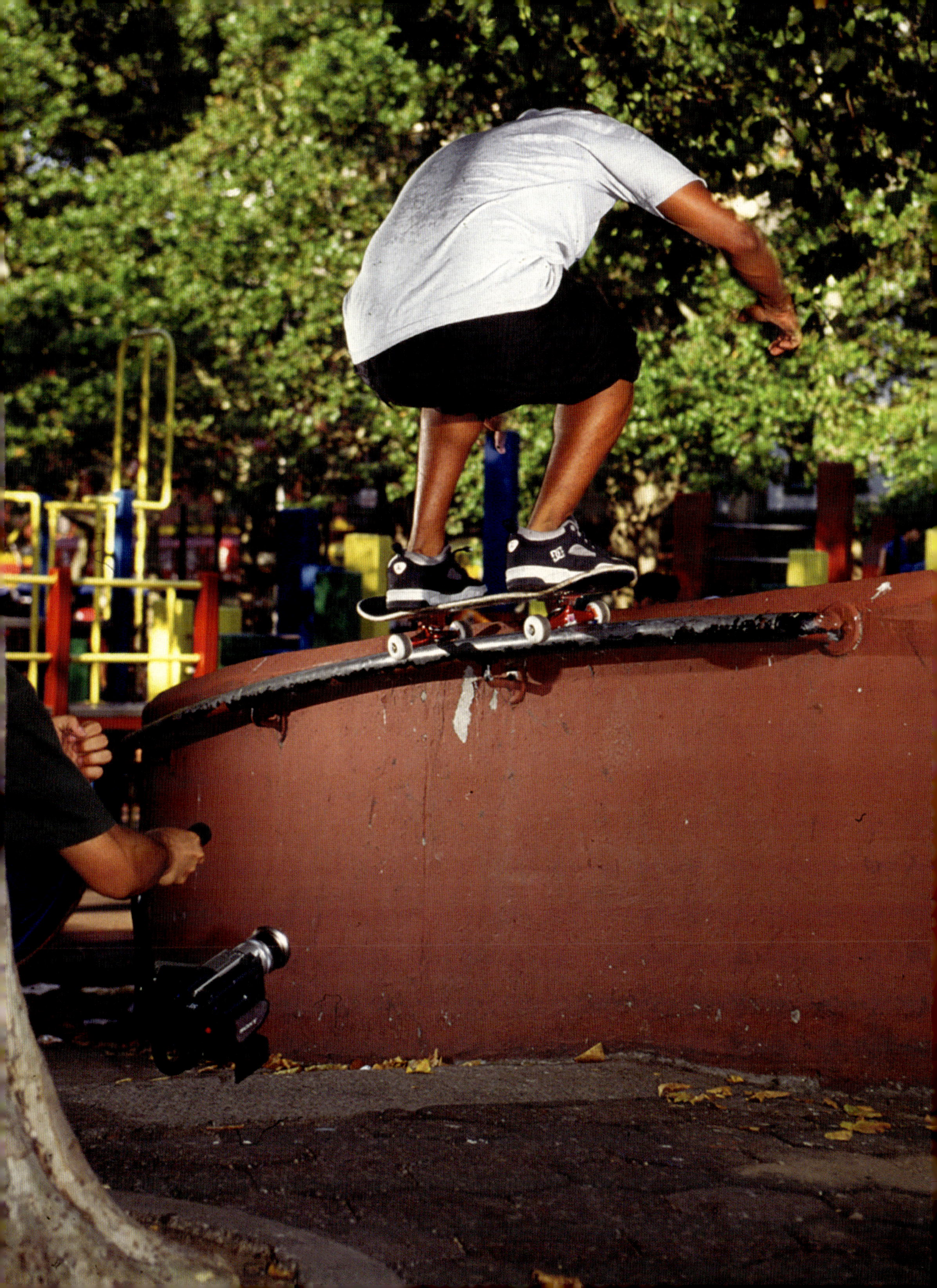

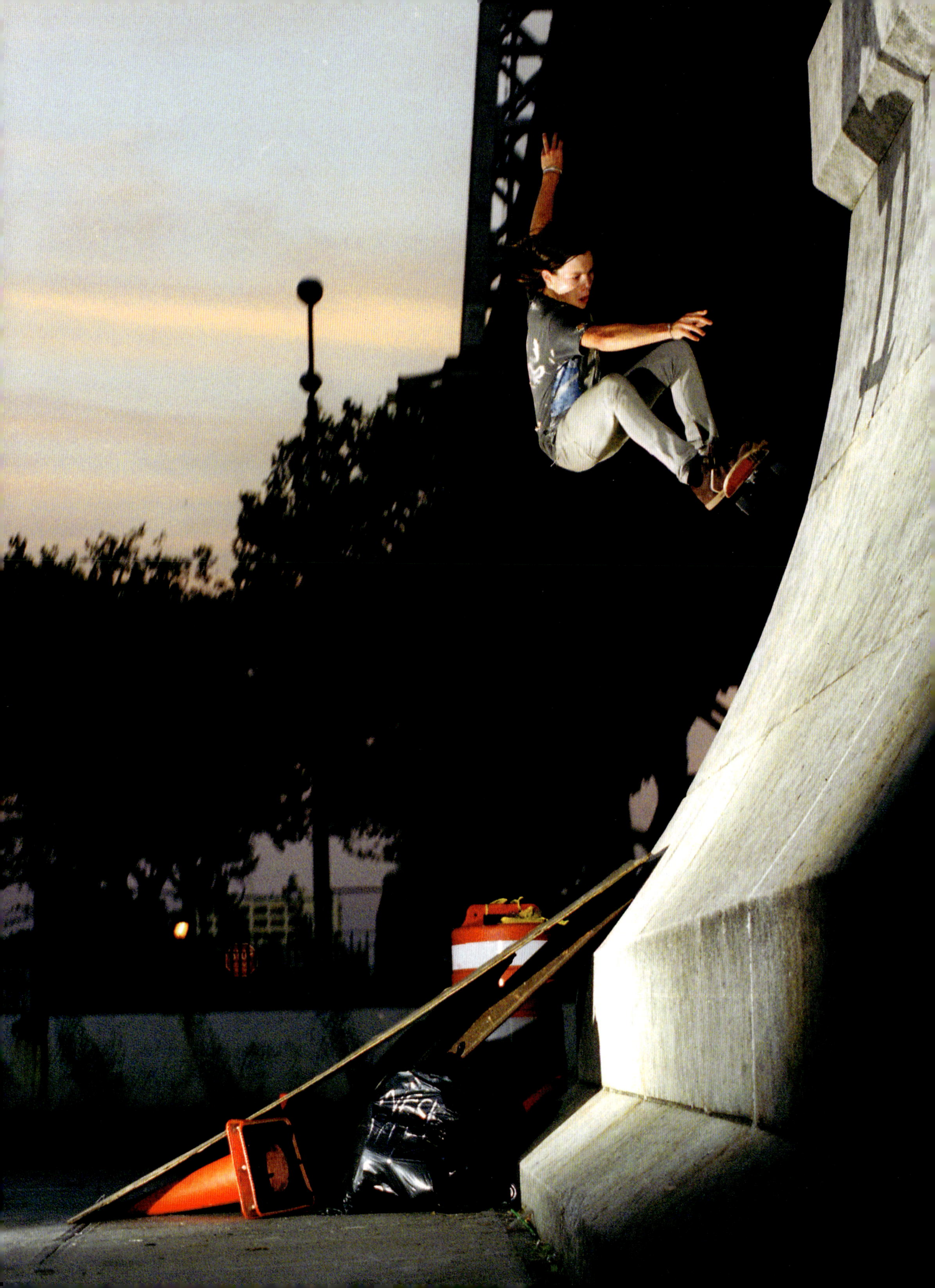

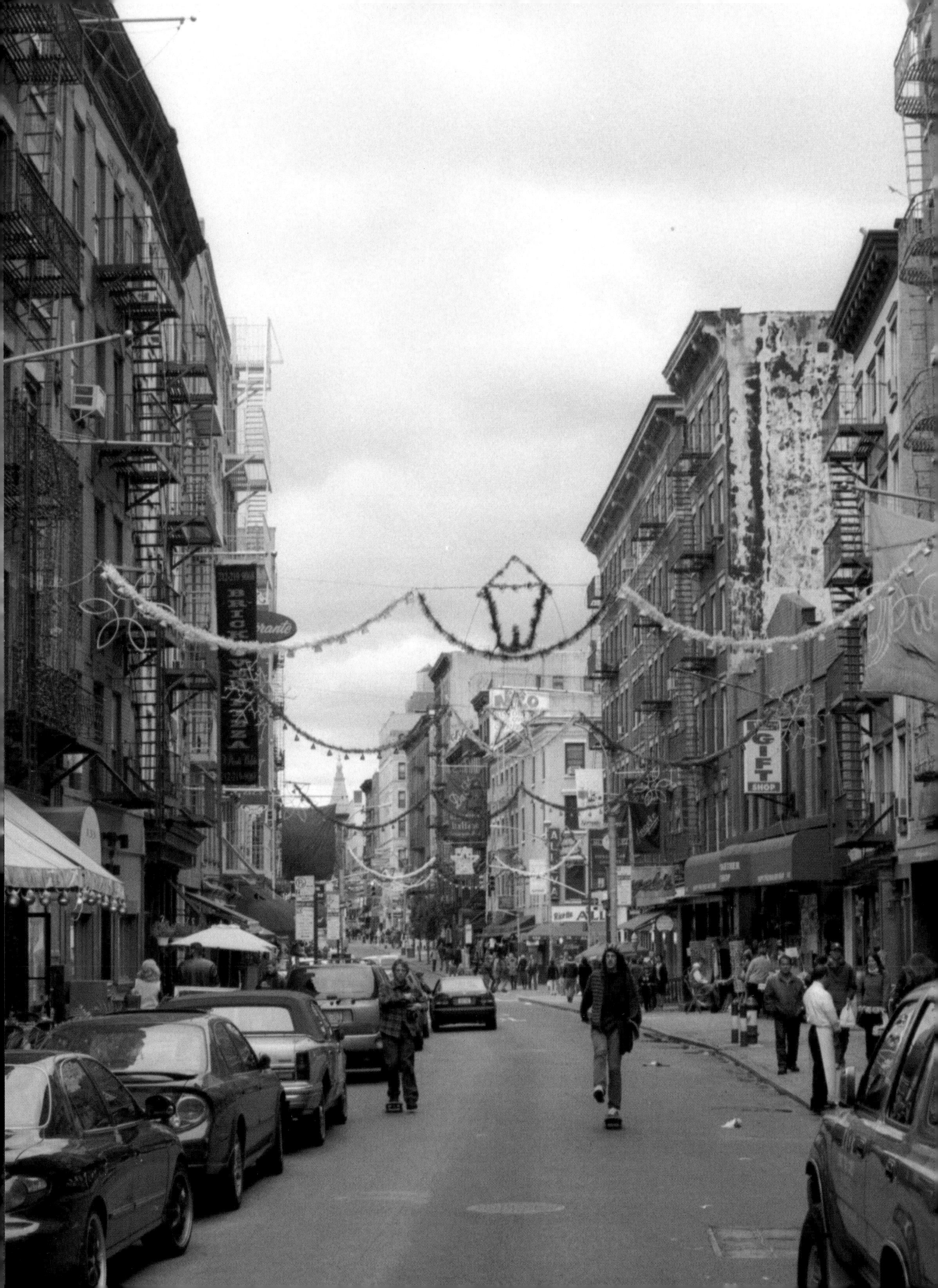
GIFT
SHOP

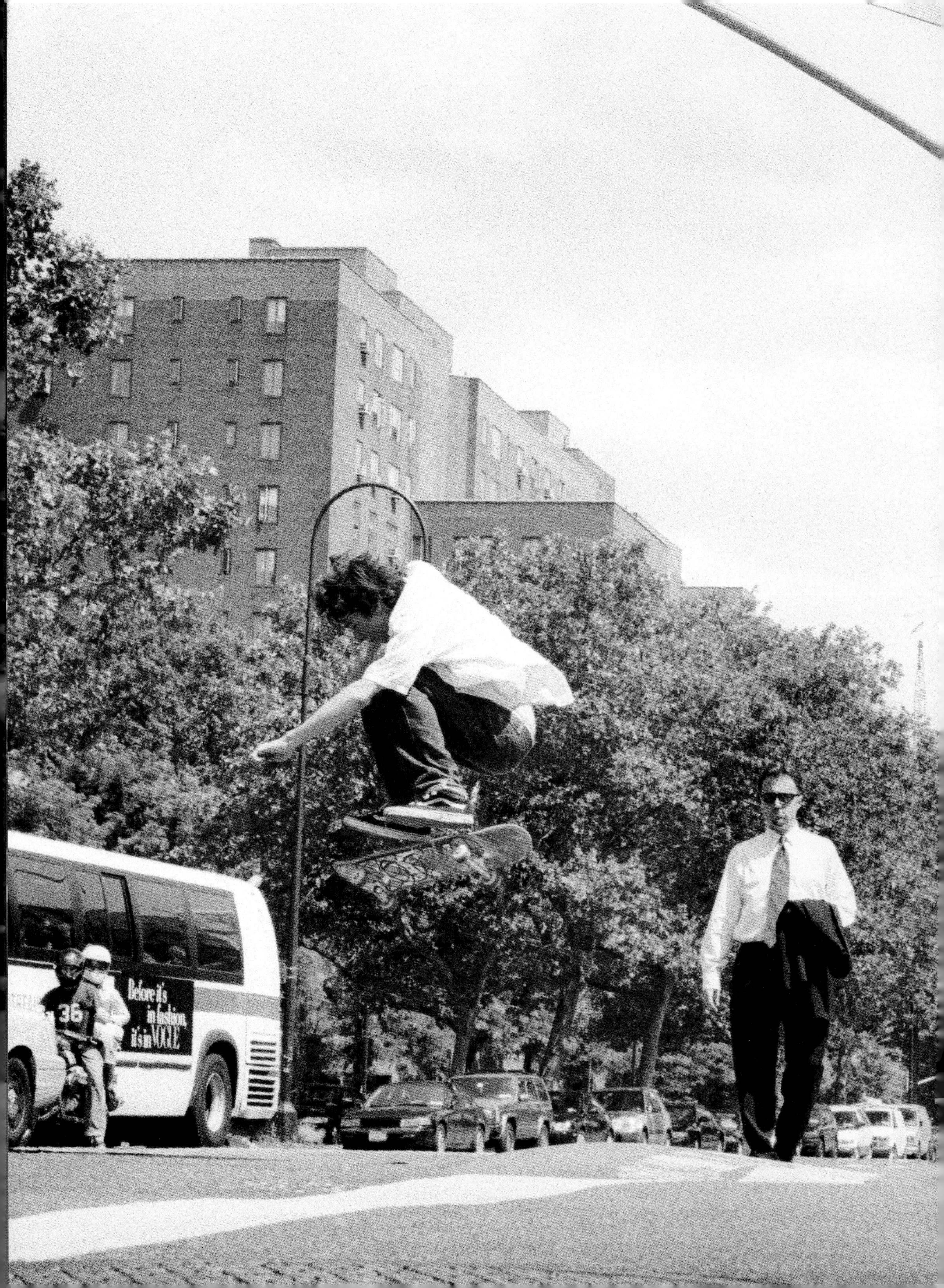
36
Before it's
in fashion,
it's in VOGUE

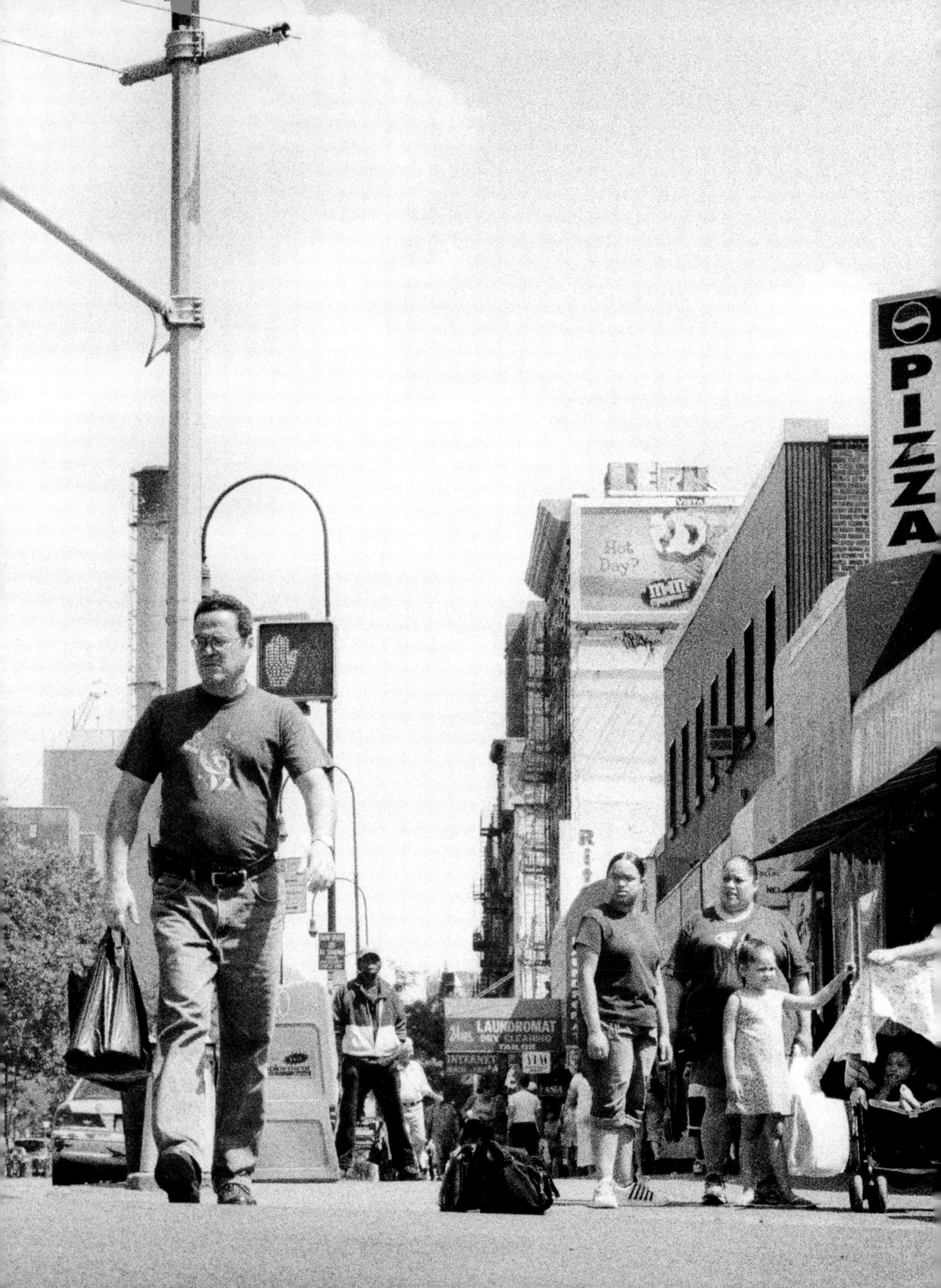
PIZZA
Hot Day?
LAUNDROMAT
DRY CLEANING
TAILOR

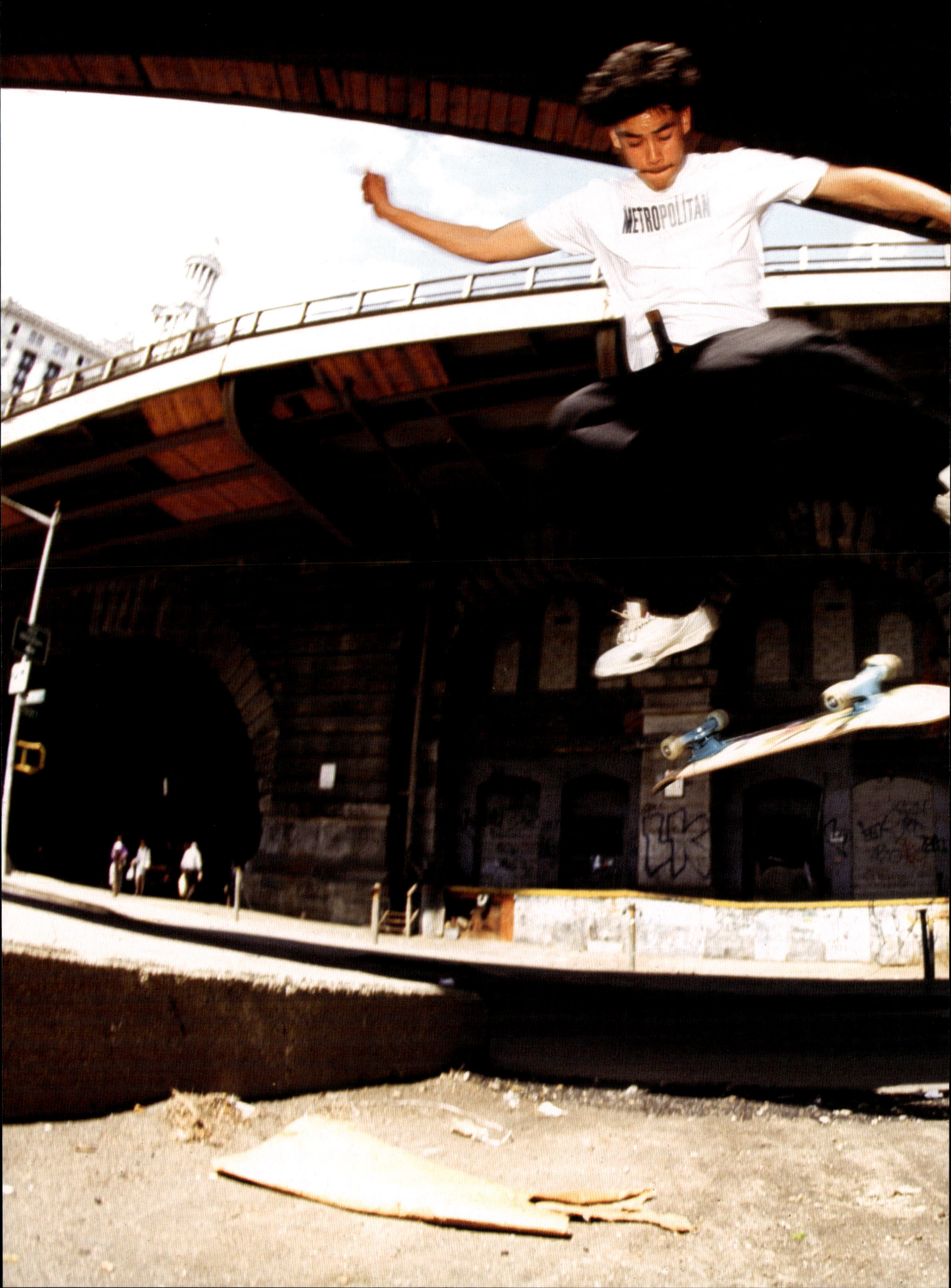
METROPOLITAN

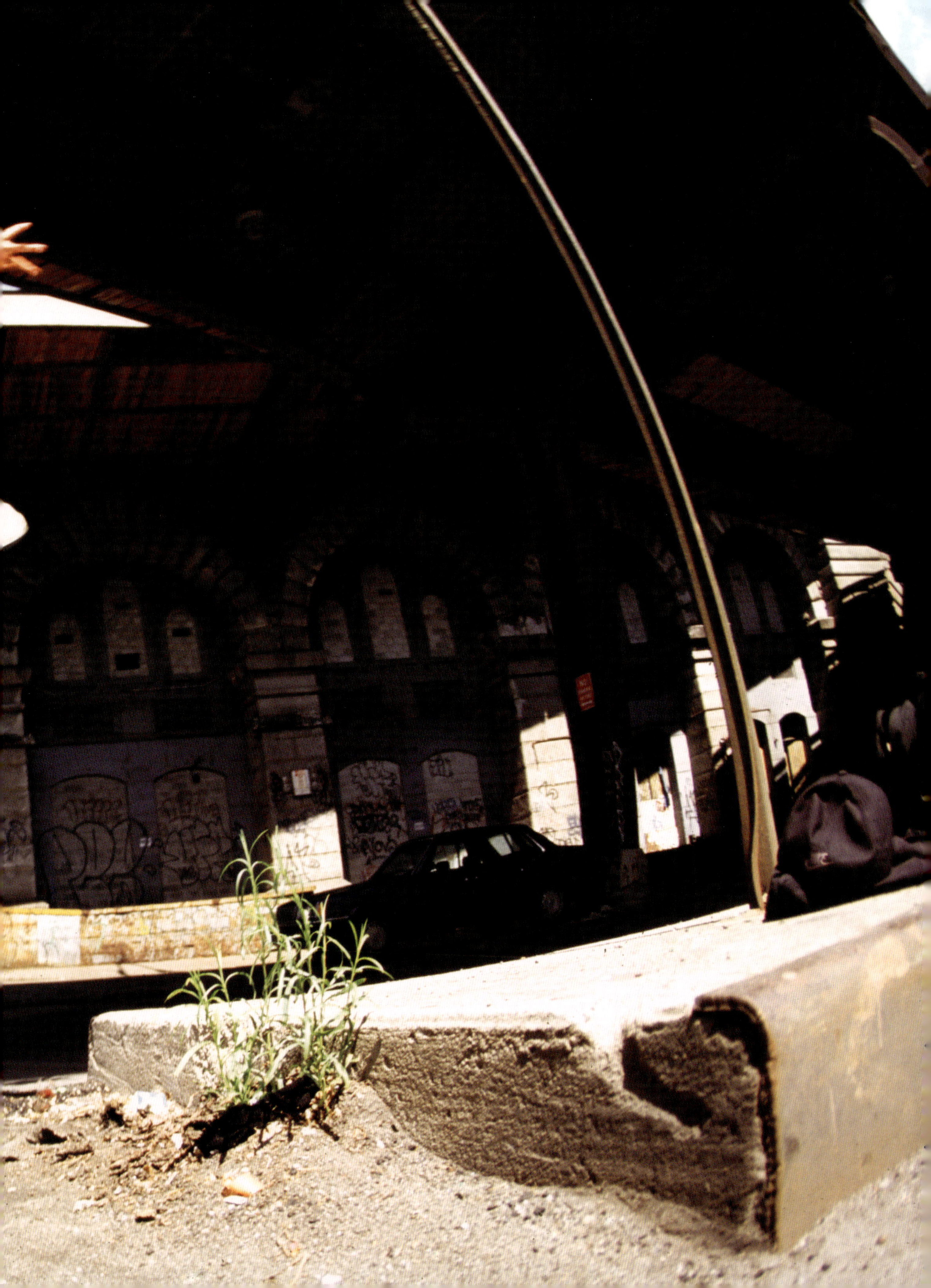

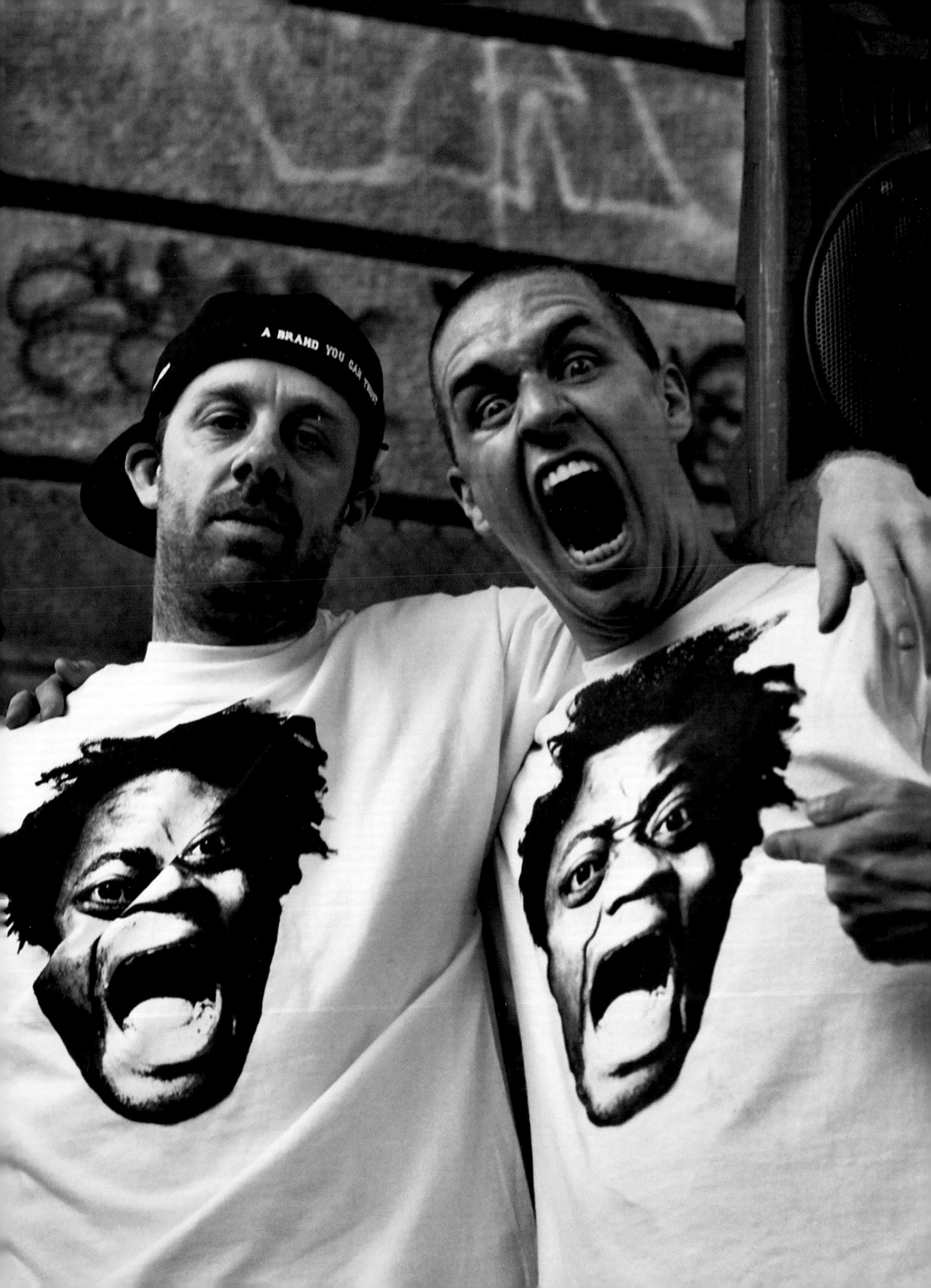
A BRAND YOU CAN

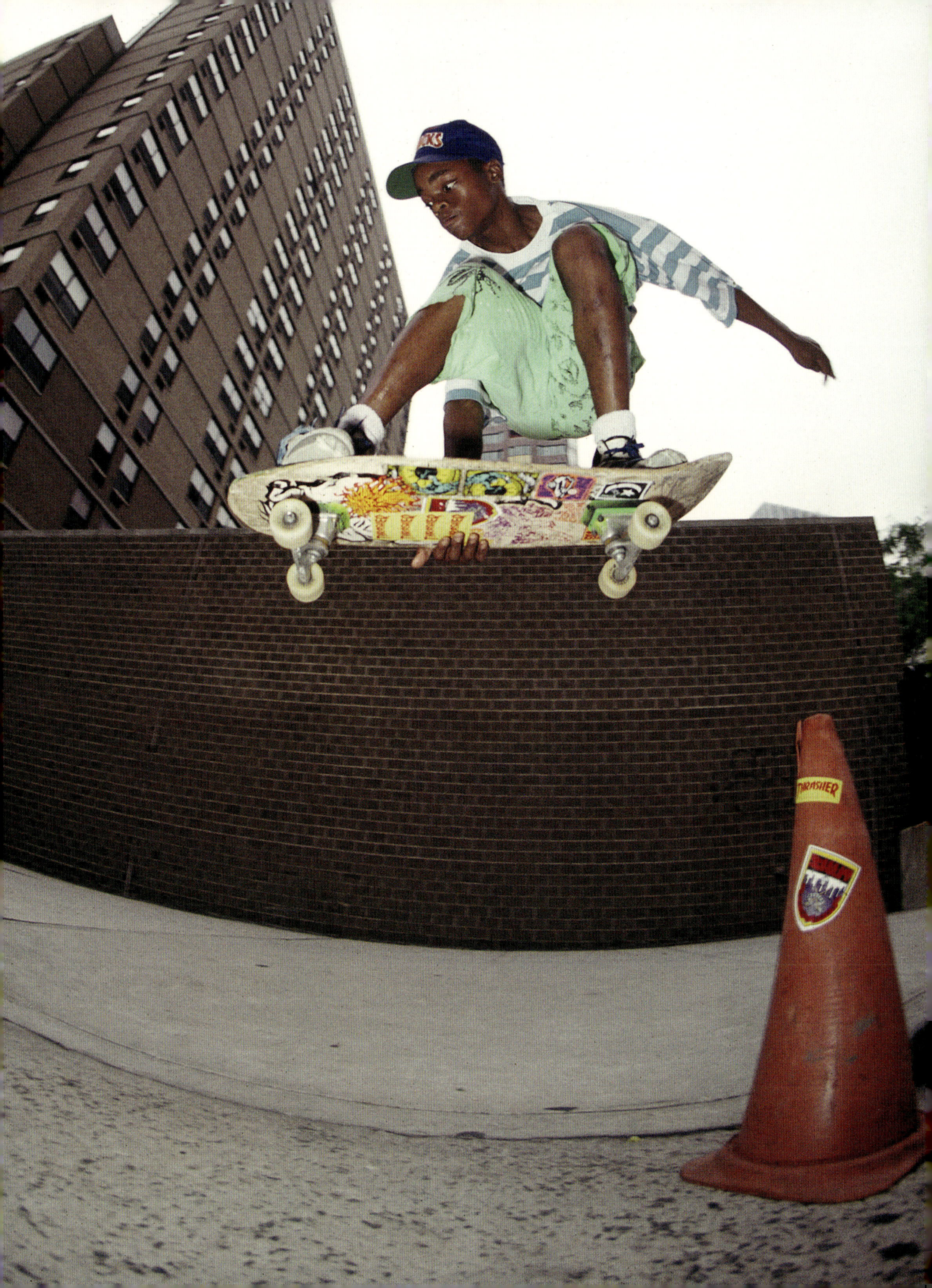
THRASHER

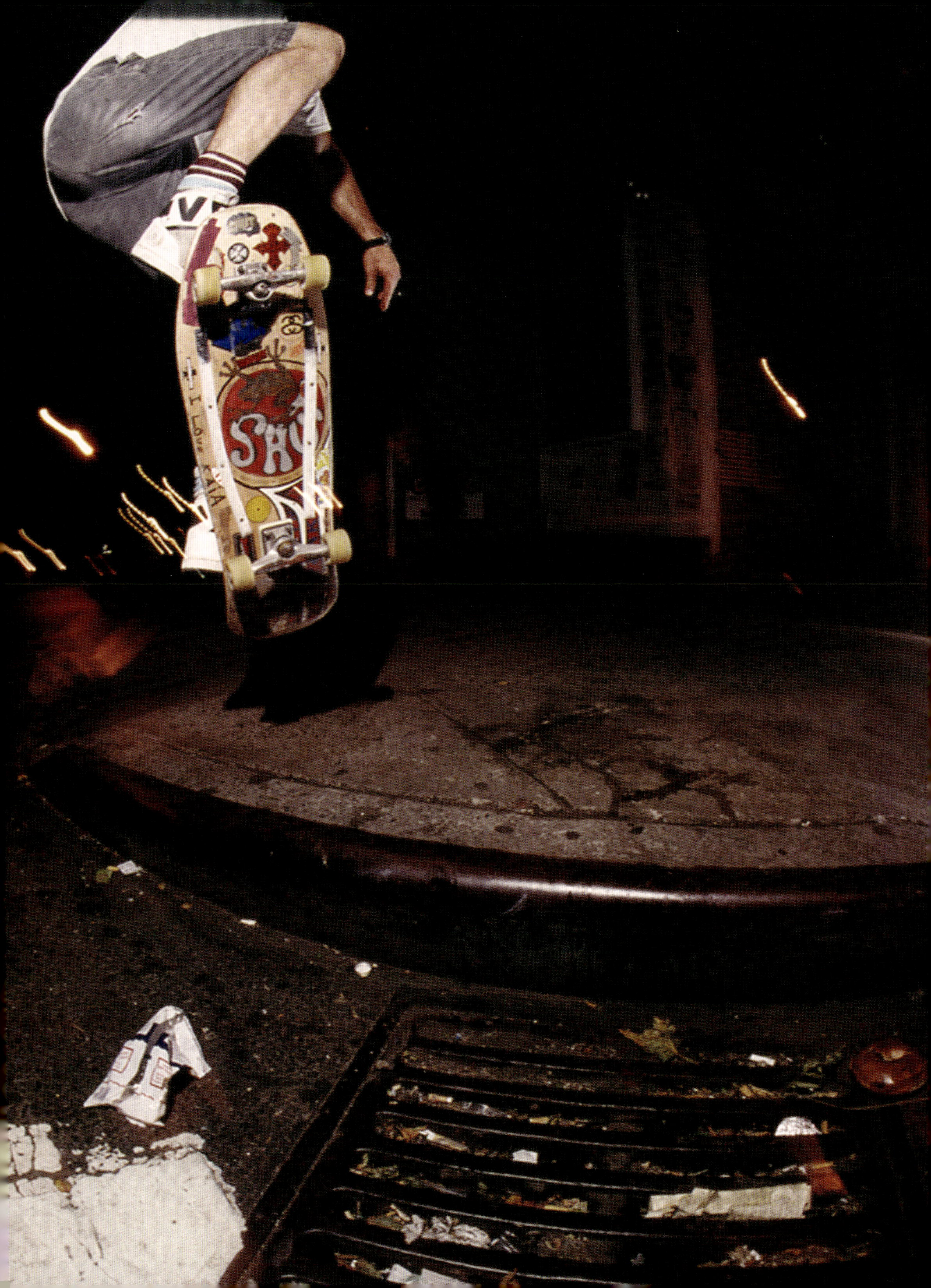
I Love KAIA

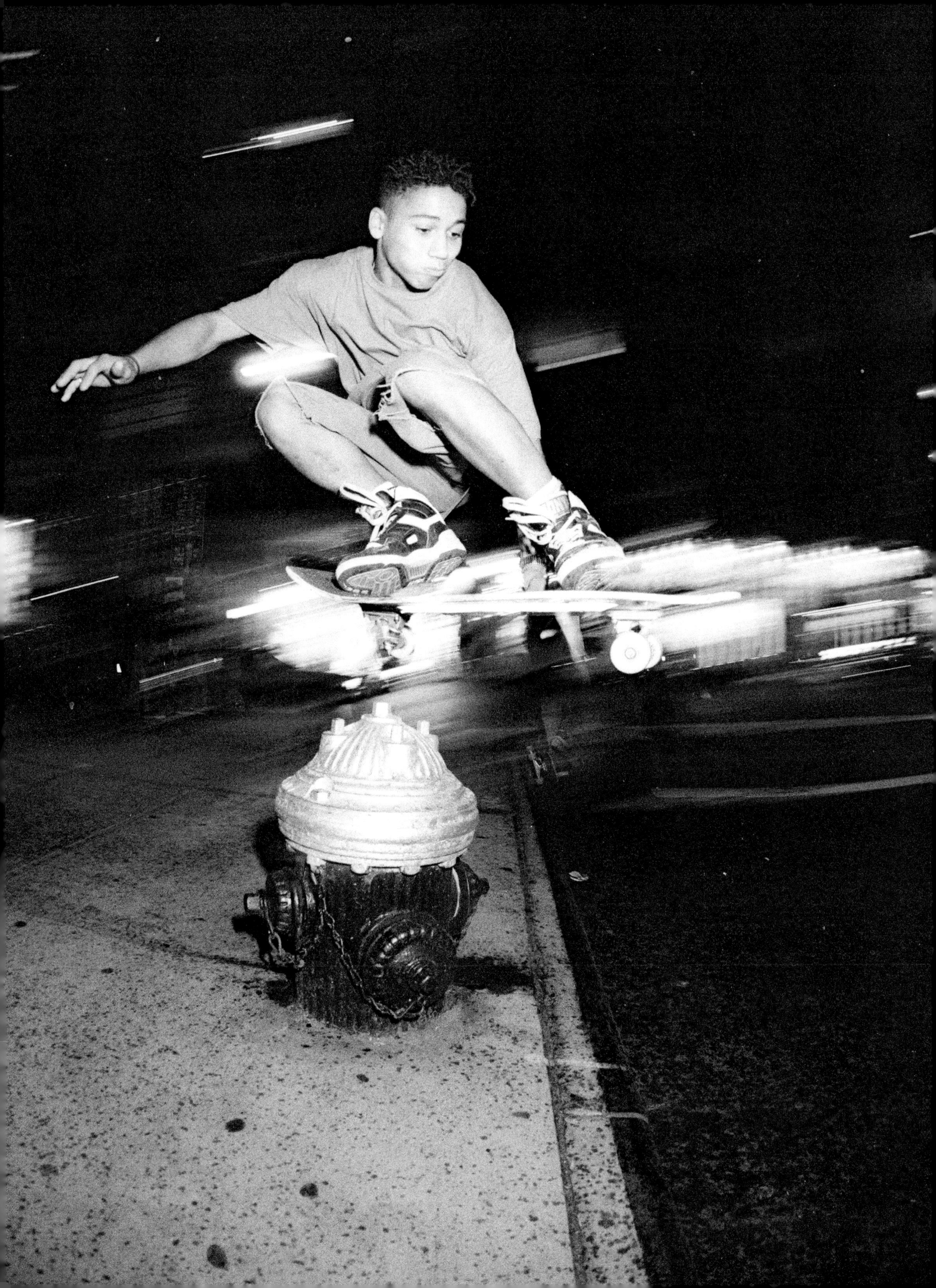

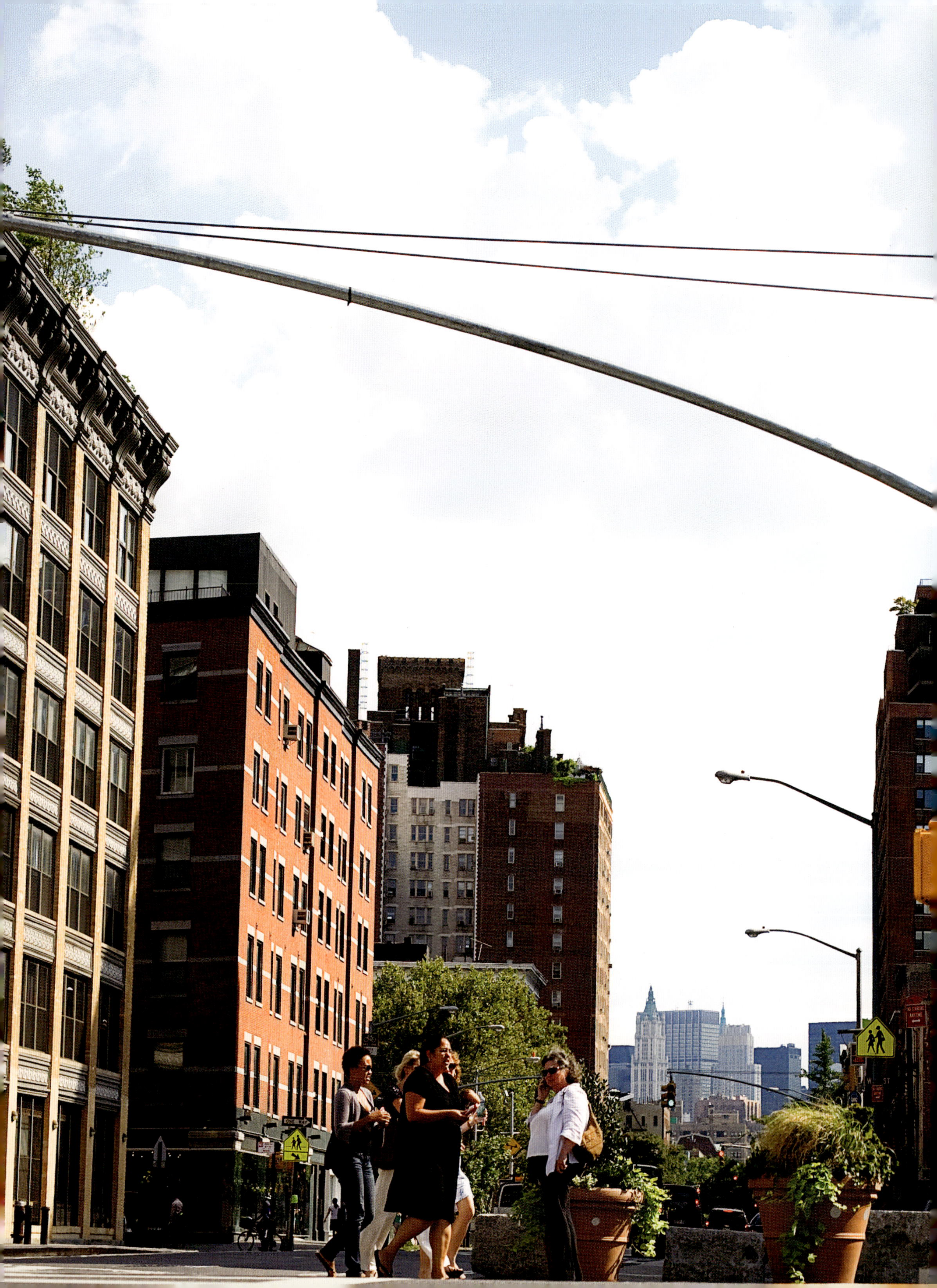

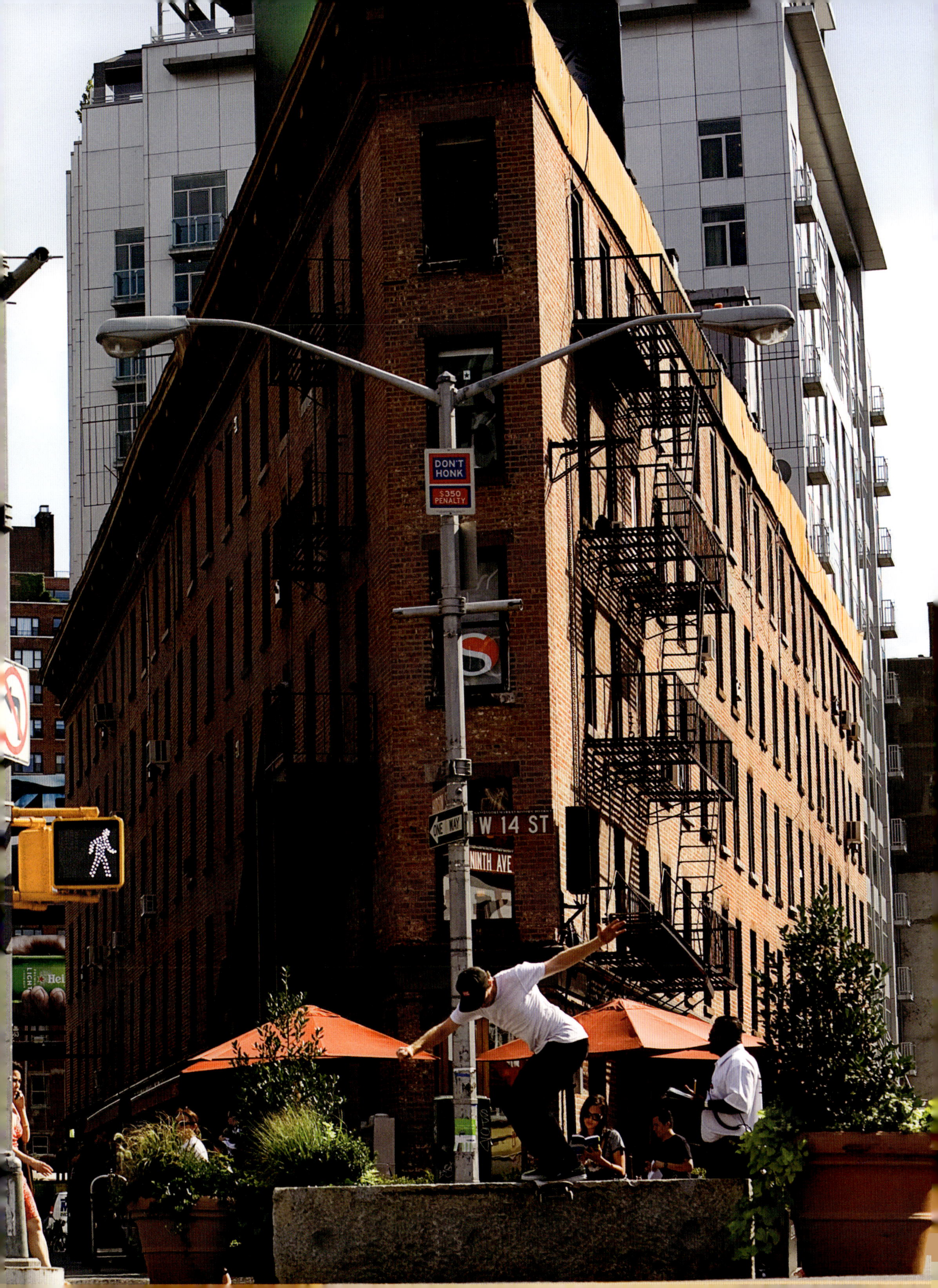

DON'T HONK
$350 PENALTY
ONE WAY
W 14 ST
NINTH AVE

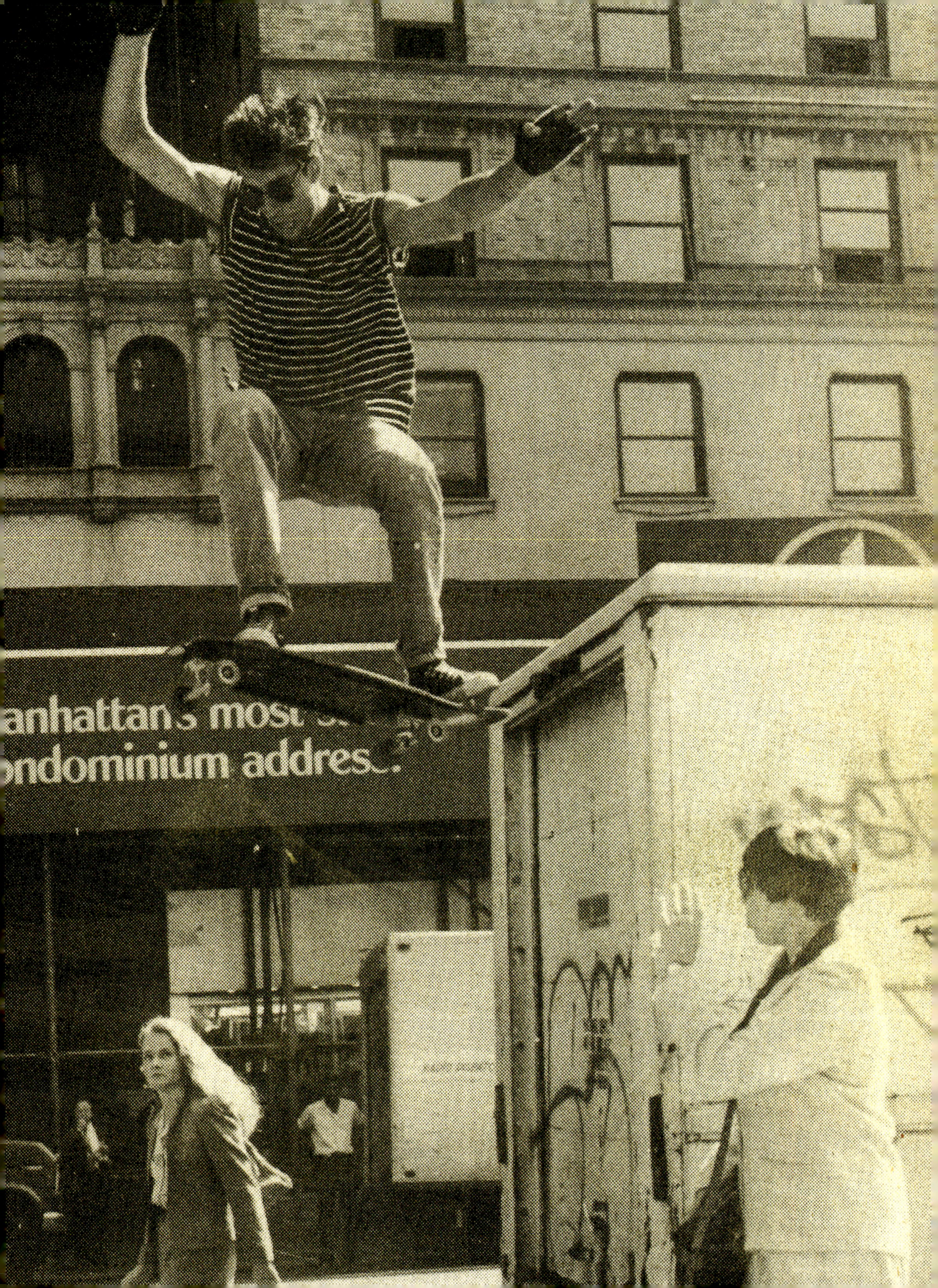
anhattan's most s
ondominium addres

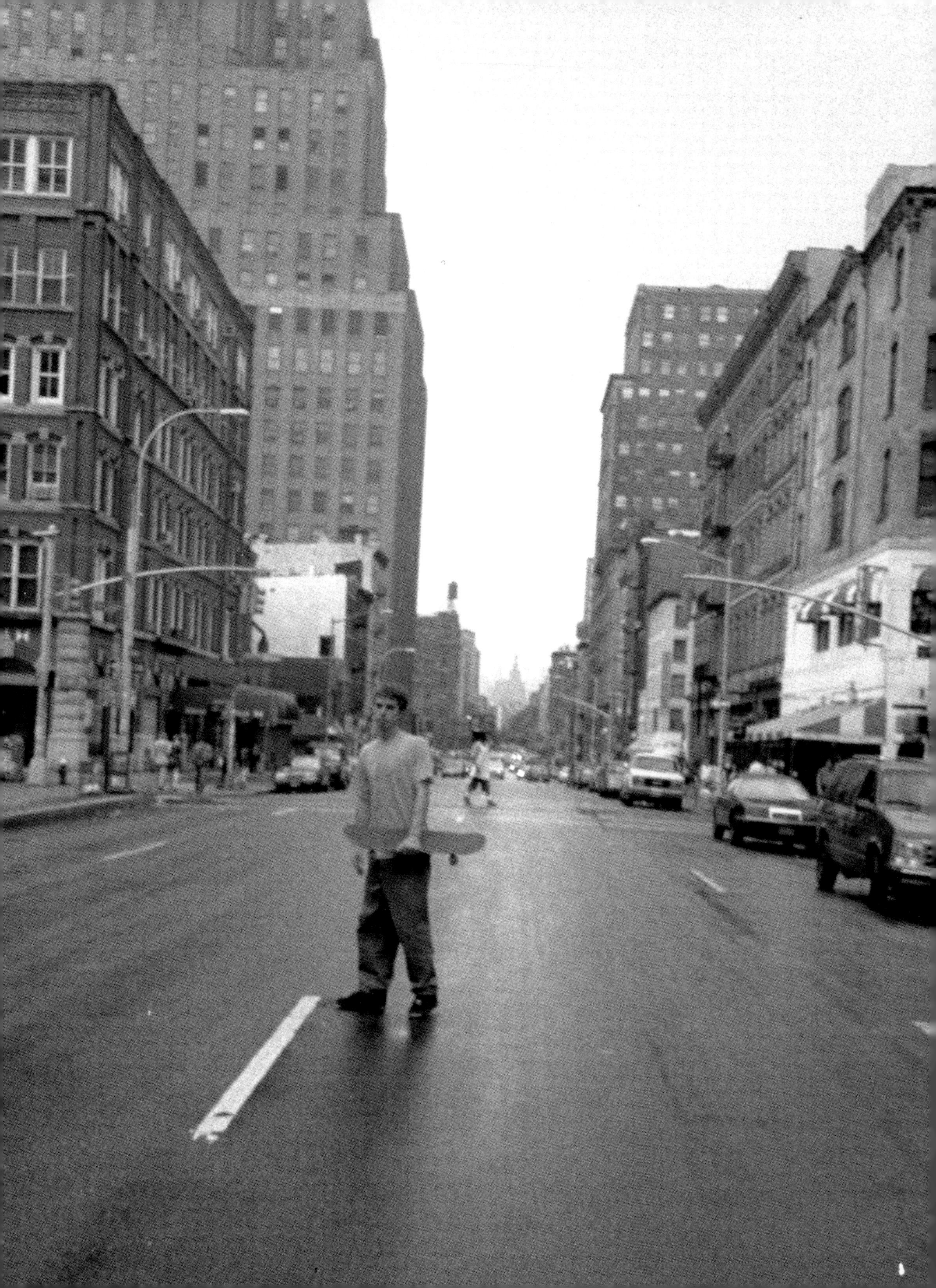

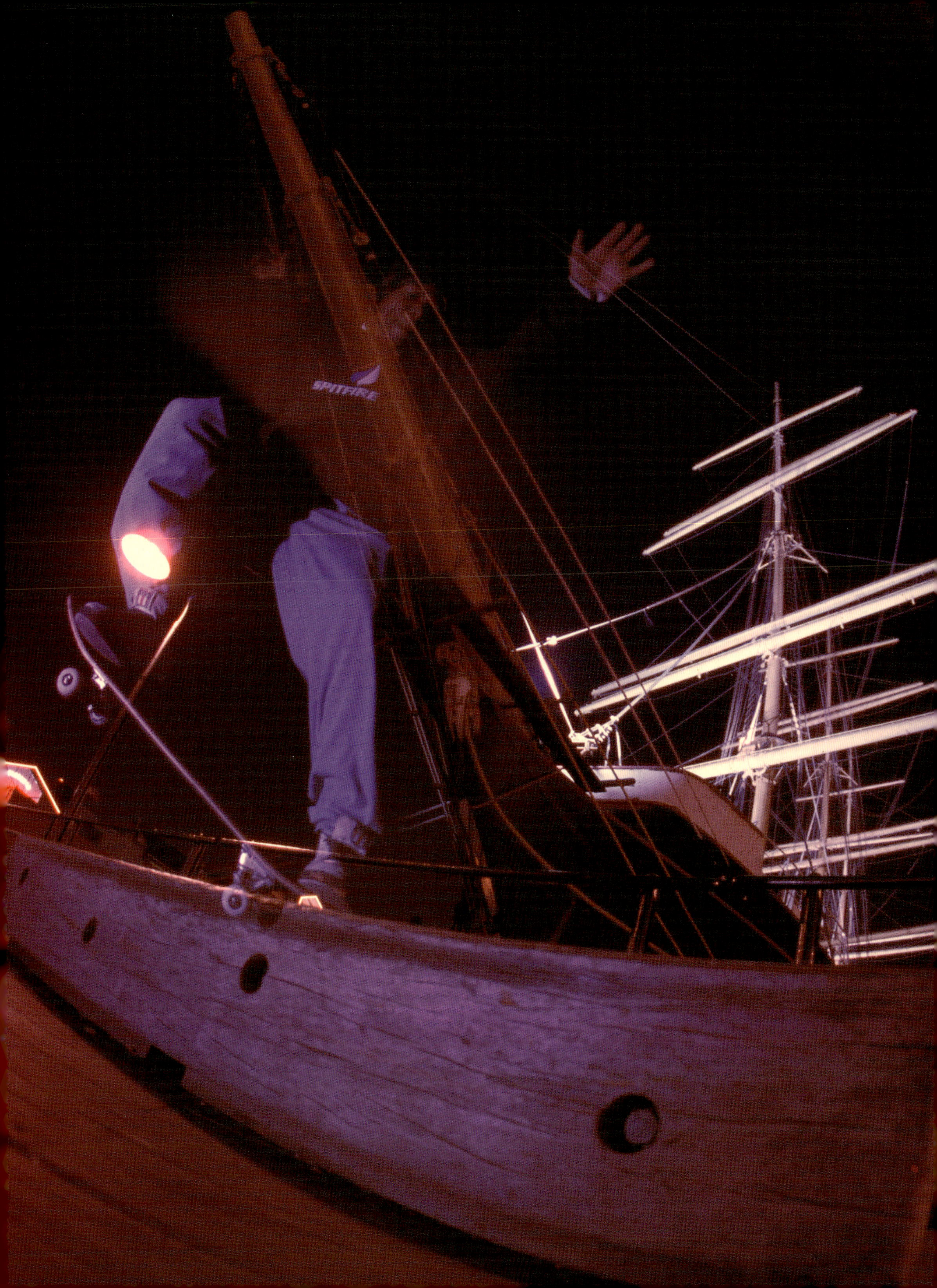
SPITFIRE

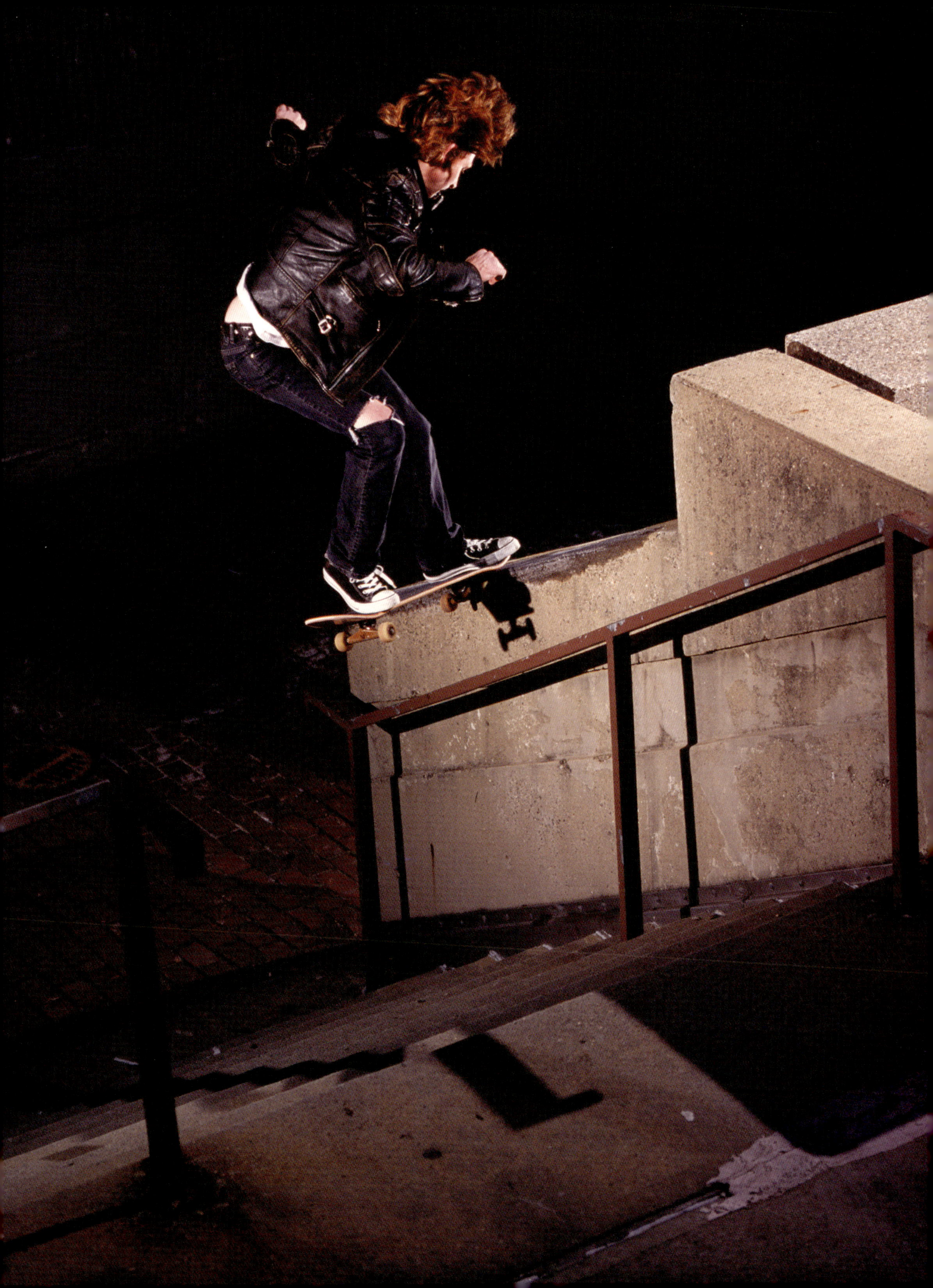

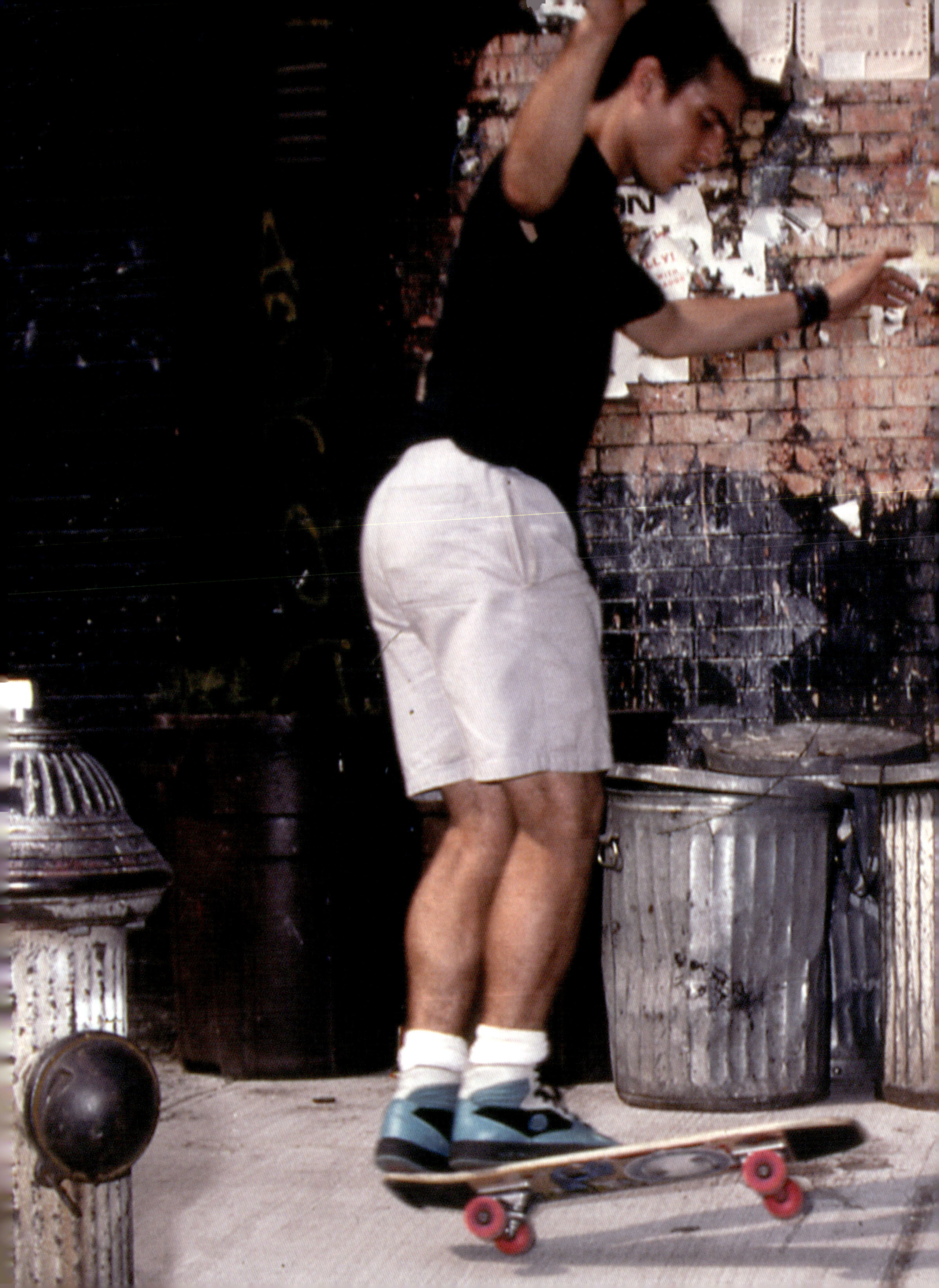

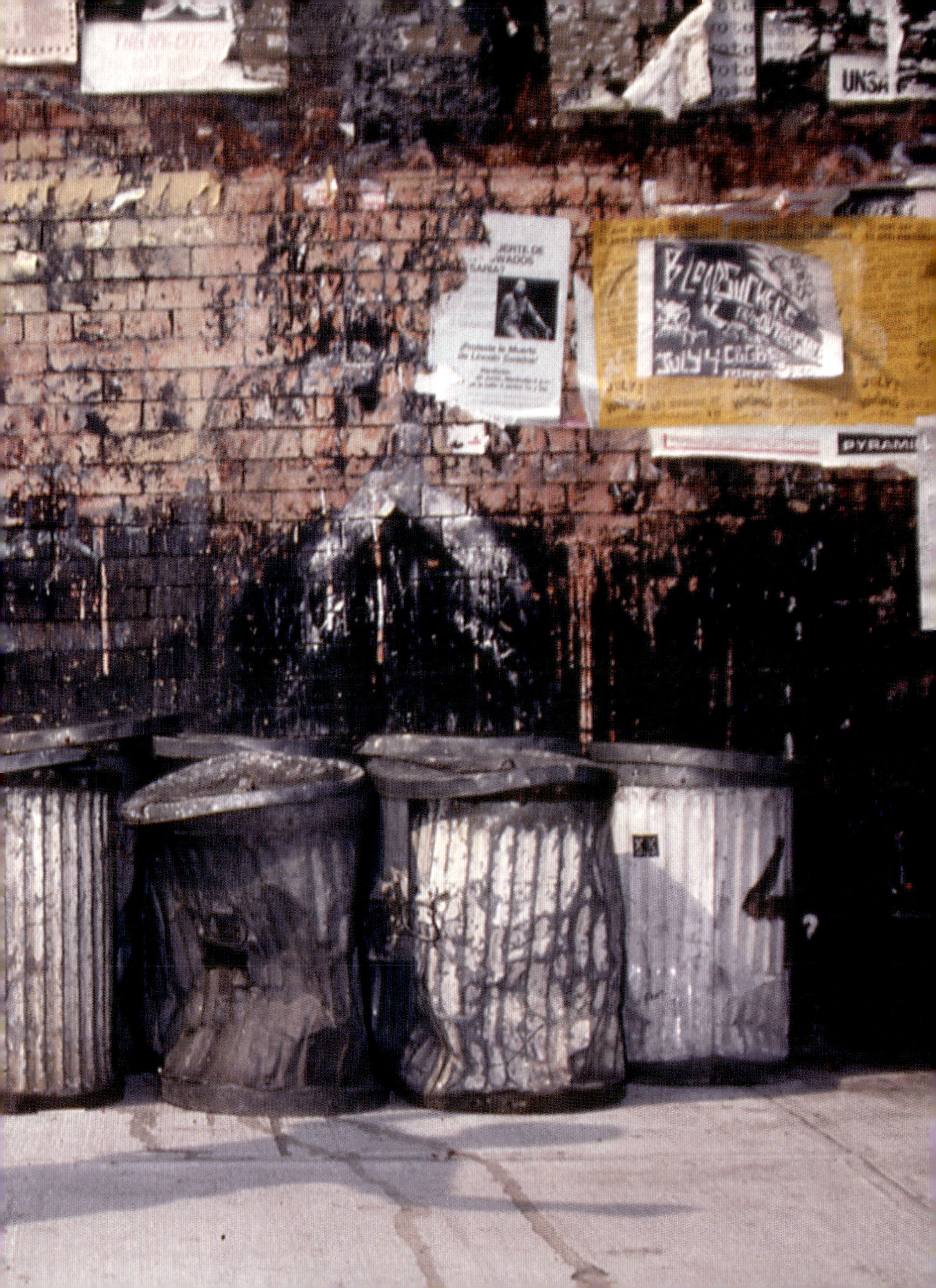
UNSA
PYRAMI

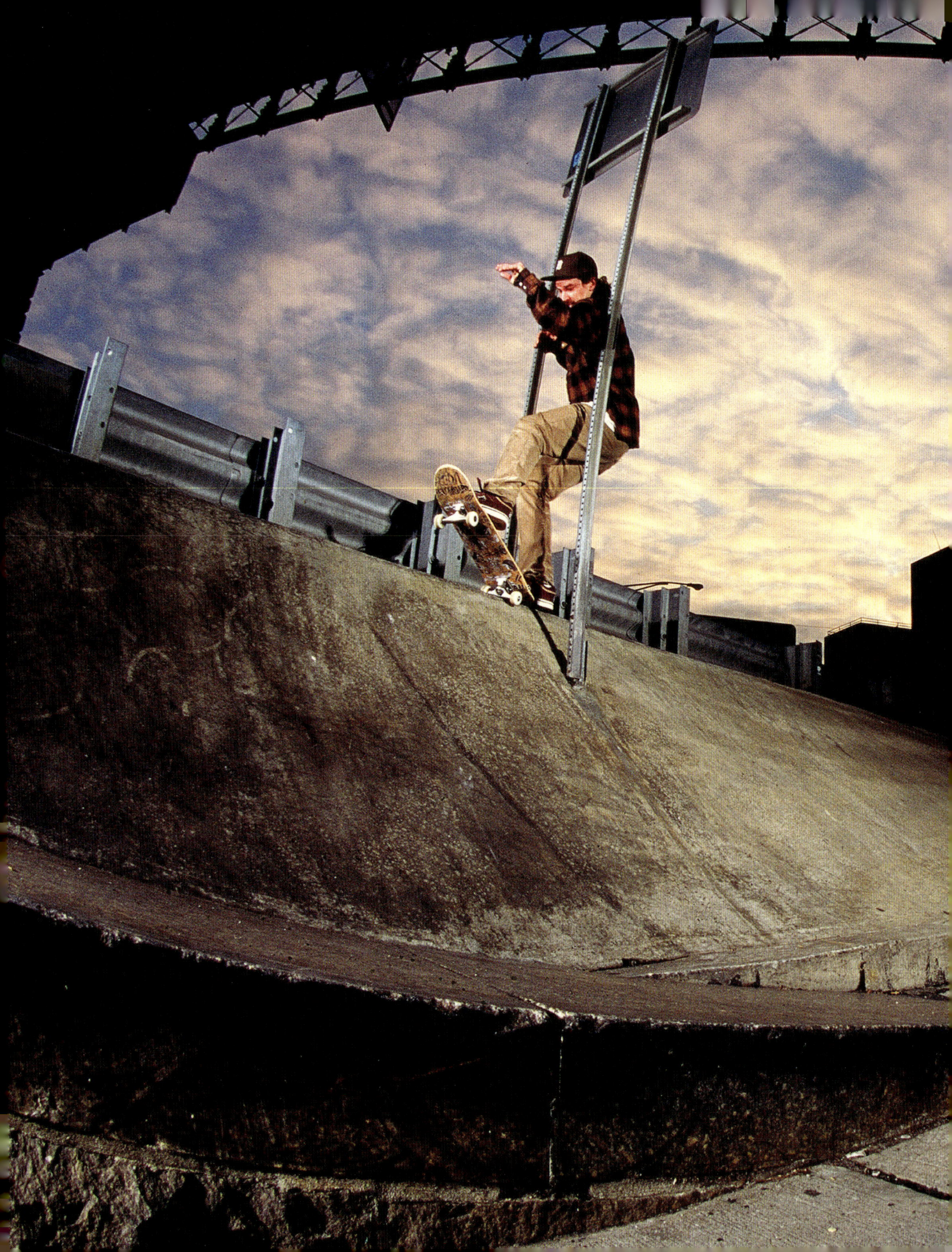

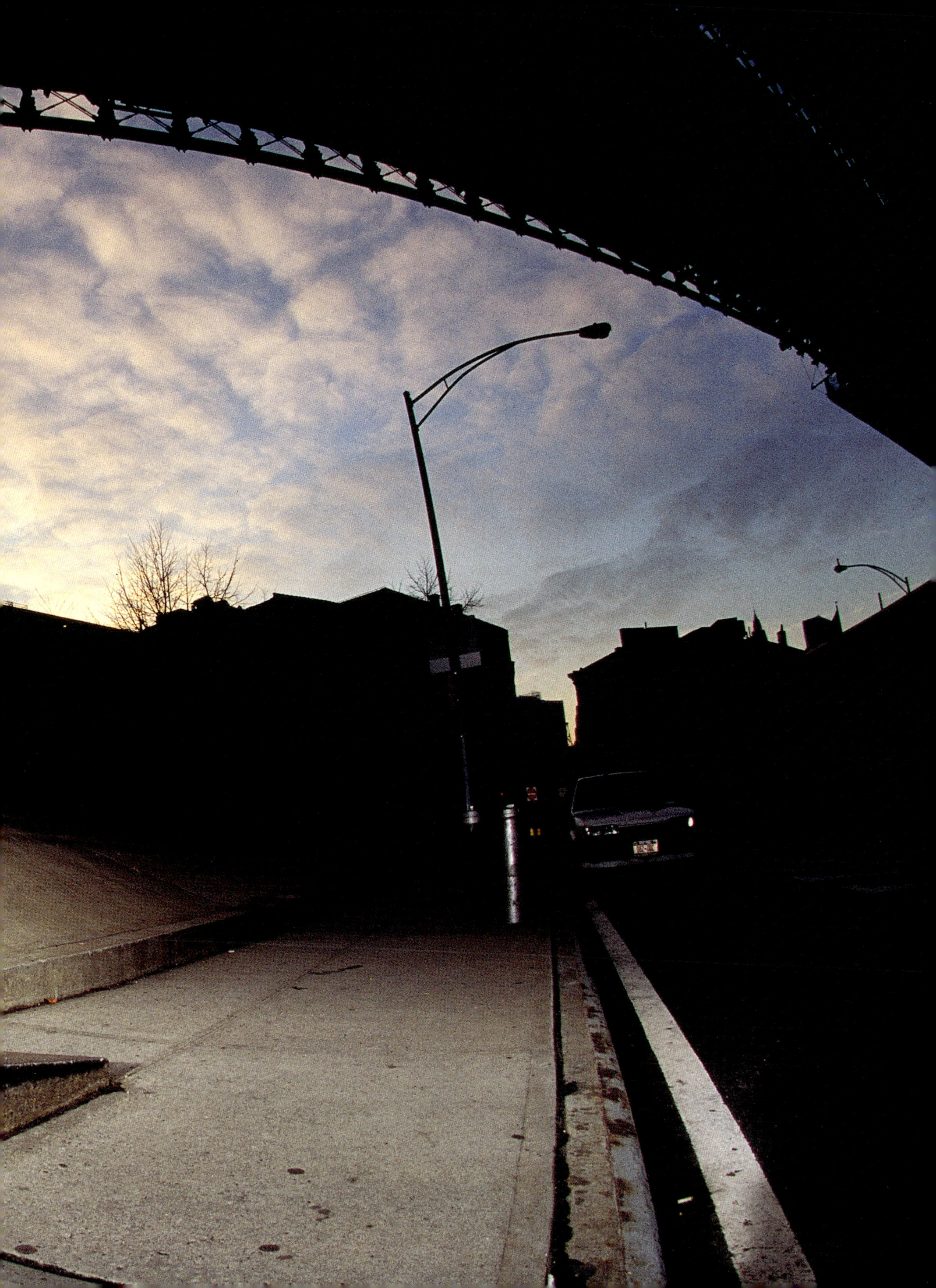

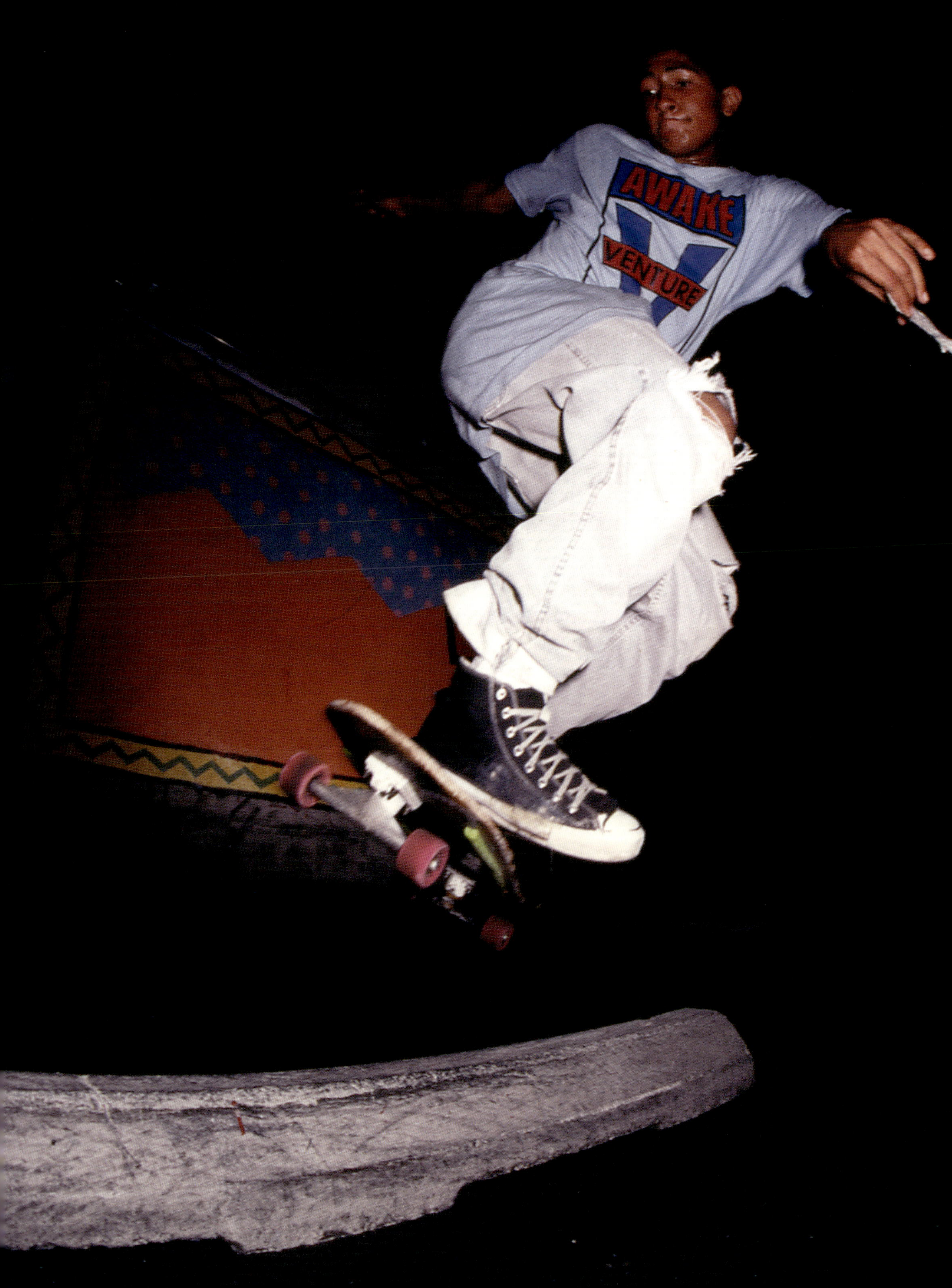
AWAKE
VENTURE

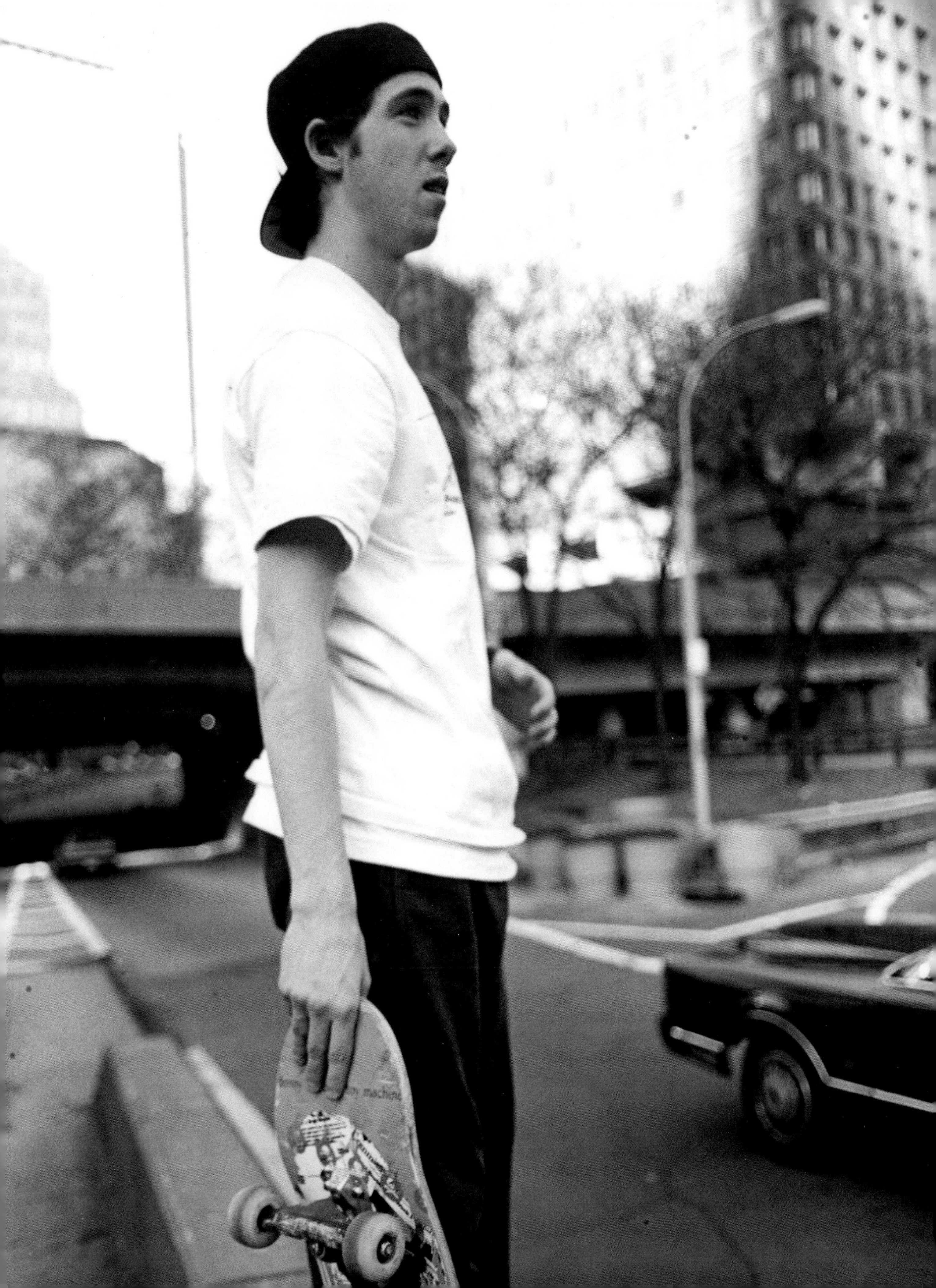

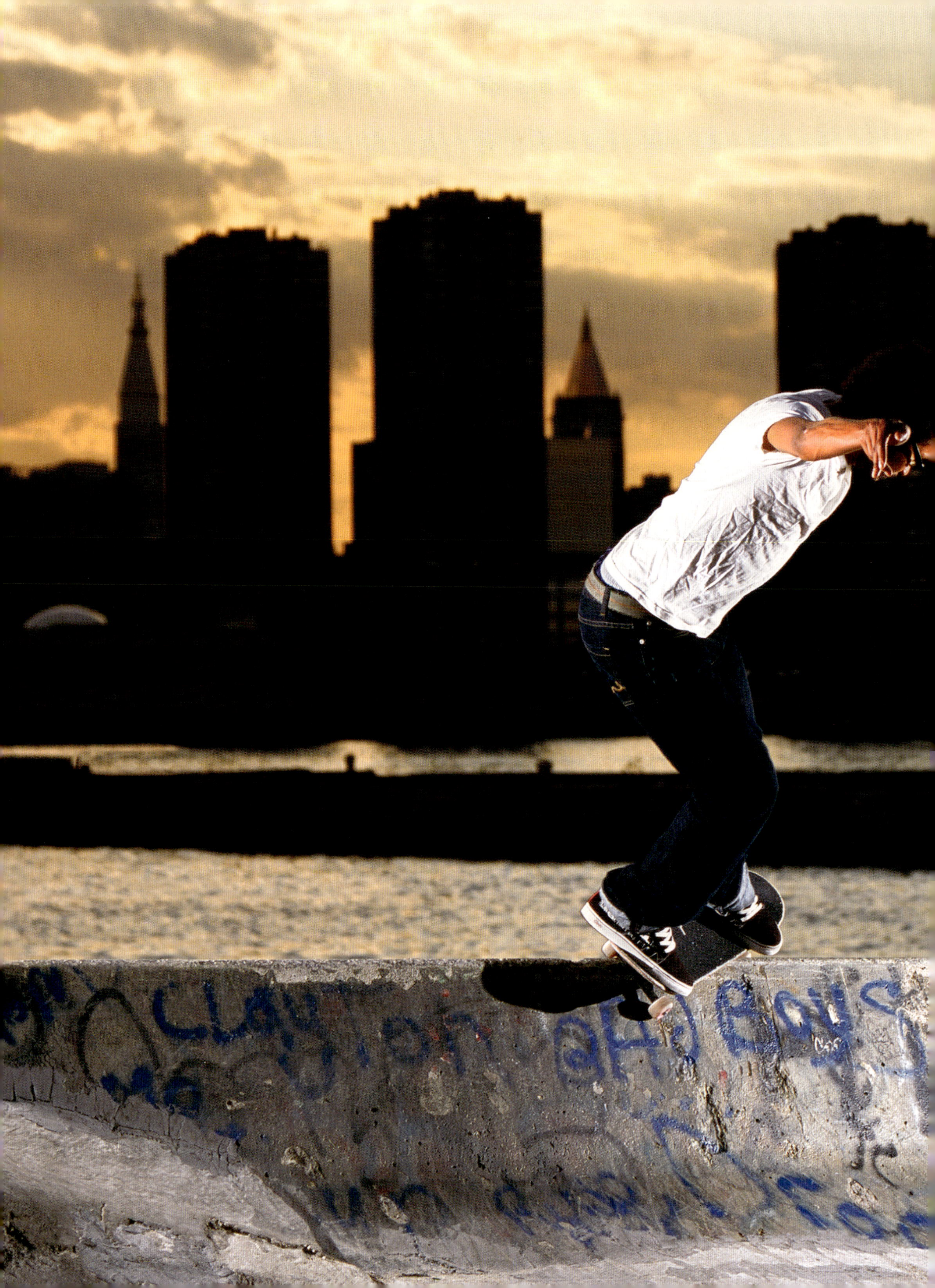

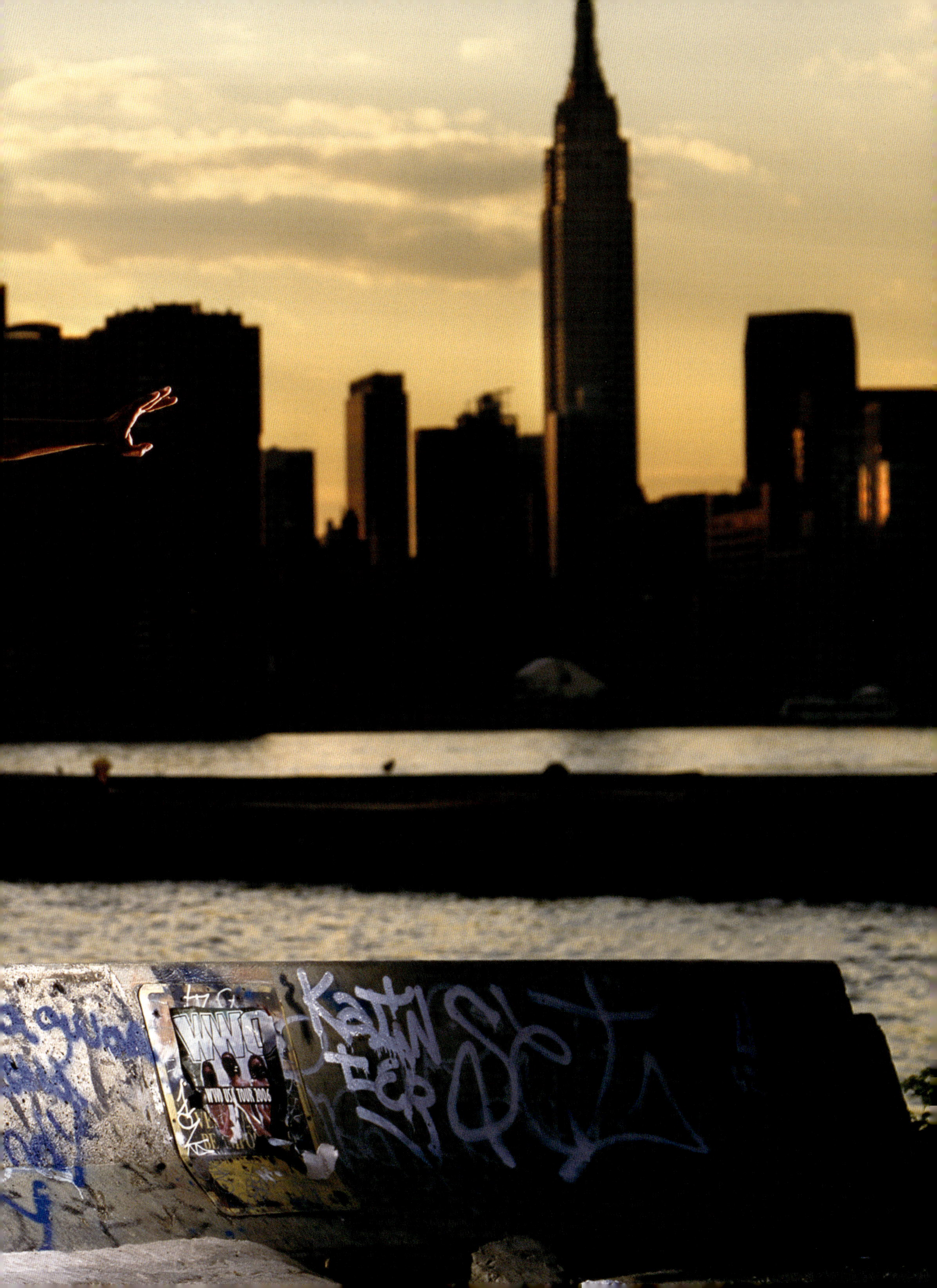
WWO
WWO USA TOUR 2006

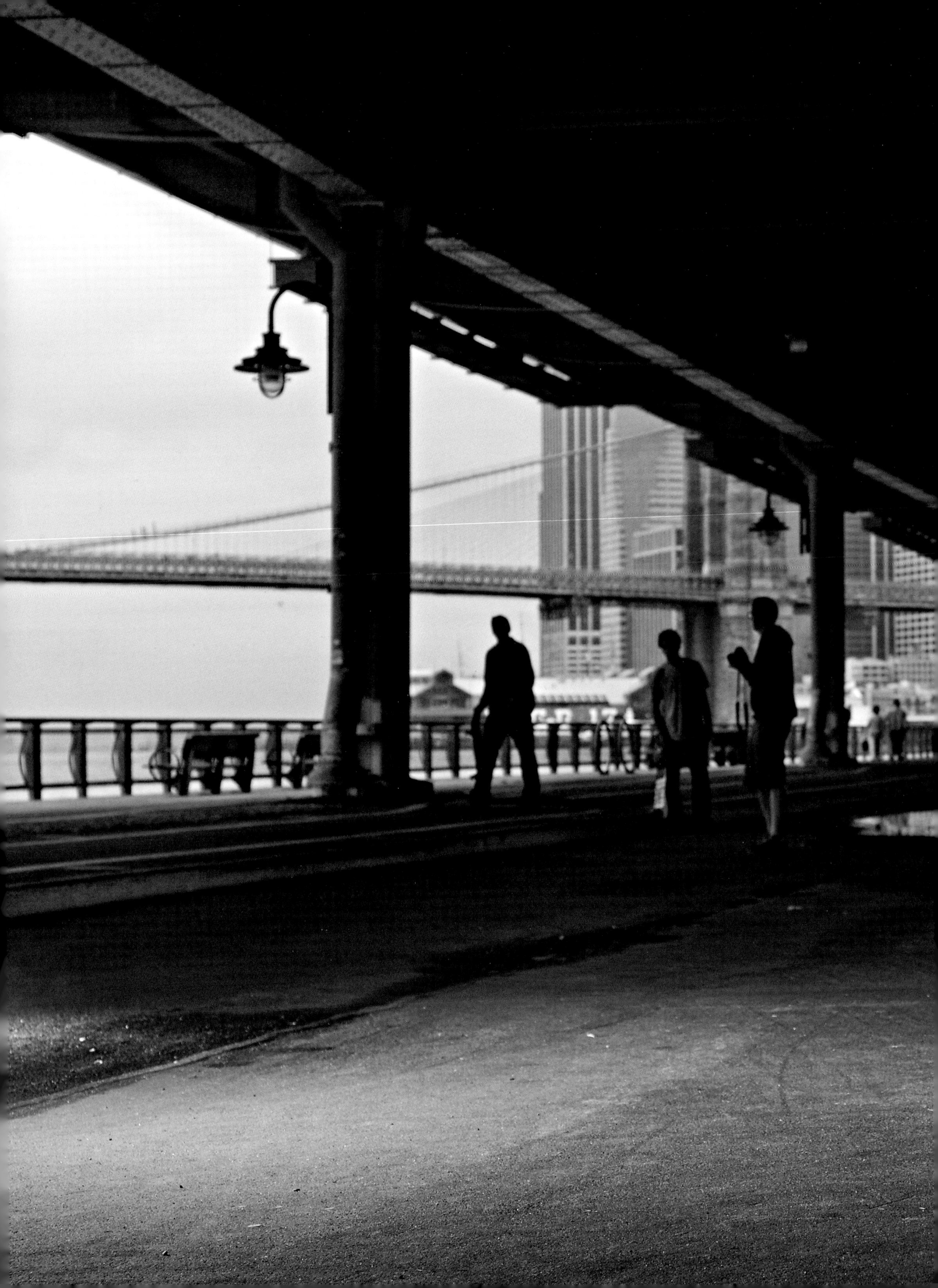

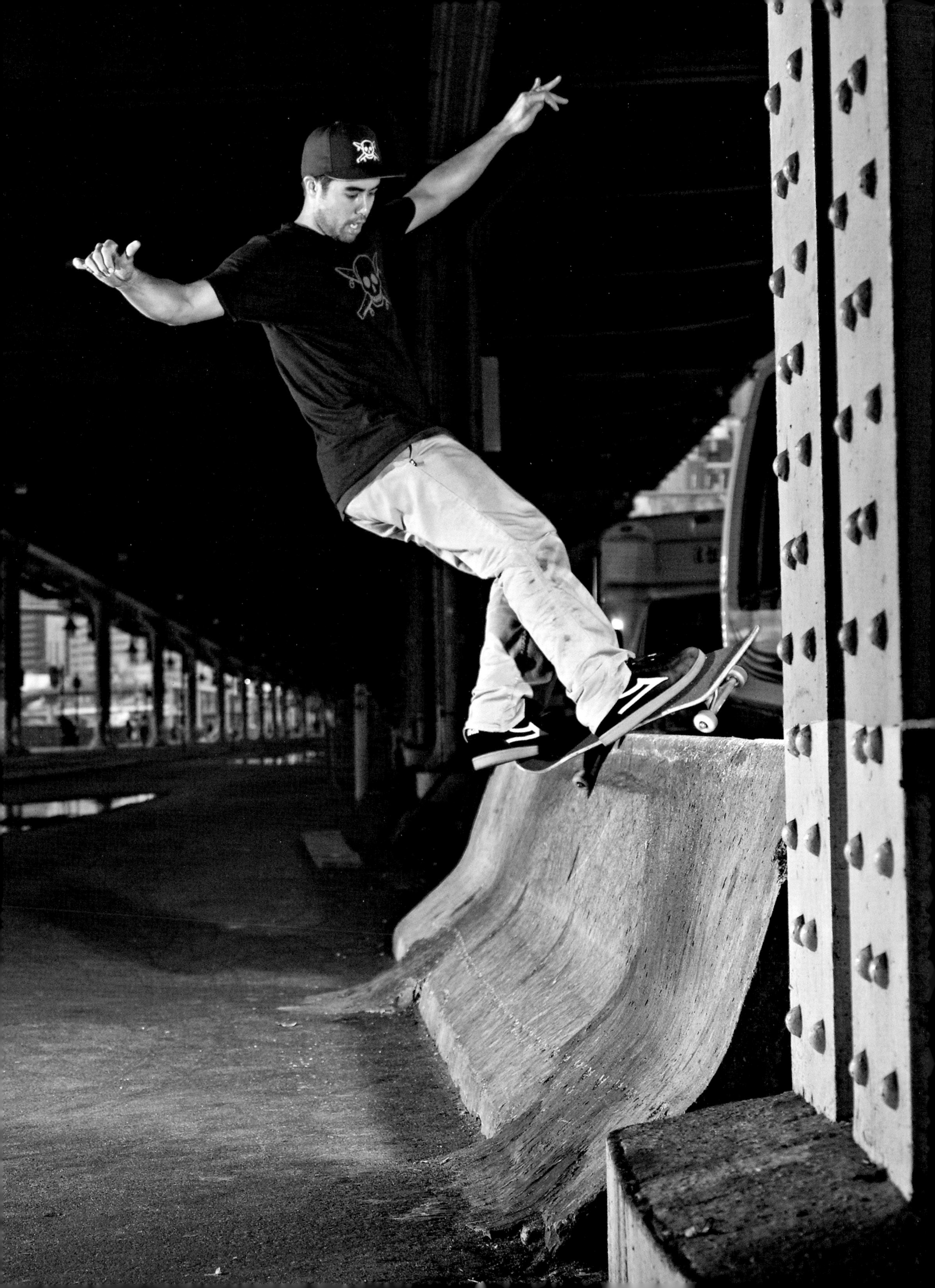

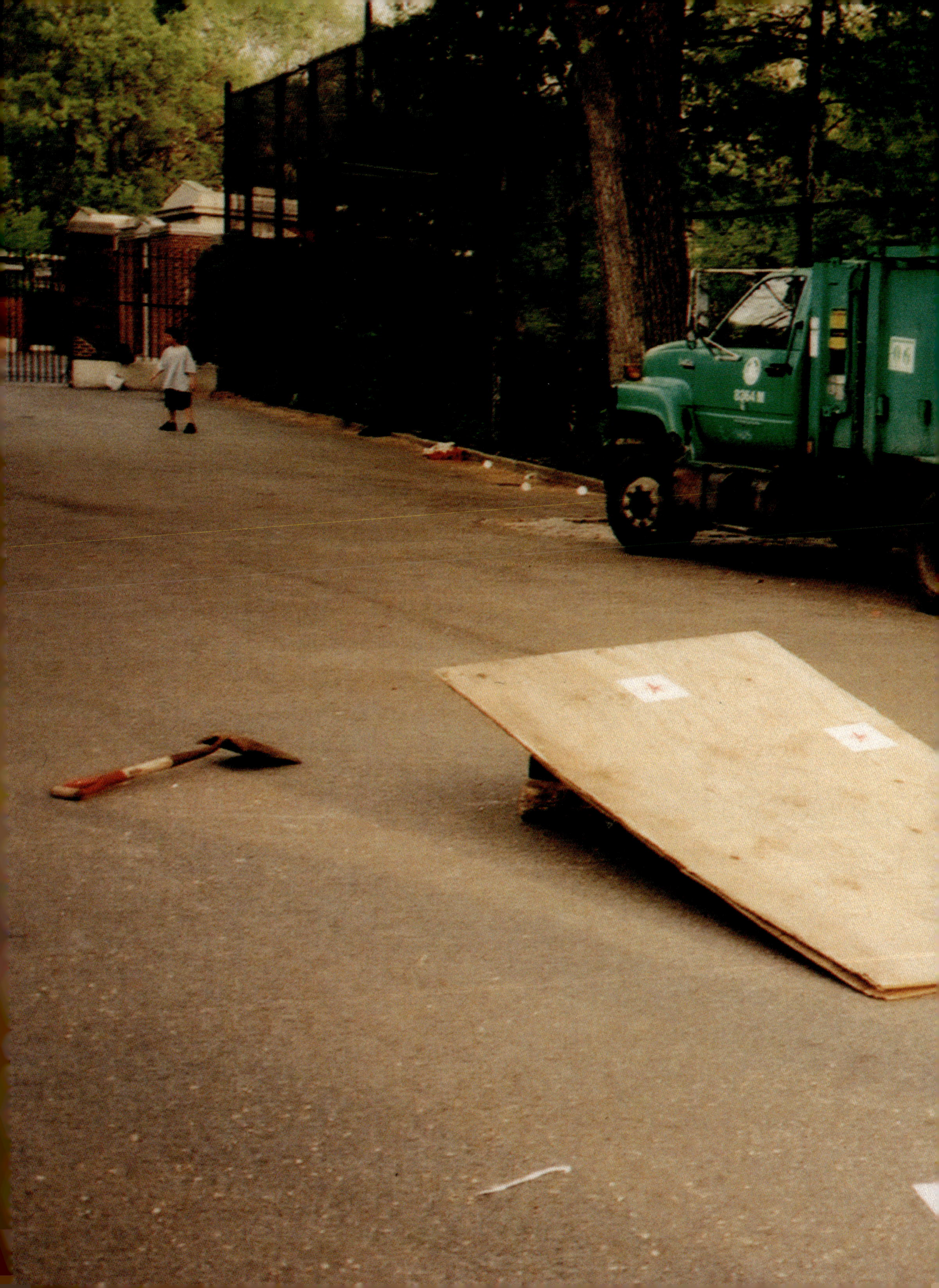

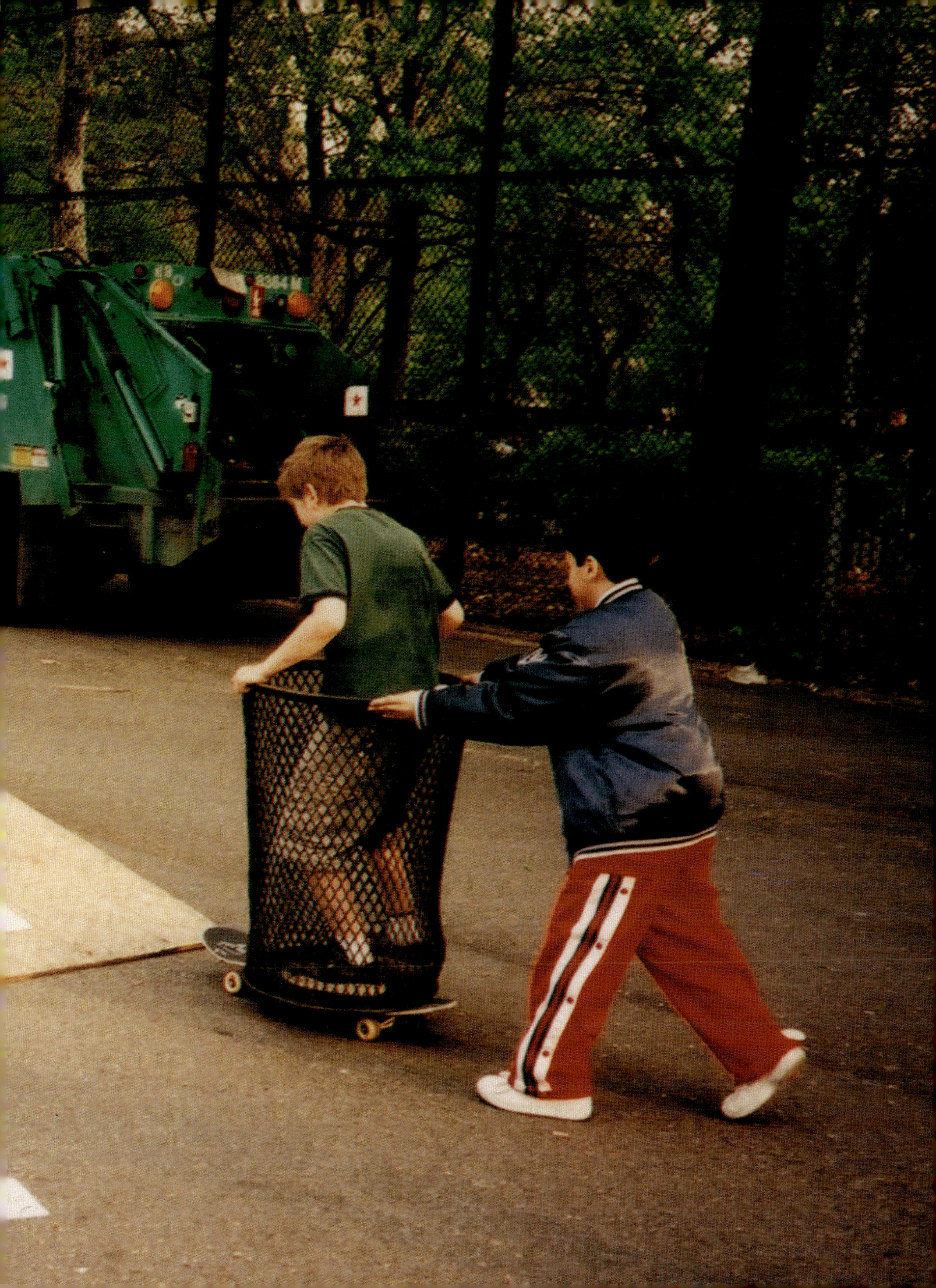

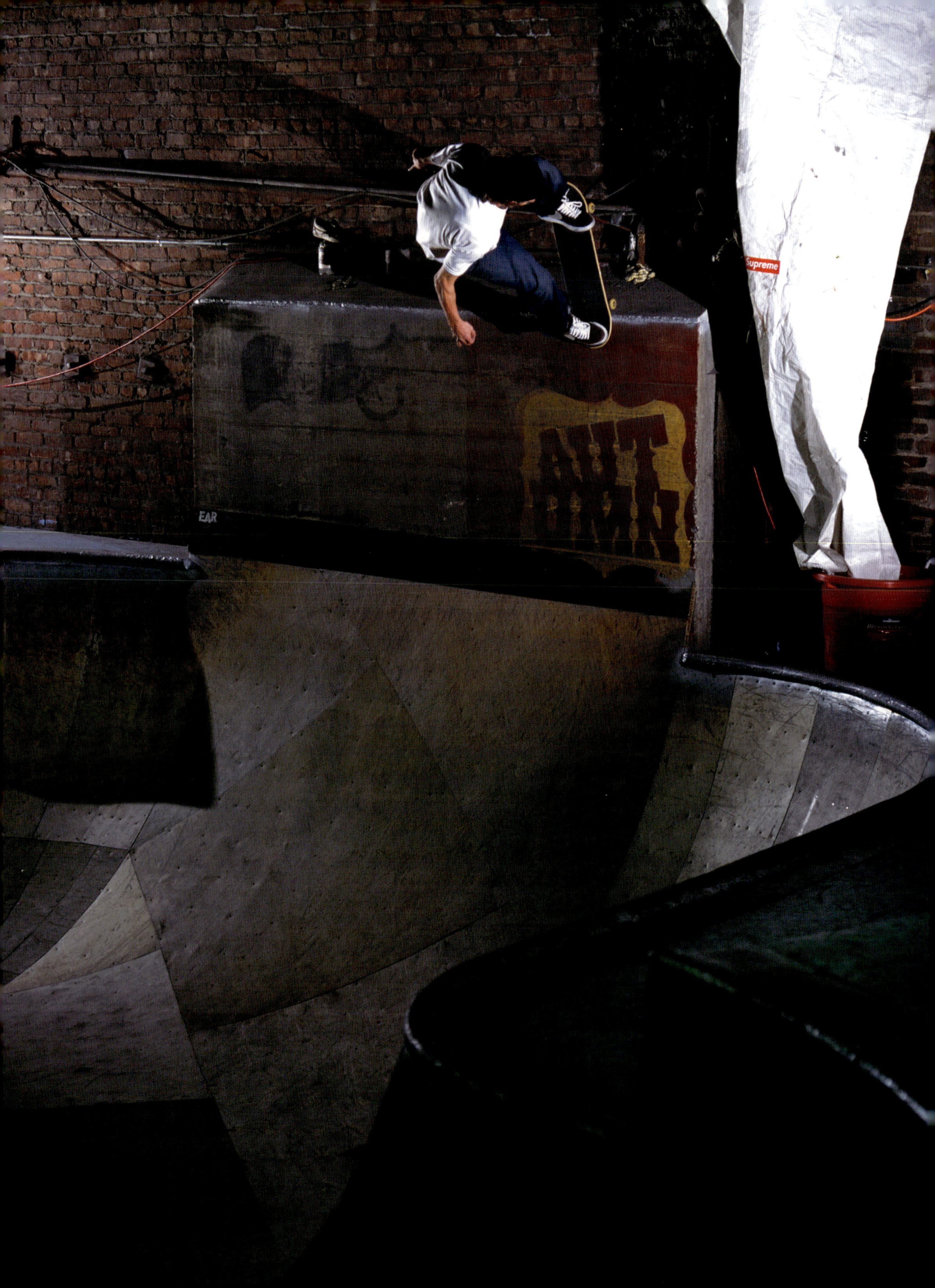
EAR
Supreme

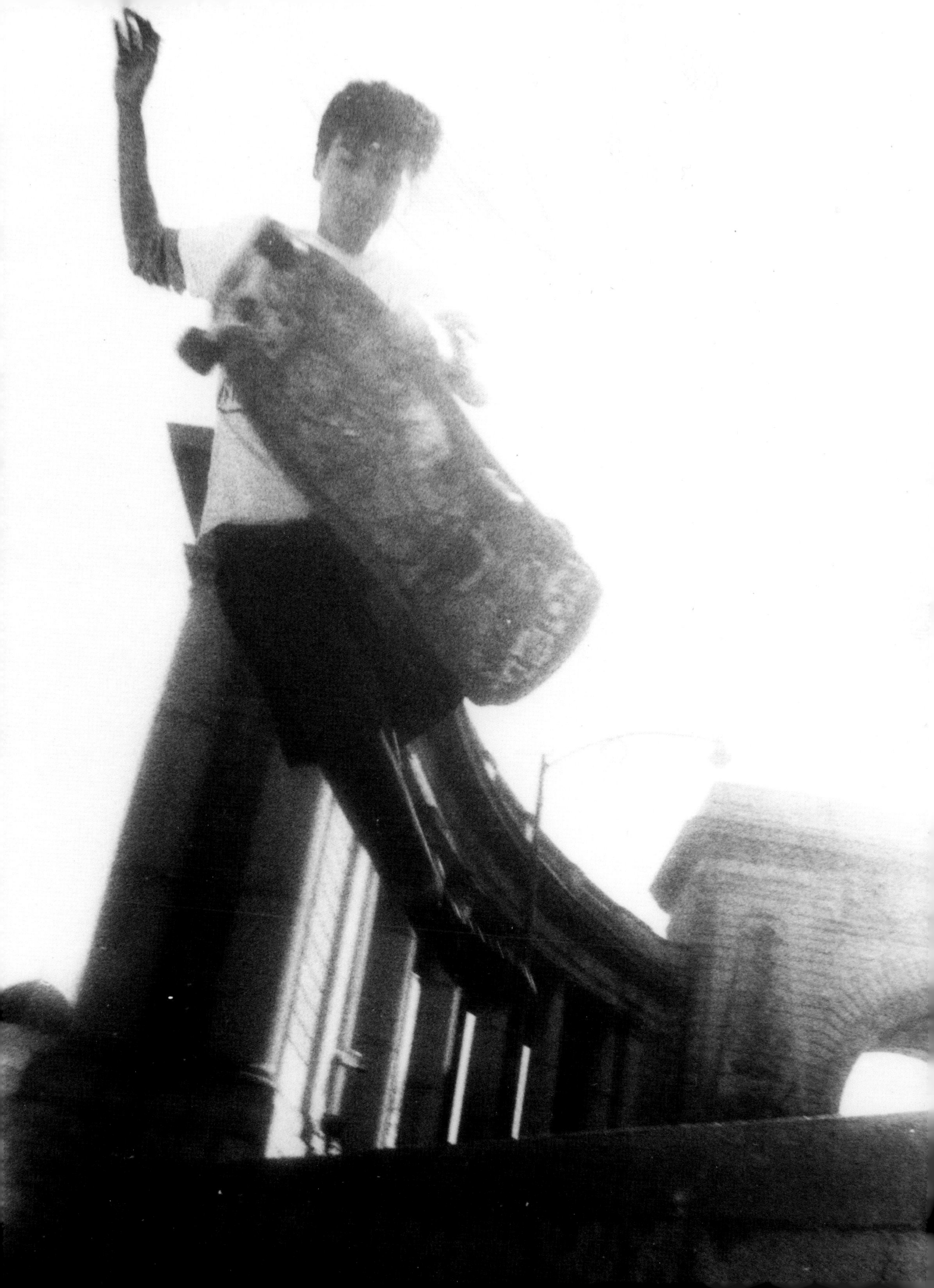

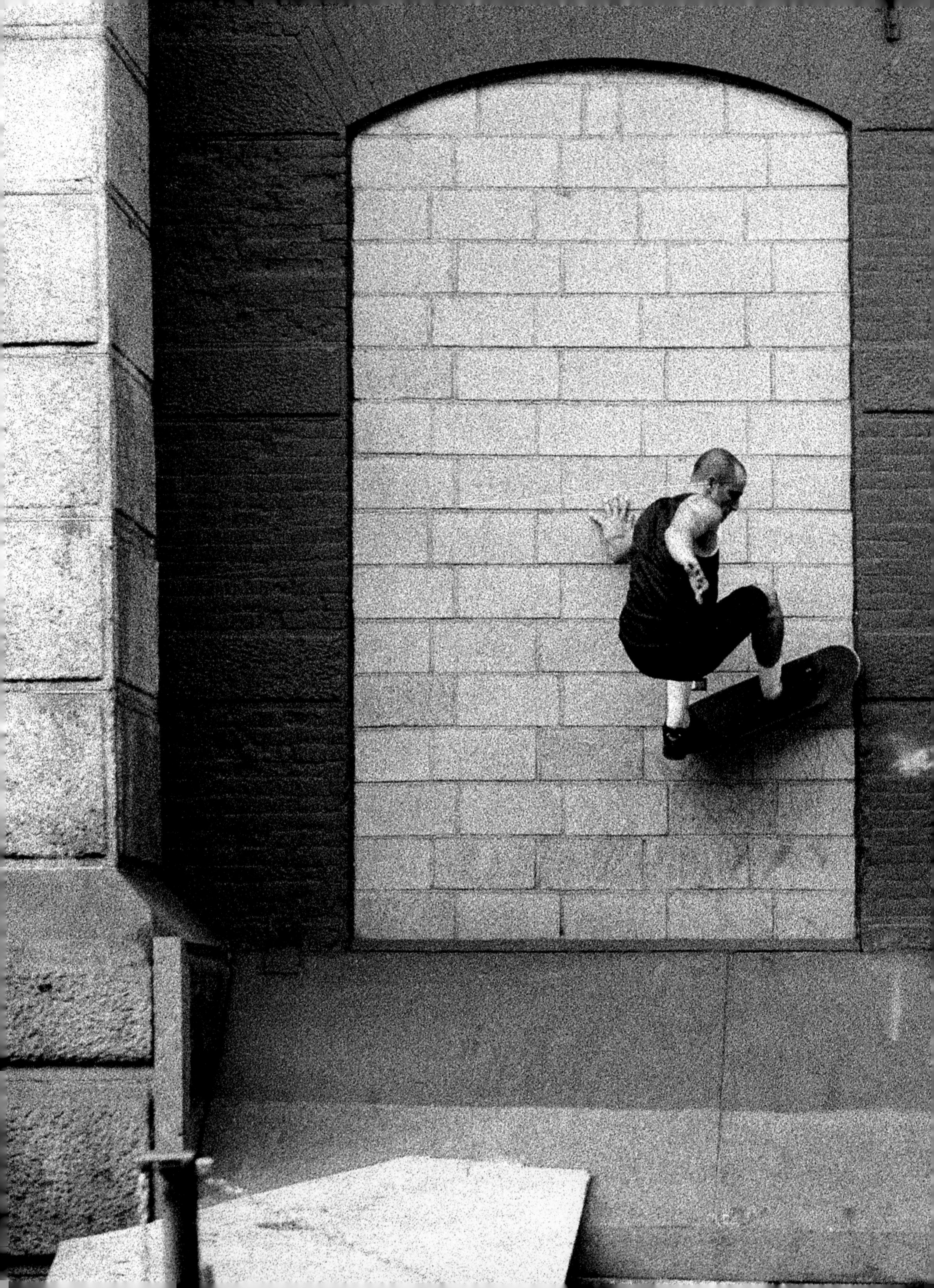

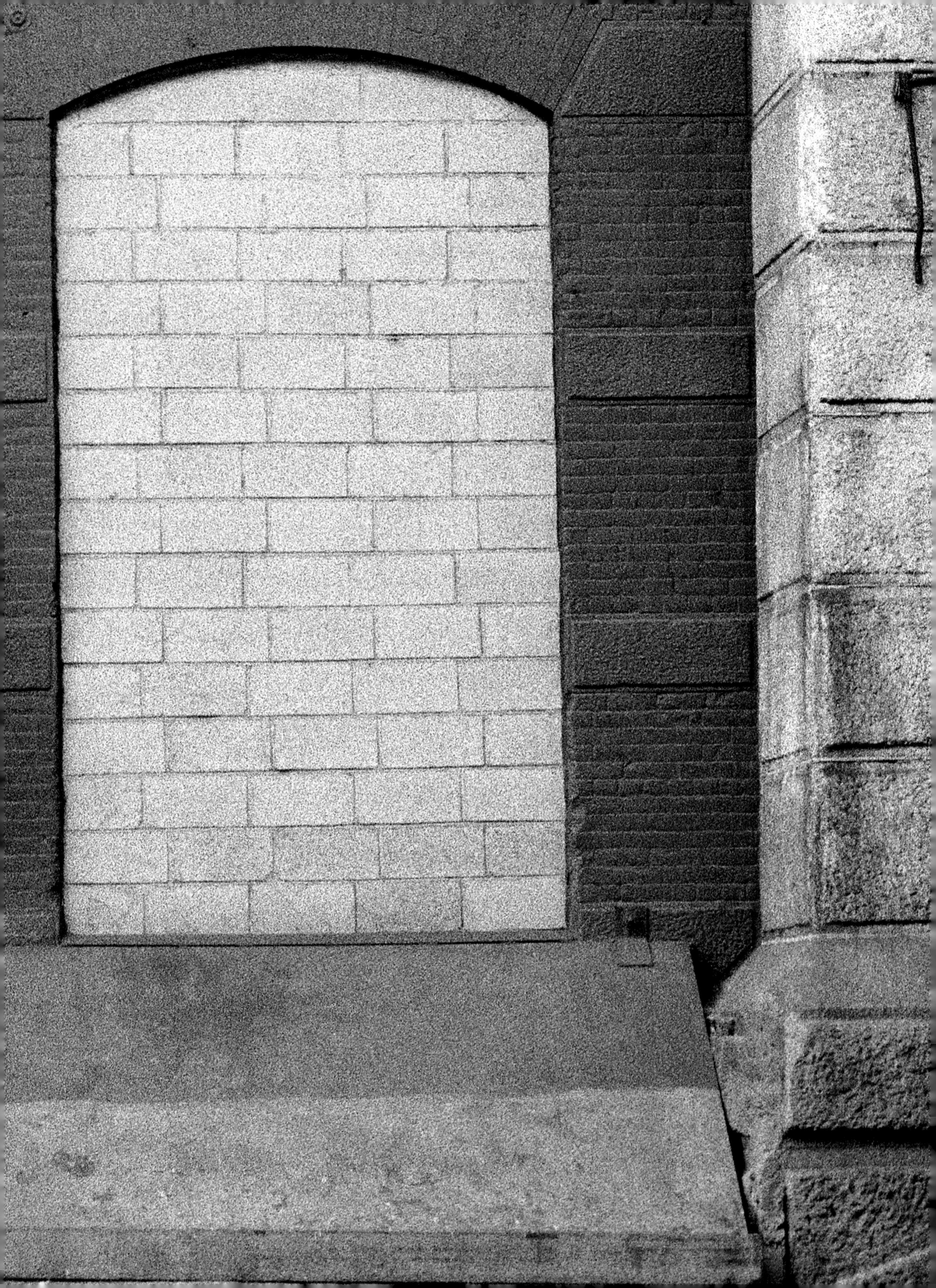

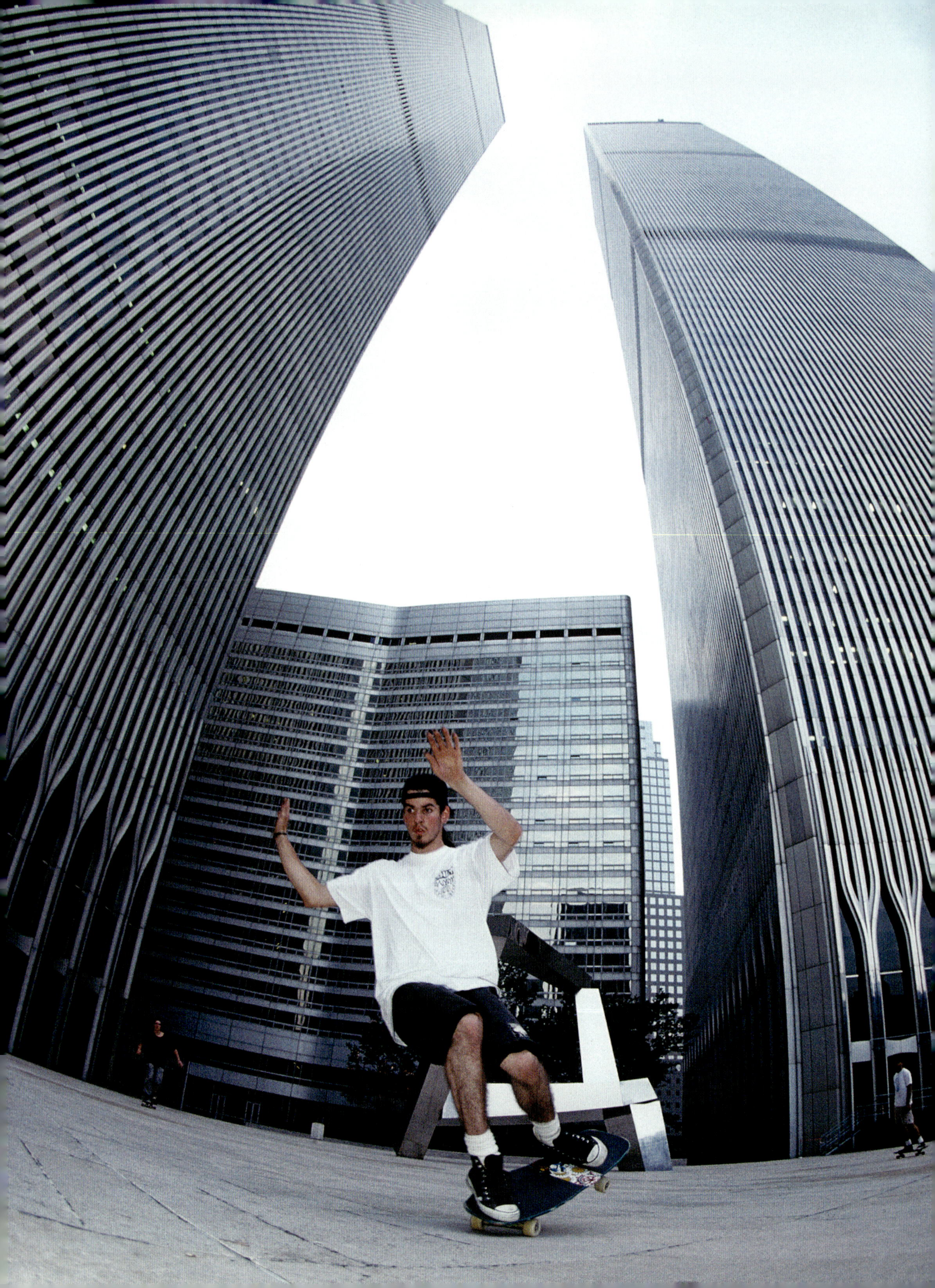

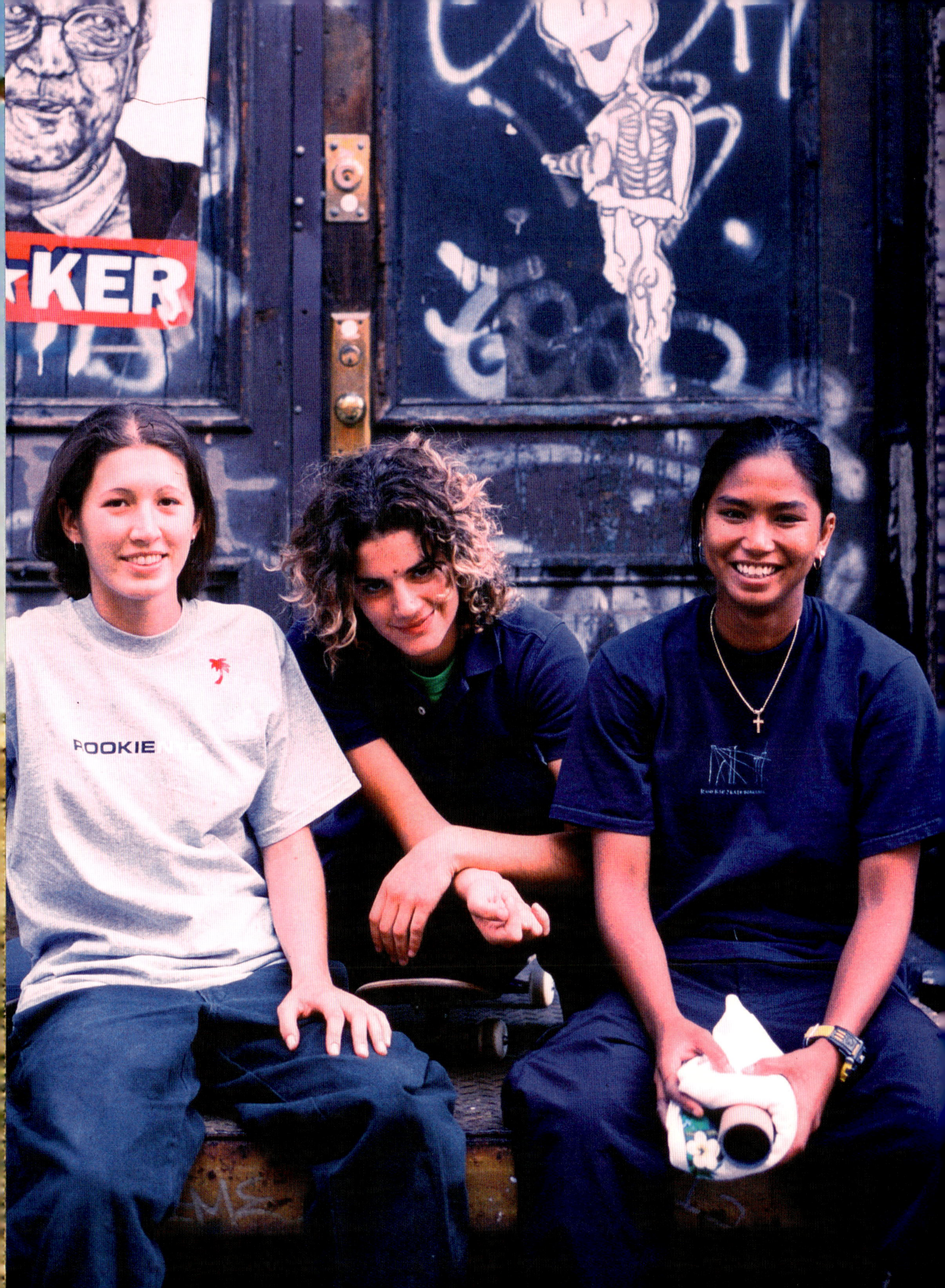
KER
ROOKIE

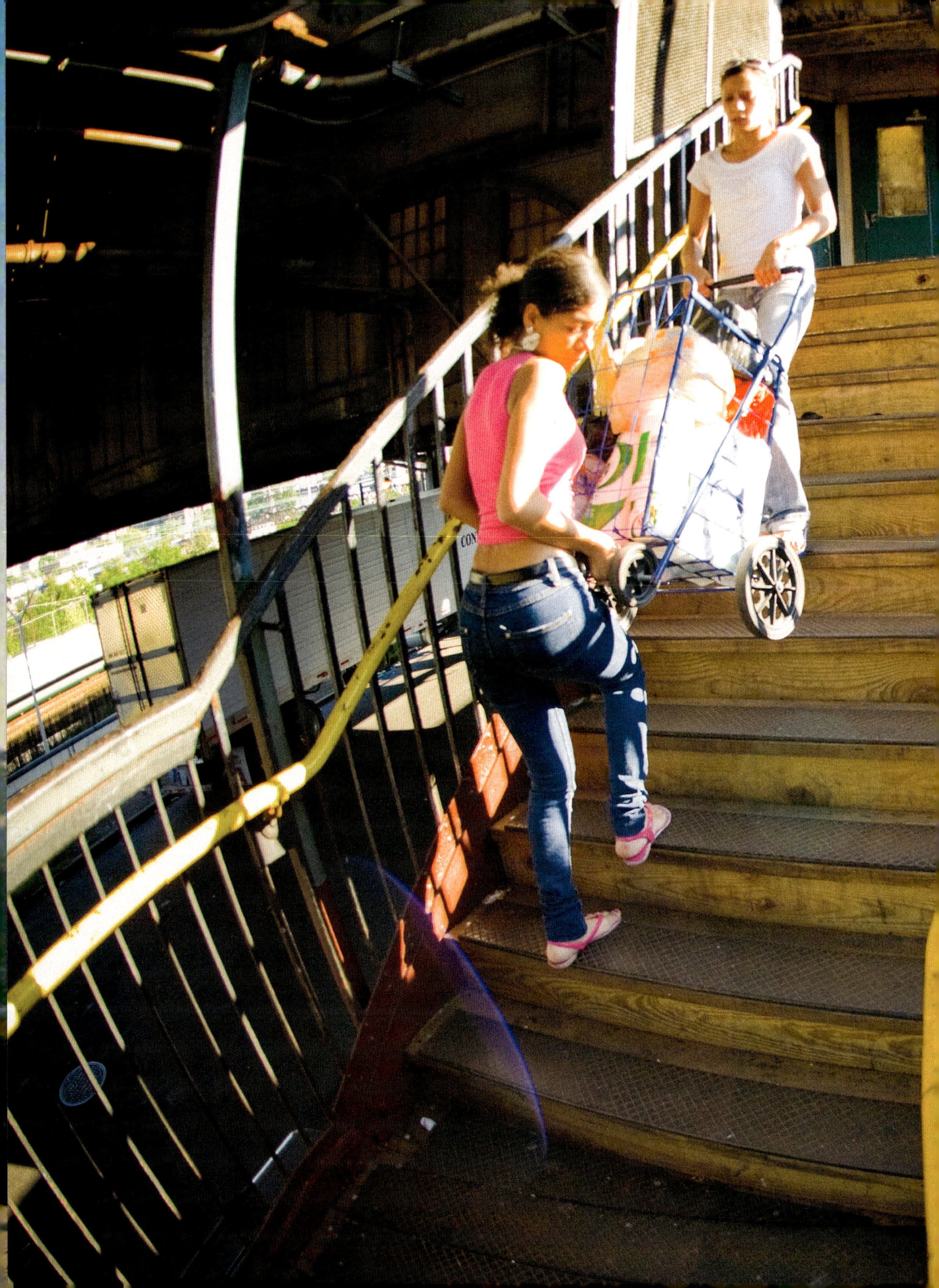

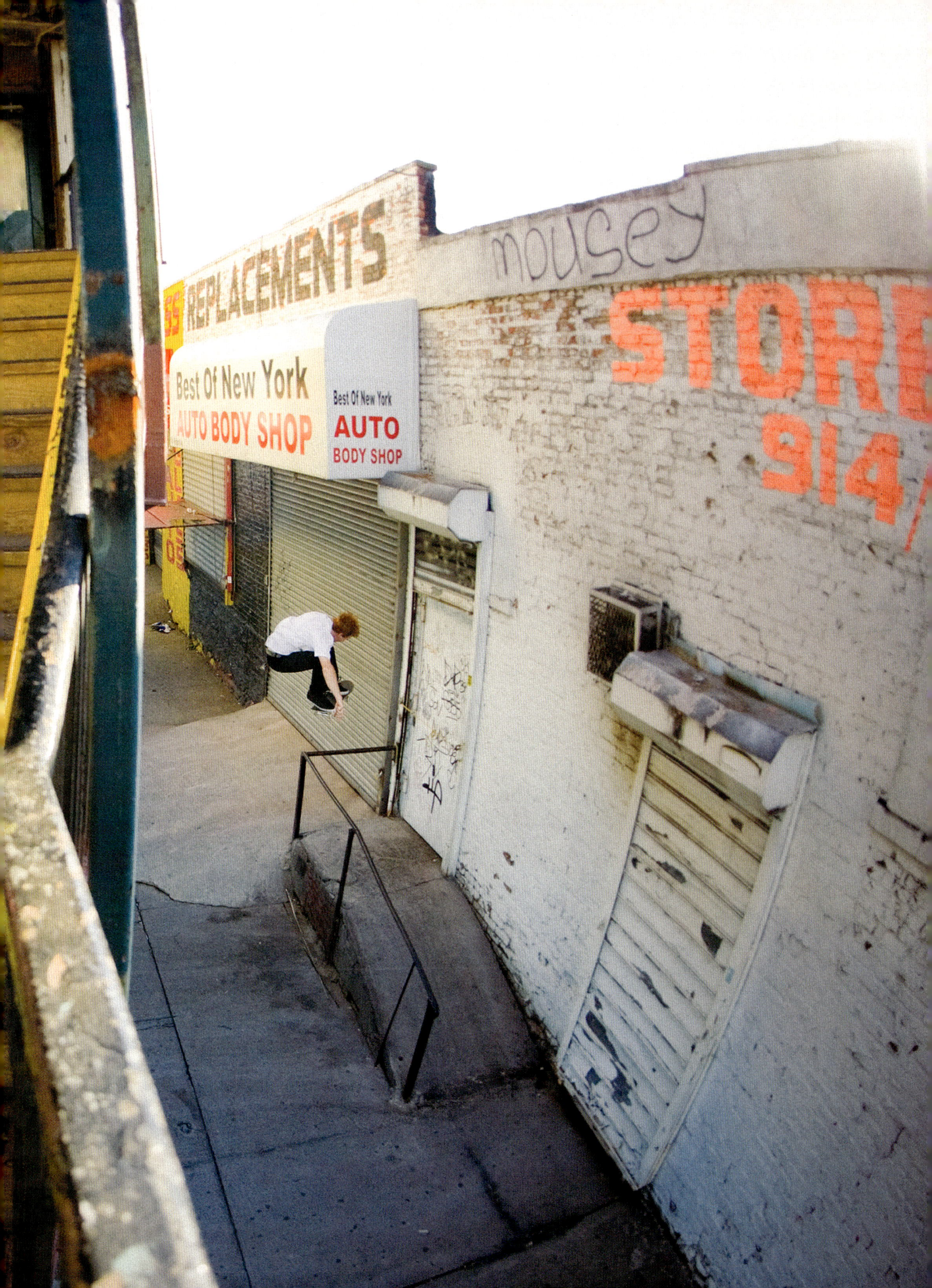
REPLACEMENTS
Best Of New York
AUTO BODY SHOP
Best Of New York
AUTO
BODY SHOP
mousey
914

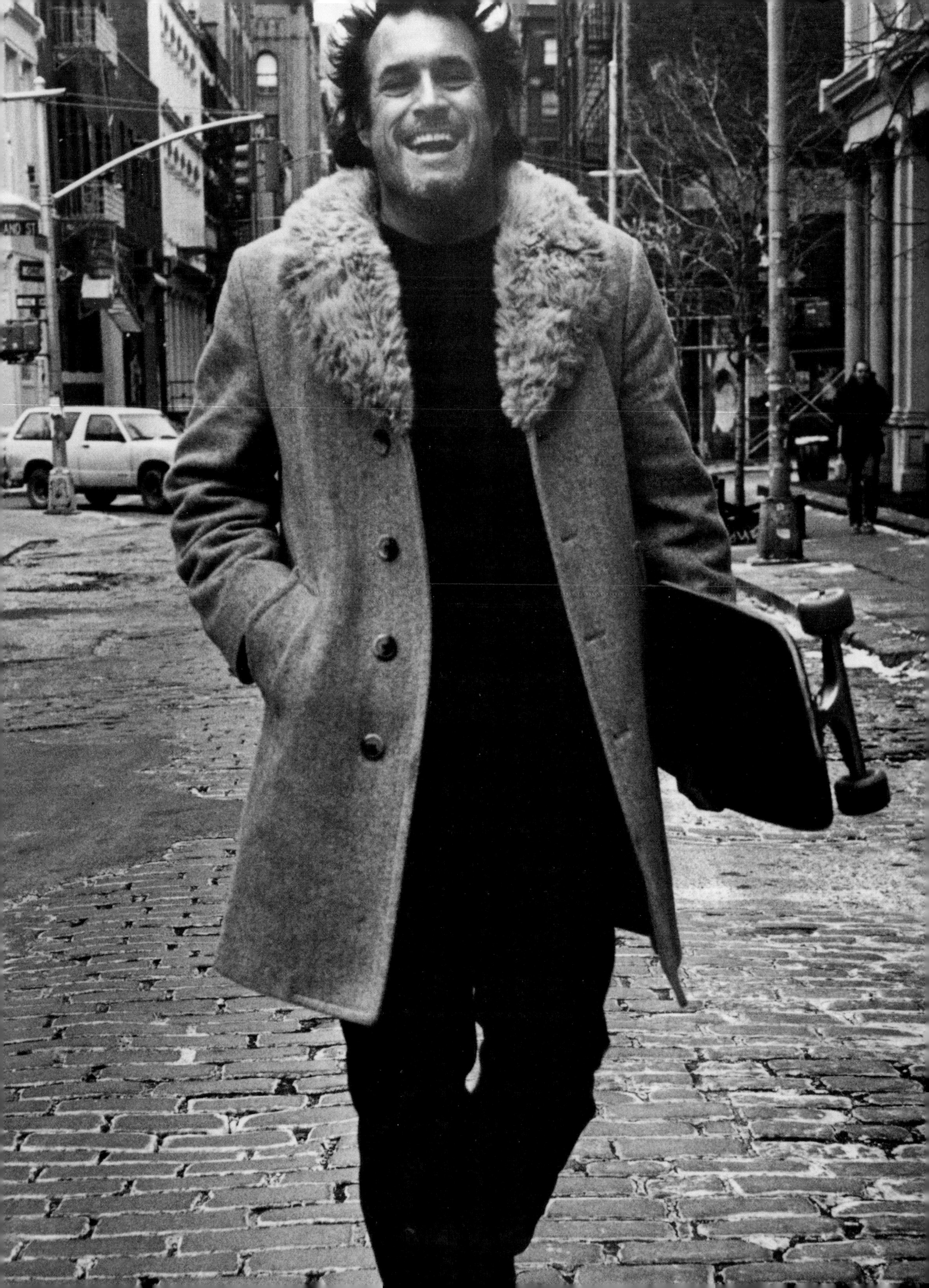

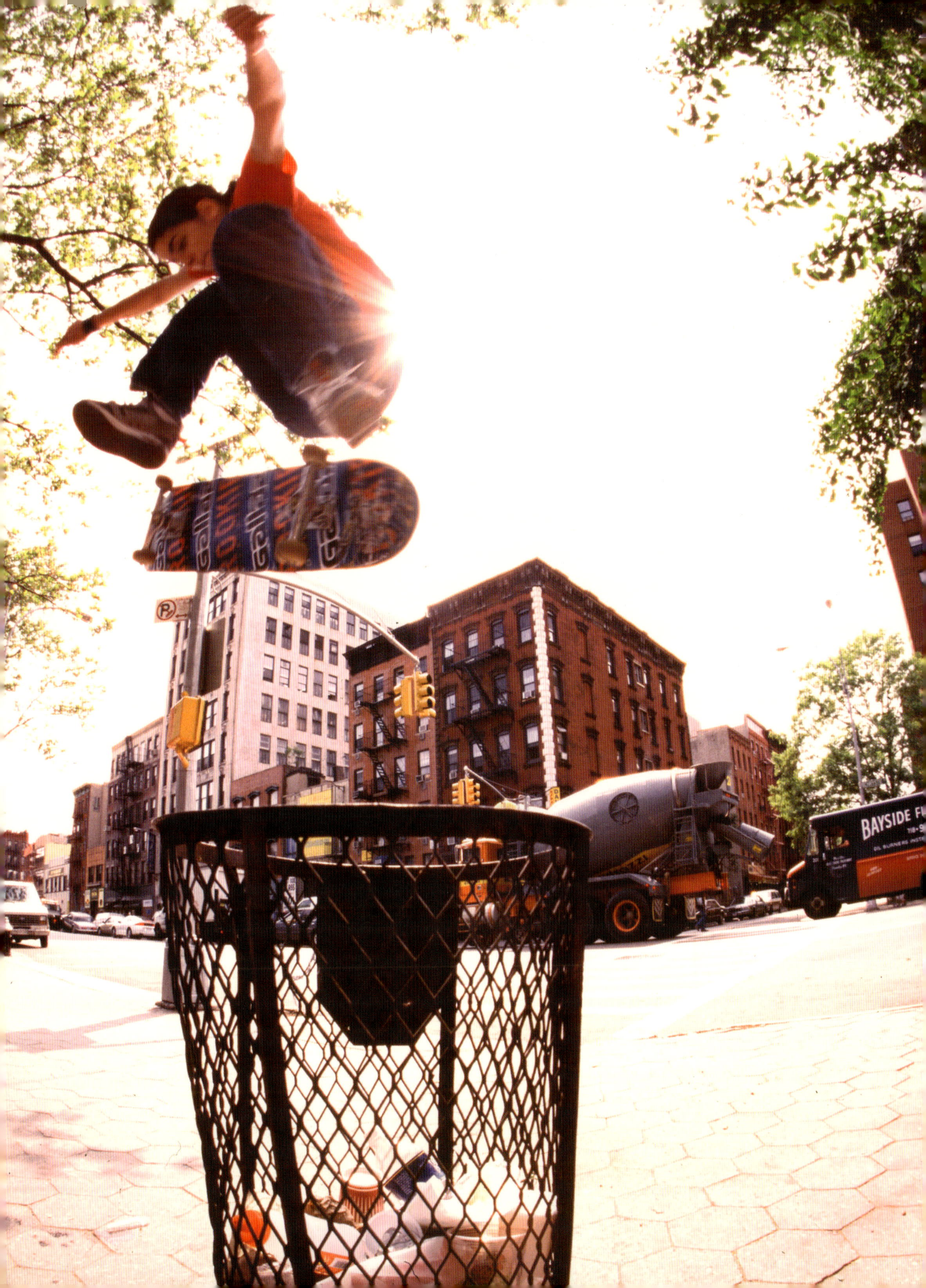
BAYSIDE

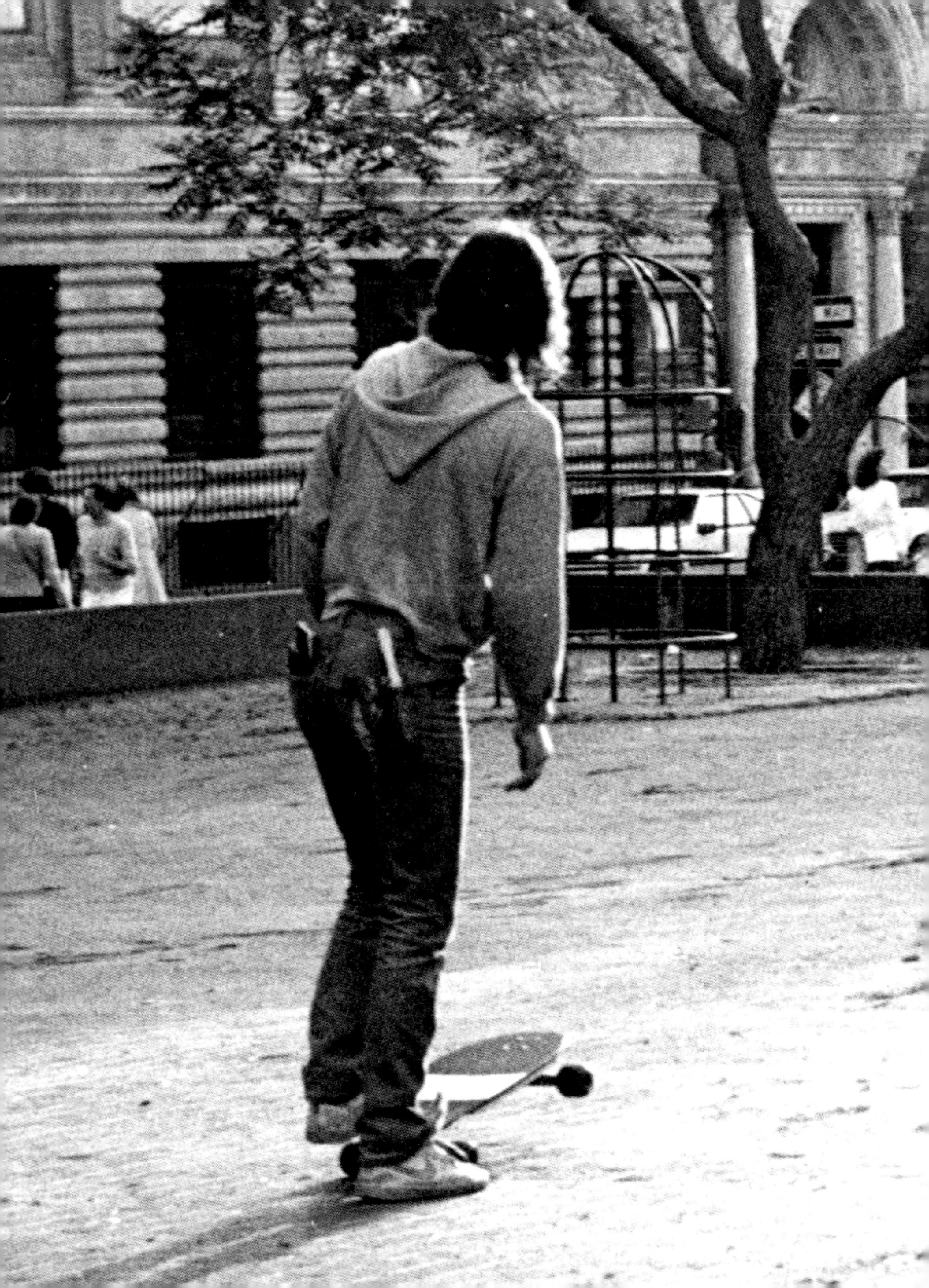

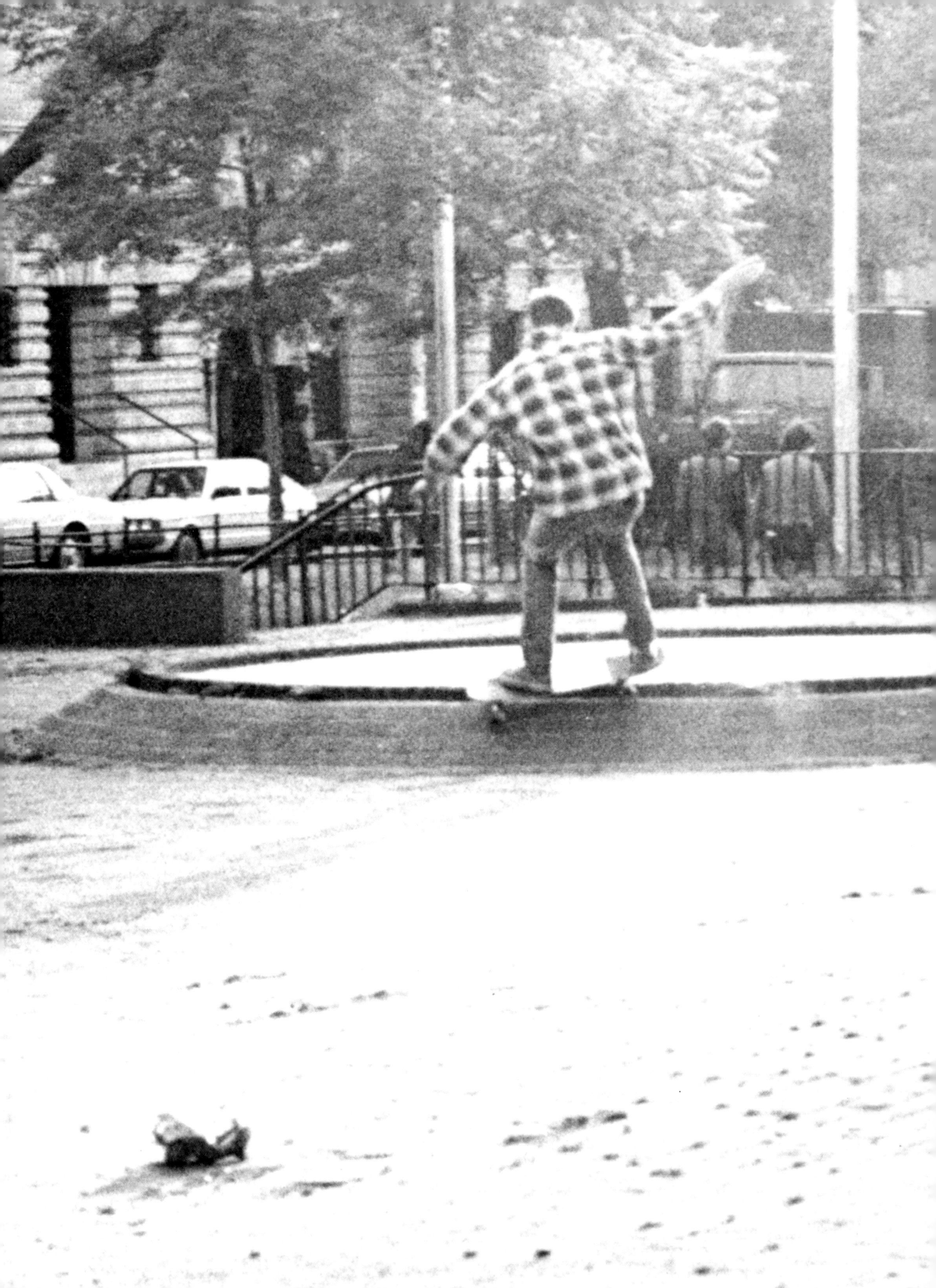

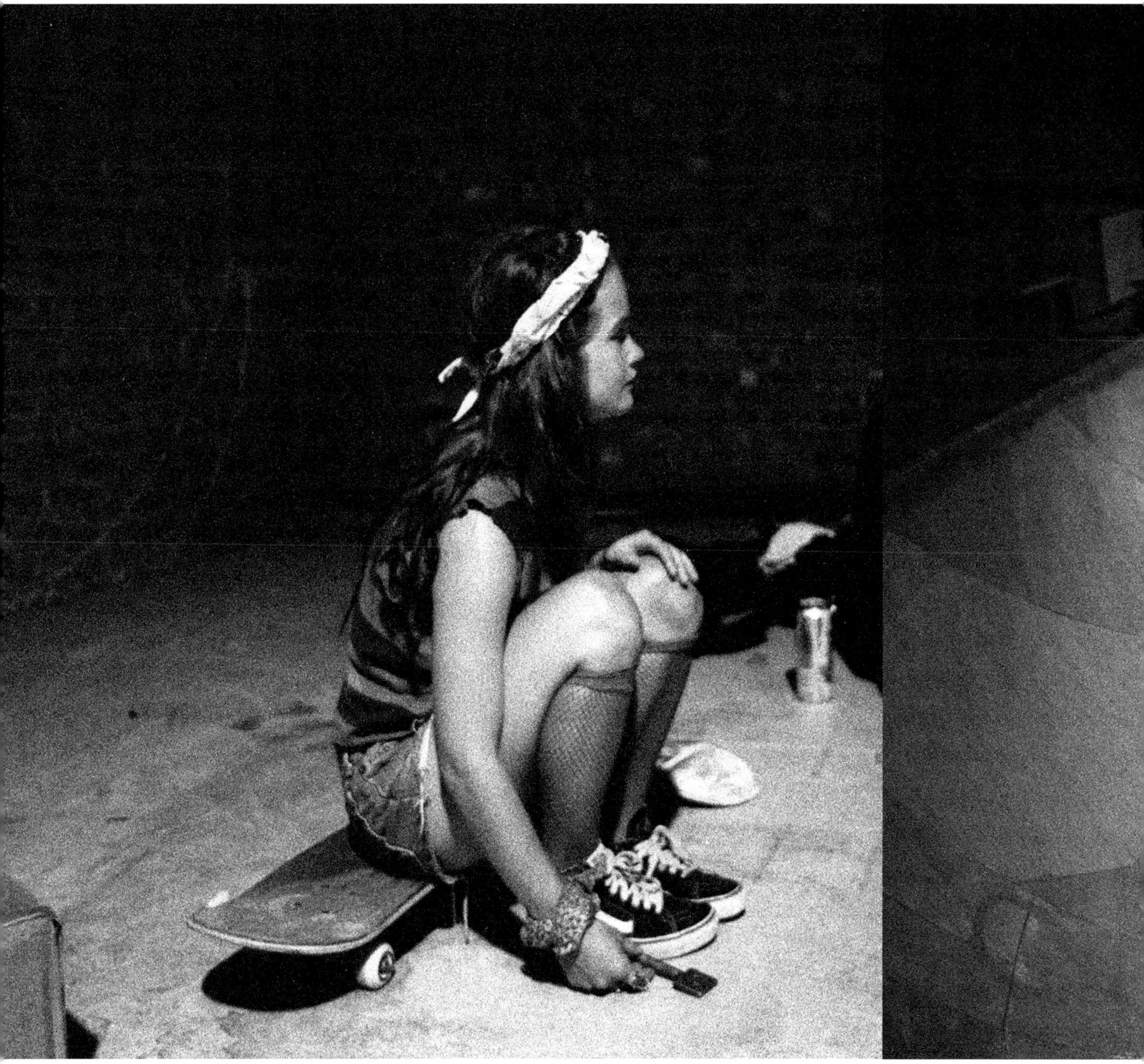

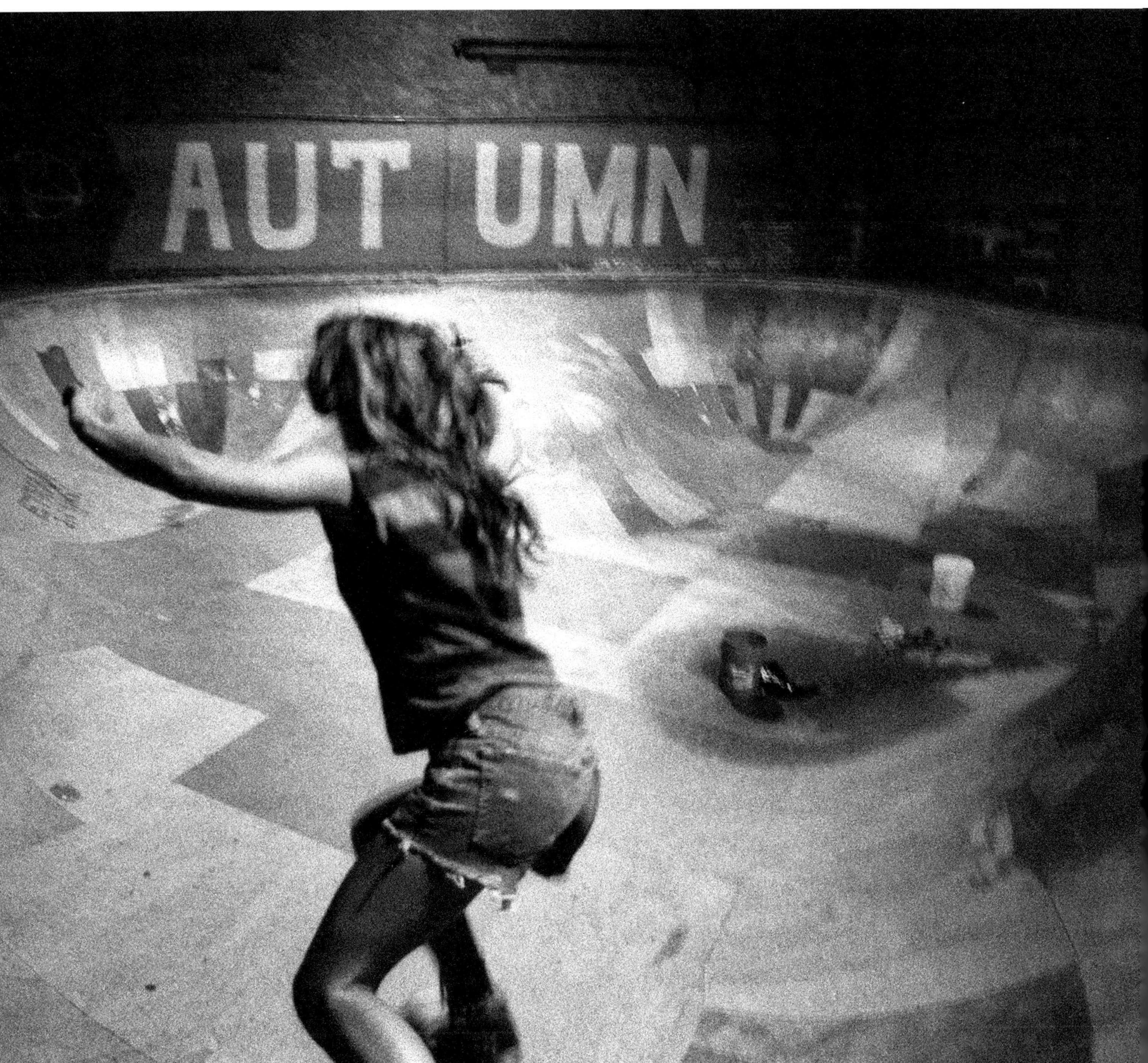
AUT UMN

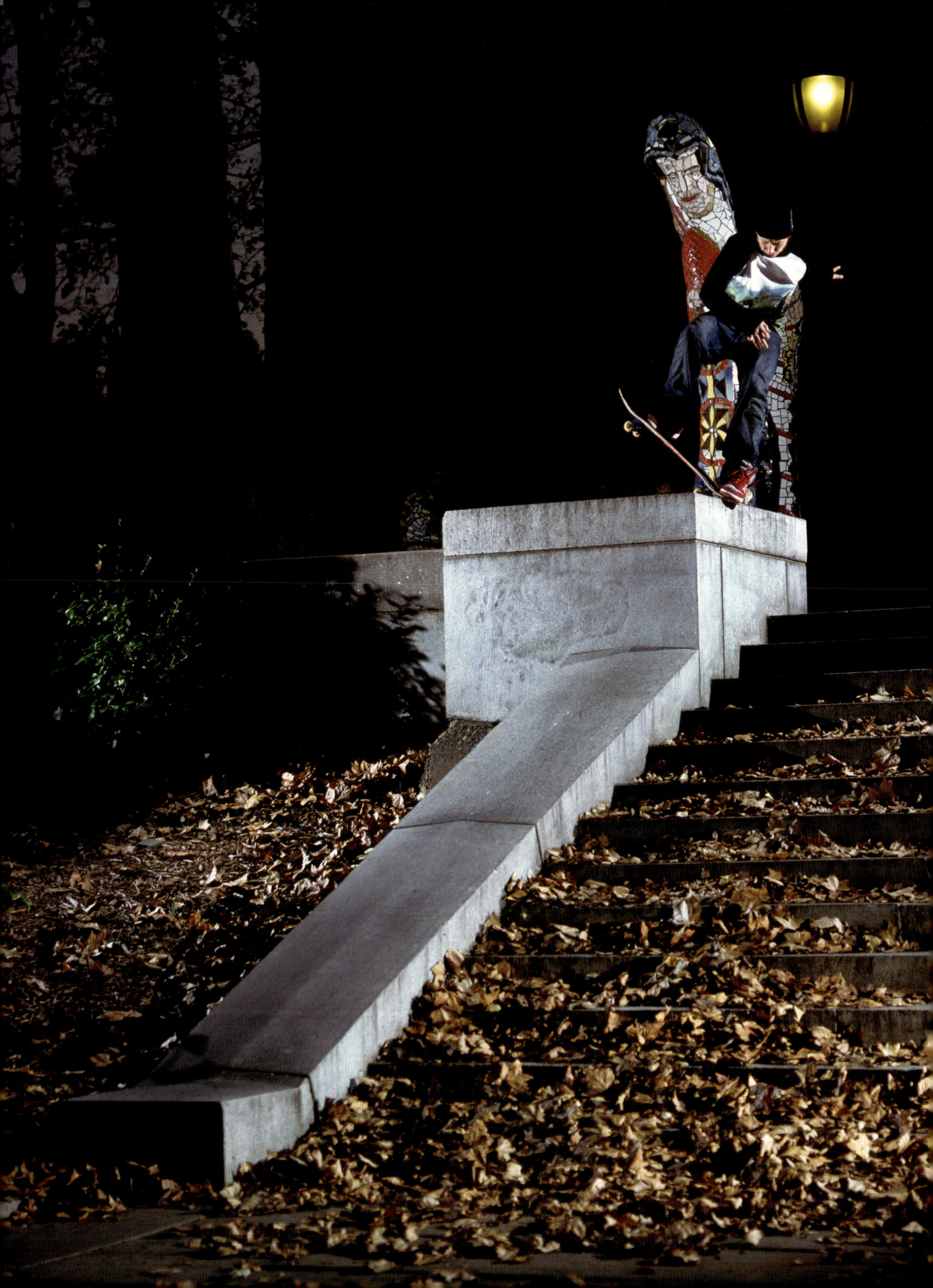

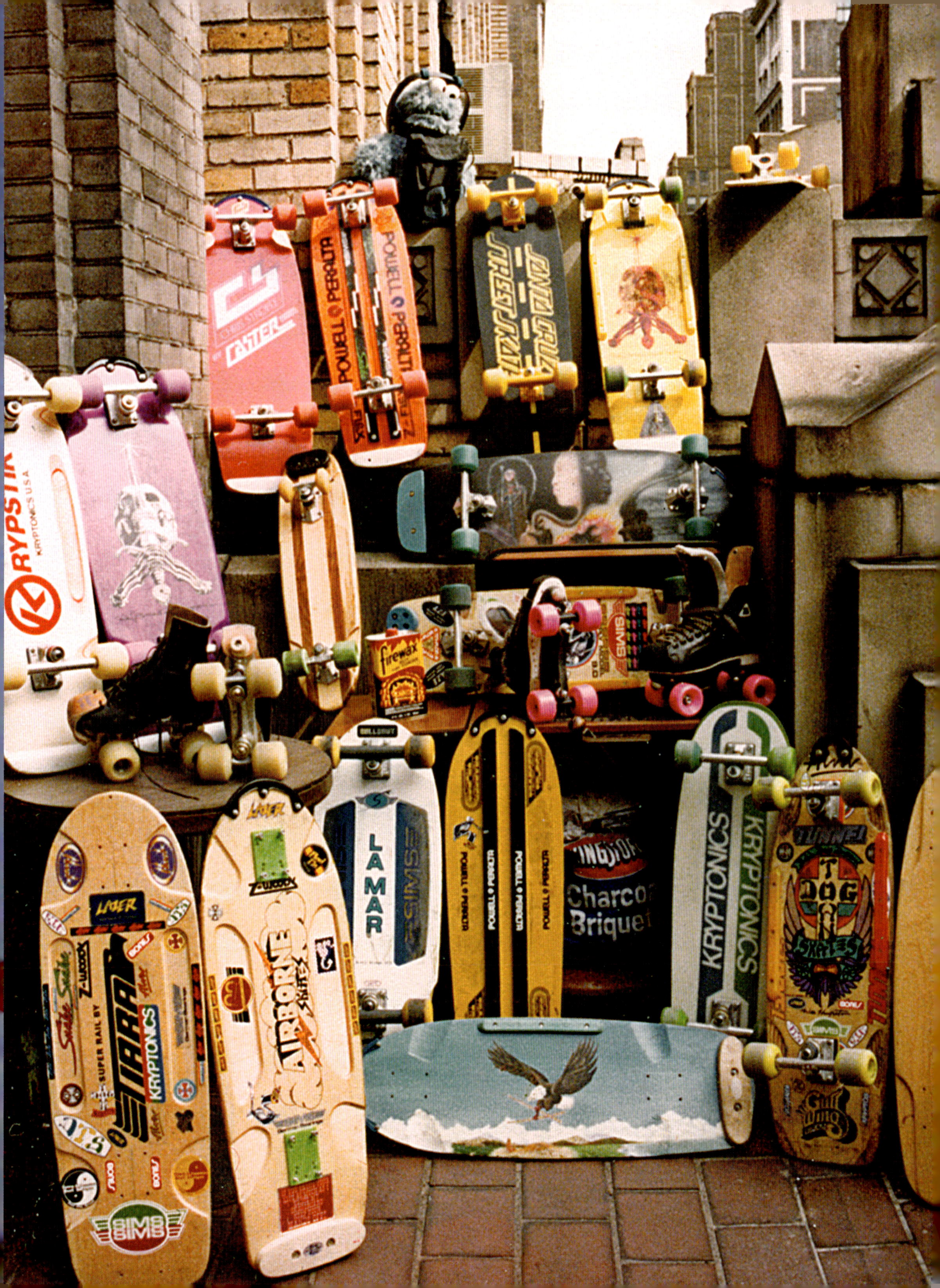

CASTER
POWELL PERALTA
POWELL PERALTA
SANTA CRUZ
STREET SKATE
KRYPSTIK
KRYPTONICS U.S.A
firewax
SIMS
LASER
Z-WOOD
KRYPTONICS
SUPER RAIL BY
AIRBORNE SKATES
LA MAR
SIMS
POWELL PERALTA
KRYPTONICS
KRYPTONICS
T DOG
SKATES
SIMS
SIMS

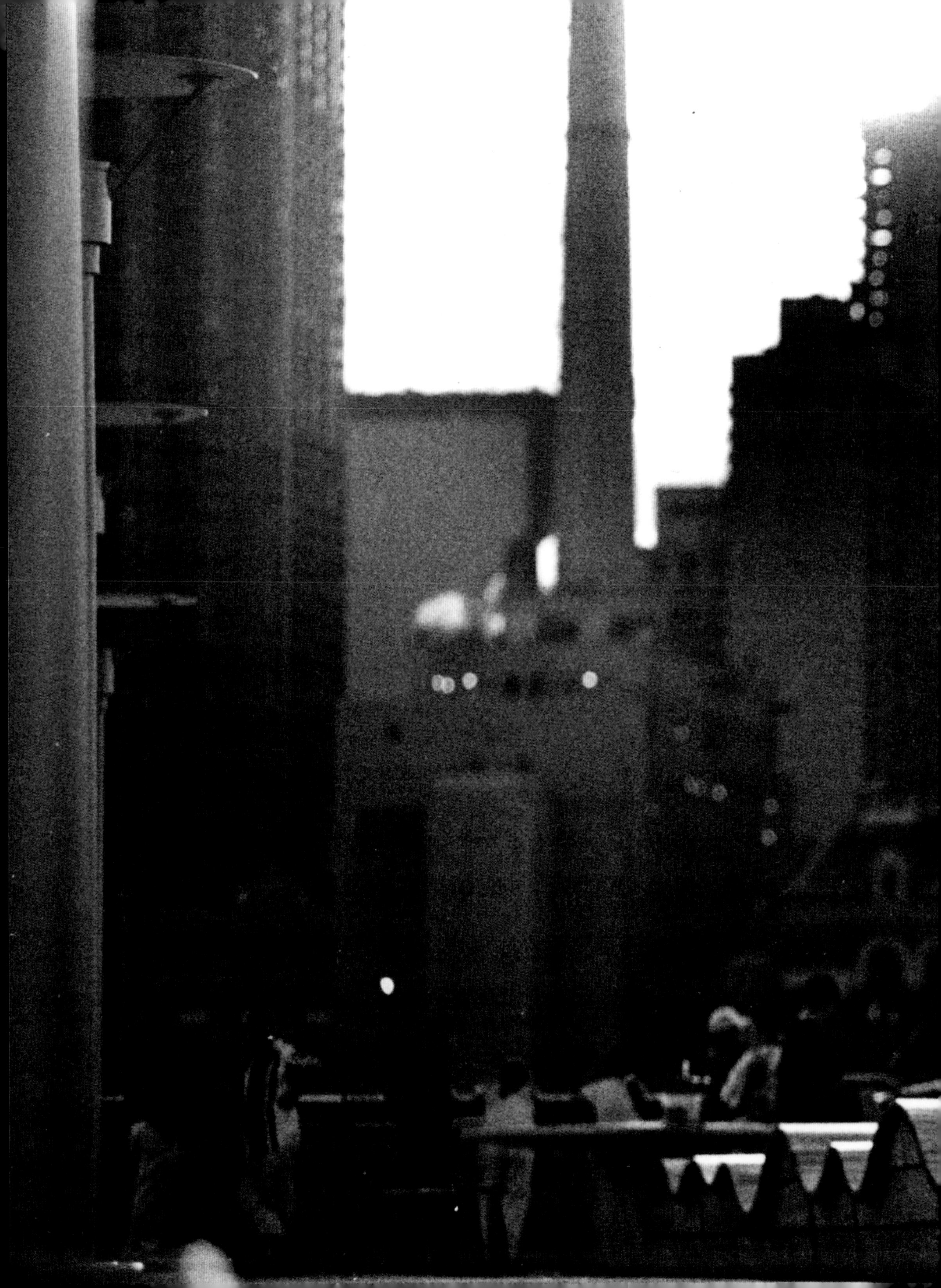

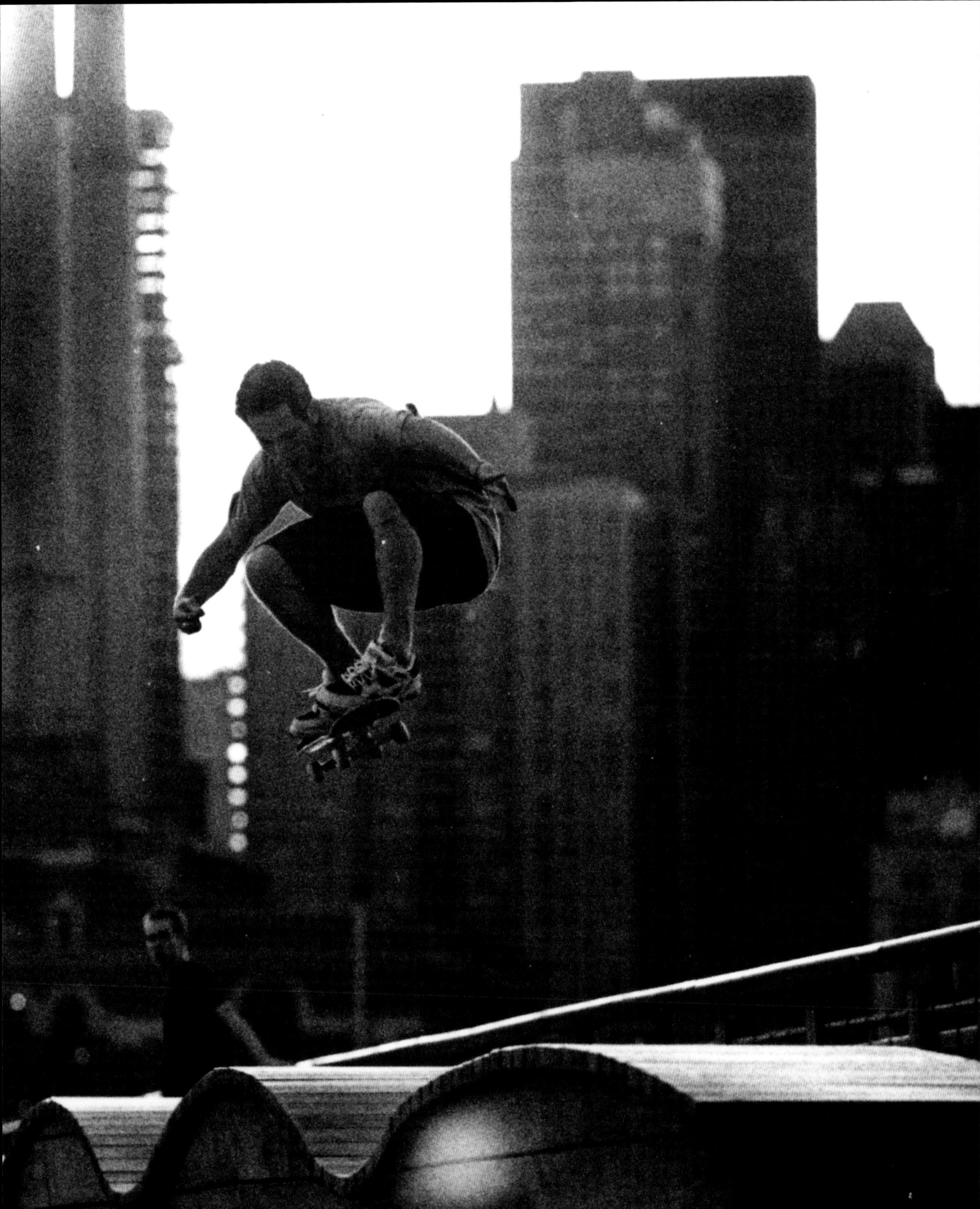

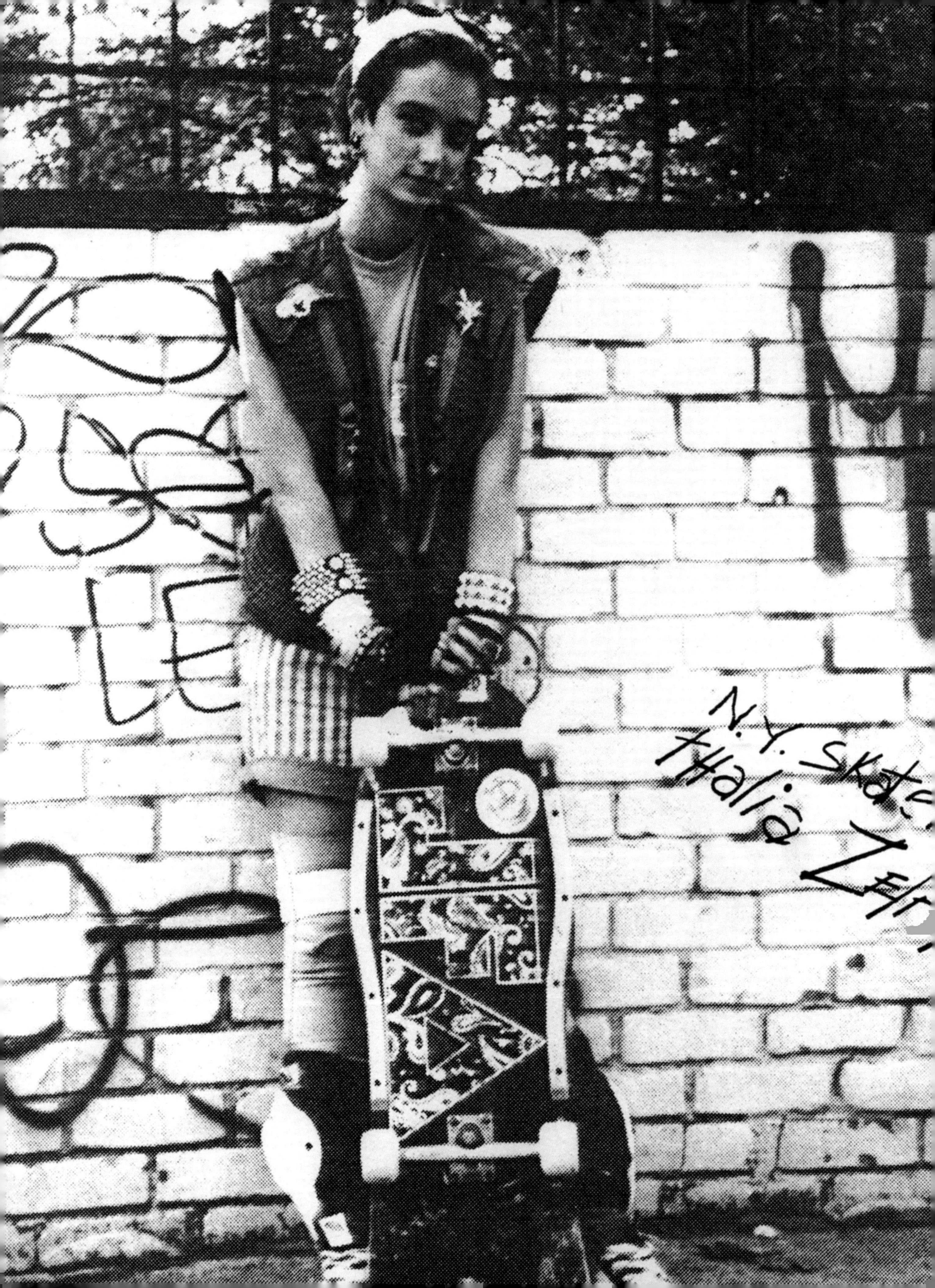
N.Y. Skate,
Thalia

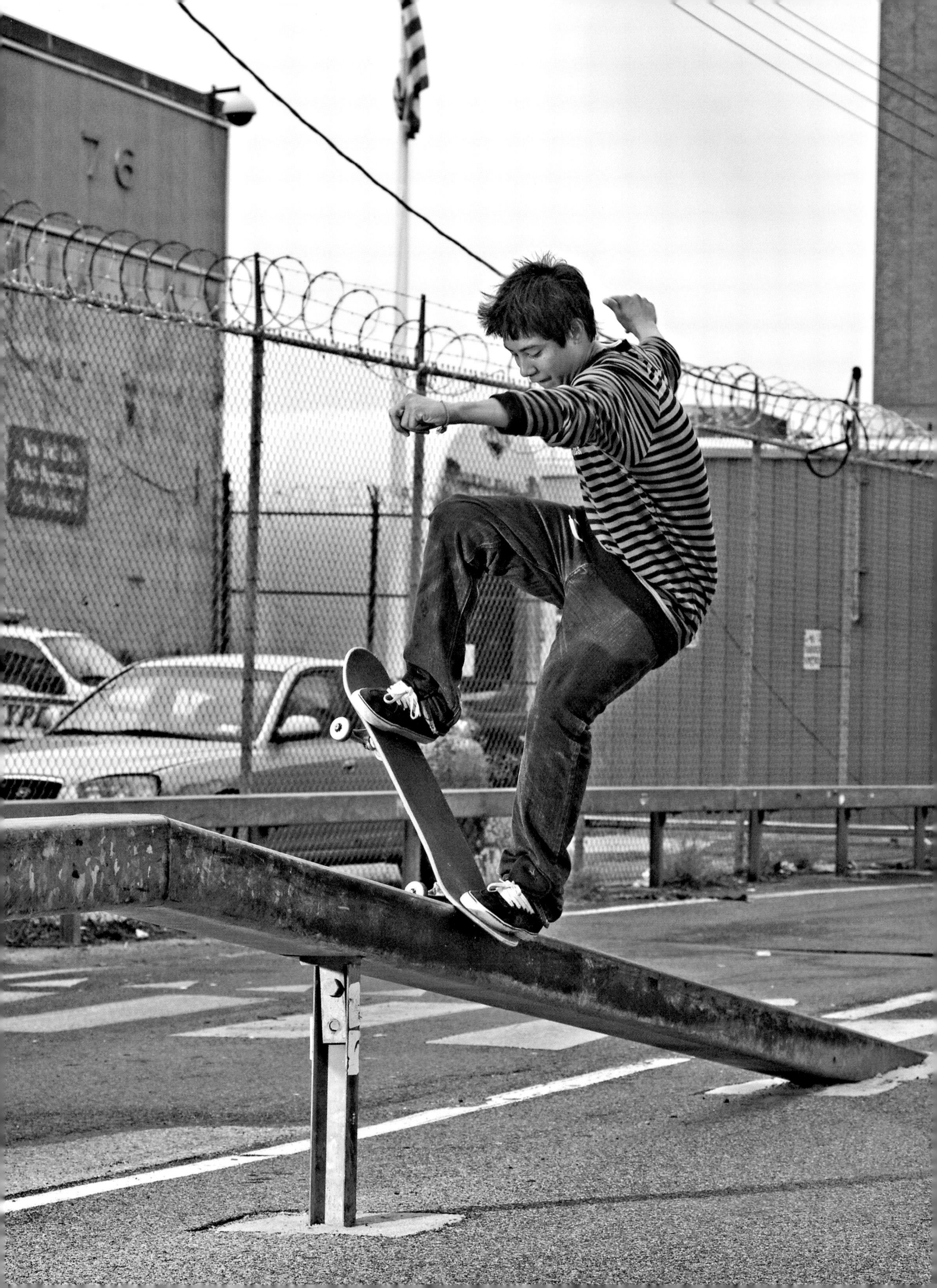
76

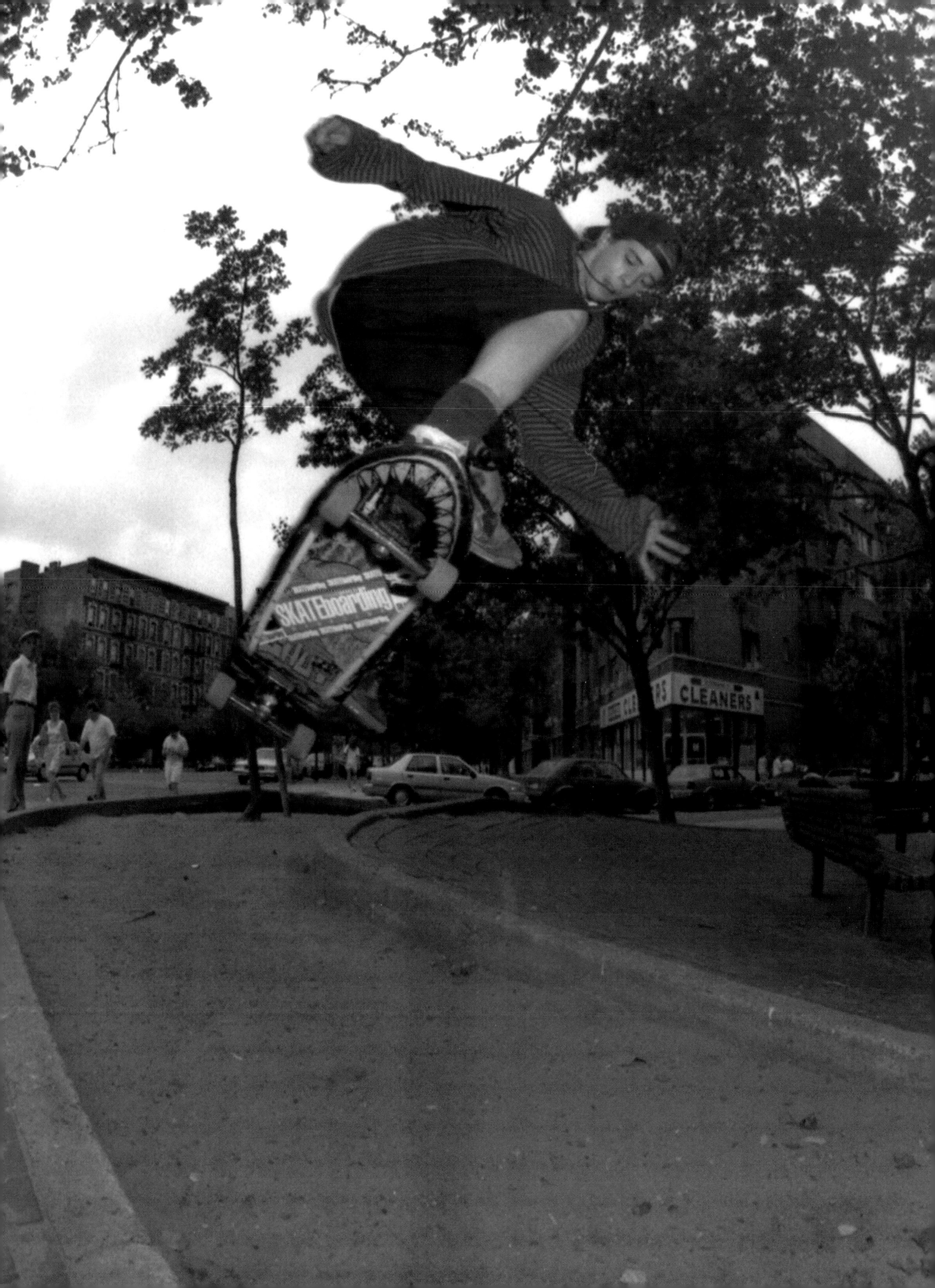
SKATEboarding
CLEANERS

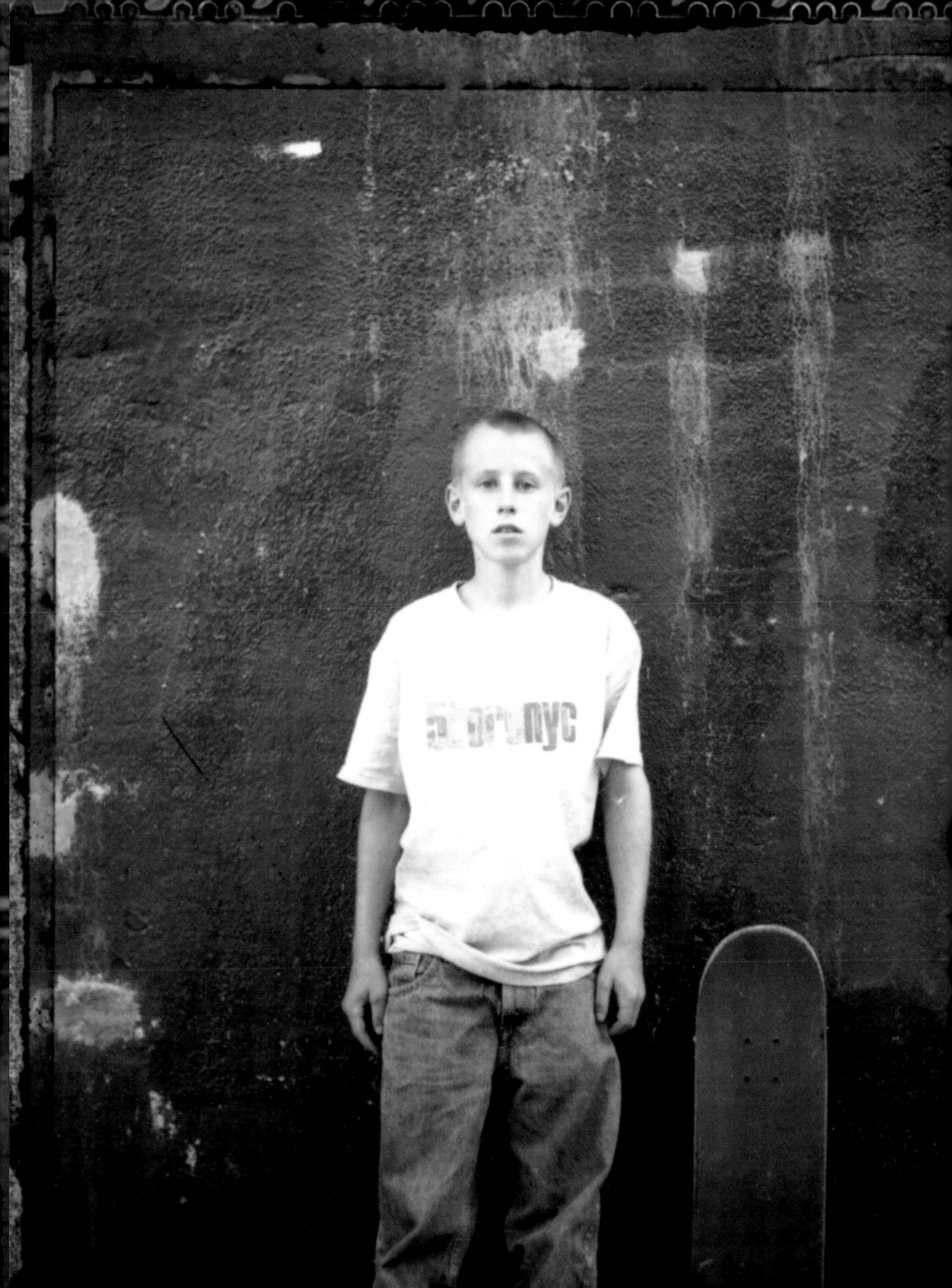
nyc

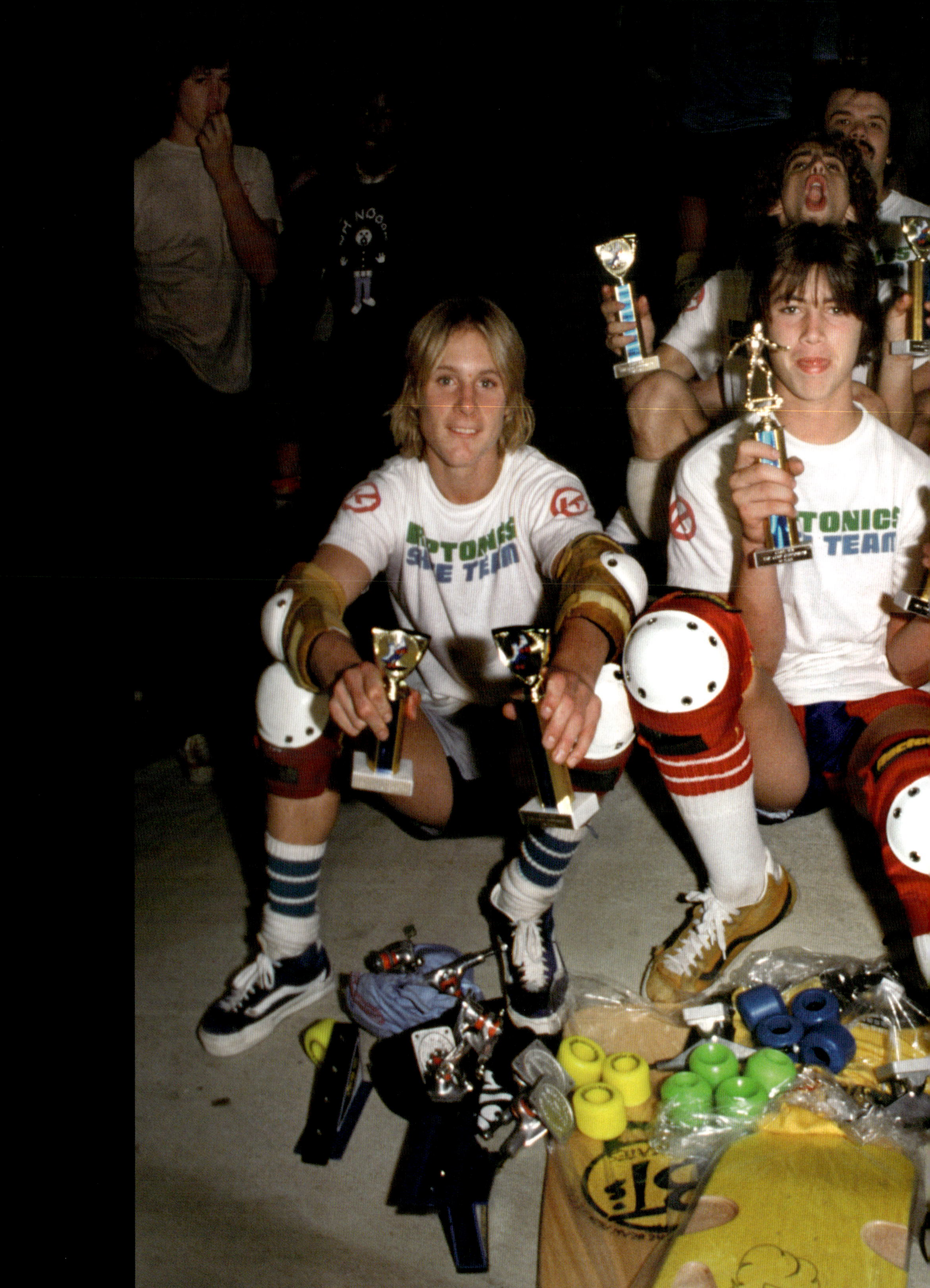
TONICS
TEAM

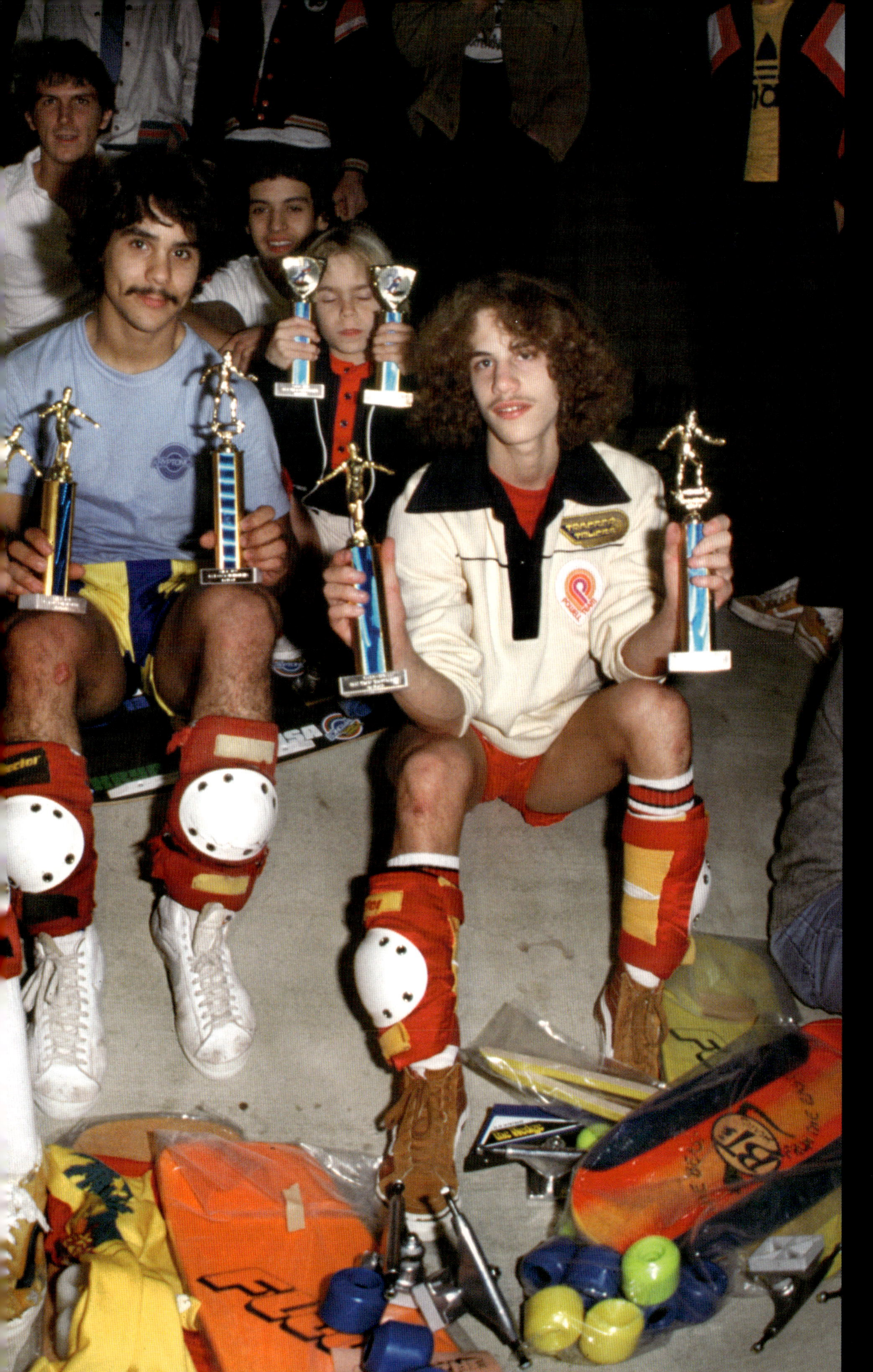

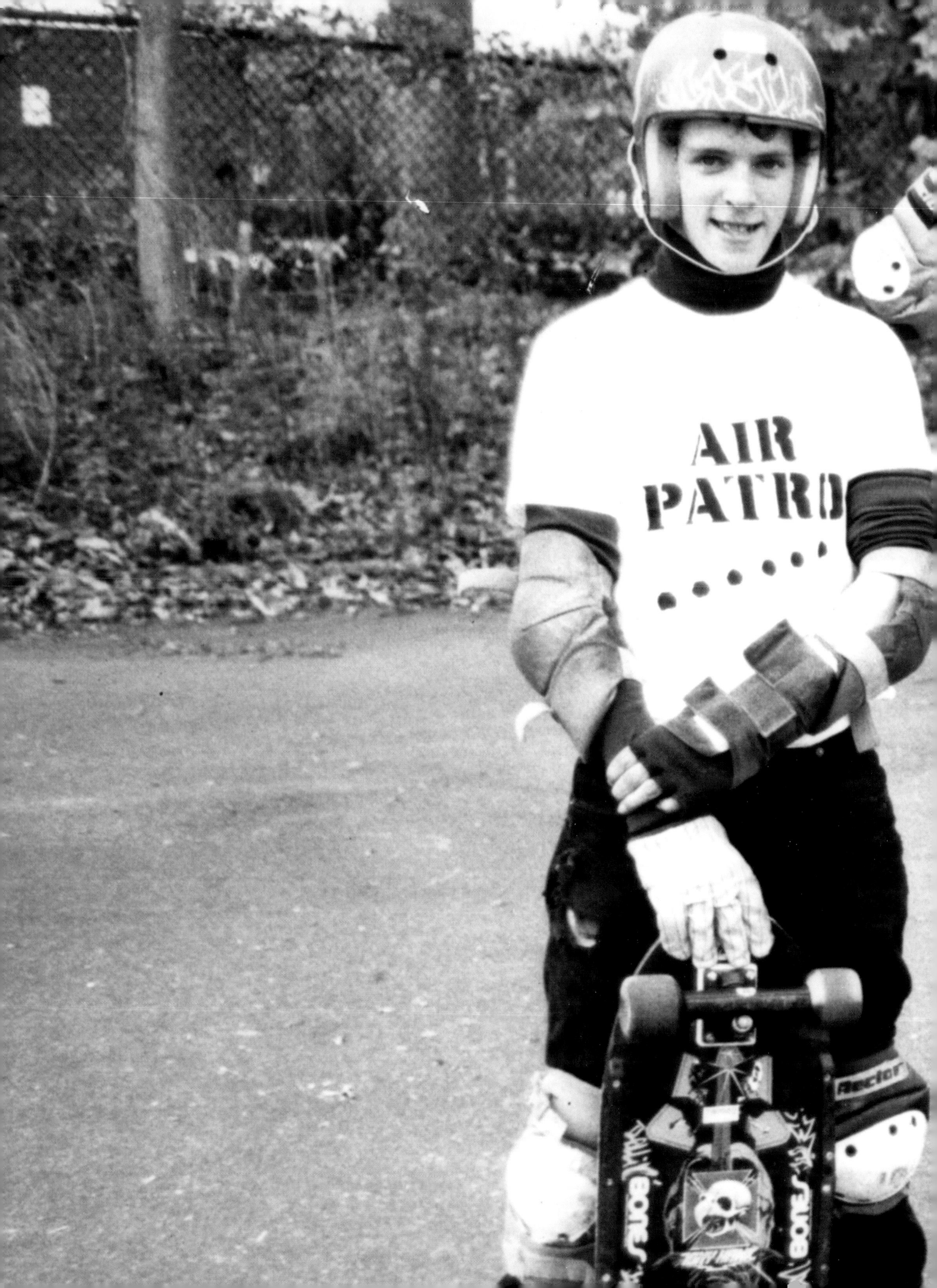
AIR
PATRO
Rector

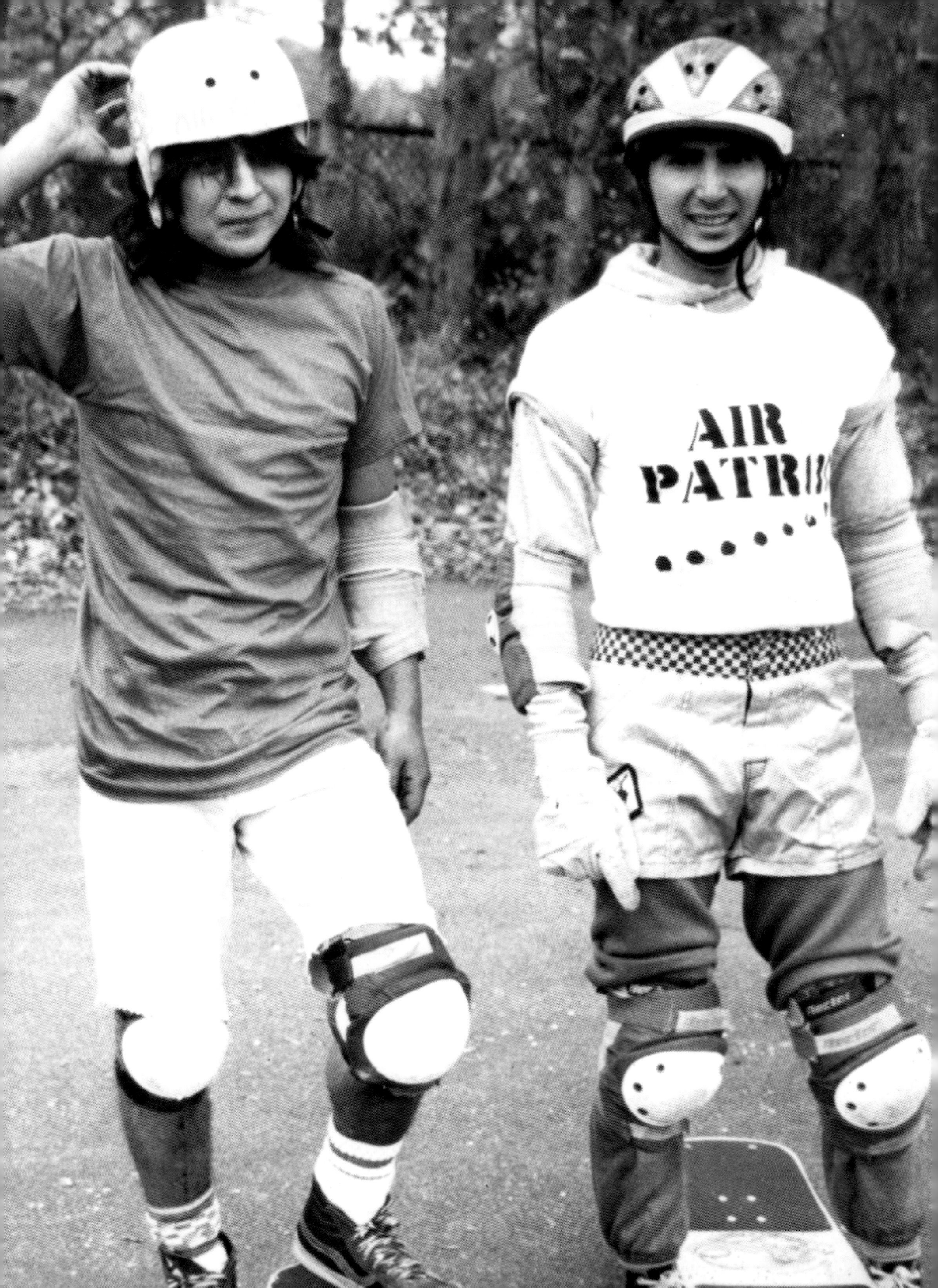
AIR
PATRI

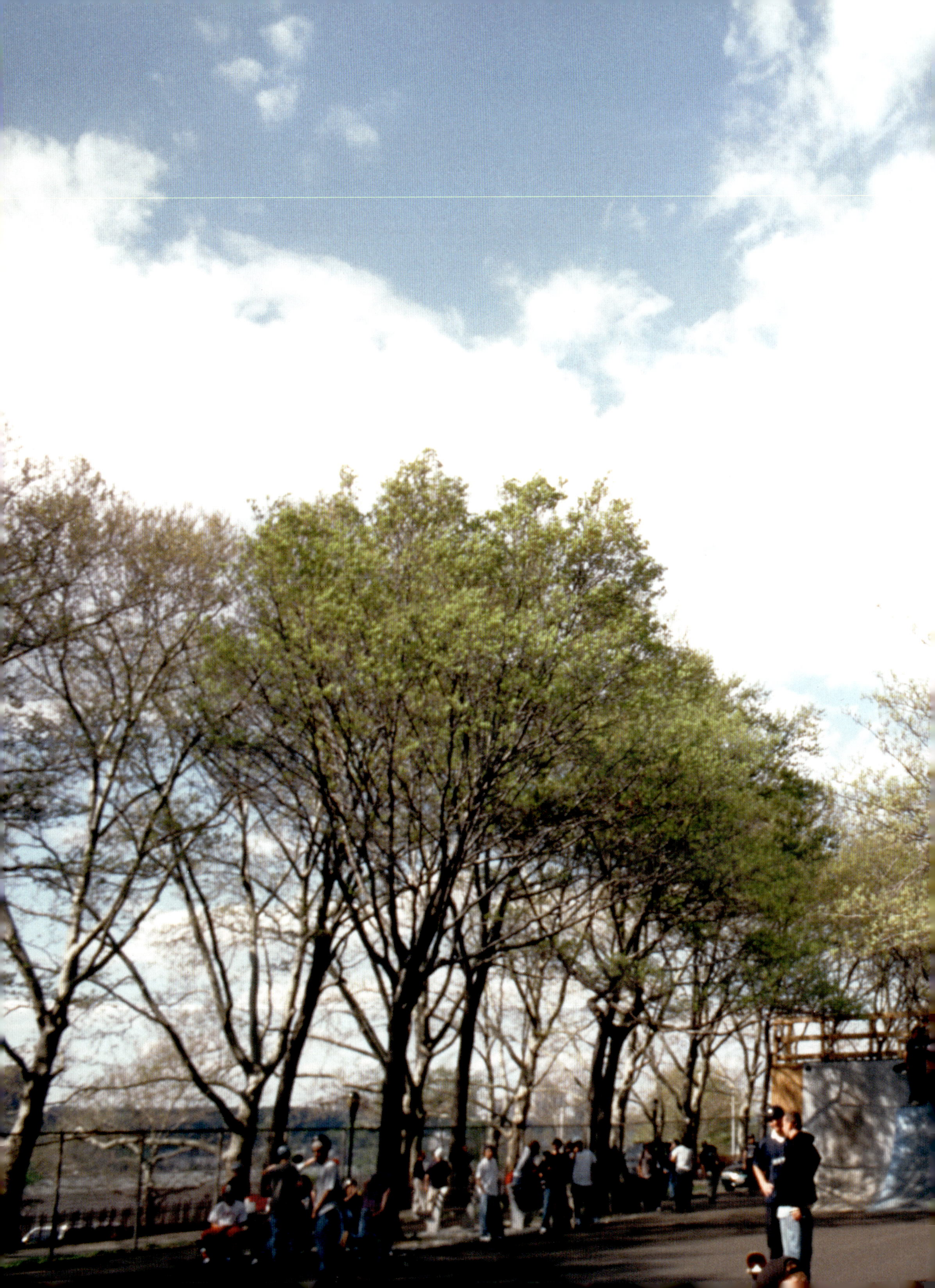

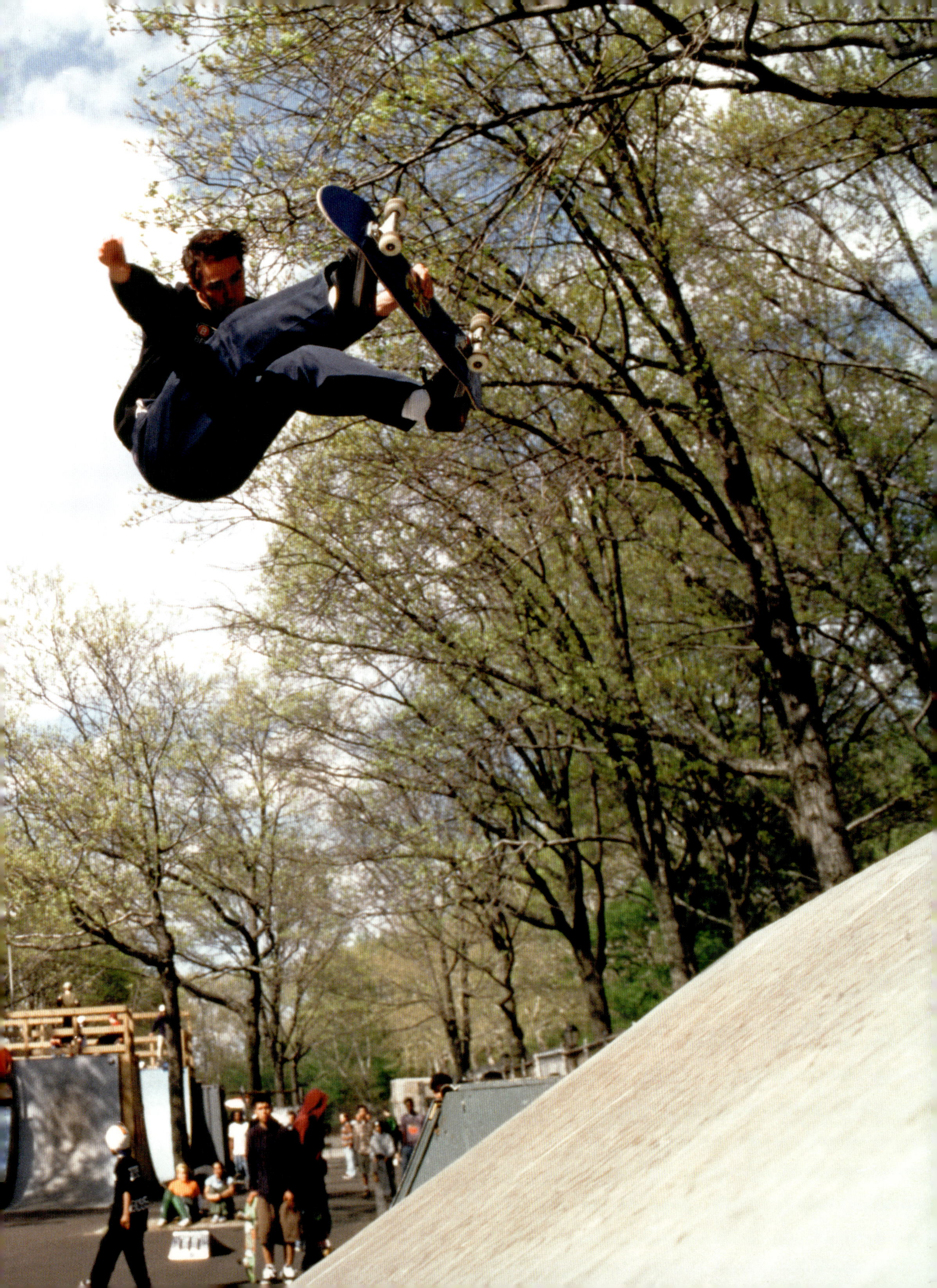

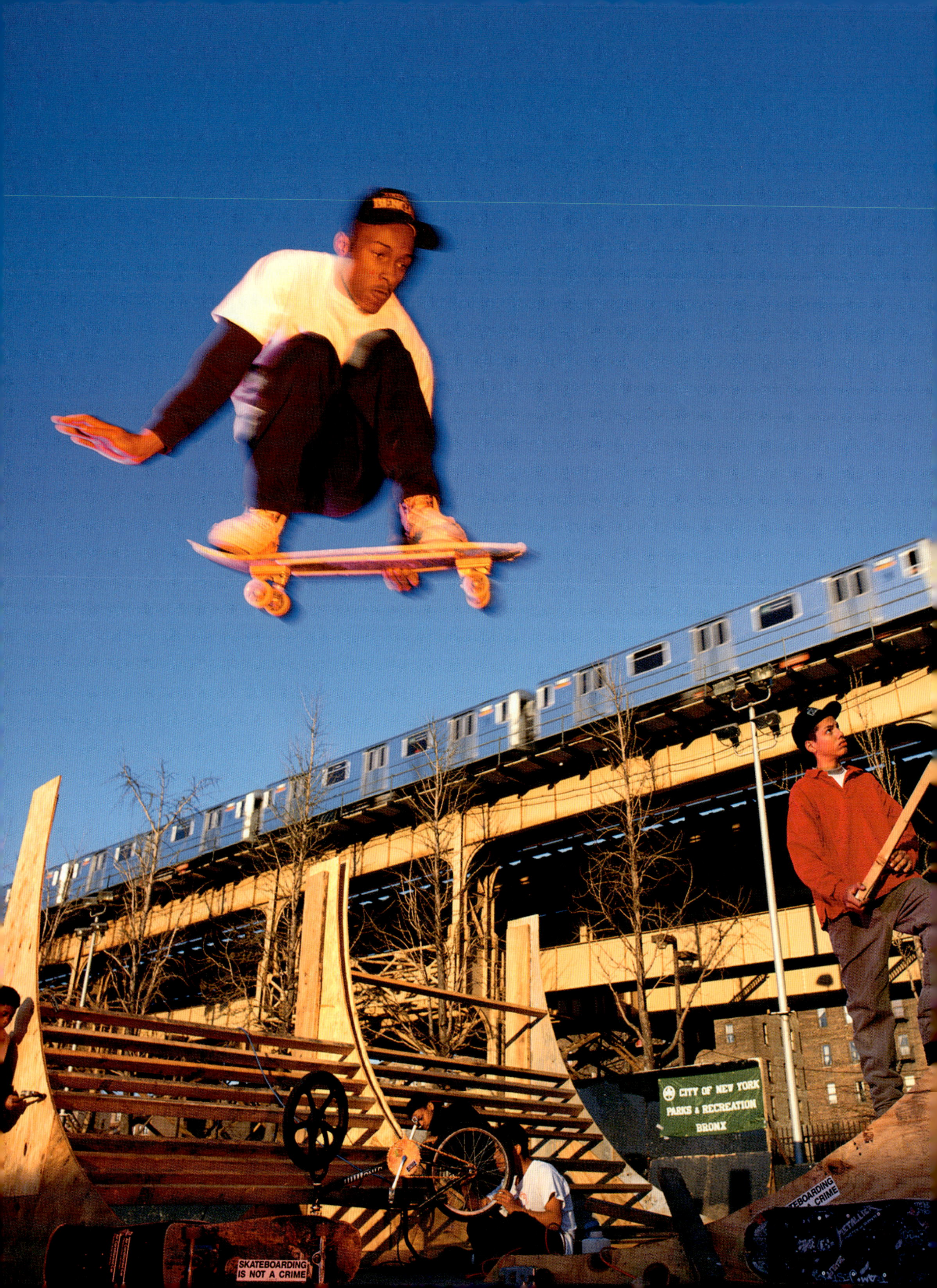
CITY OF NEW YORK
PARKS & RECREATION
BRONX
SKATEBOARDING
IS NOT A CRIME

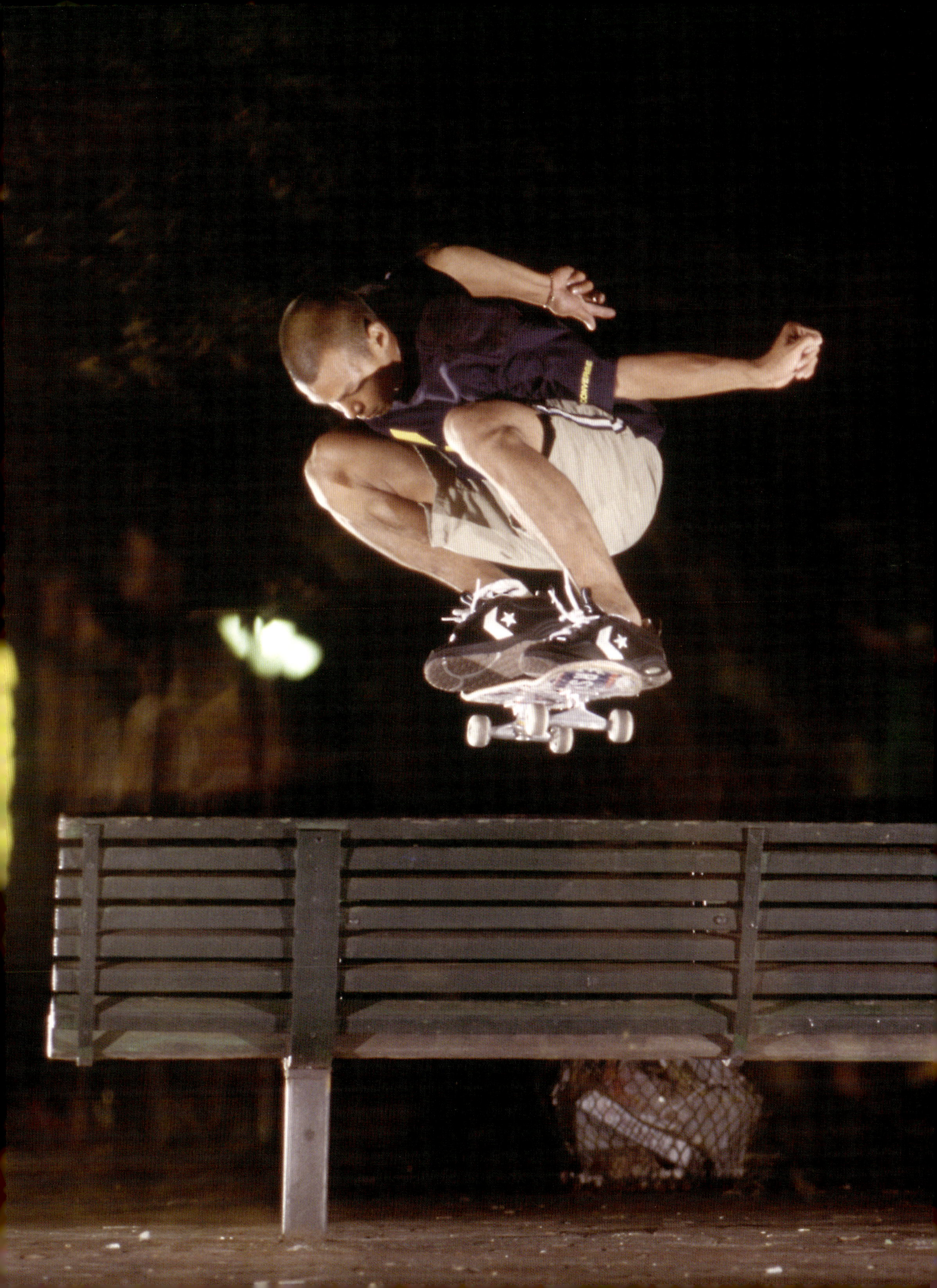

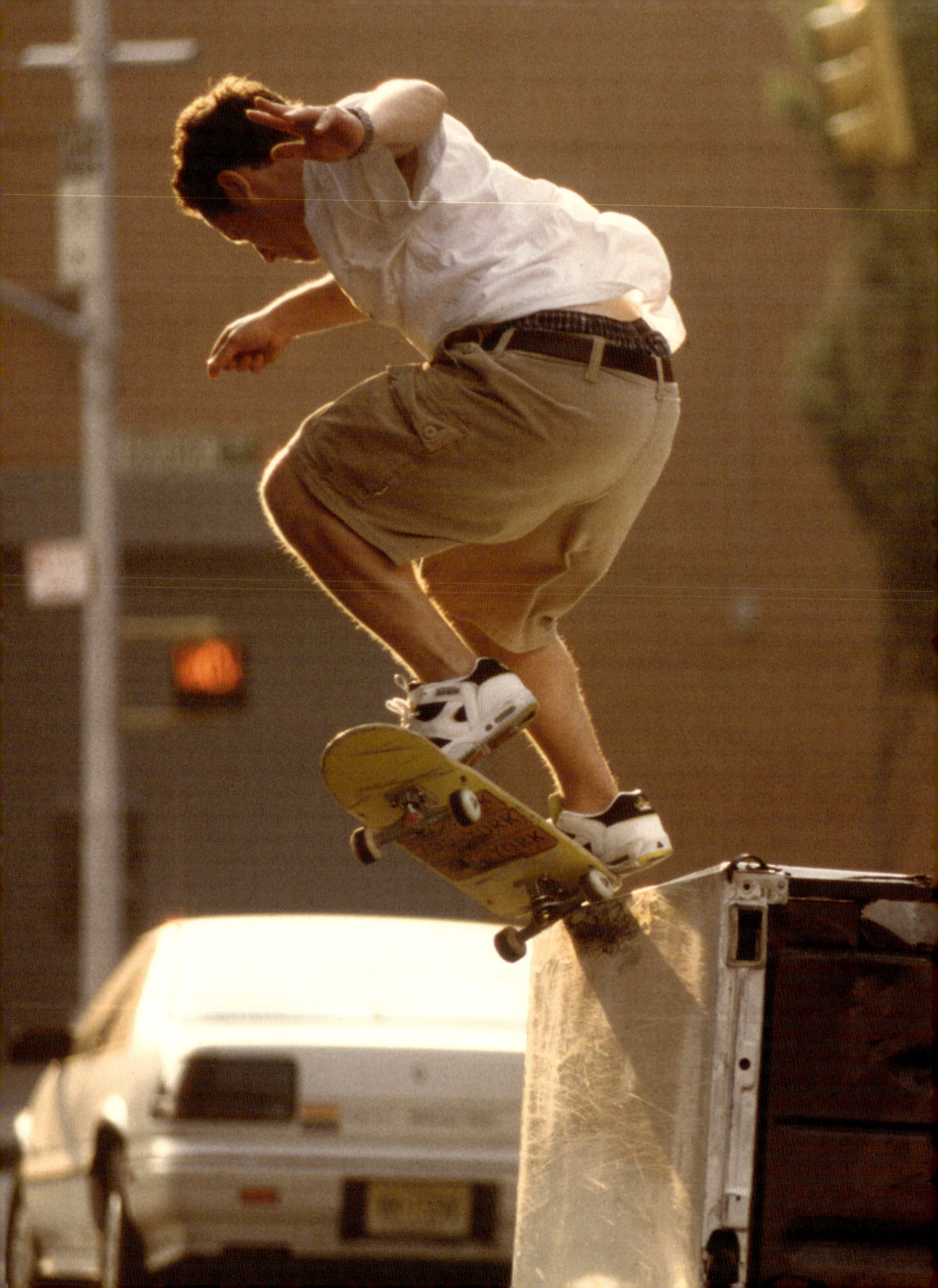

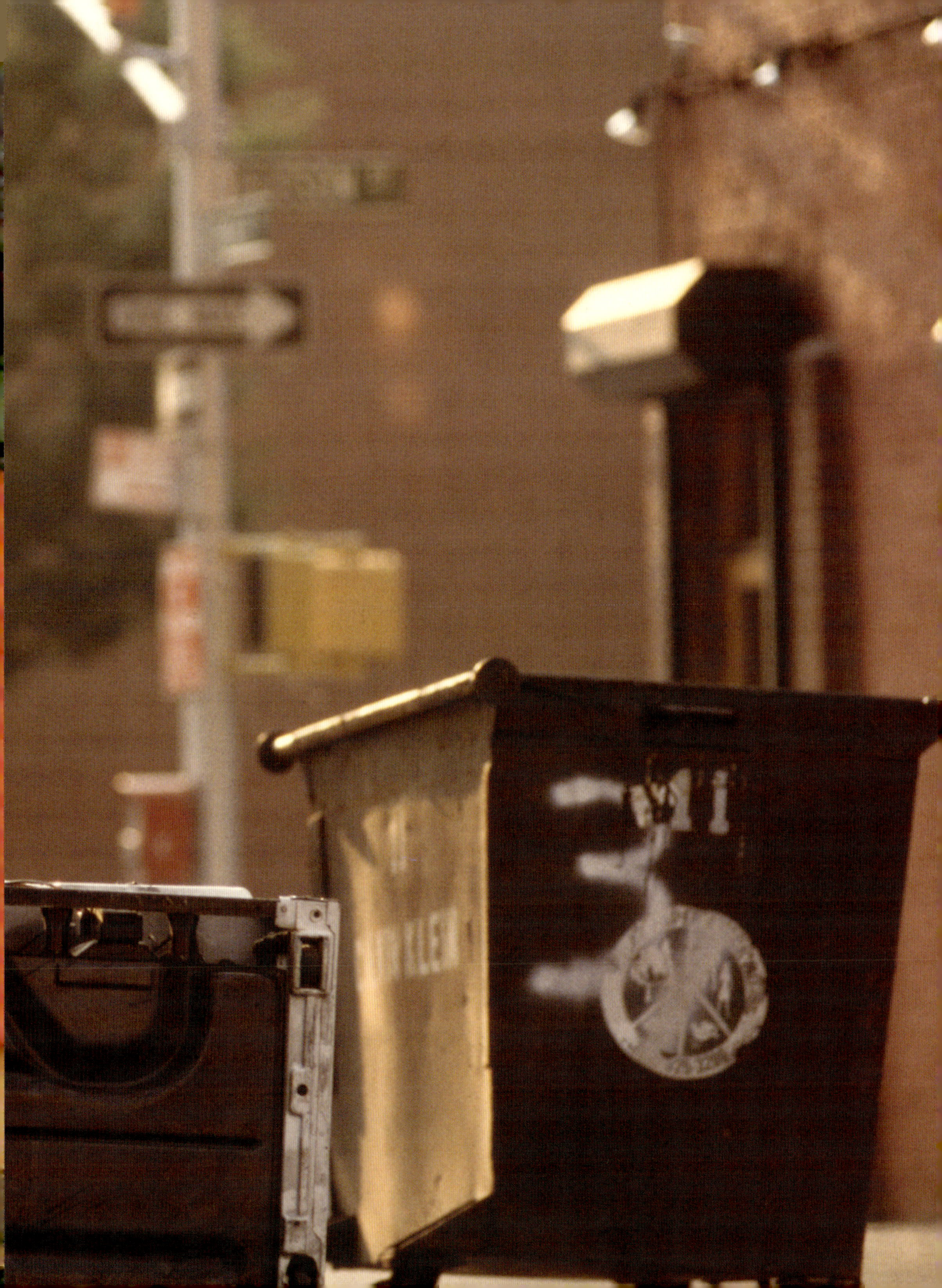

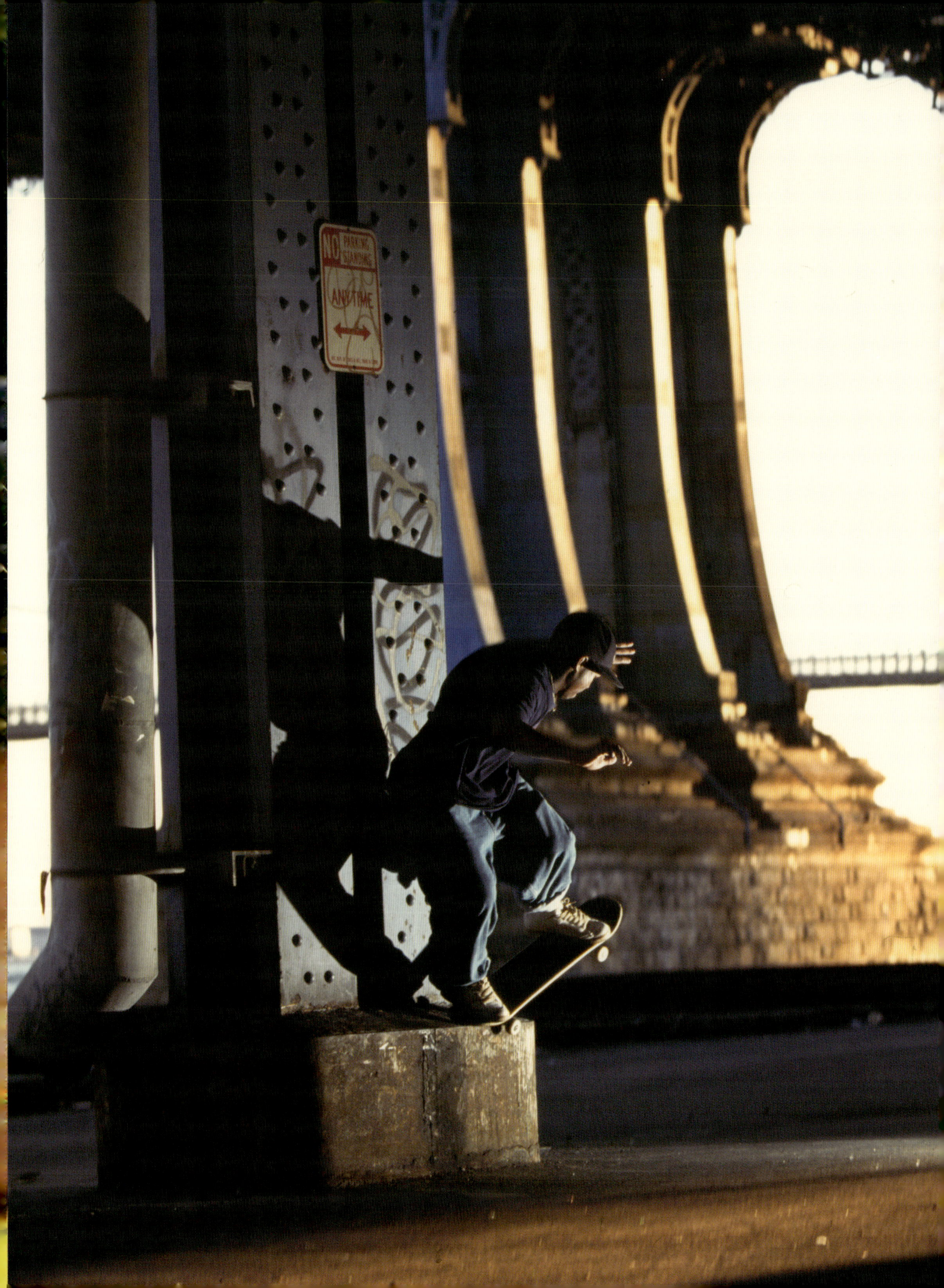
NO PARKING STANDING
ANYTIME

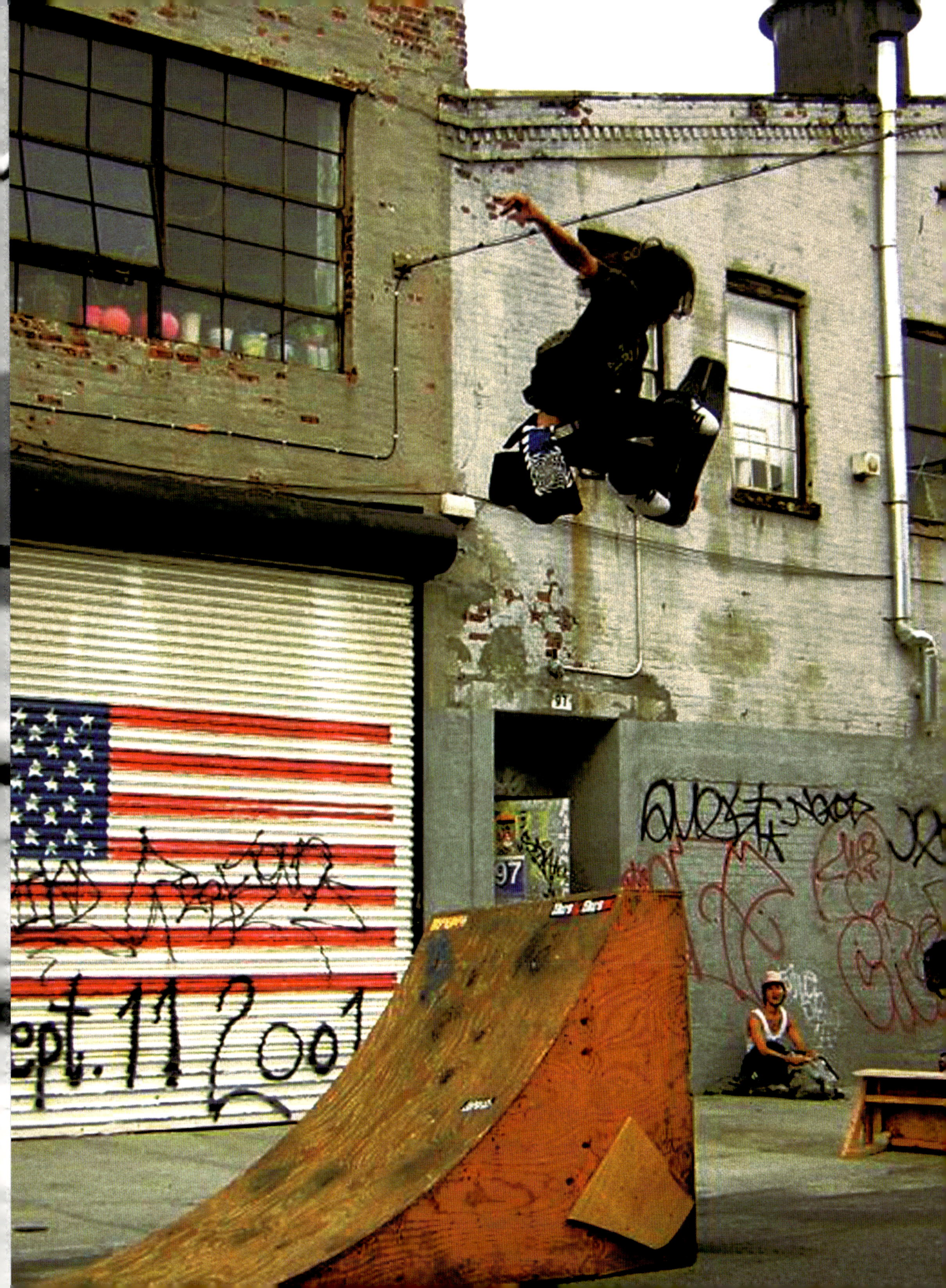
ept. 11 2001
97

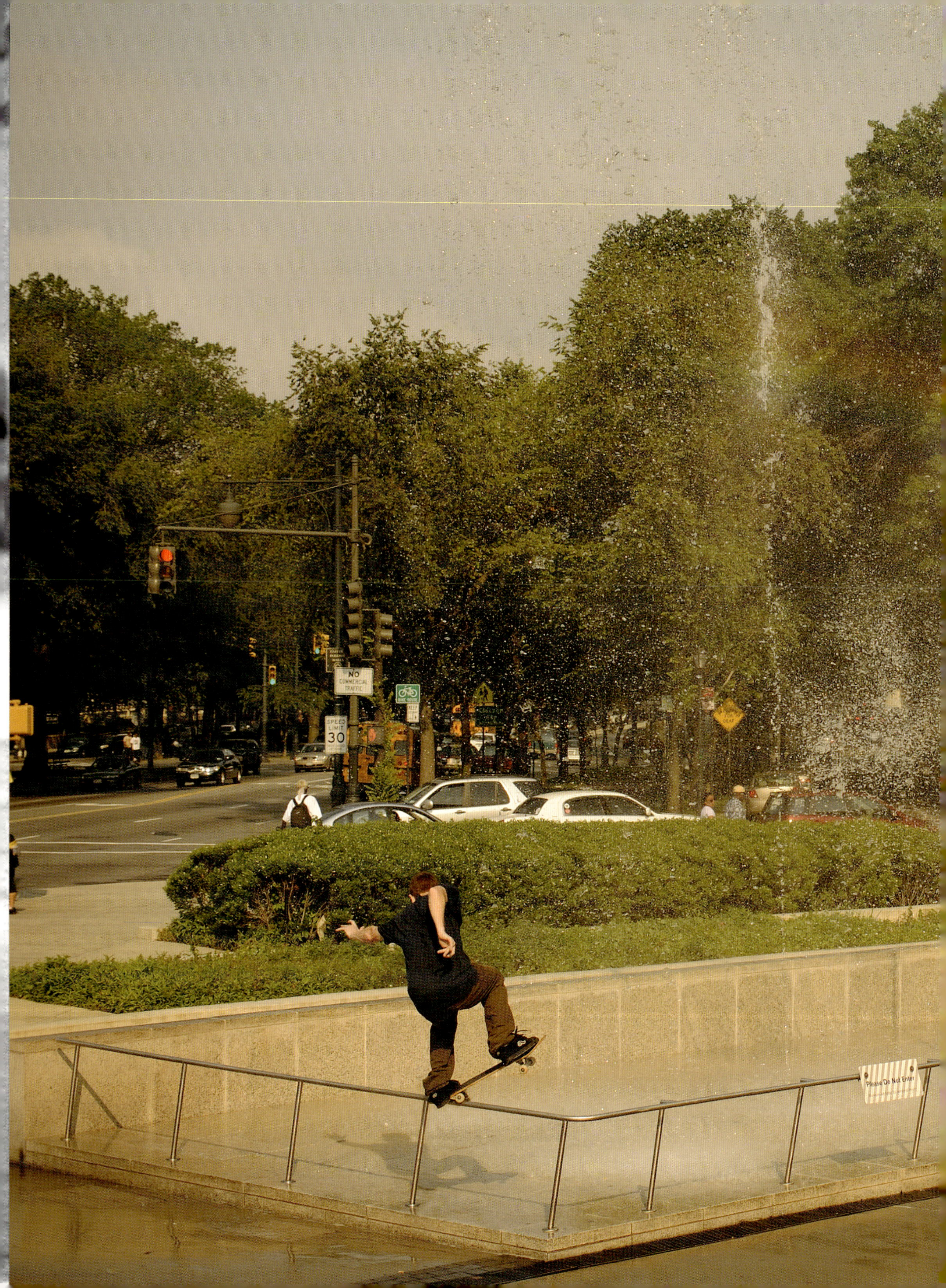
NO COMMERCIAL TRAFFIC
SPEED LIMIT 30
Please Do Not Enter

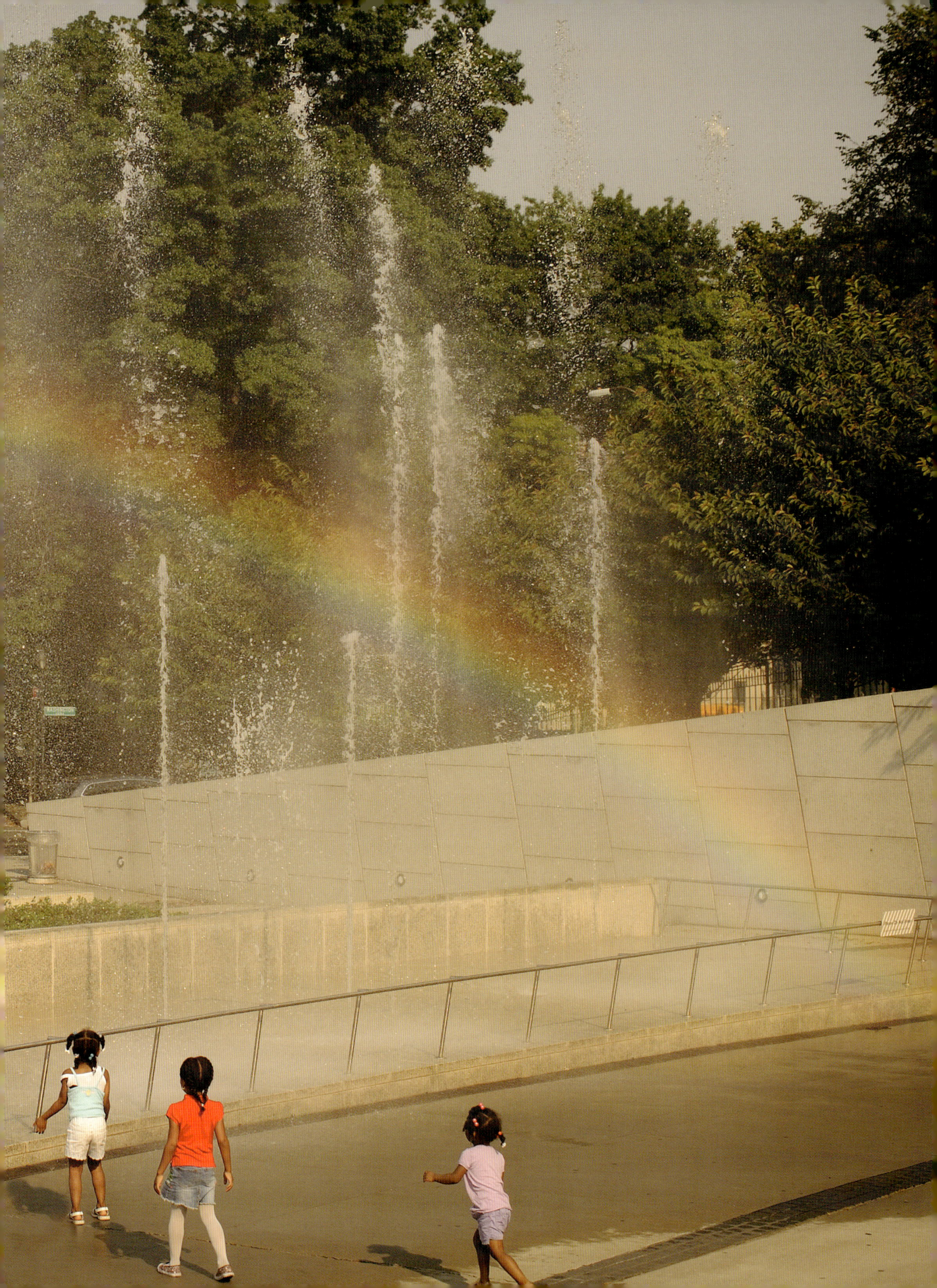

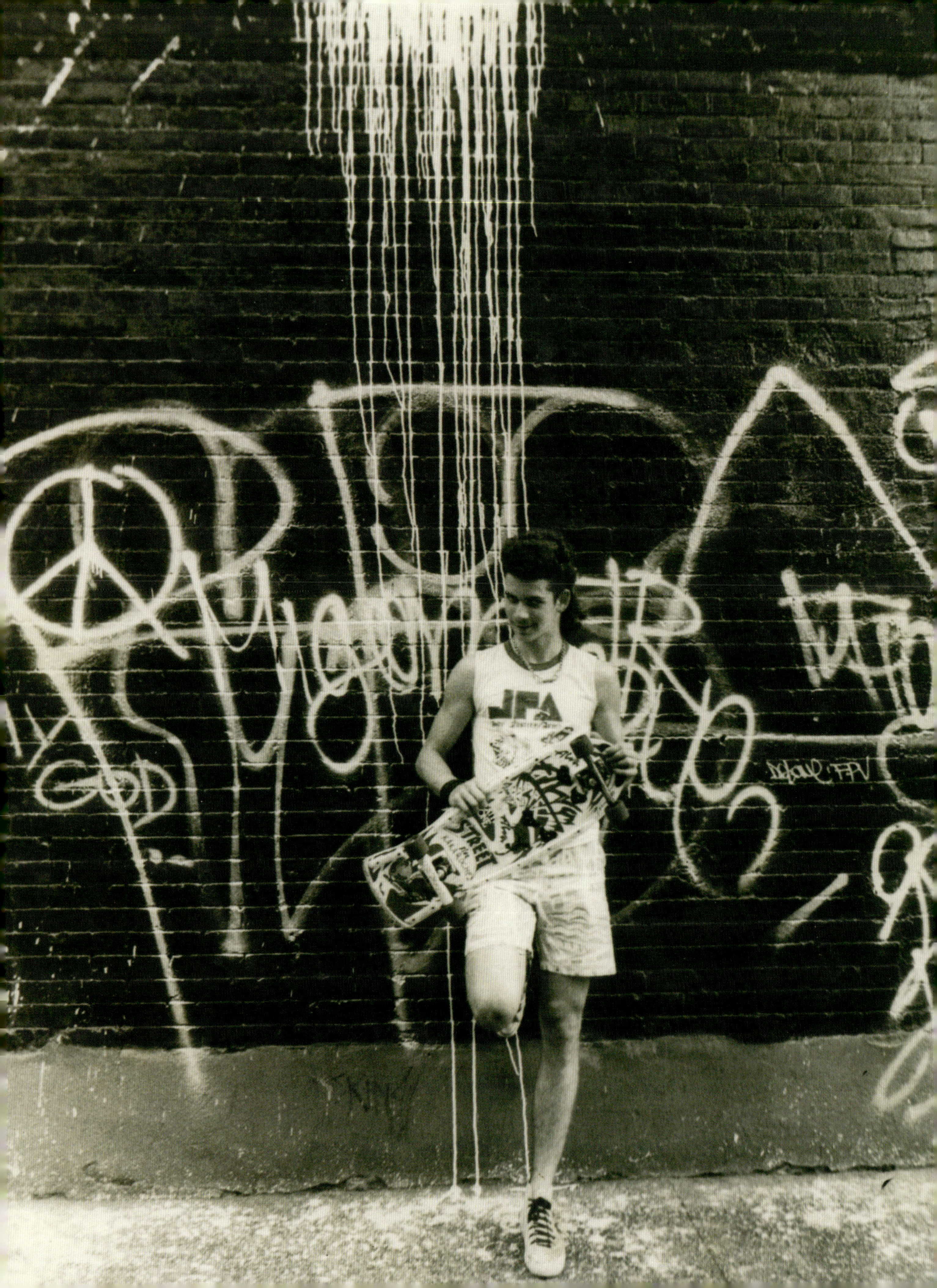
GOD
JFA
STREET

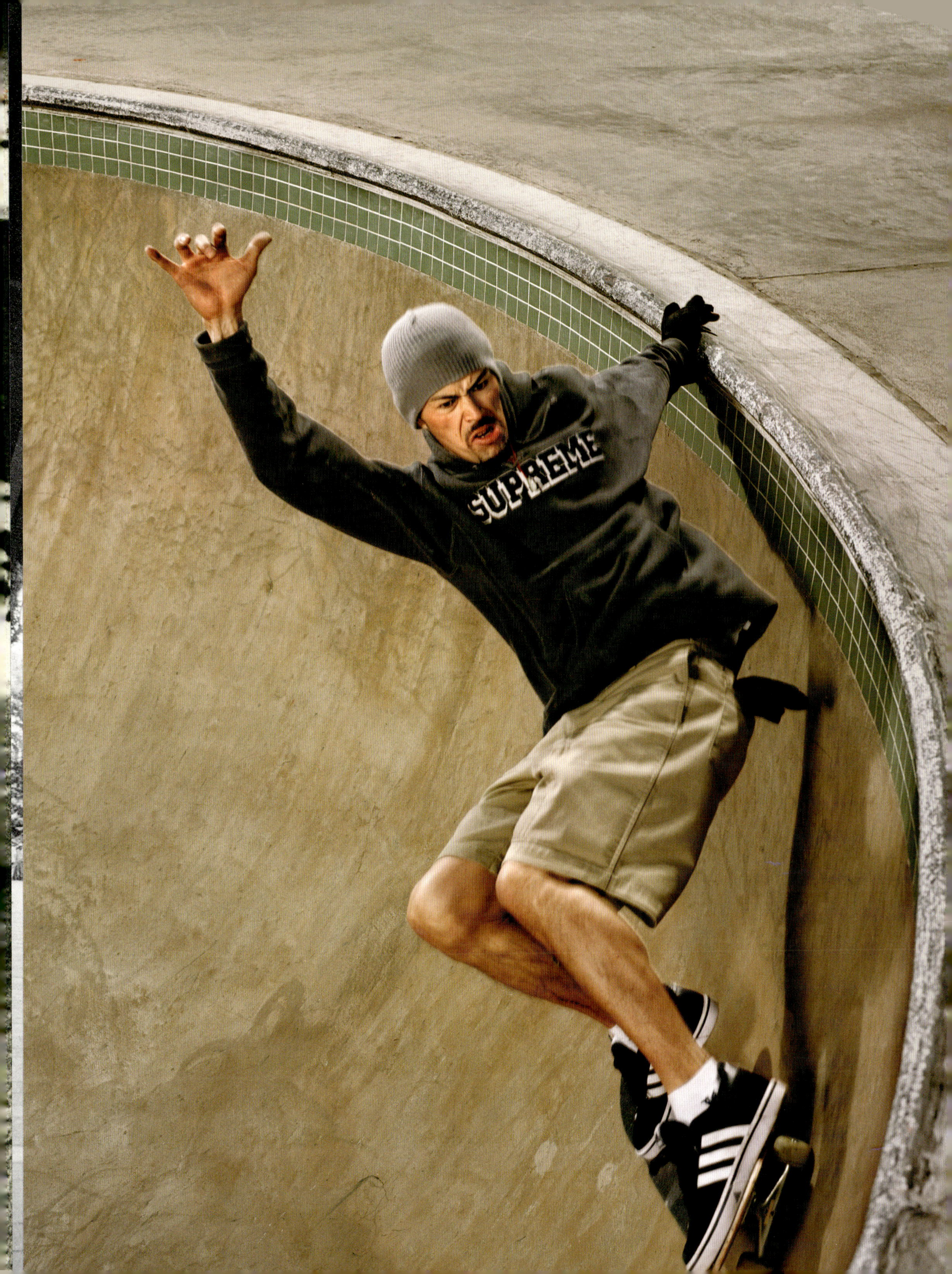
SUPREME

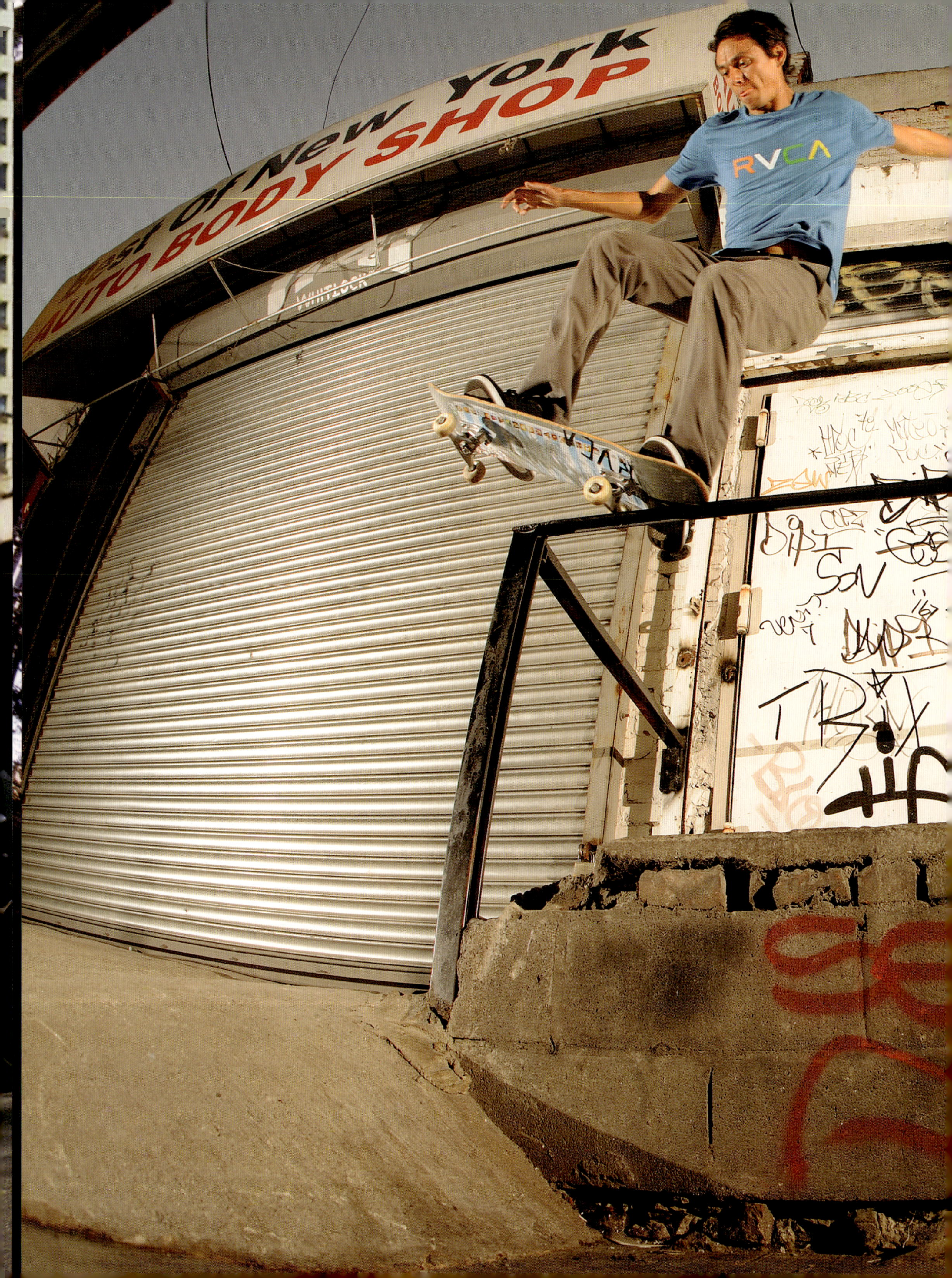
Best of New York
AUTO BODY SHOP
RVCA

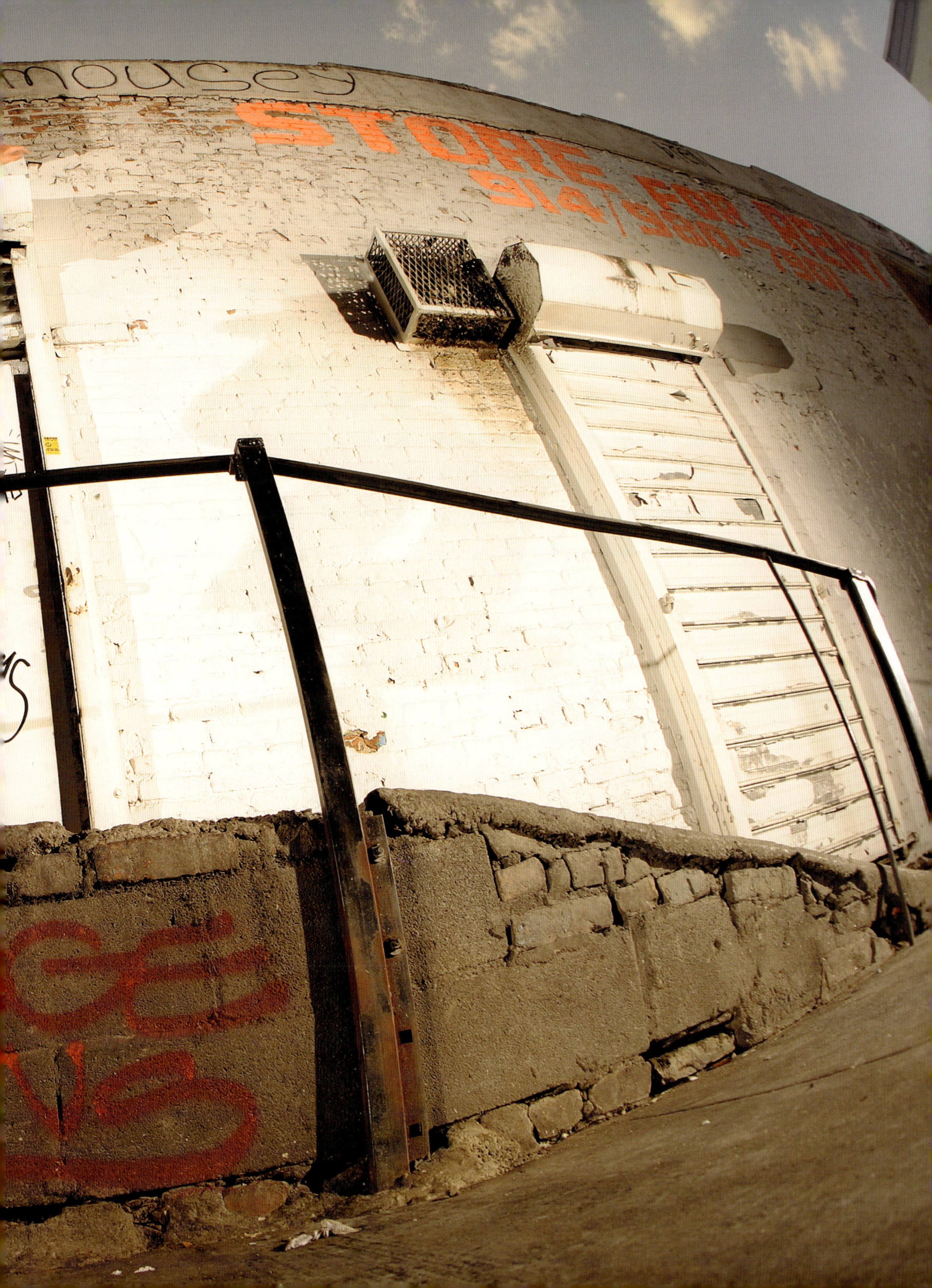
mousey
STORE FOR

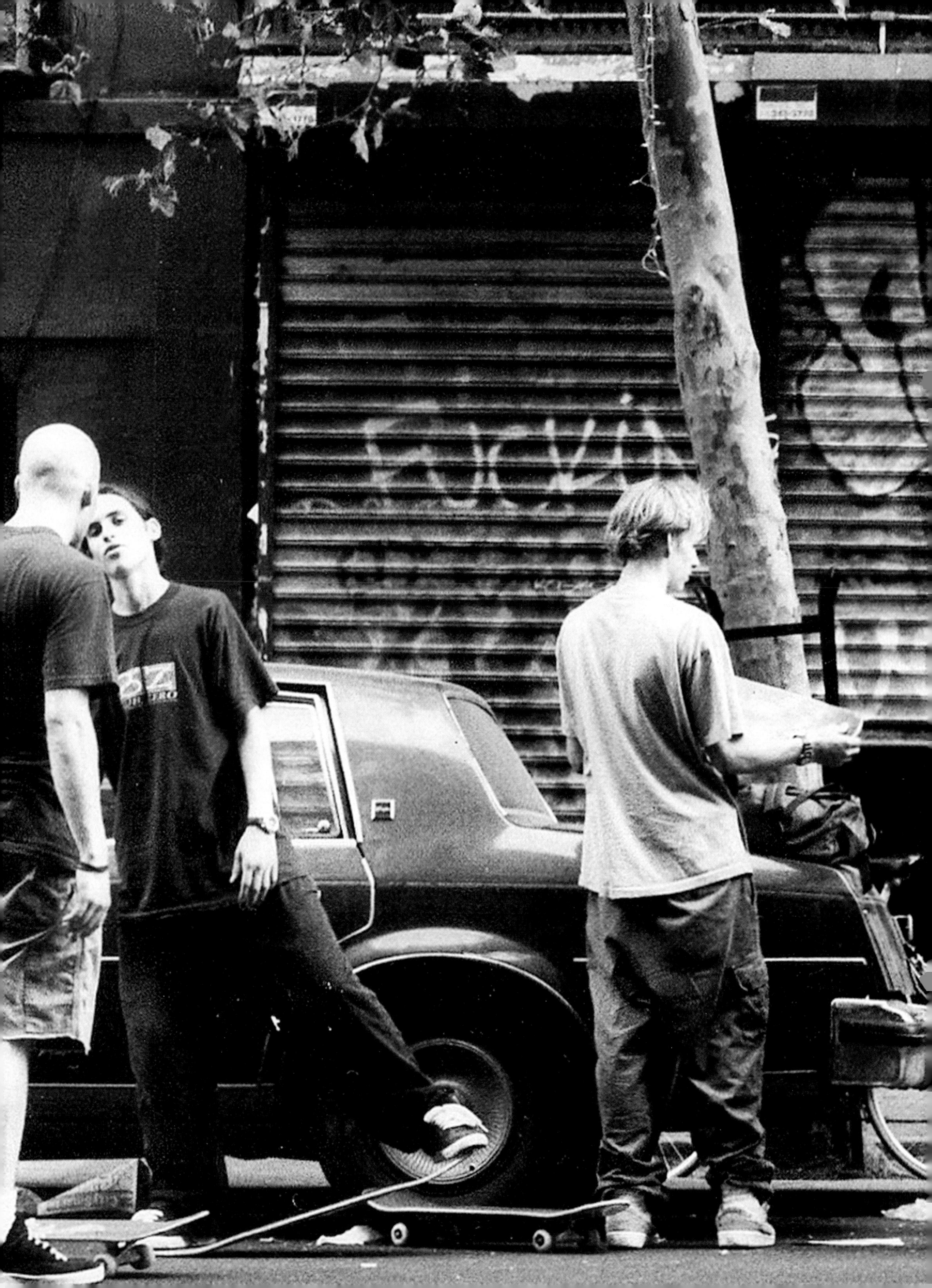

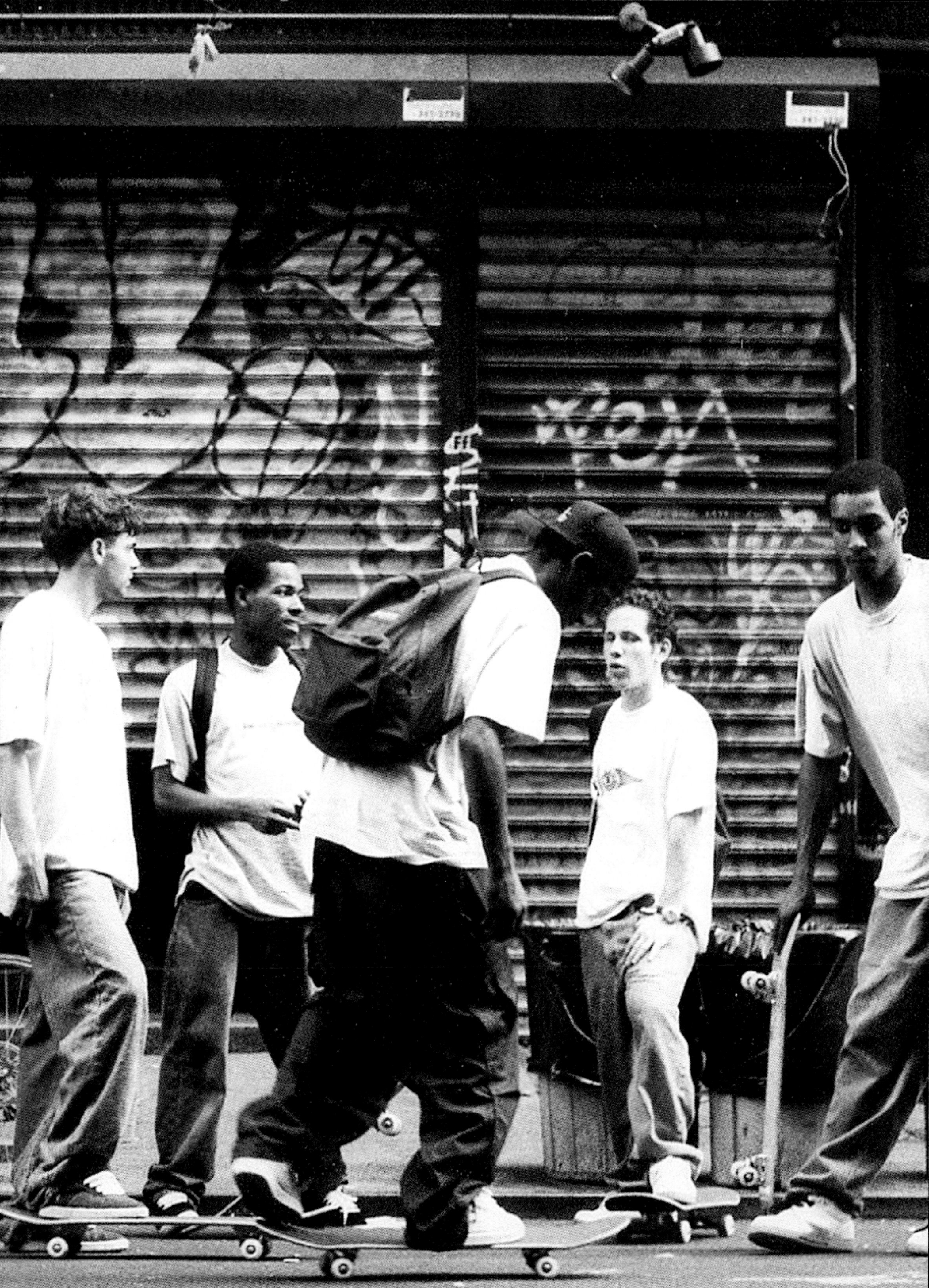

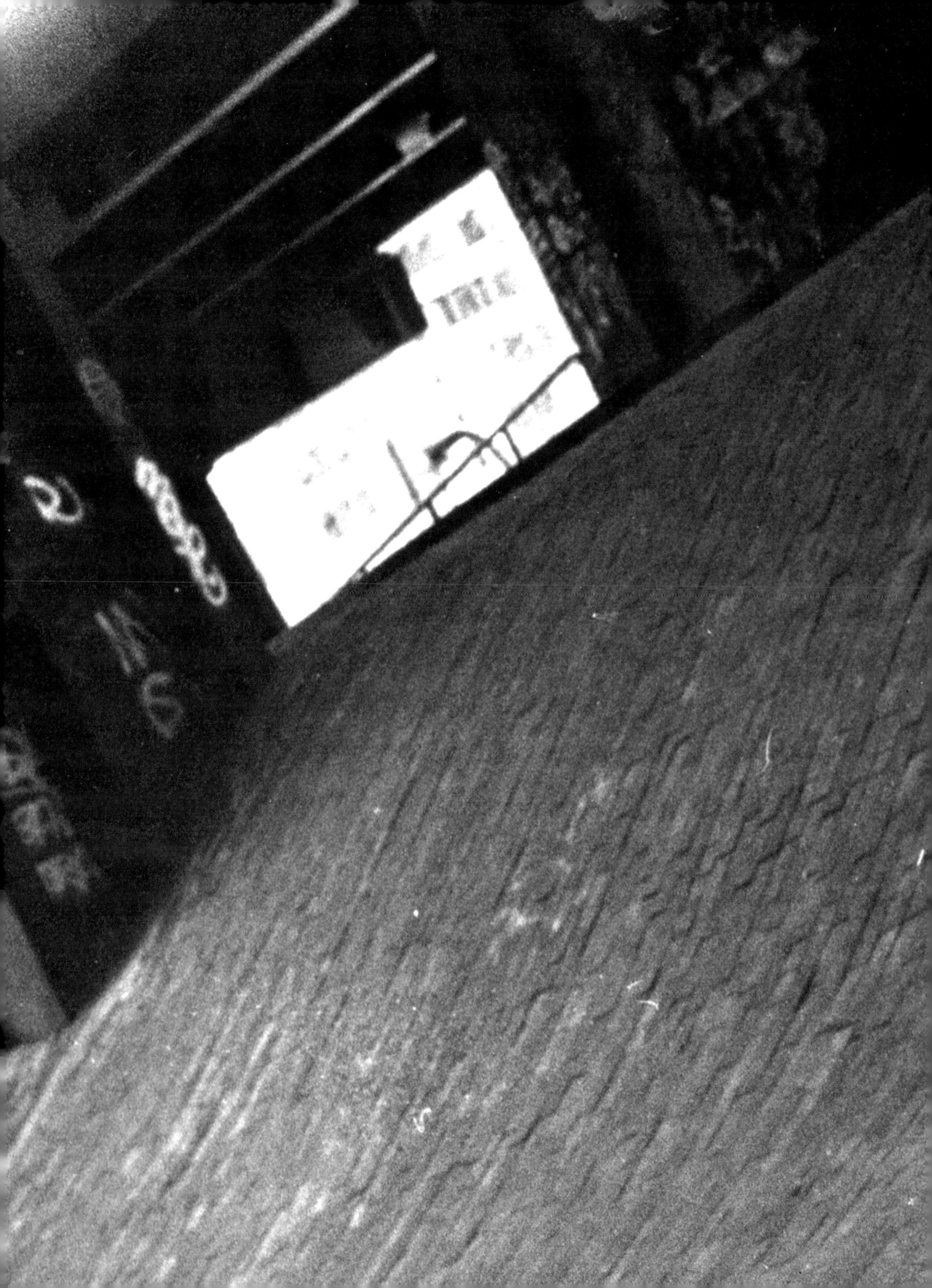

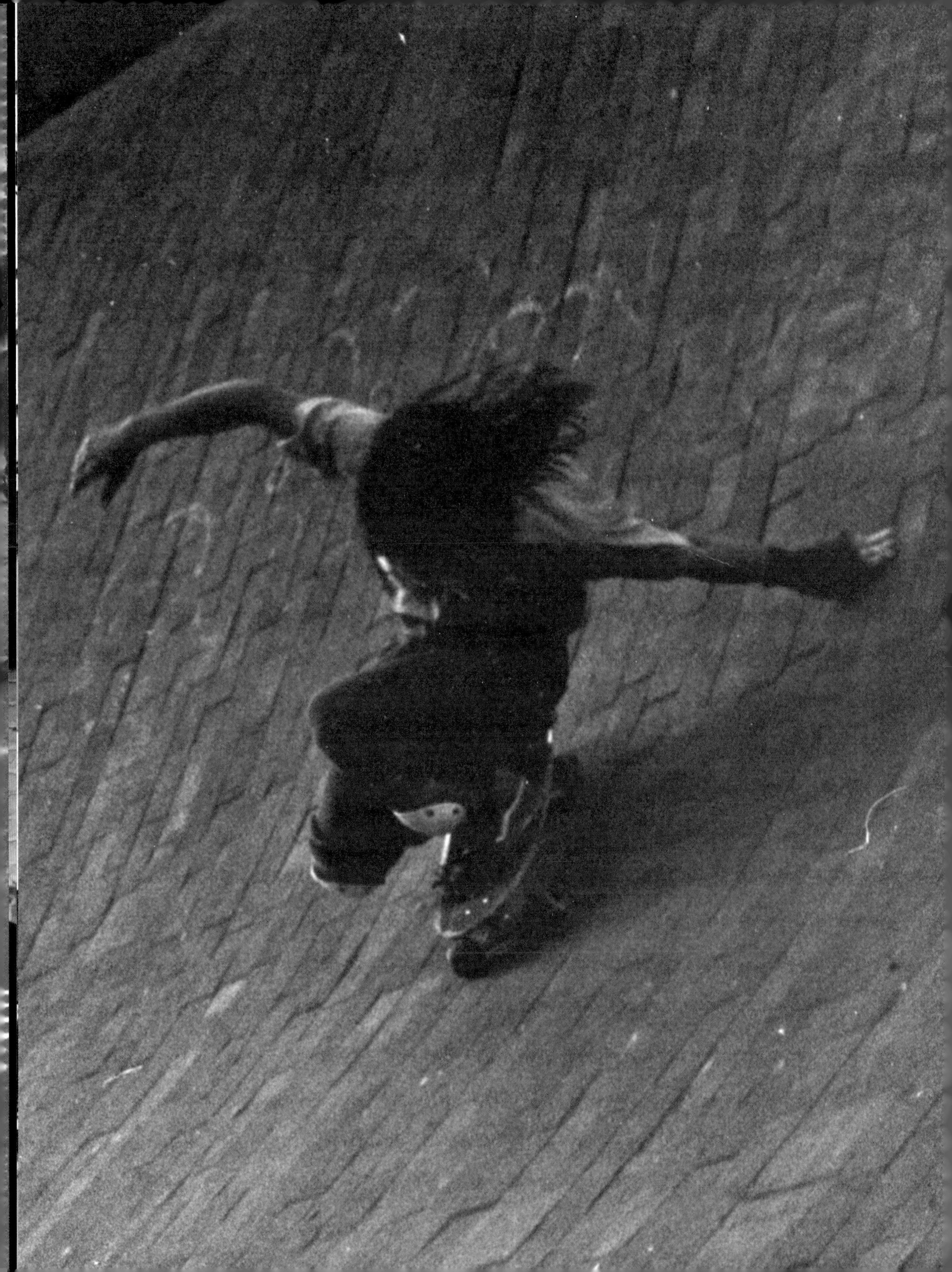

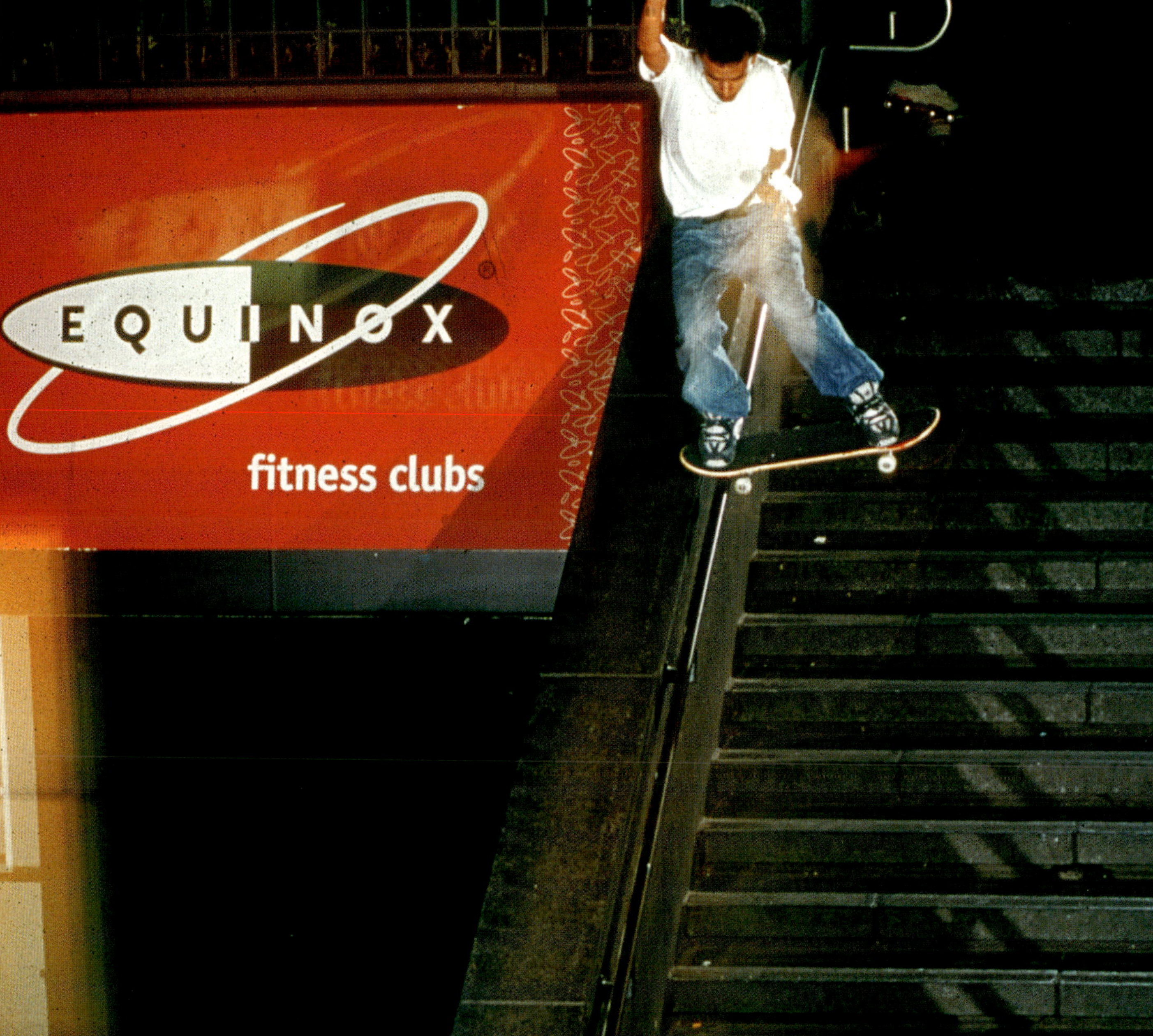
EQUINOX
fitness clubs

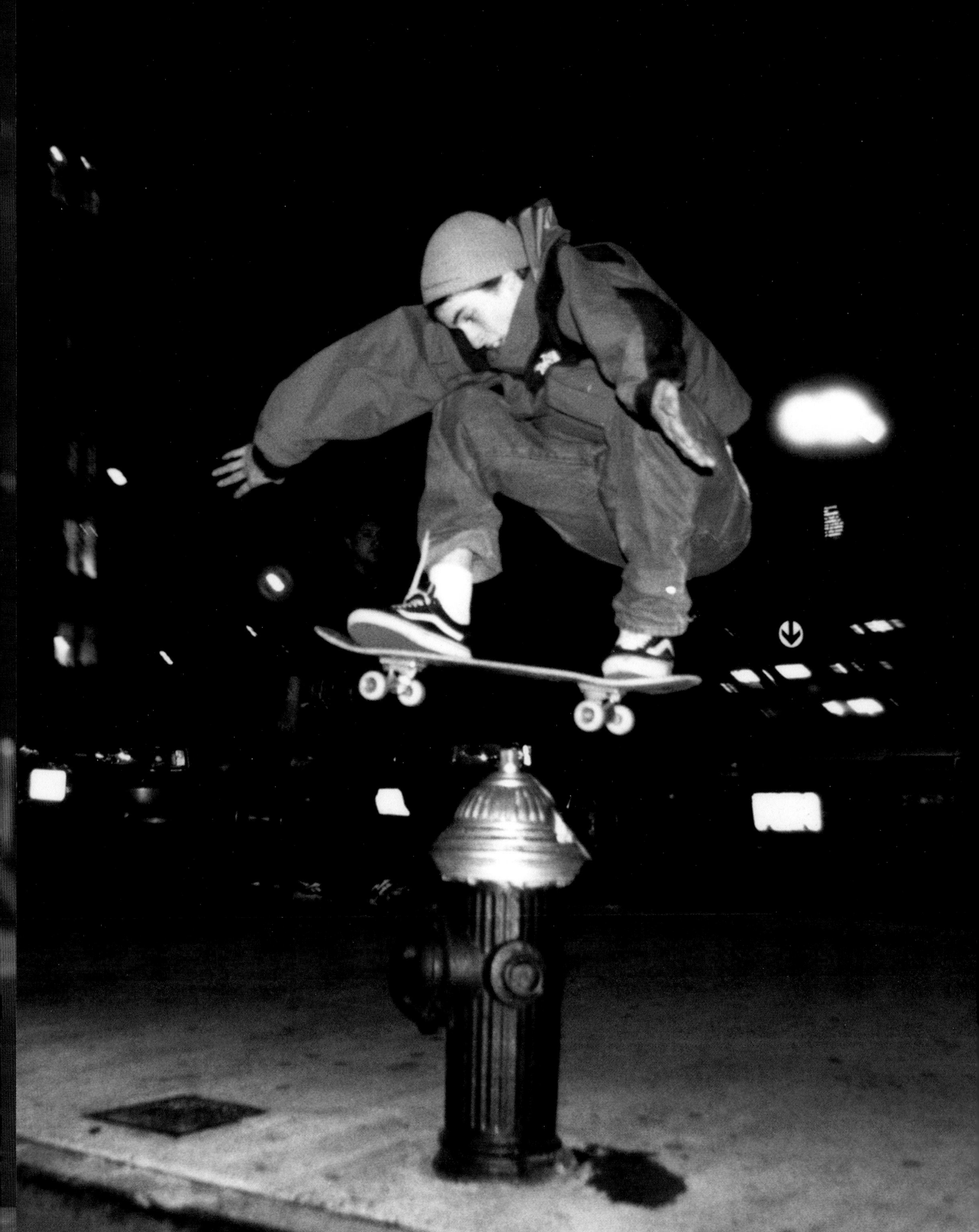

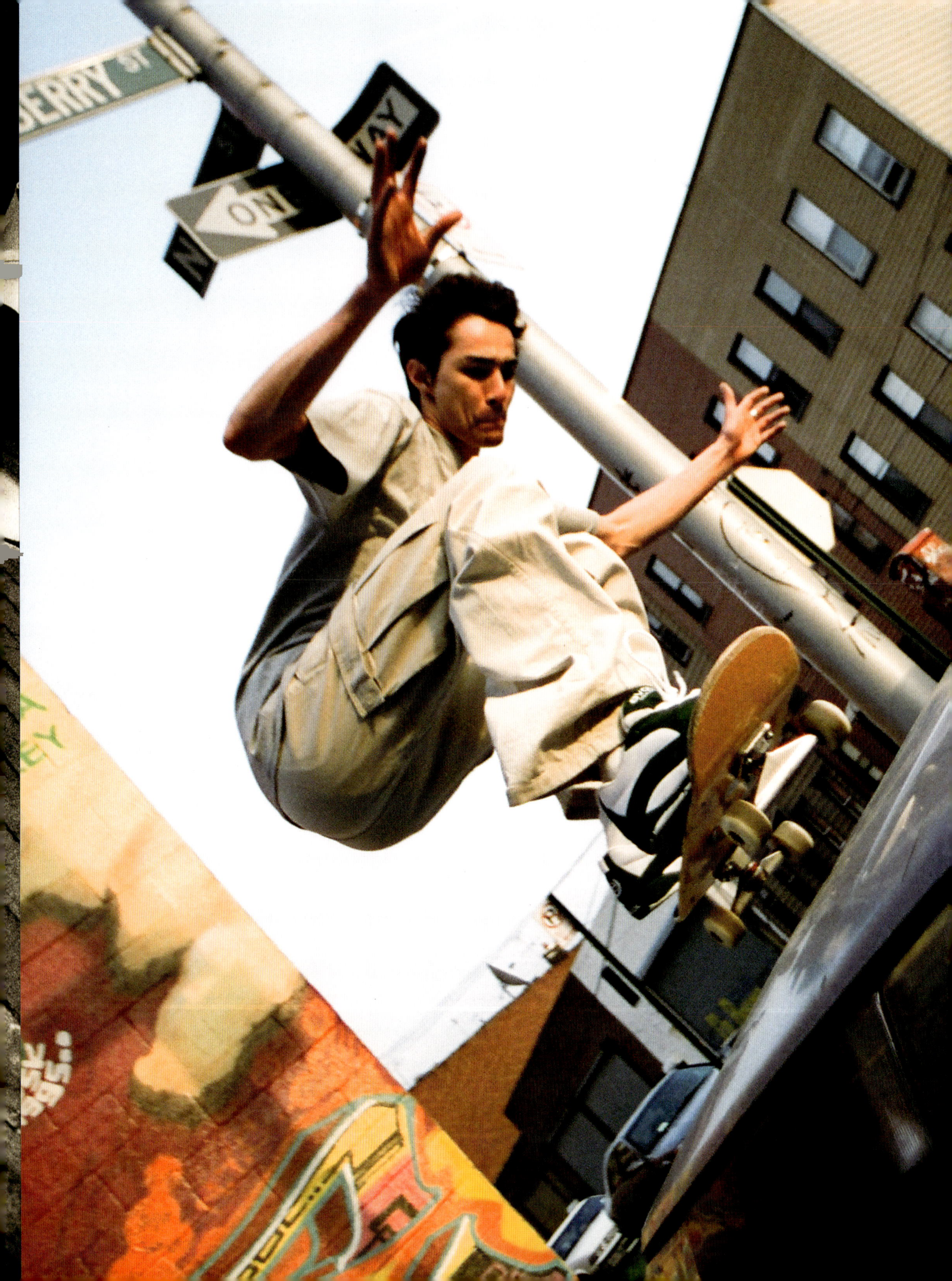

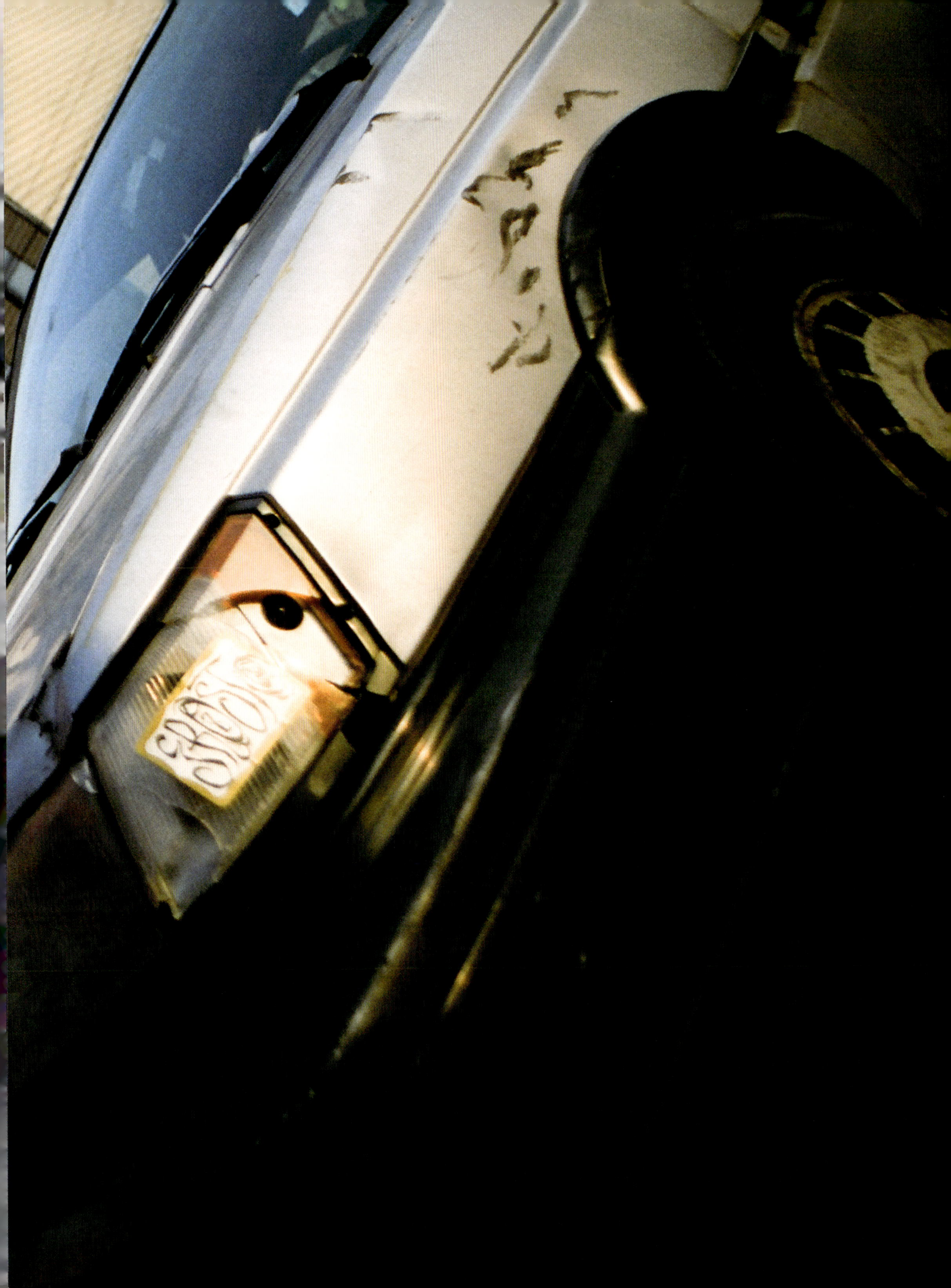

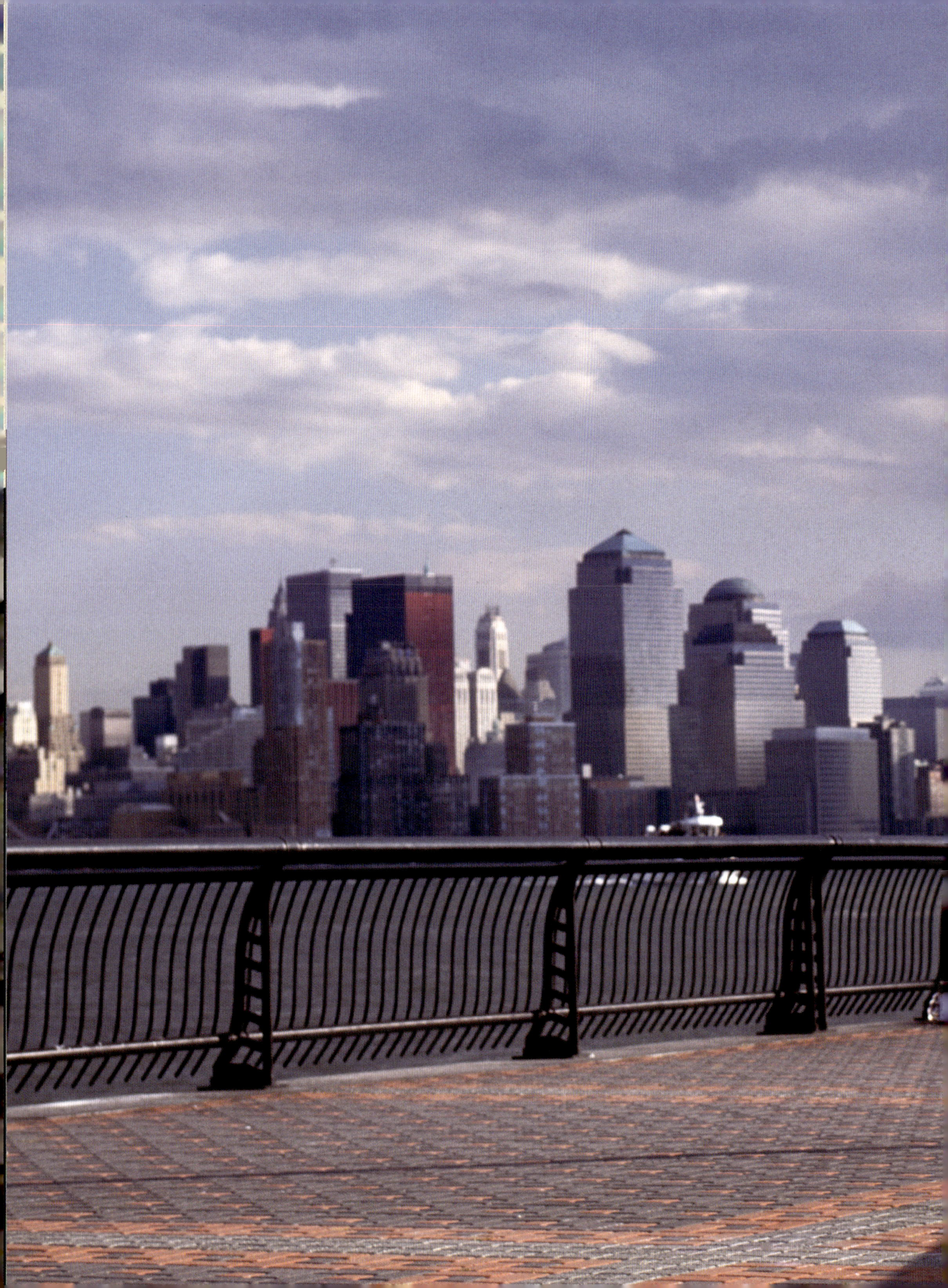

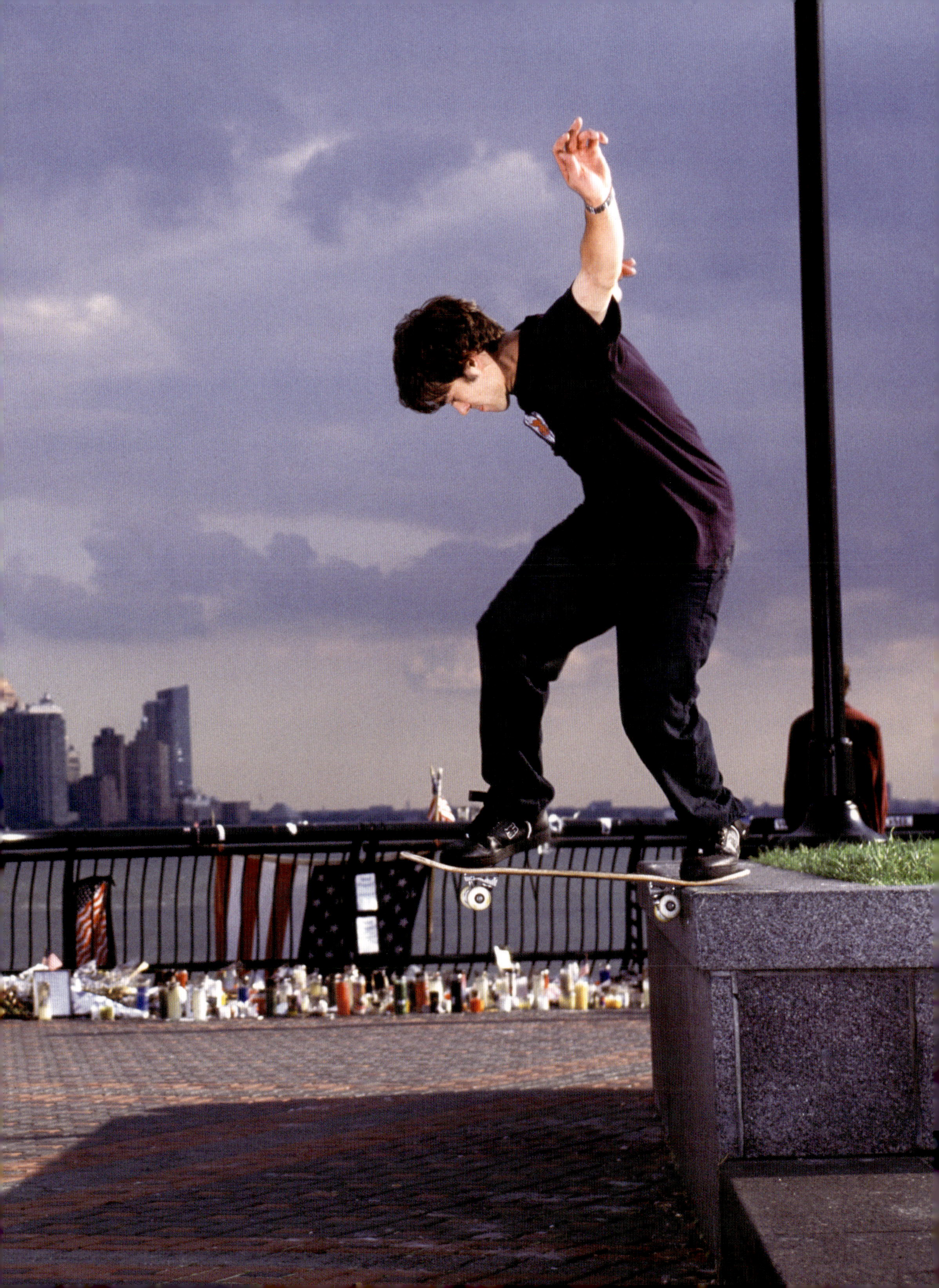

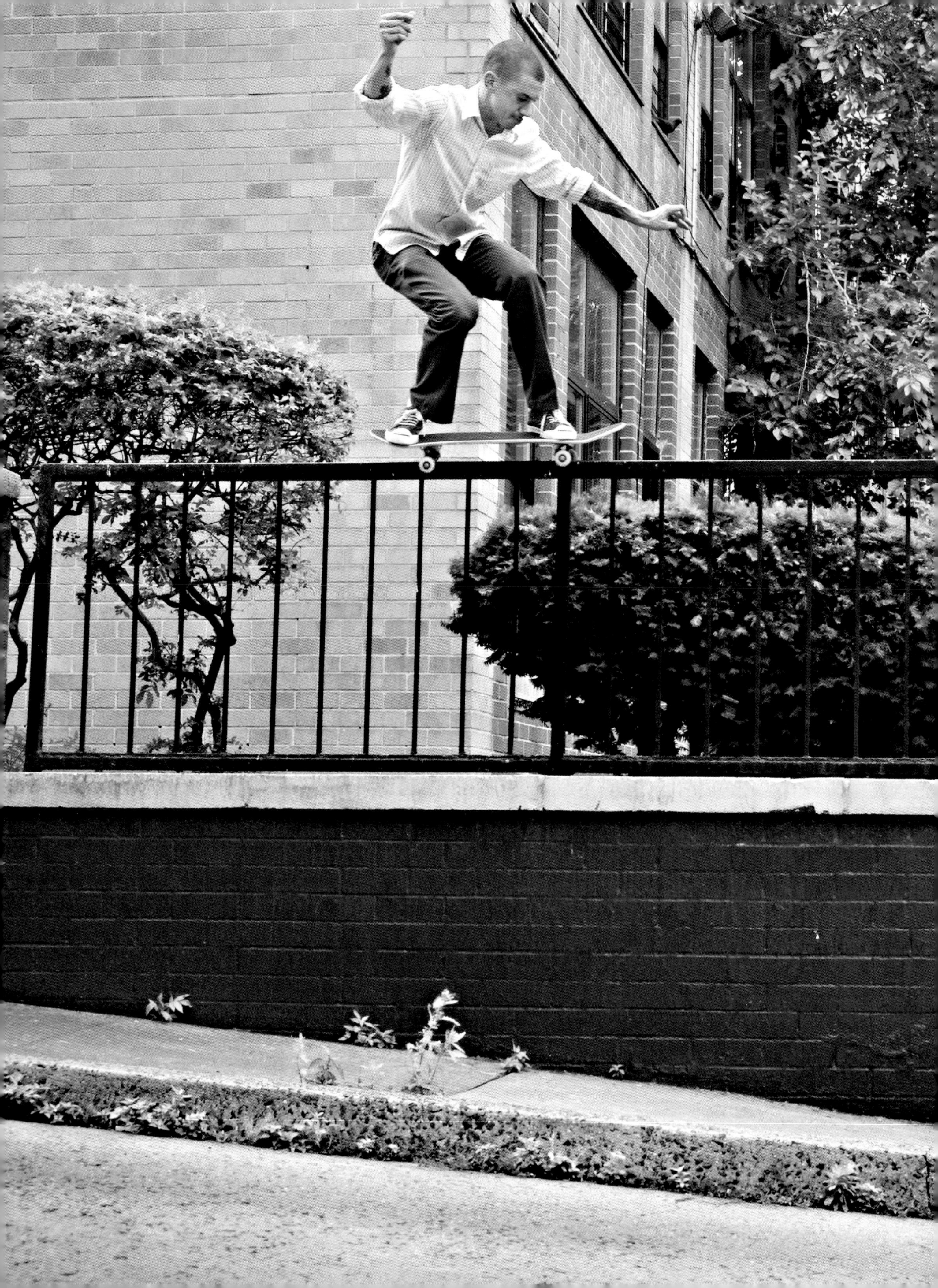

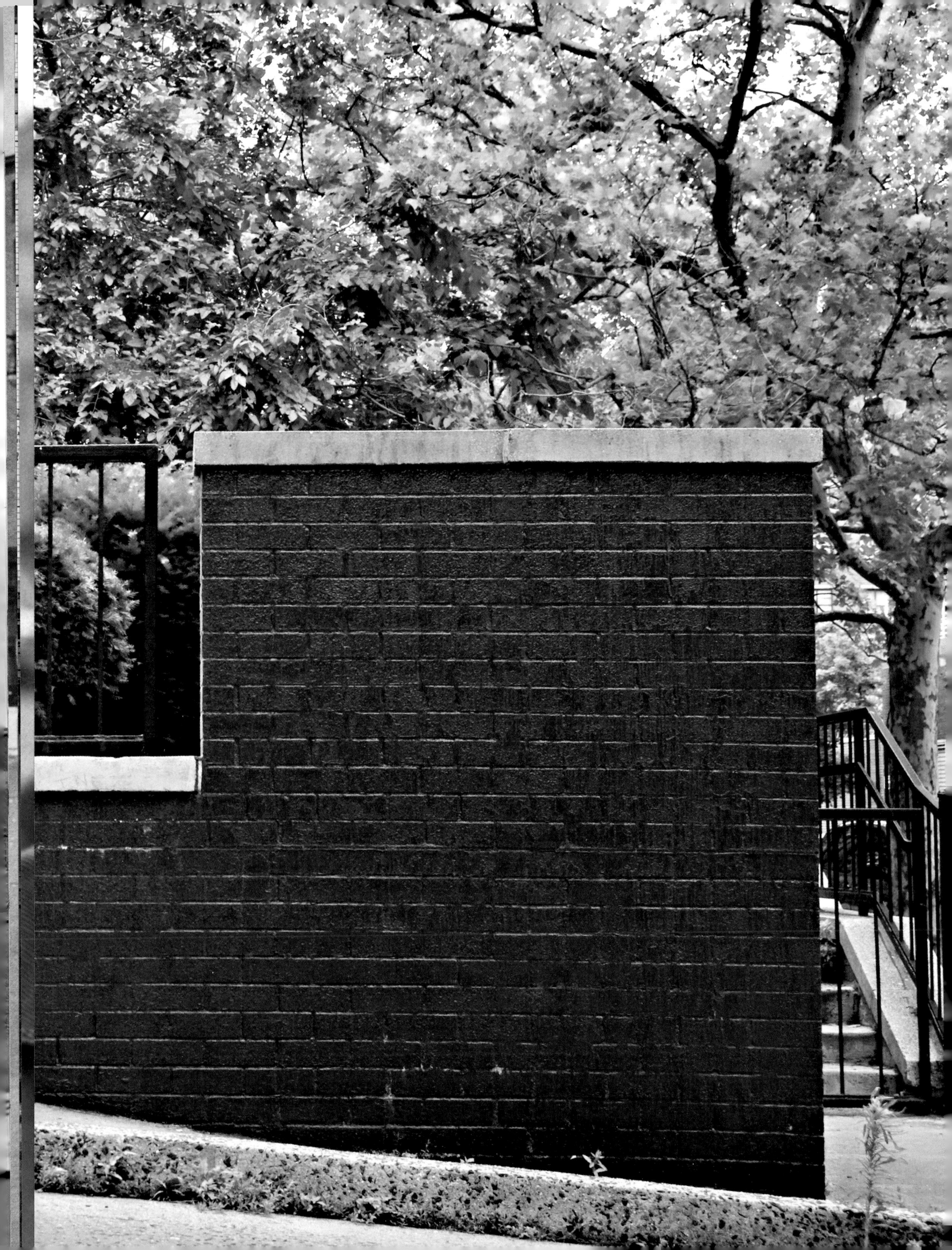

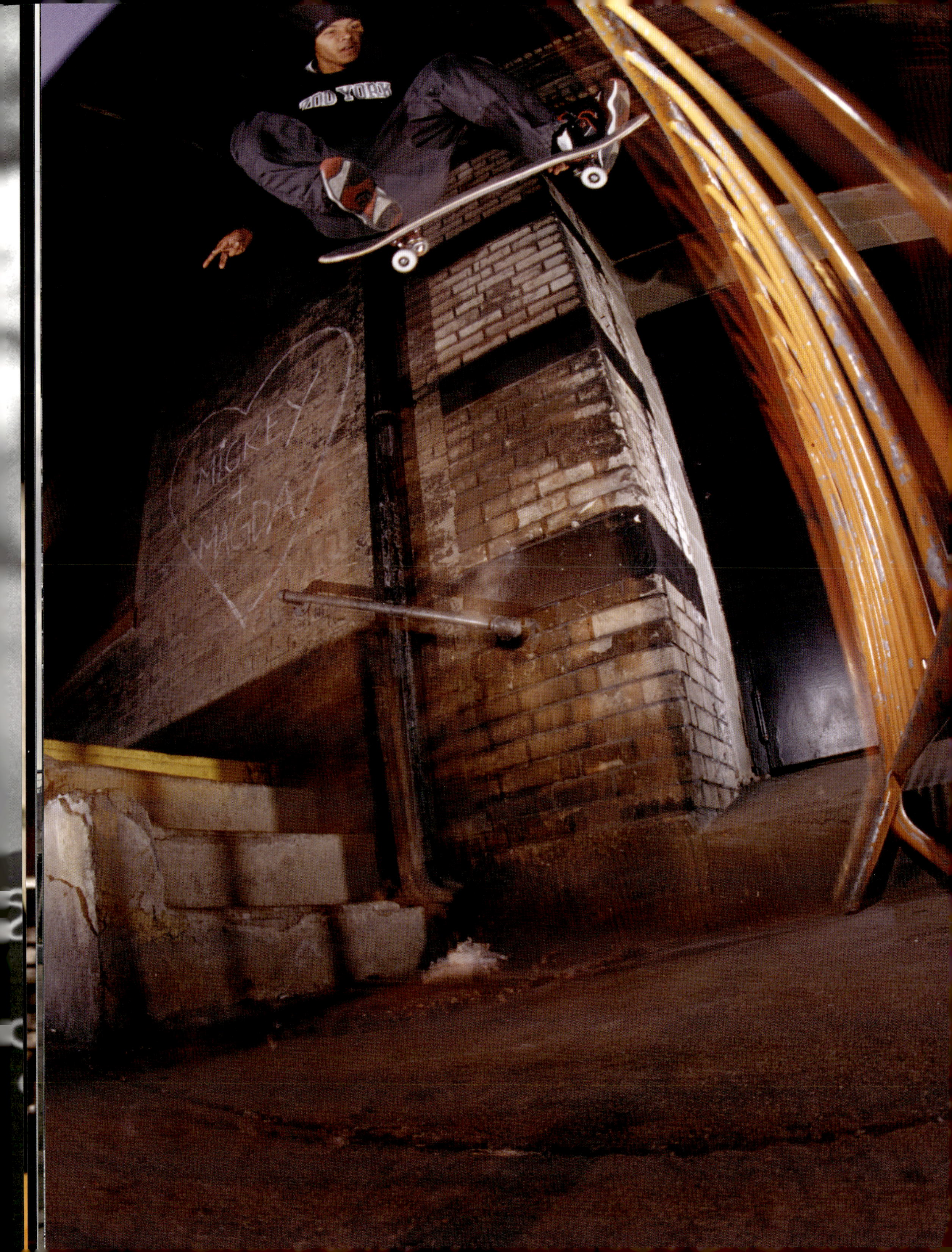
MICKEY
+
MAGDA

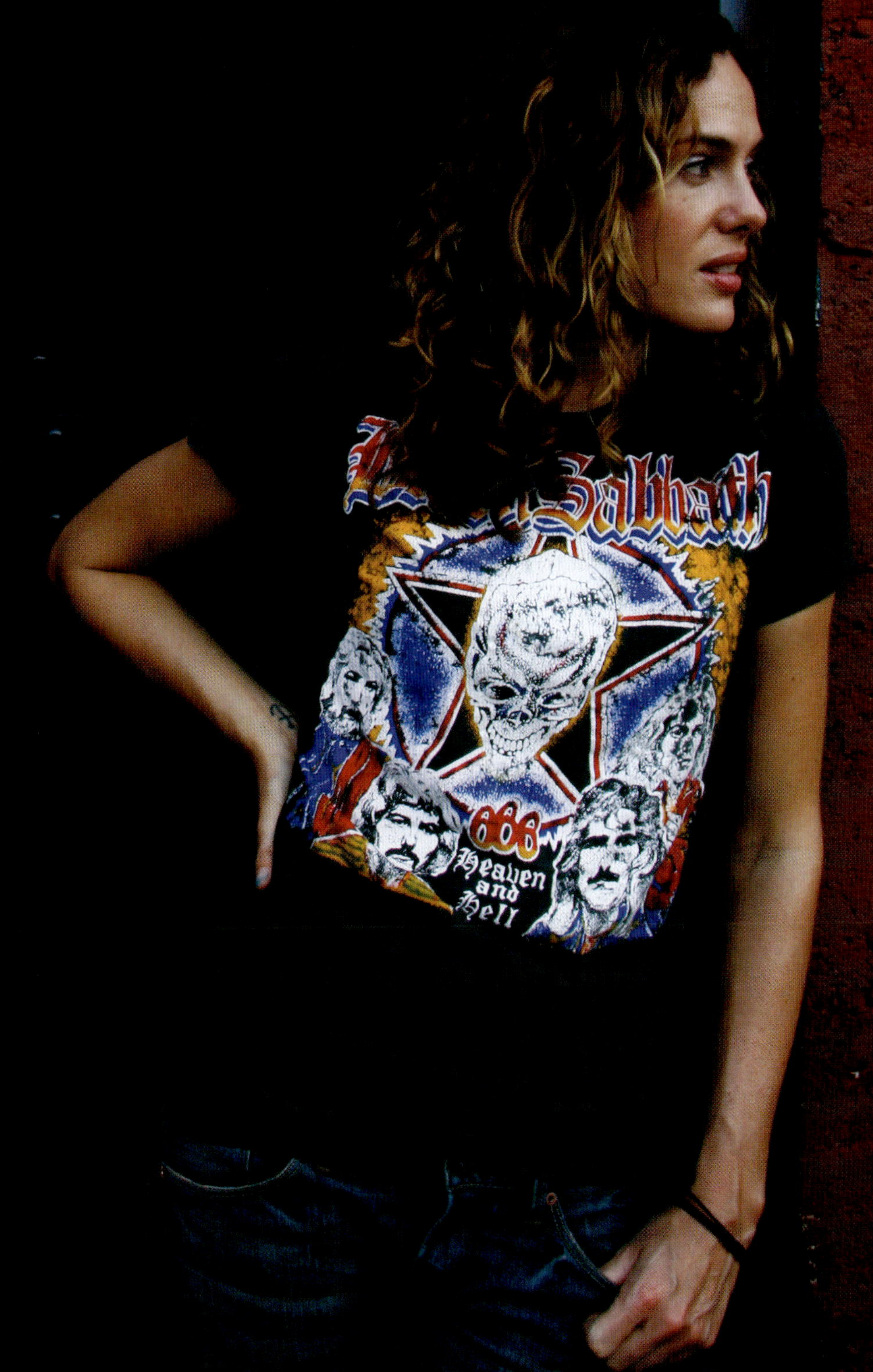
KCDC LTD
90 N 11 ST
Sabbath
666
Heaven and Hell

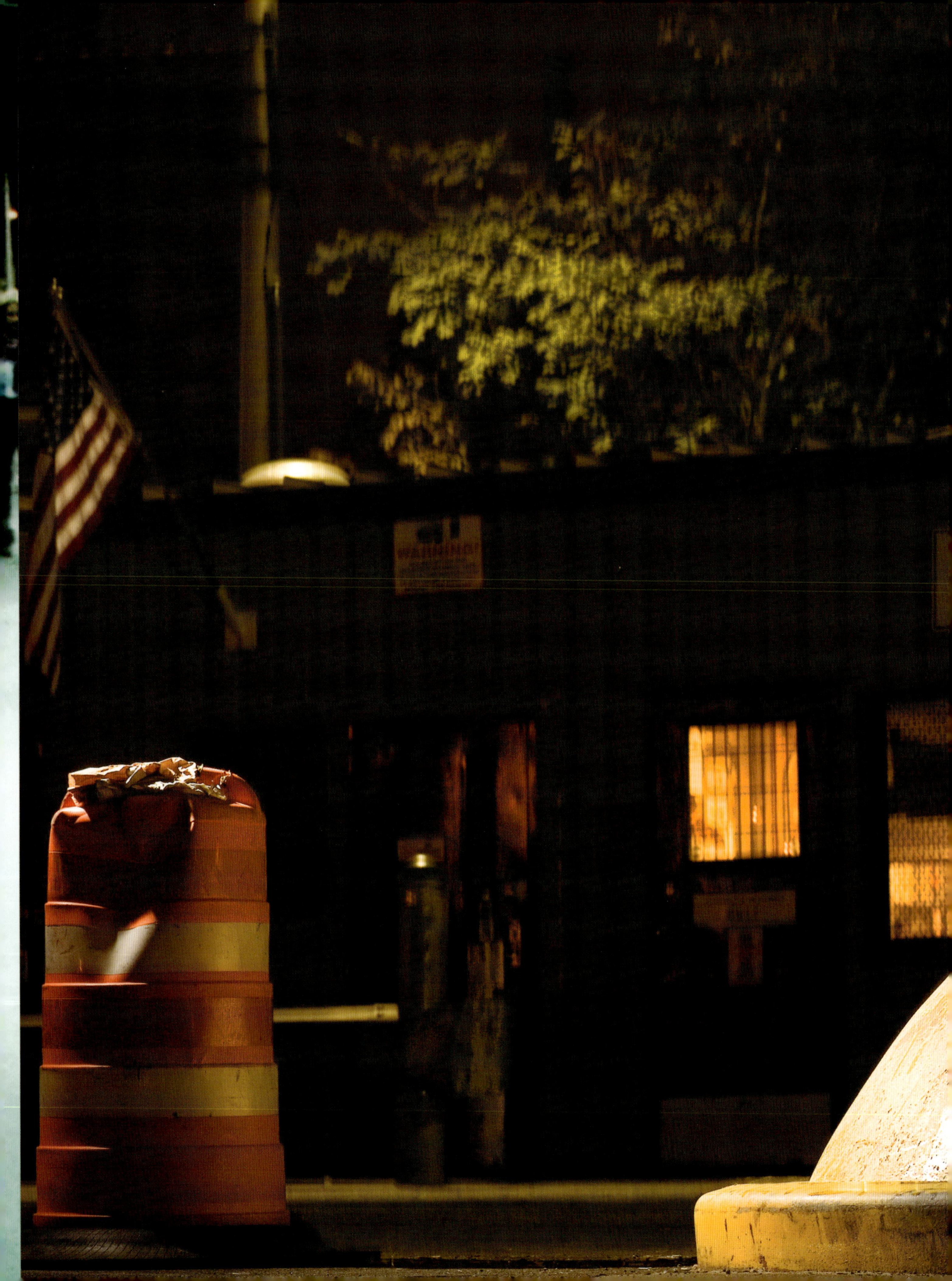

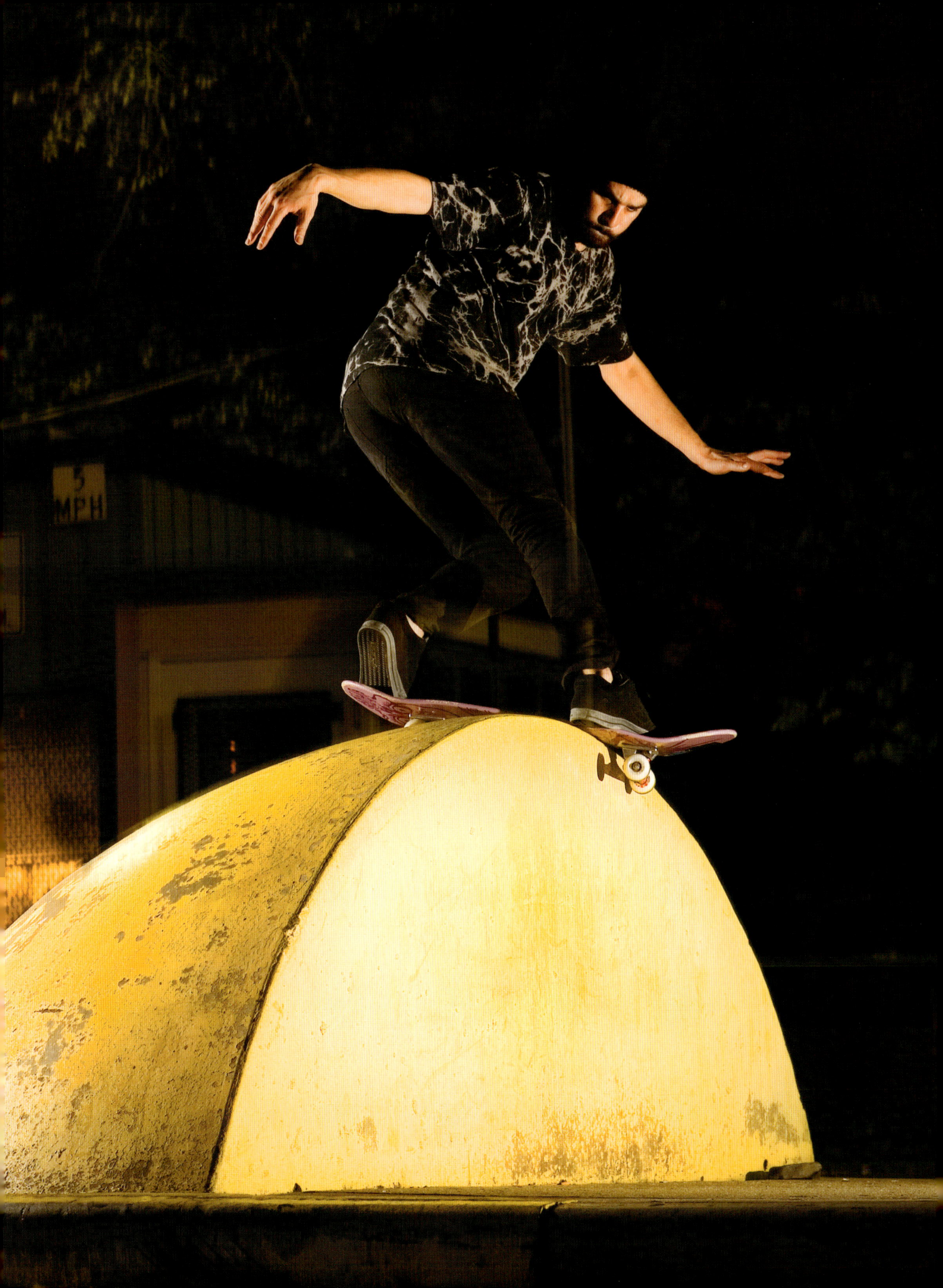
5
MPH

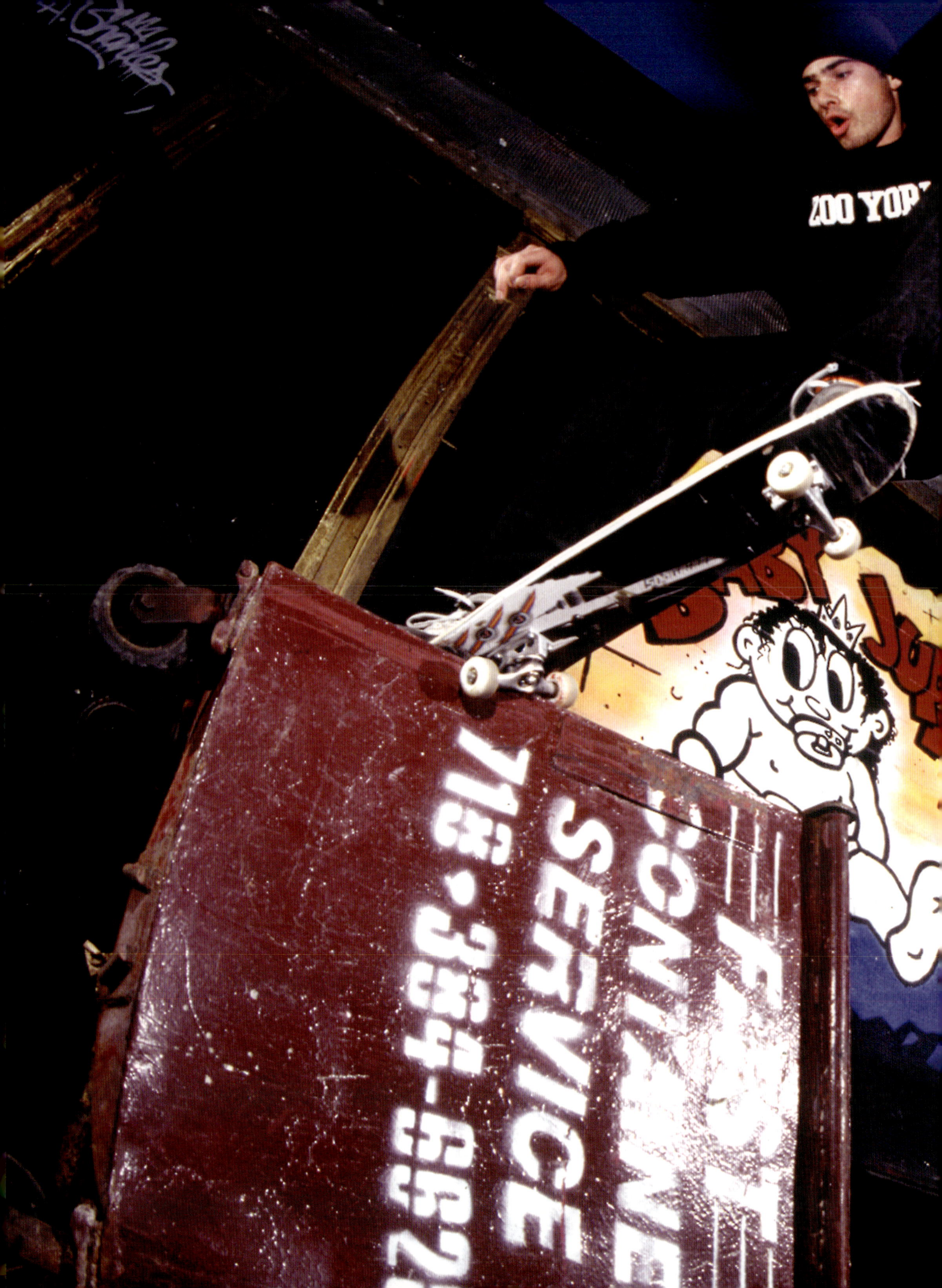
SERVICE

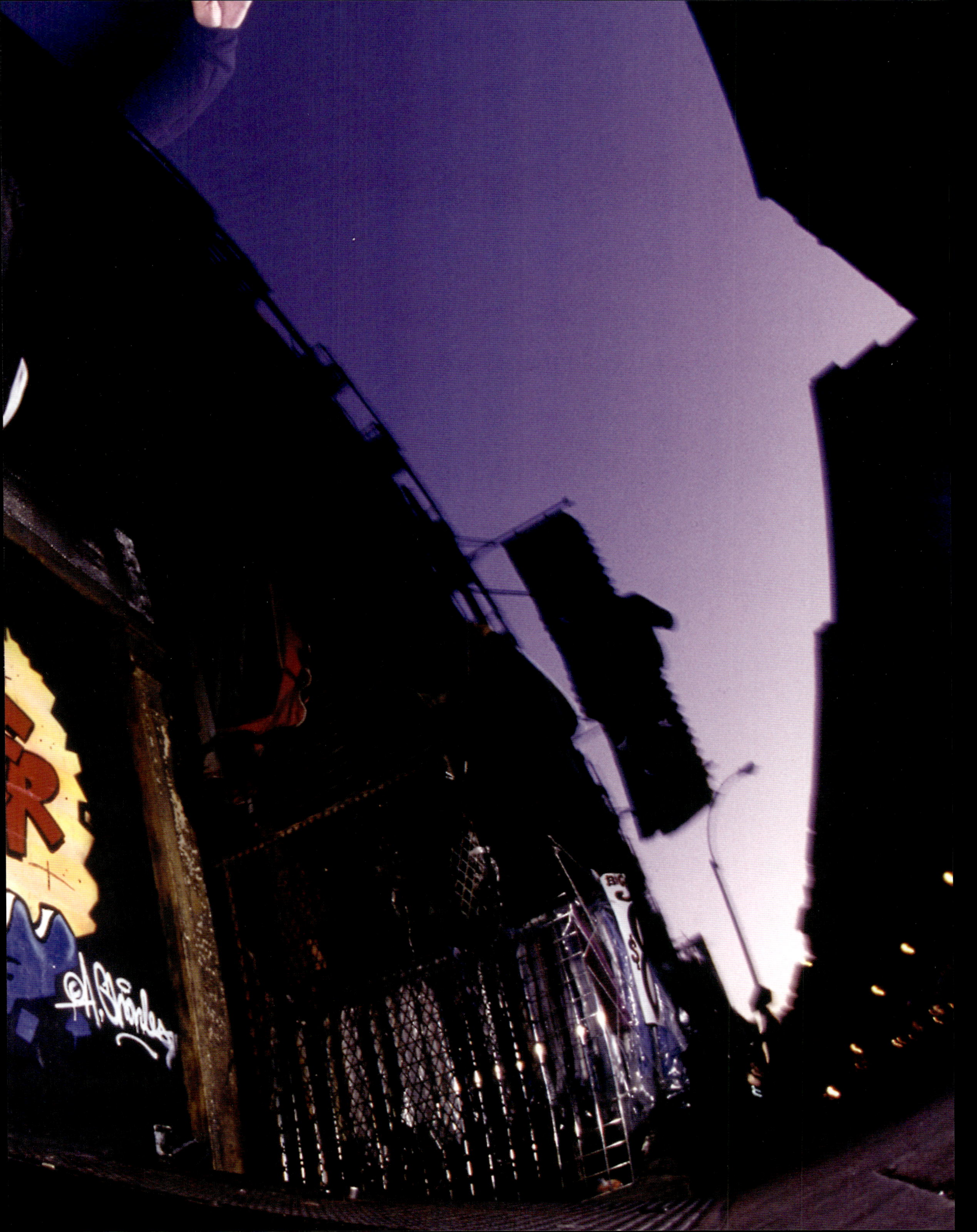

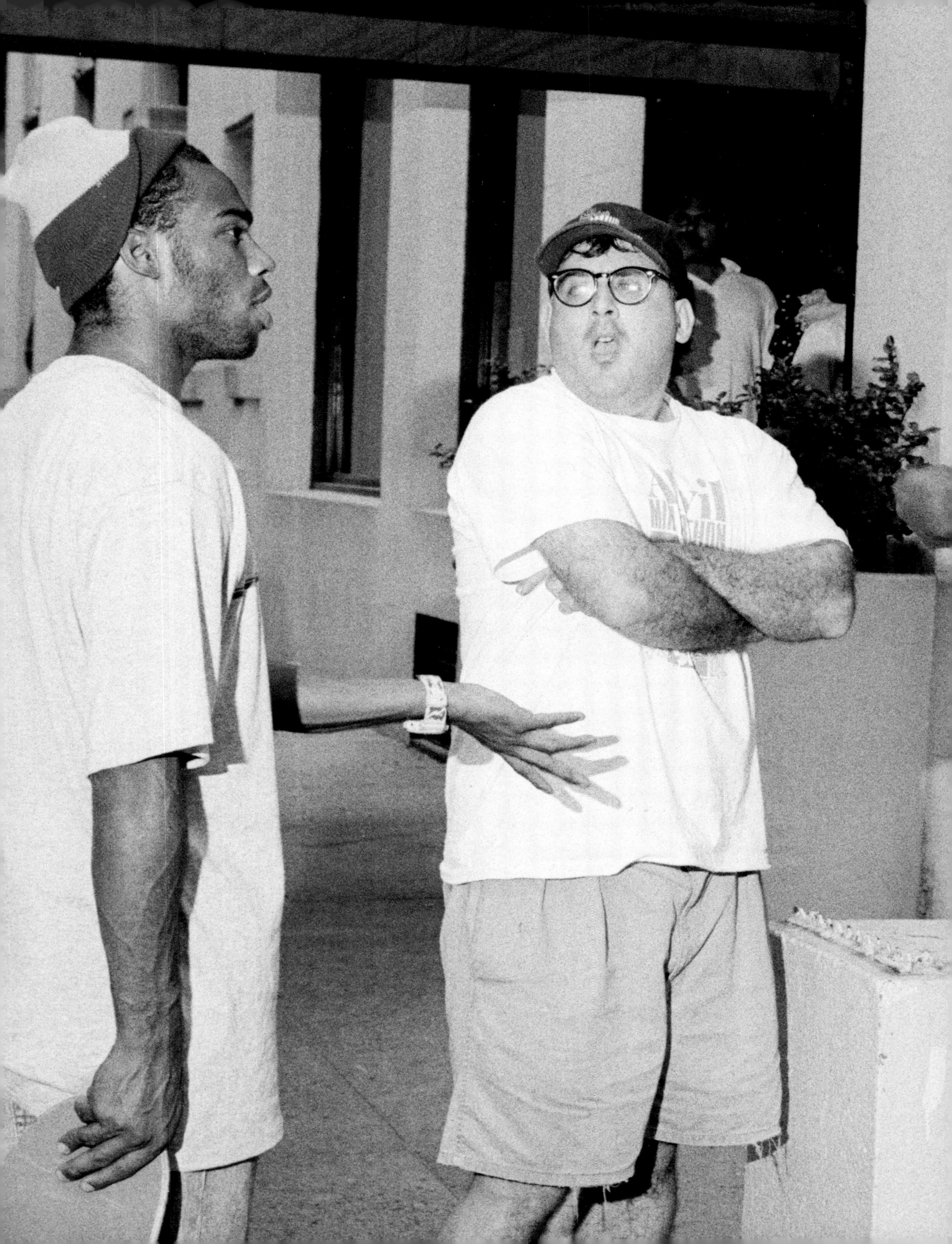

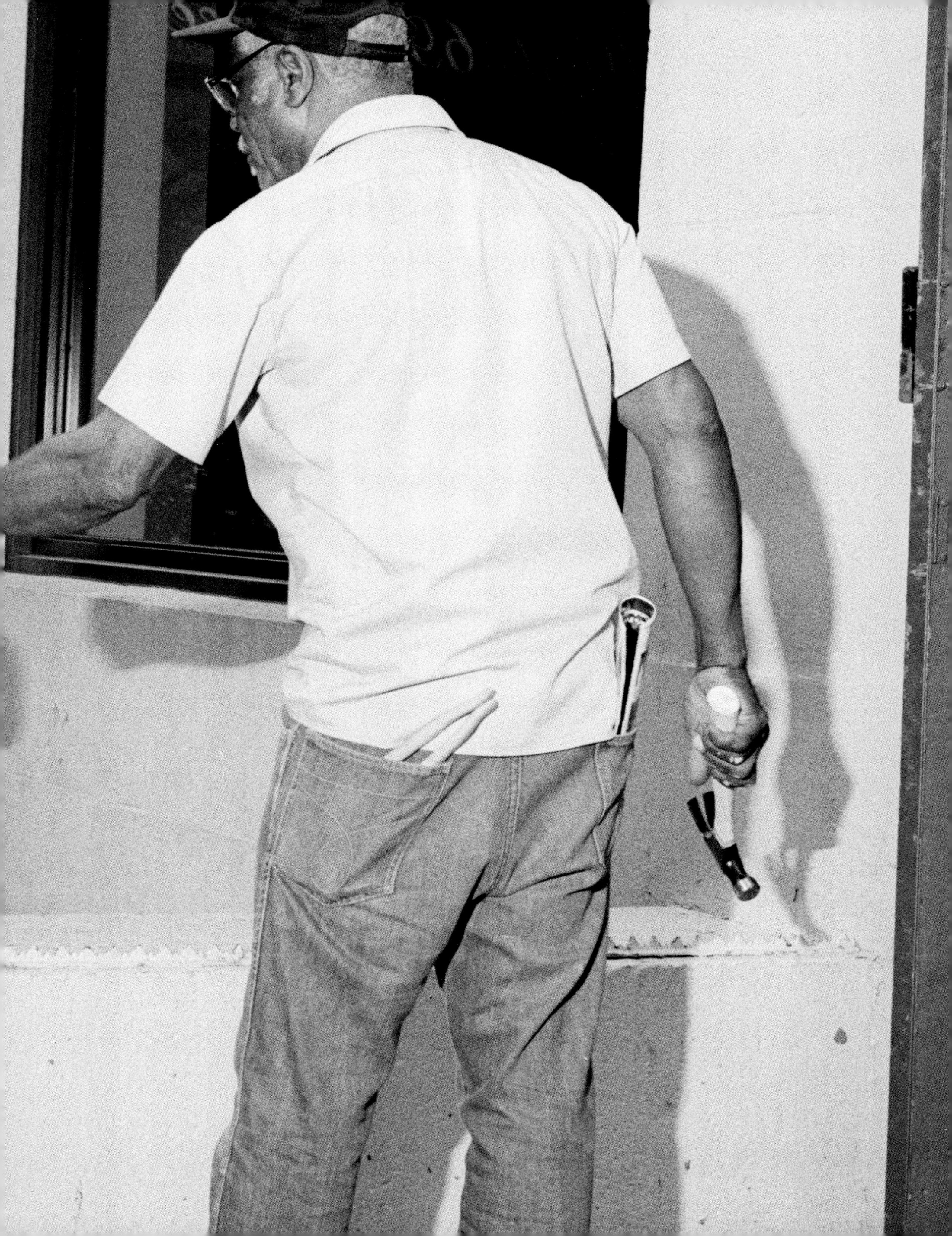

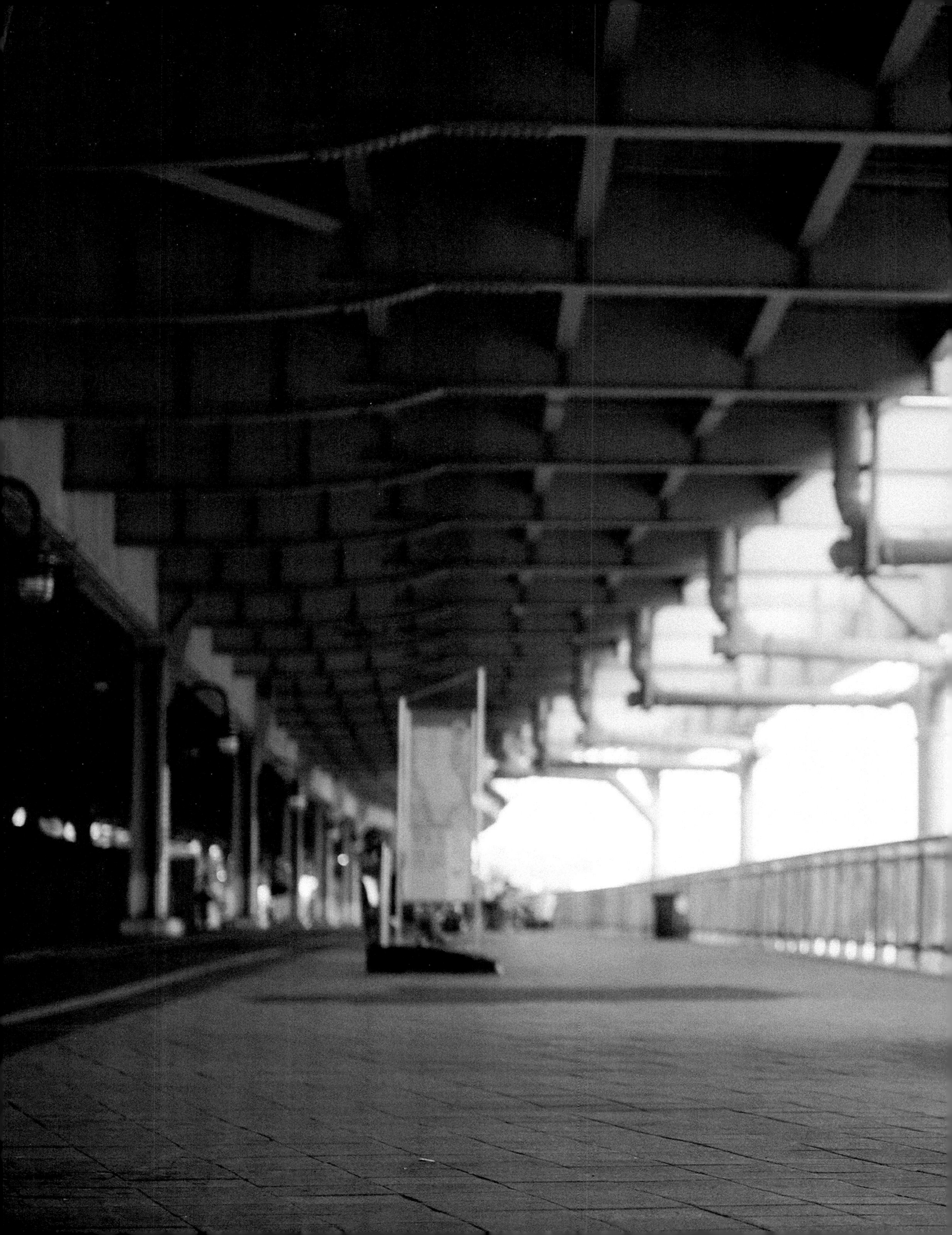

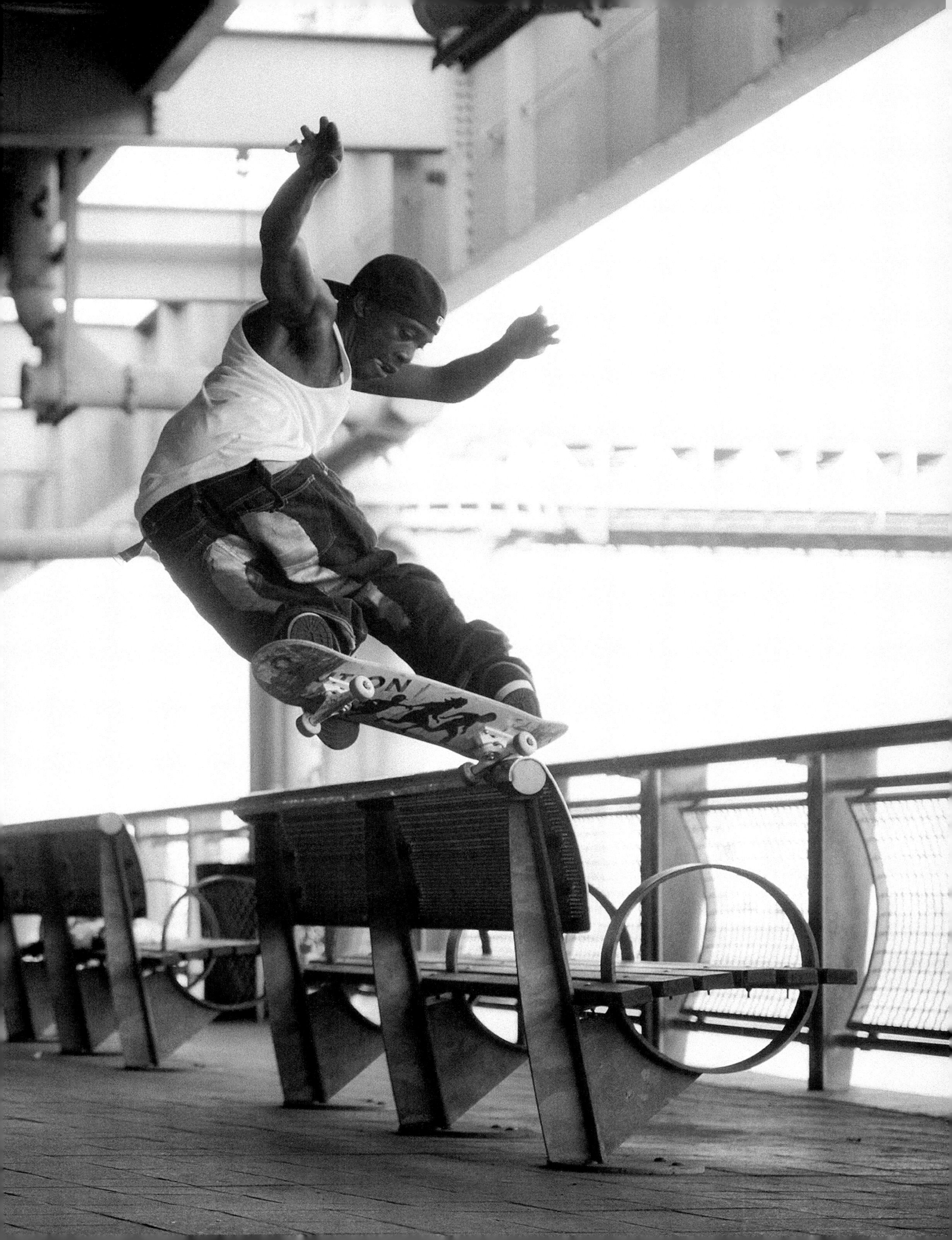

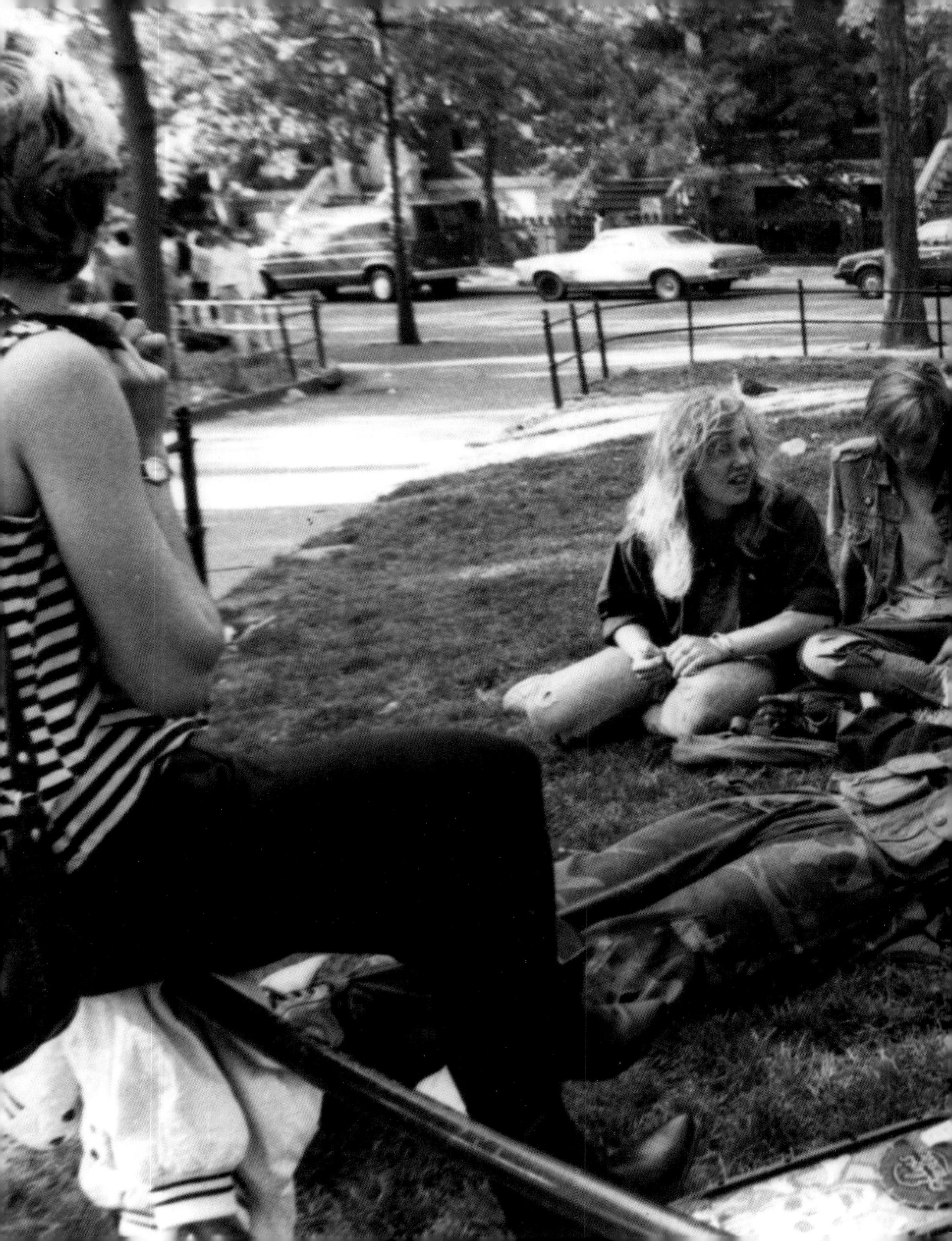

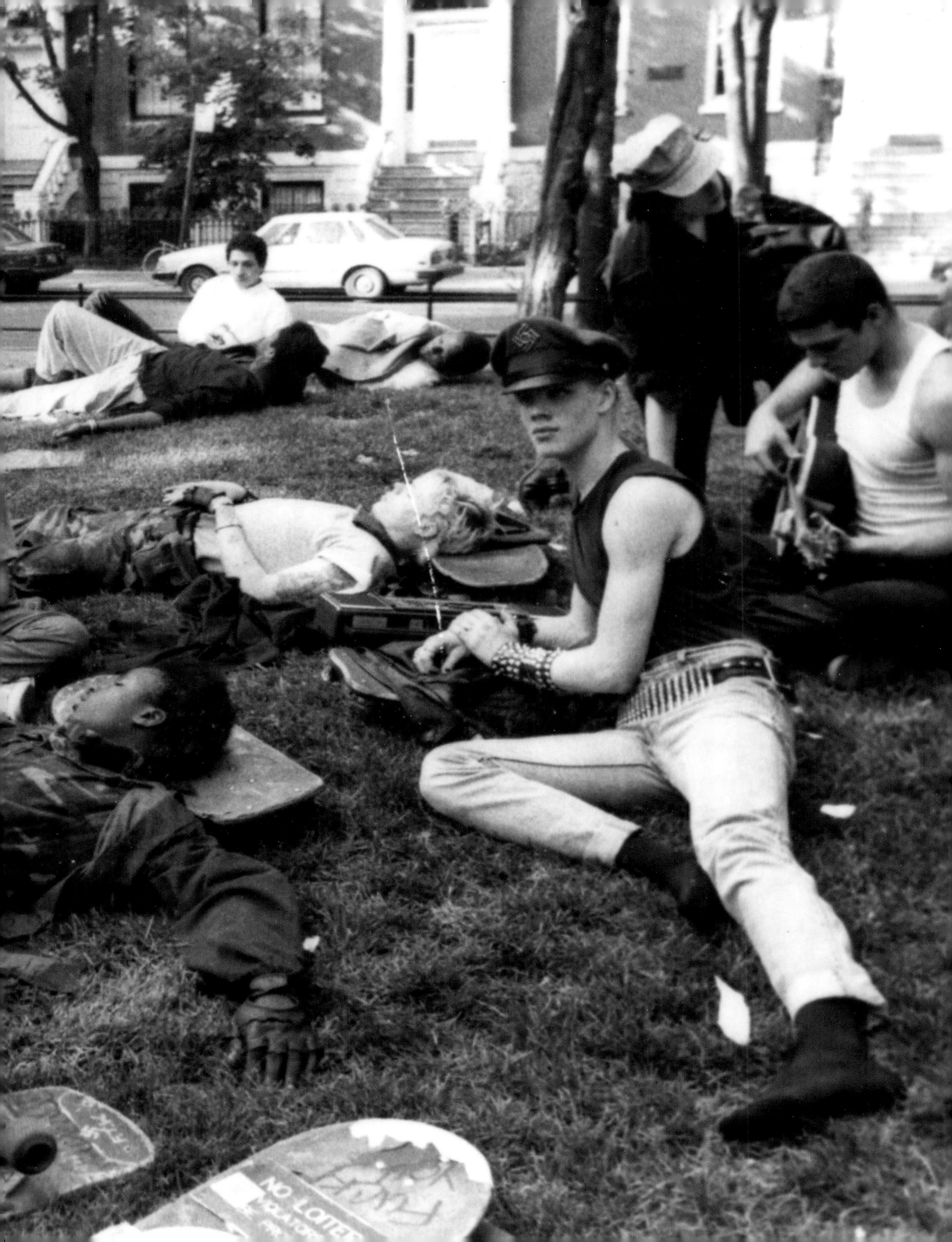
NO LOITER

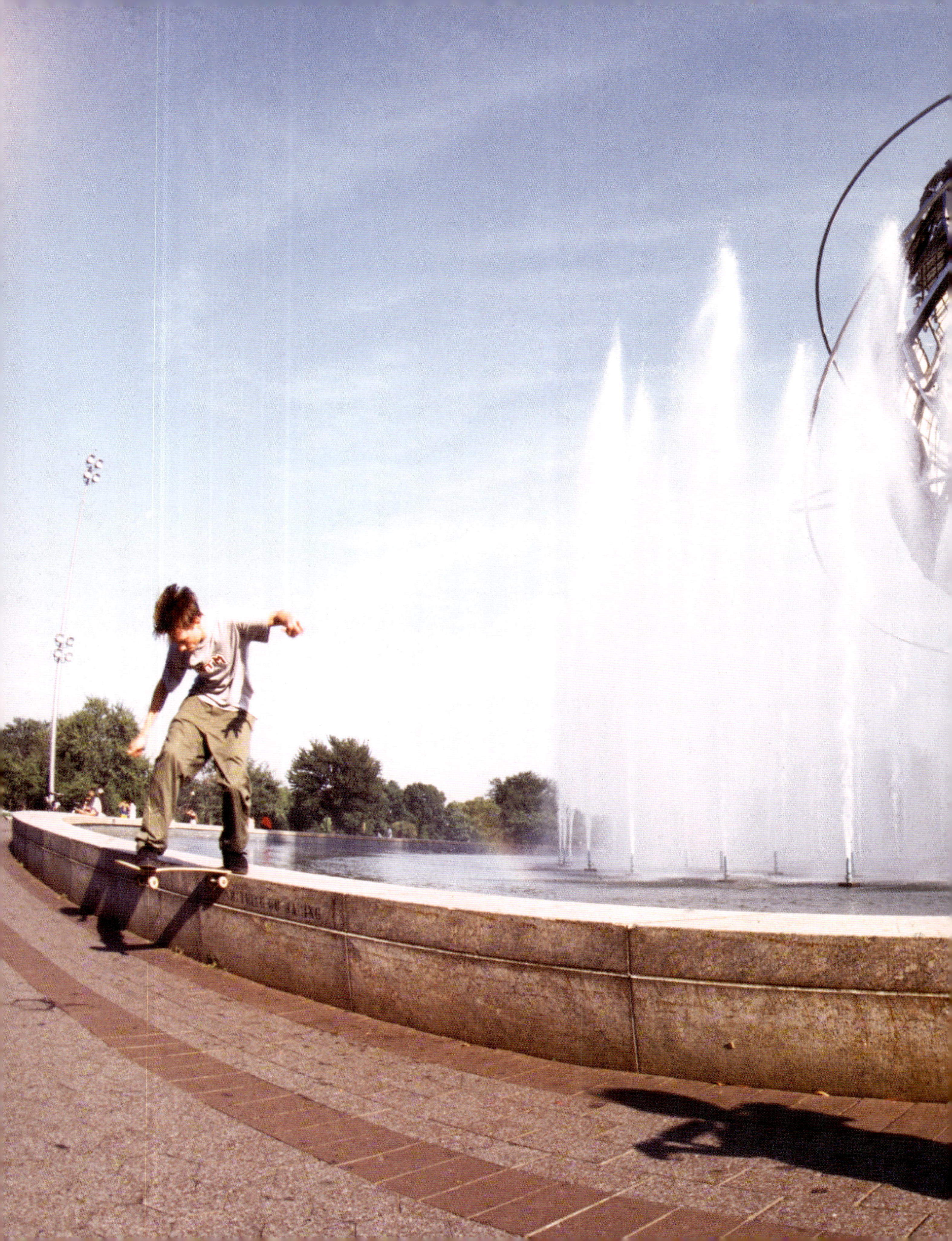

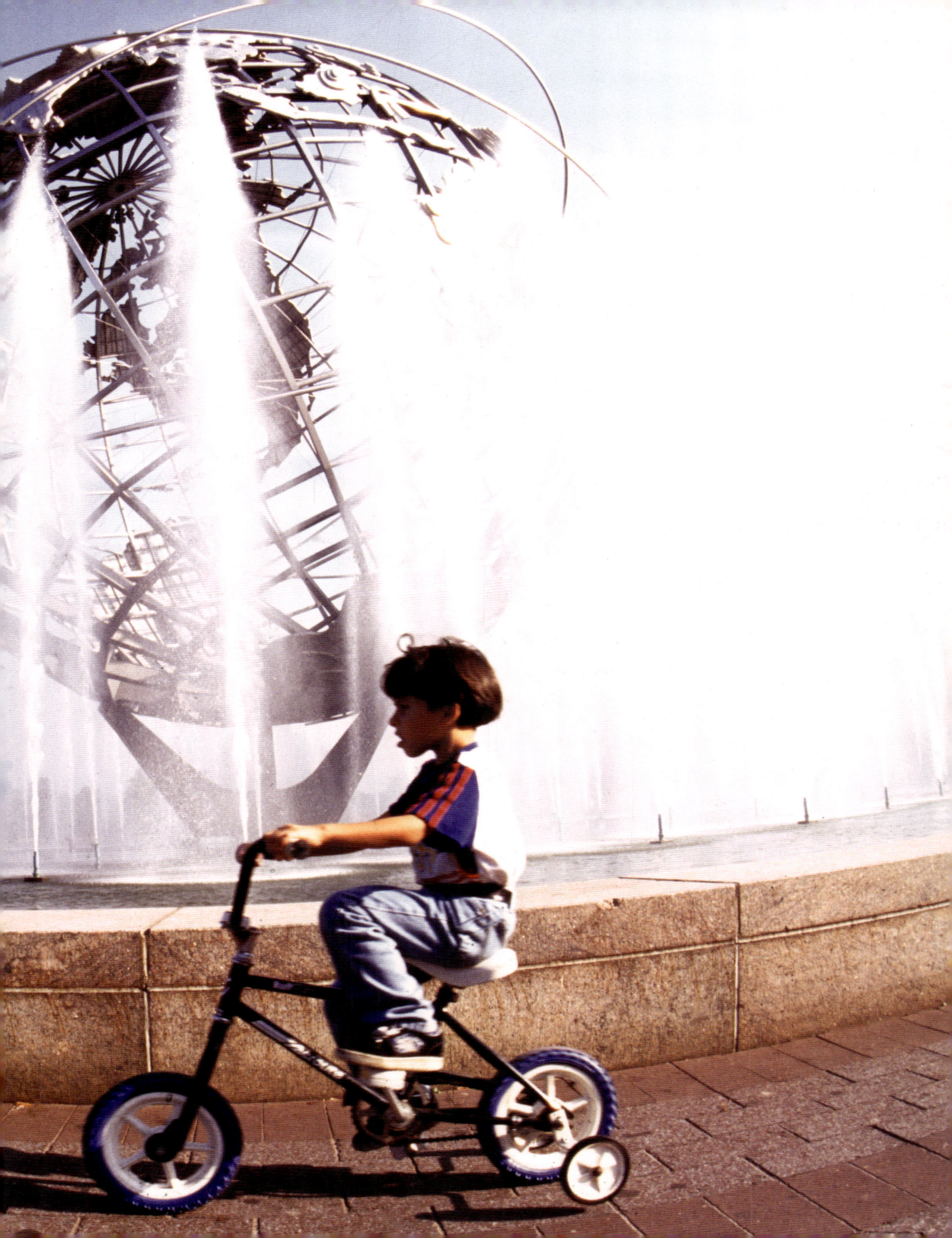

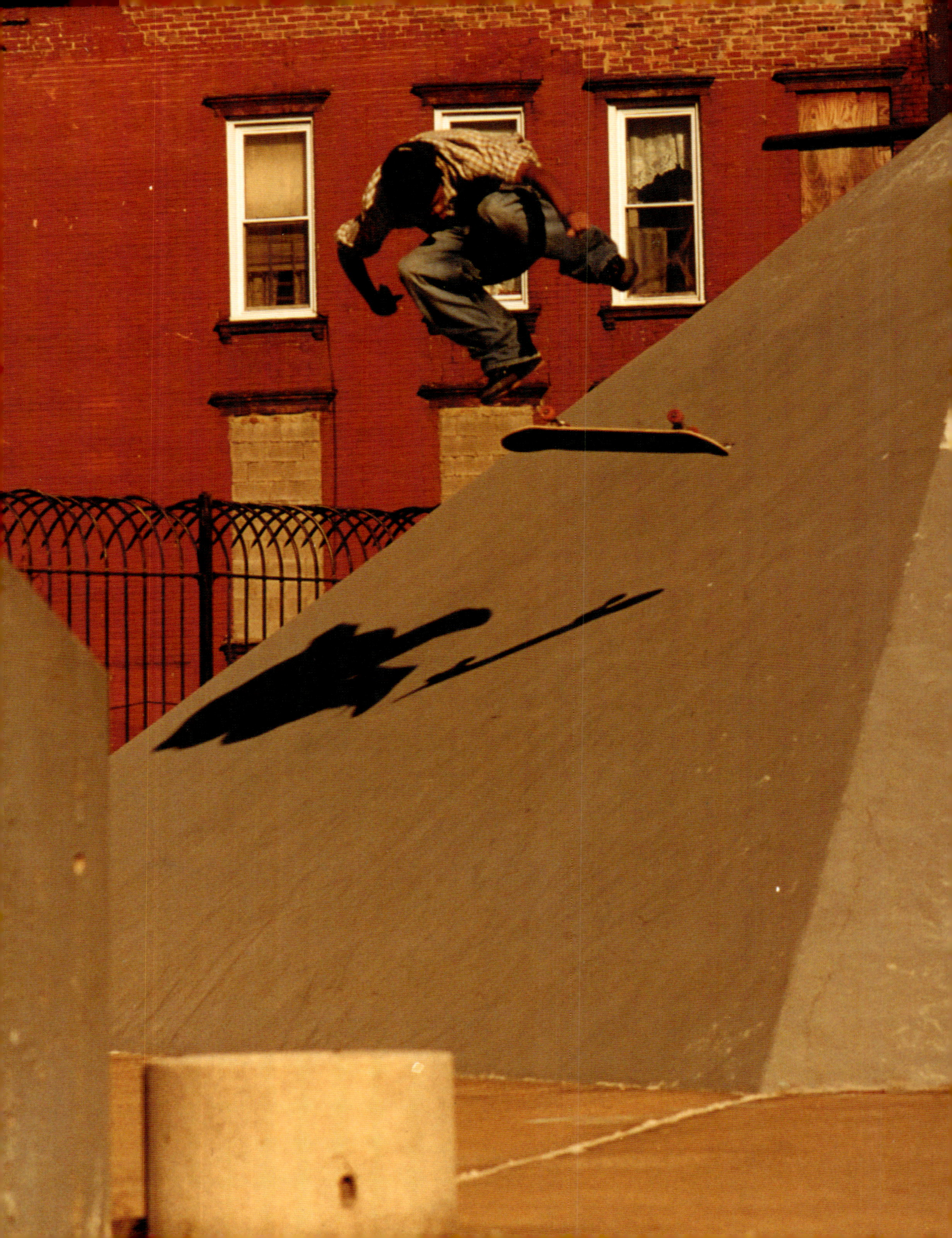

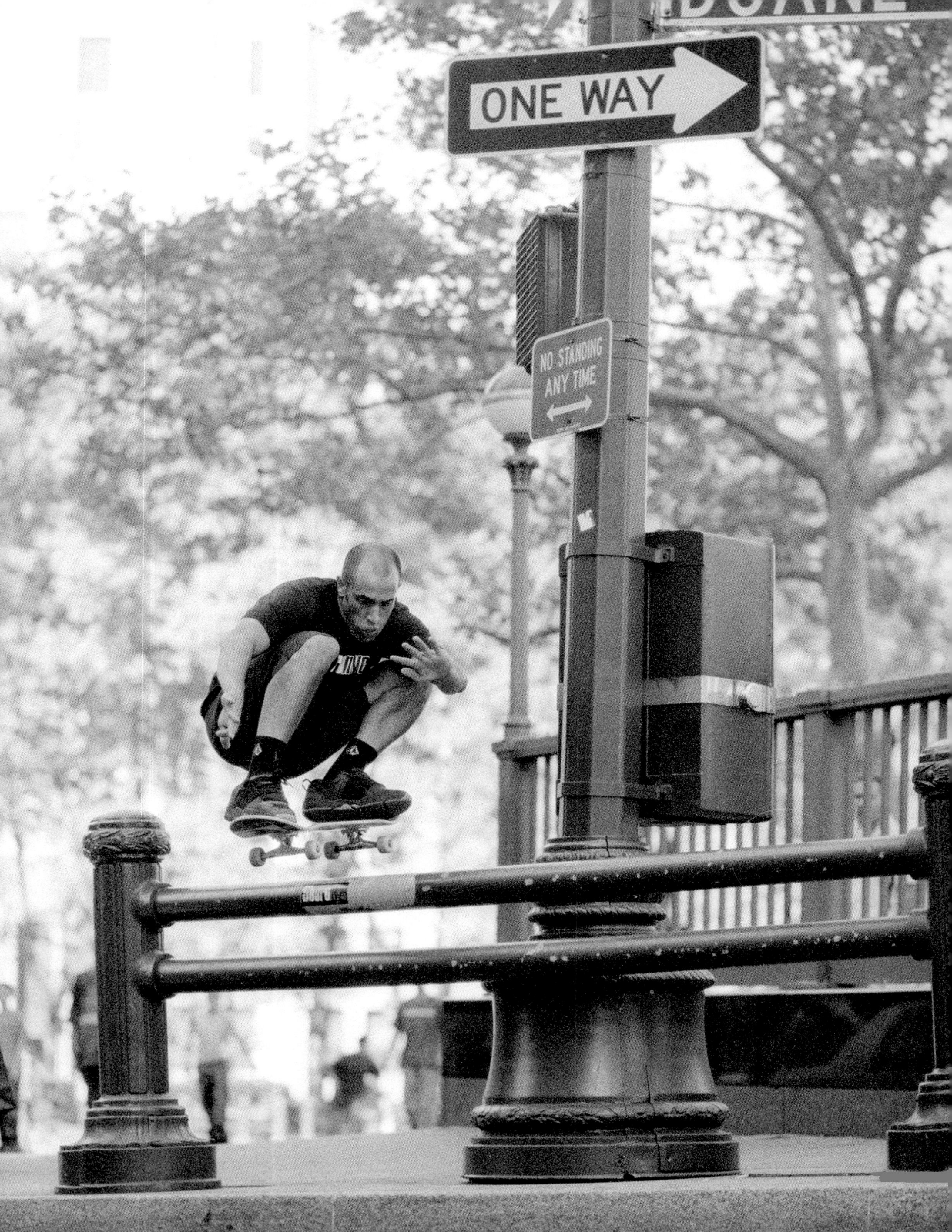
ONE WAY
NO STANDING
ANY TIME

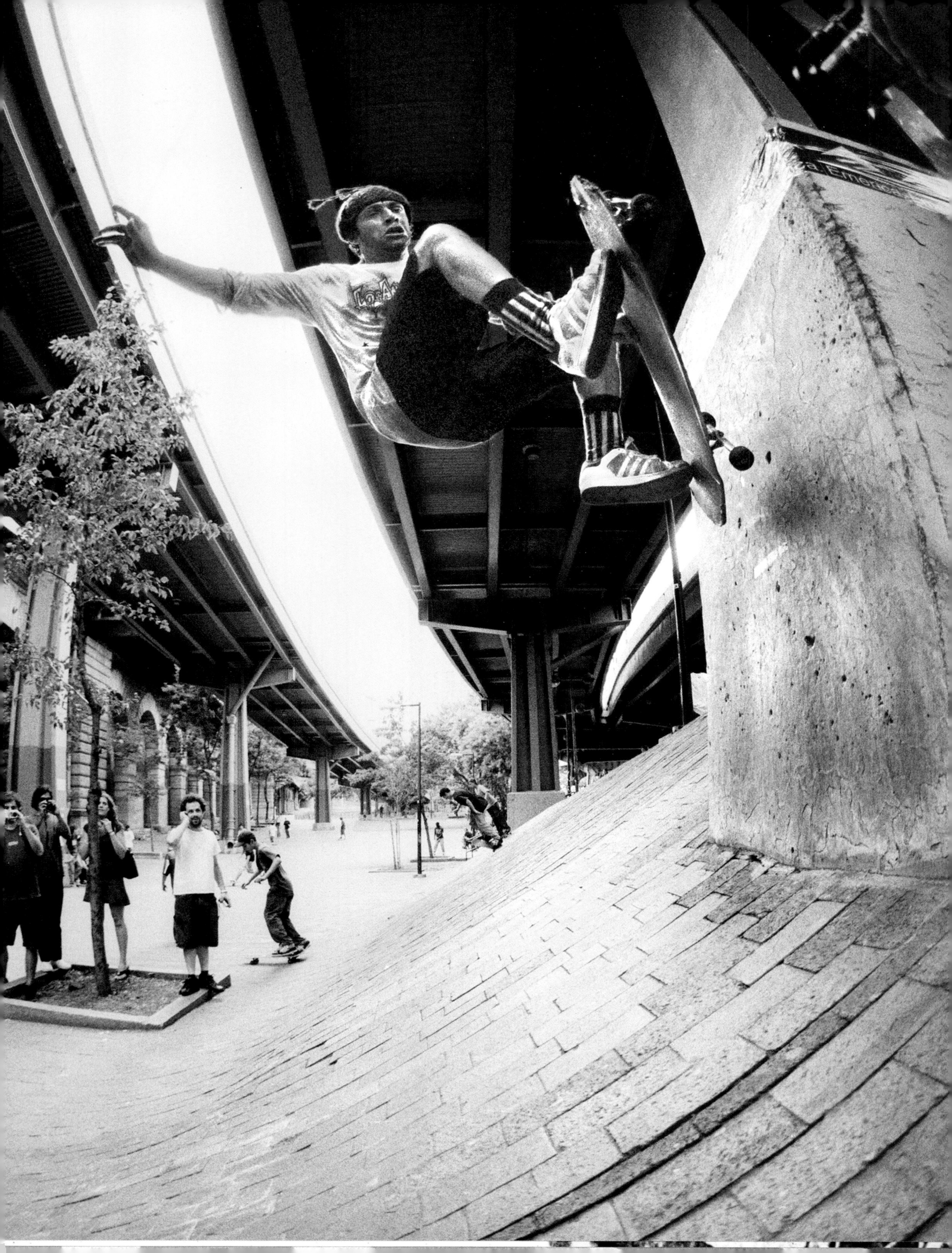

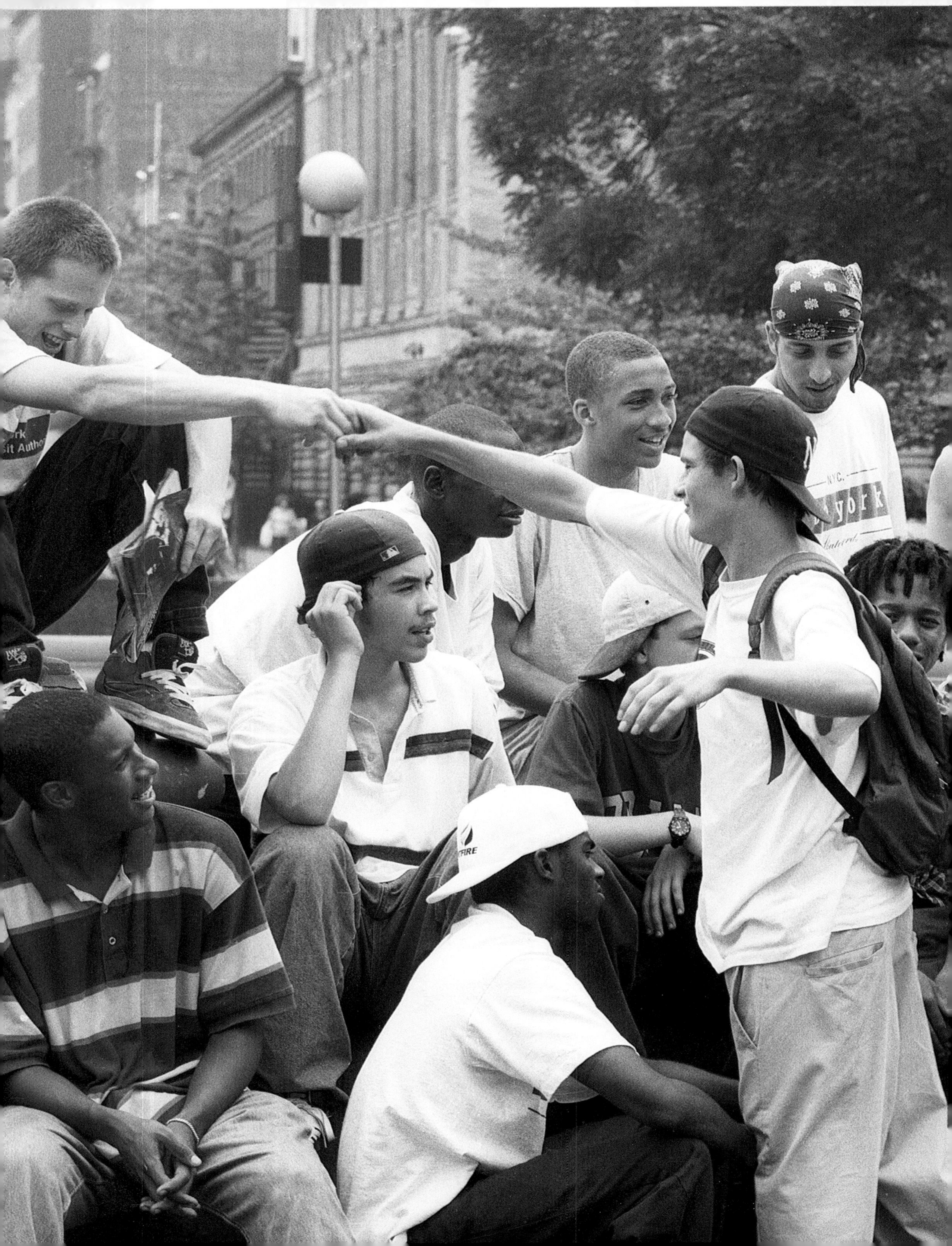

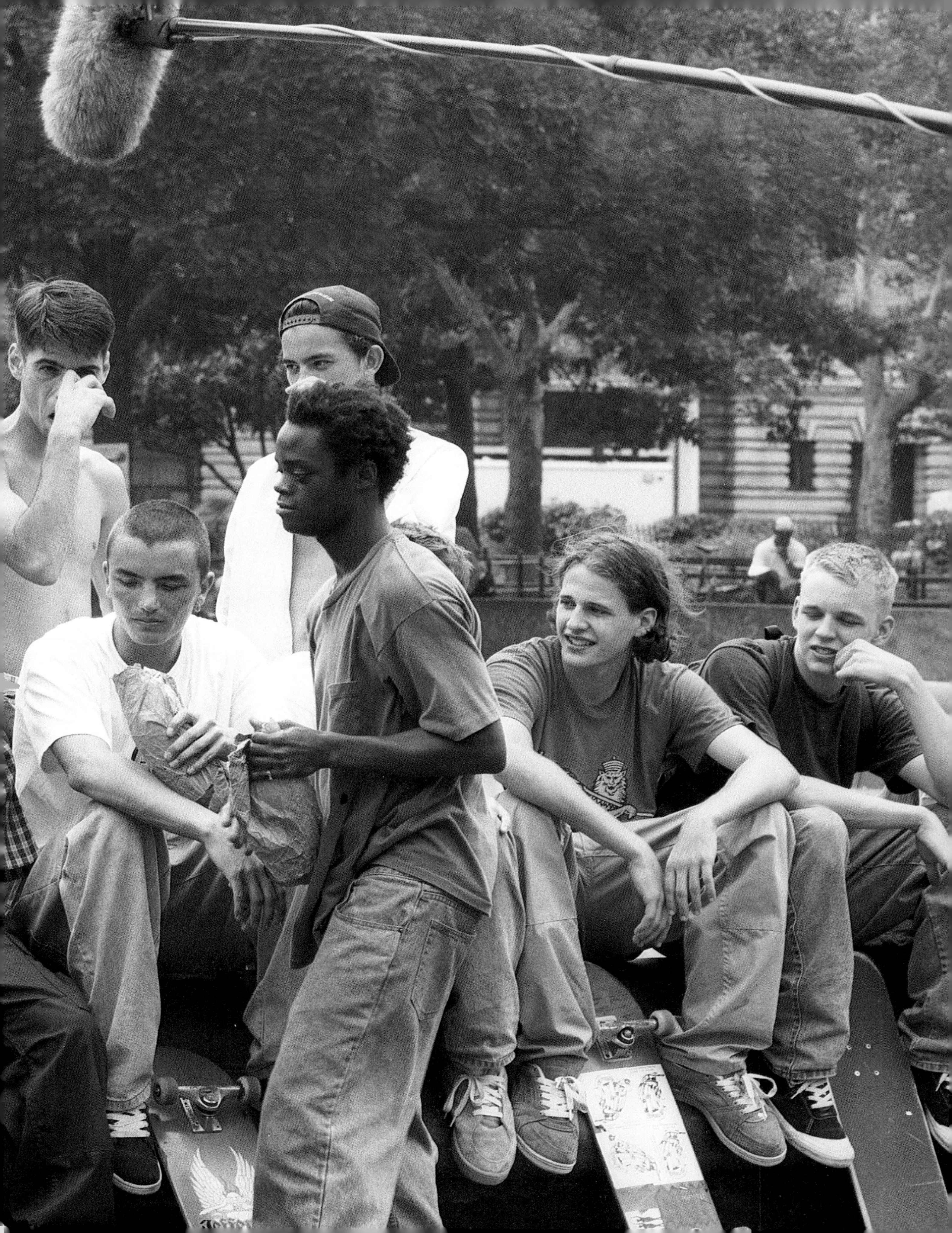

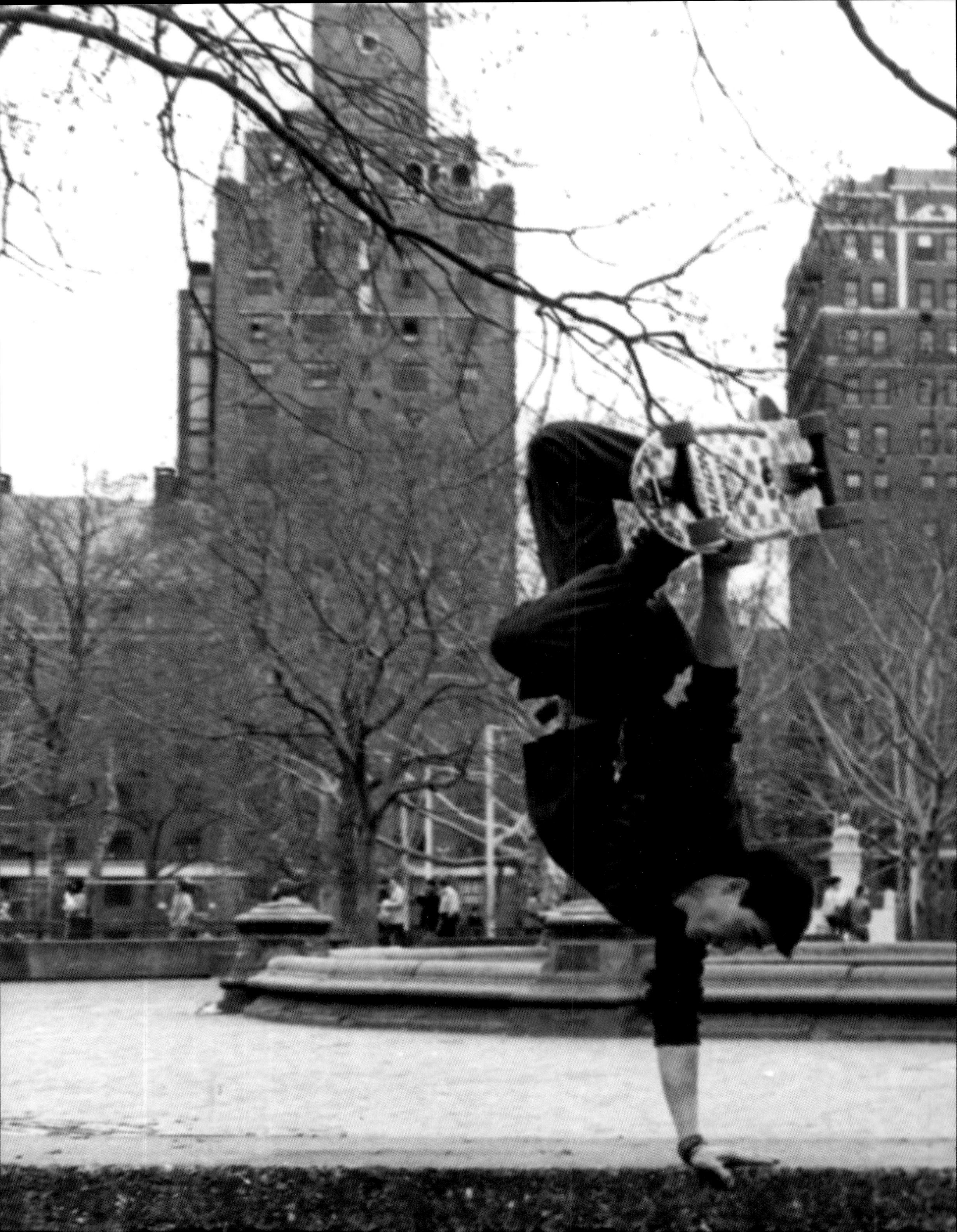

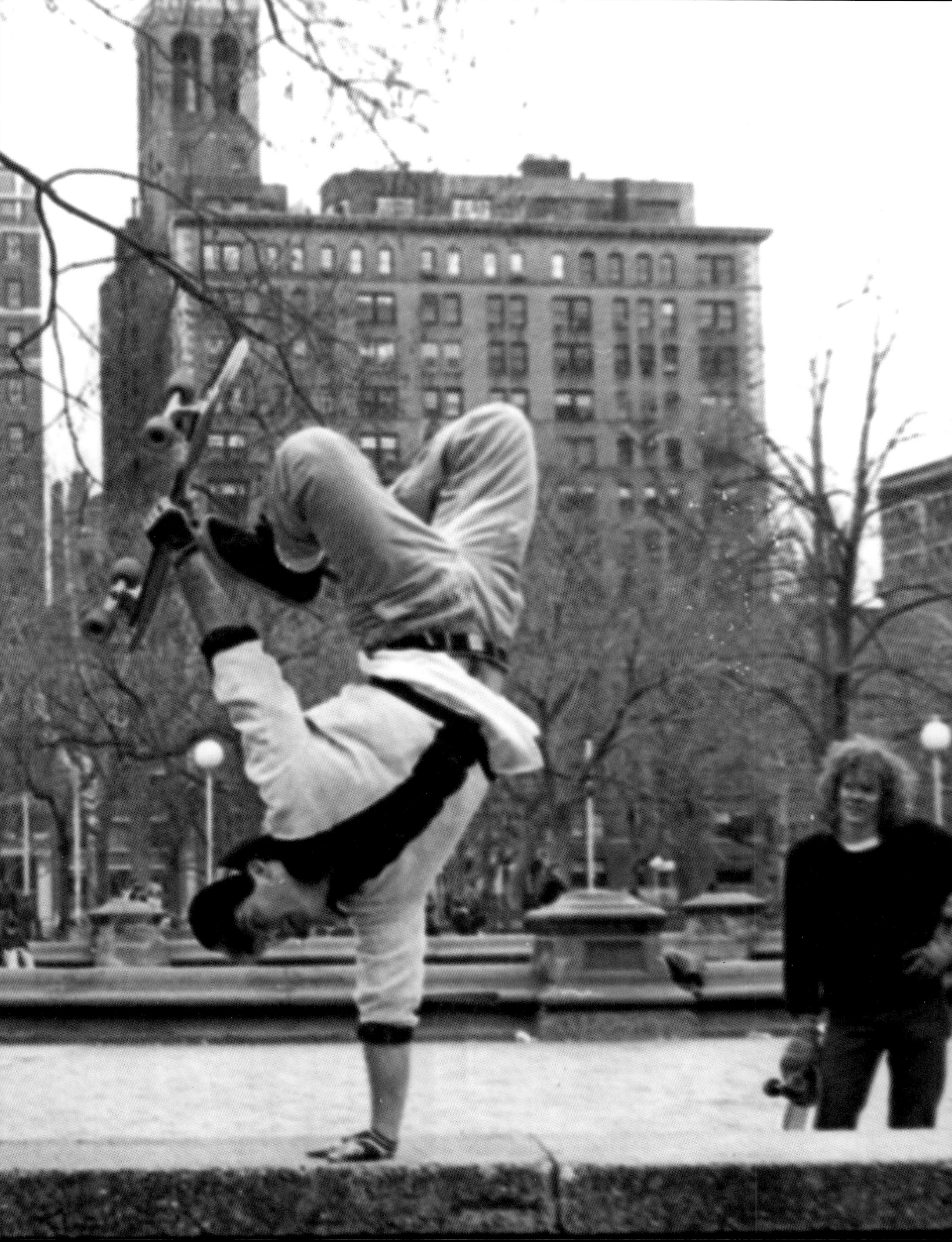

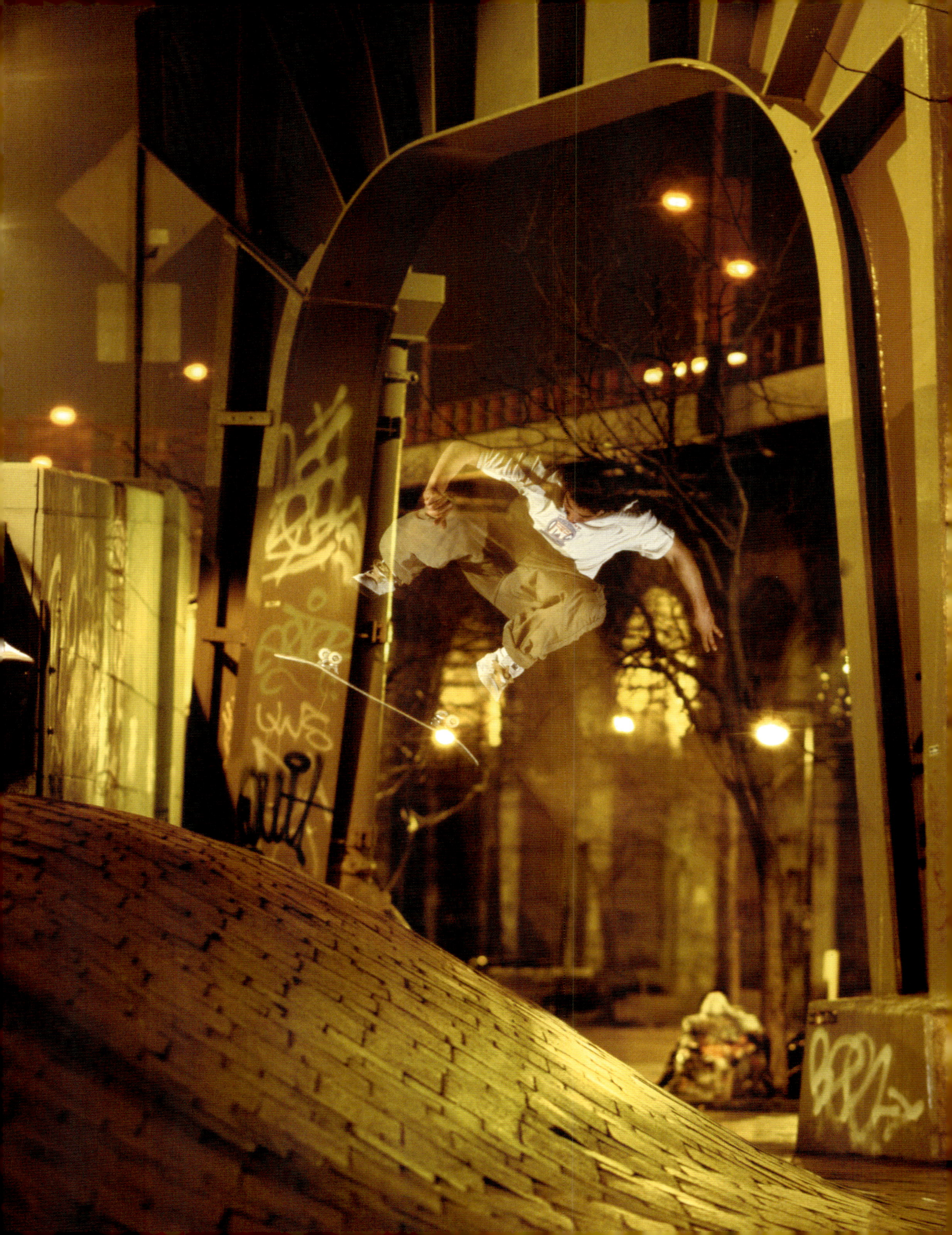

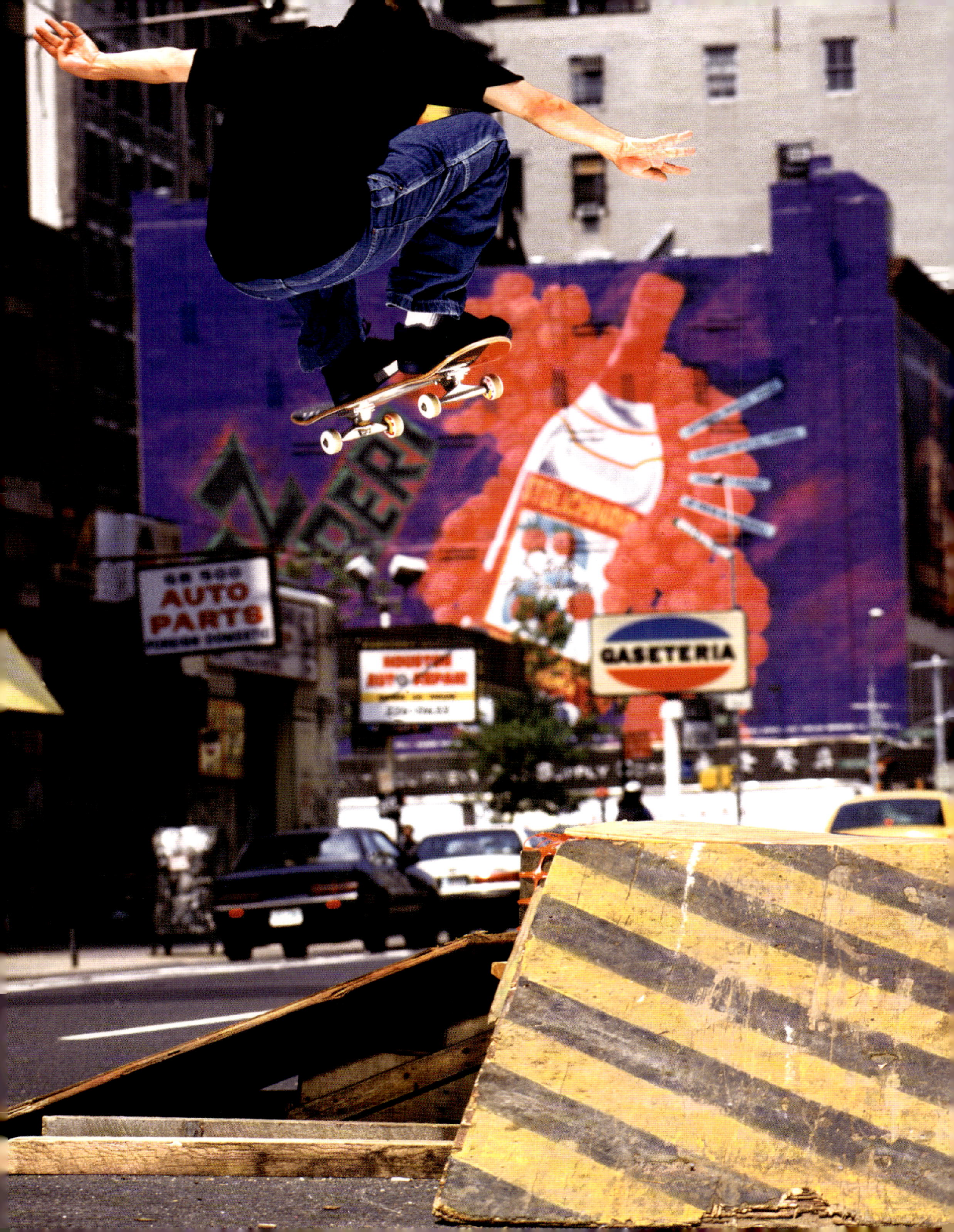
AUTO
PARTS
GASETERIA

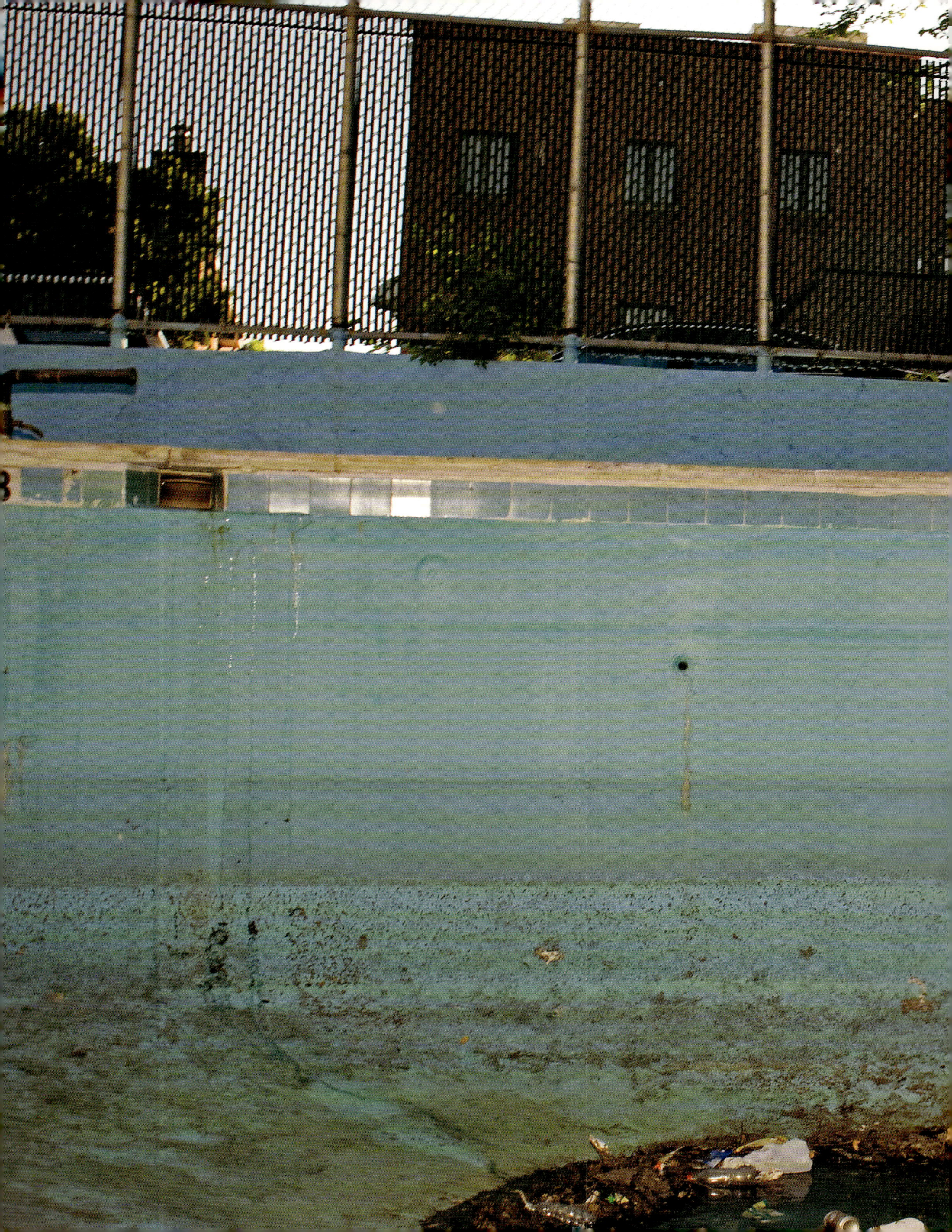

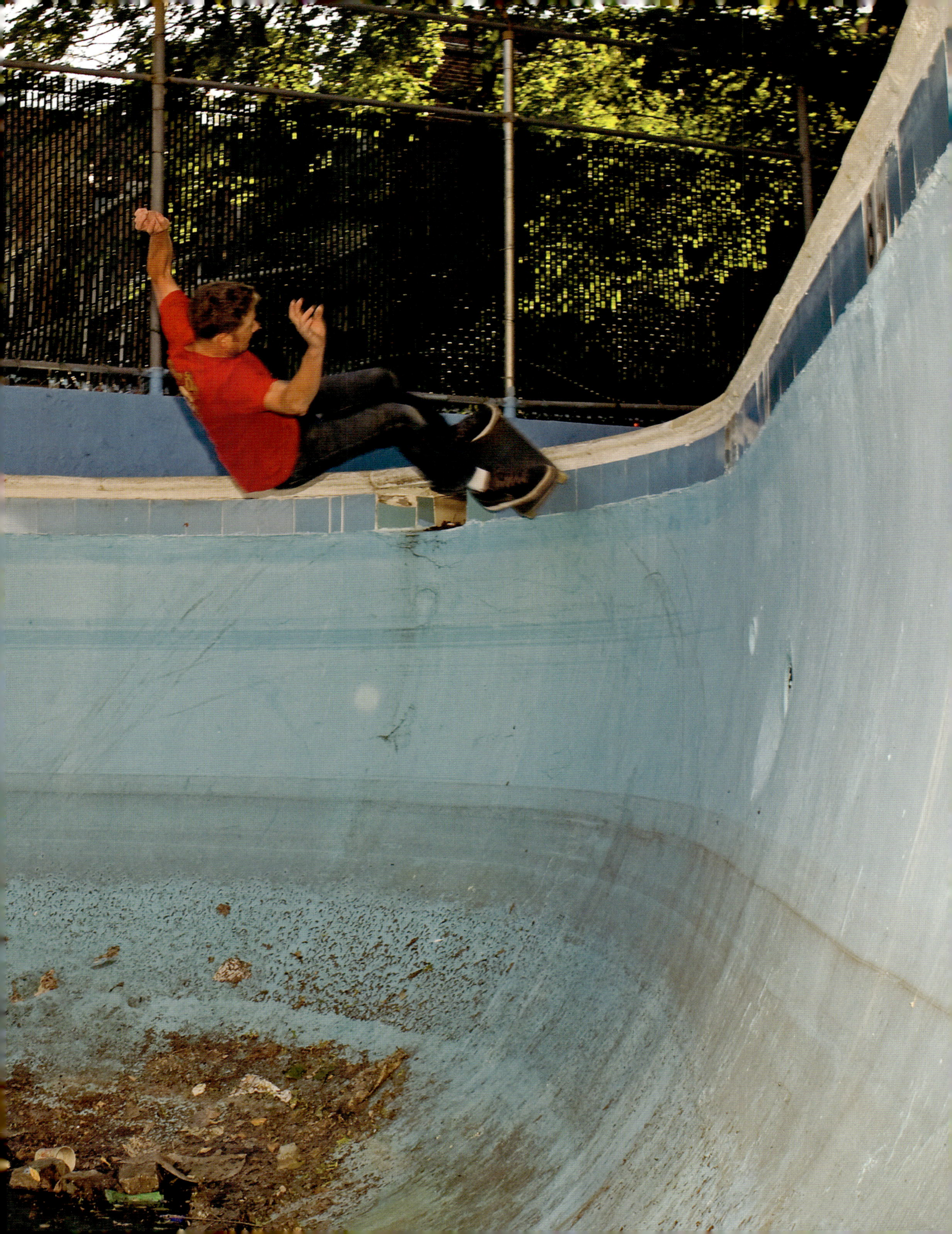

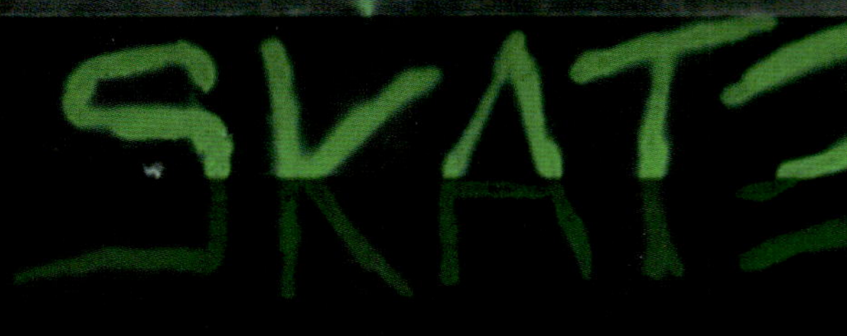
SKAT

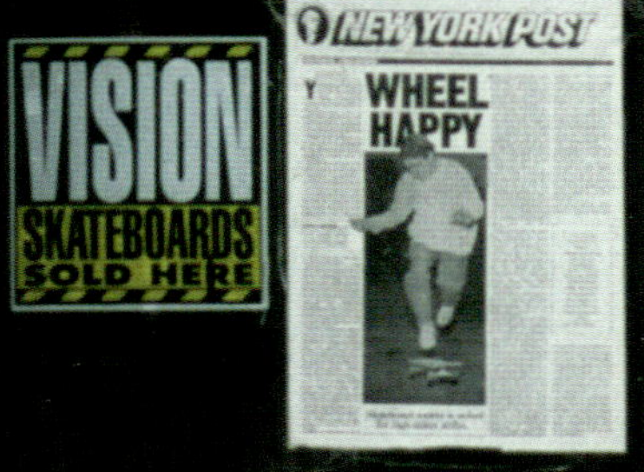
VISION
SKATEBOARDS
SOLD HERE
NEW YORK POST
WHEEL HAPPY

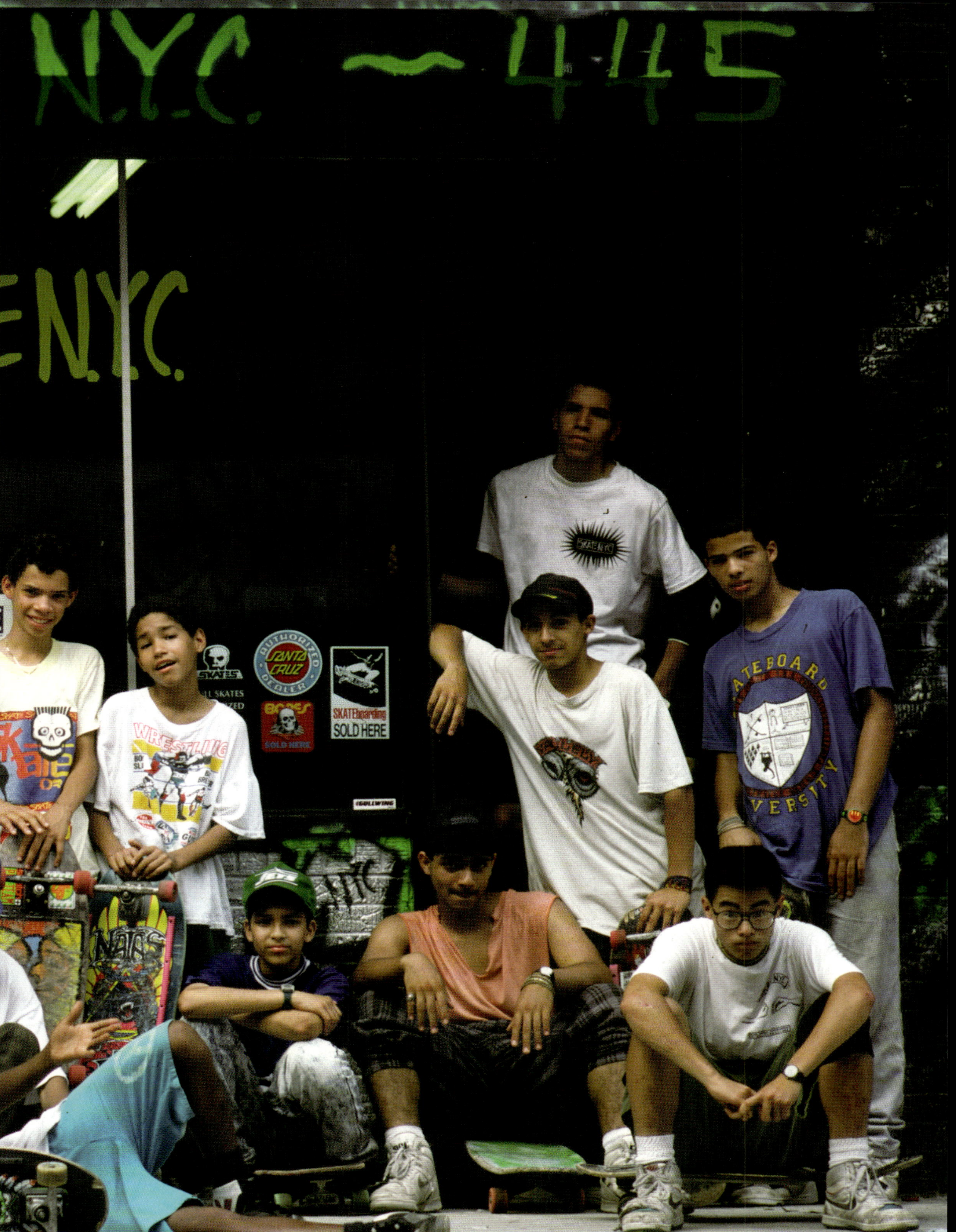

NYC ~ 445
N.Y.C.
N.Y.C.
AUTHORIZED SANTA CRUZ DEALER
SKATEboarding SOLD HERE
WRESTLING
SKATE NYC
SKATEBOARD UNIVERSITY
NATAS

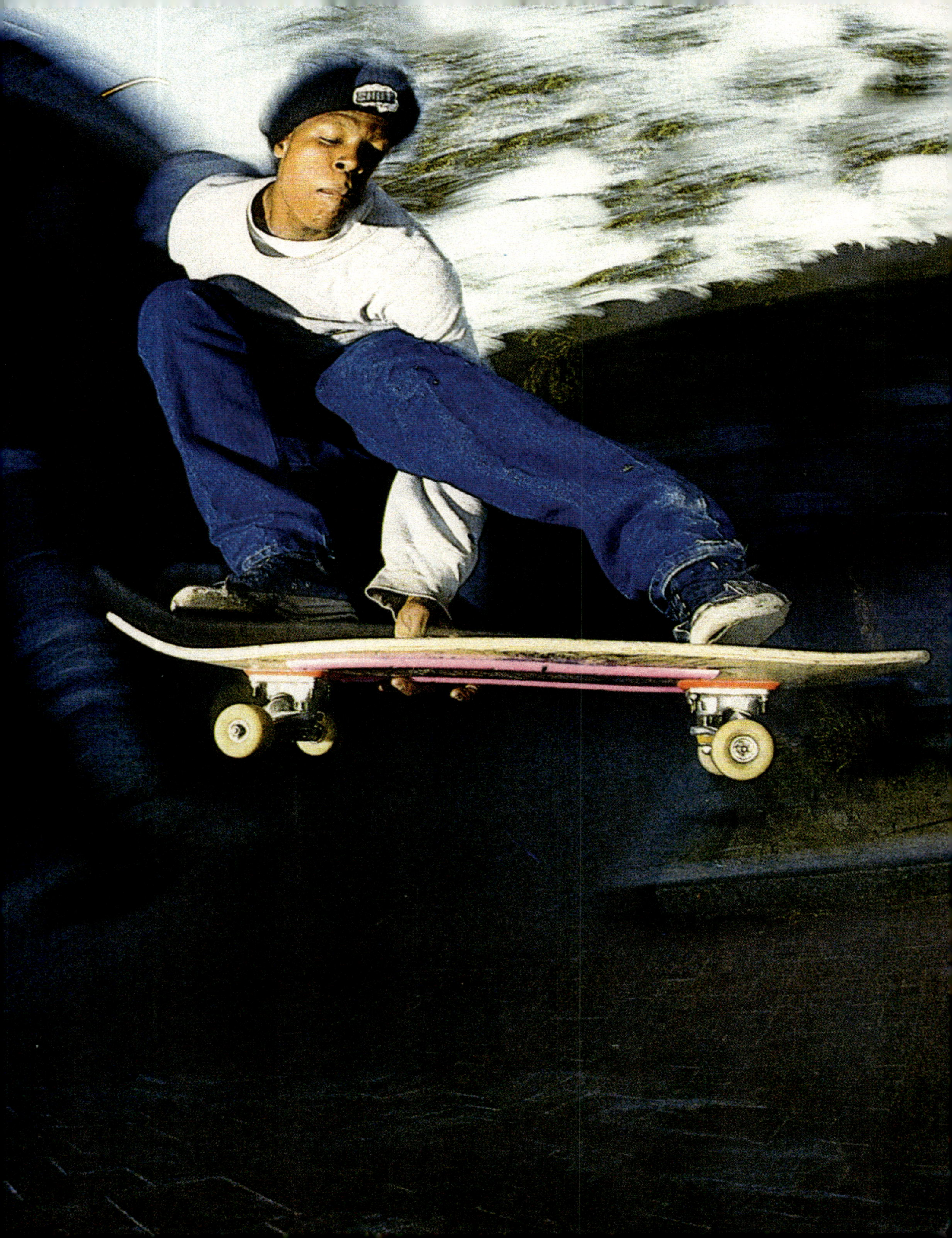

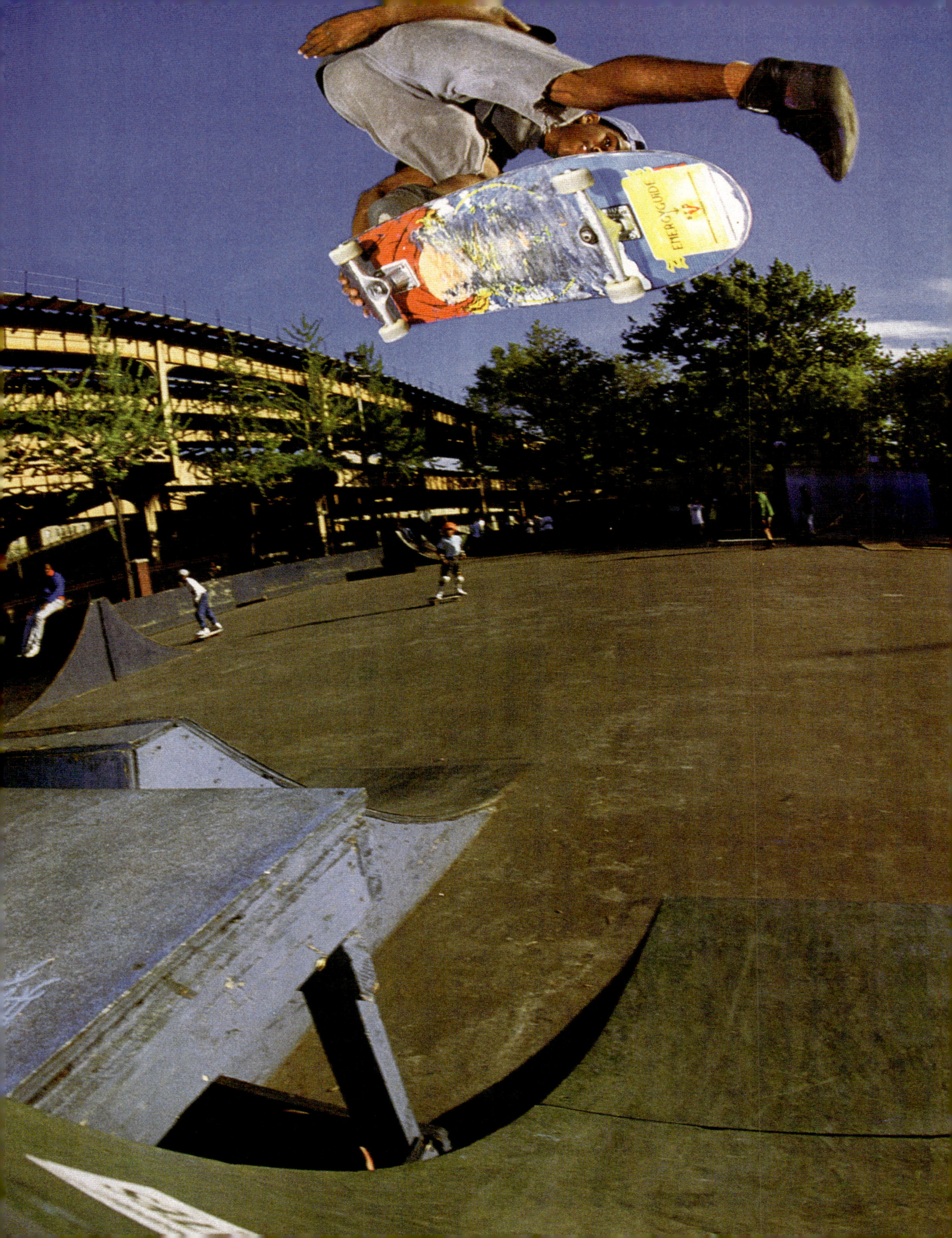
ENERGYGUIDE

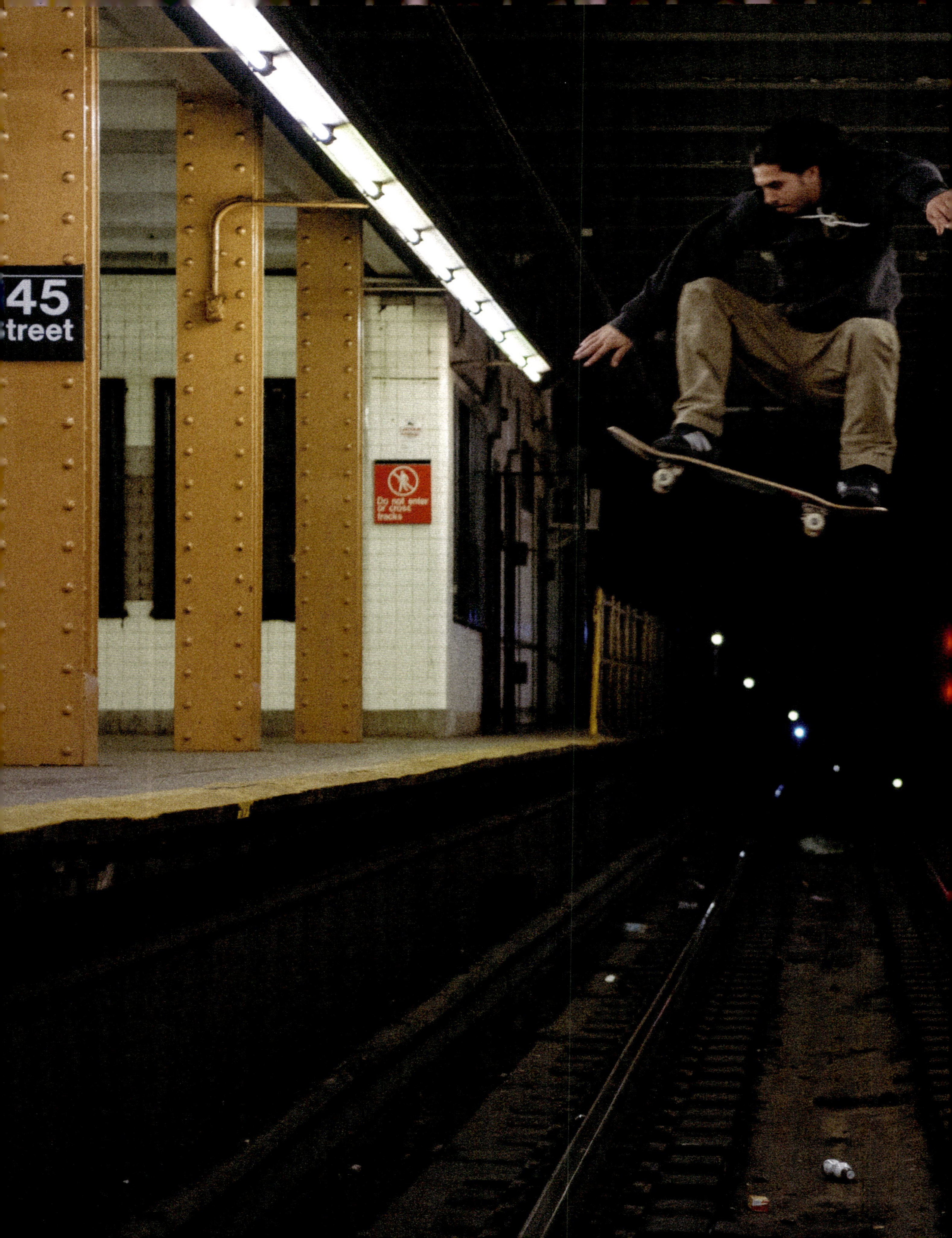
45
treet
Do not enter or cross tracks

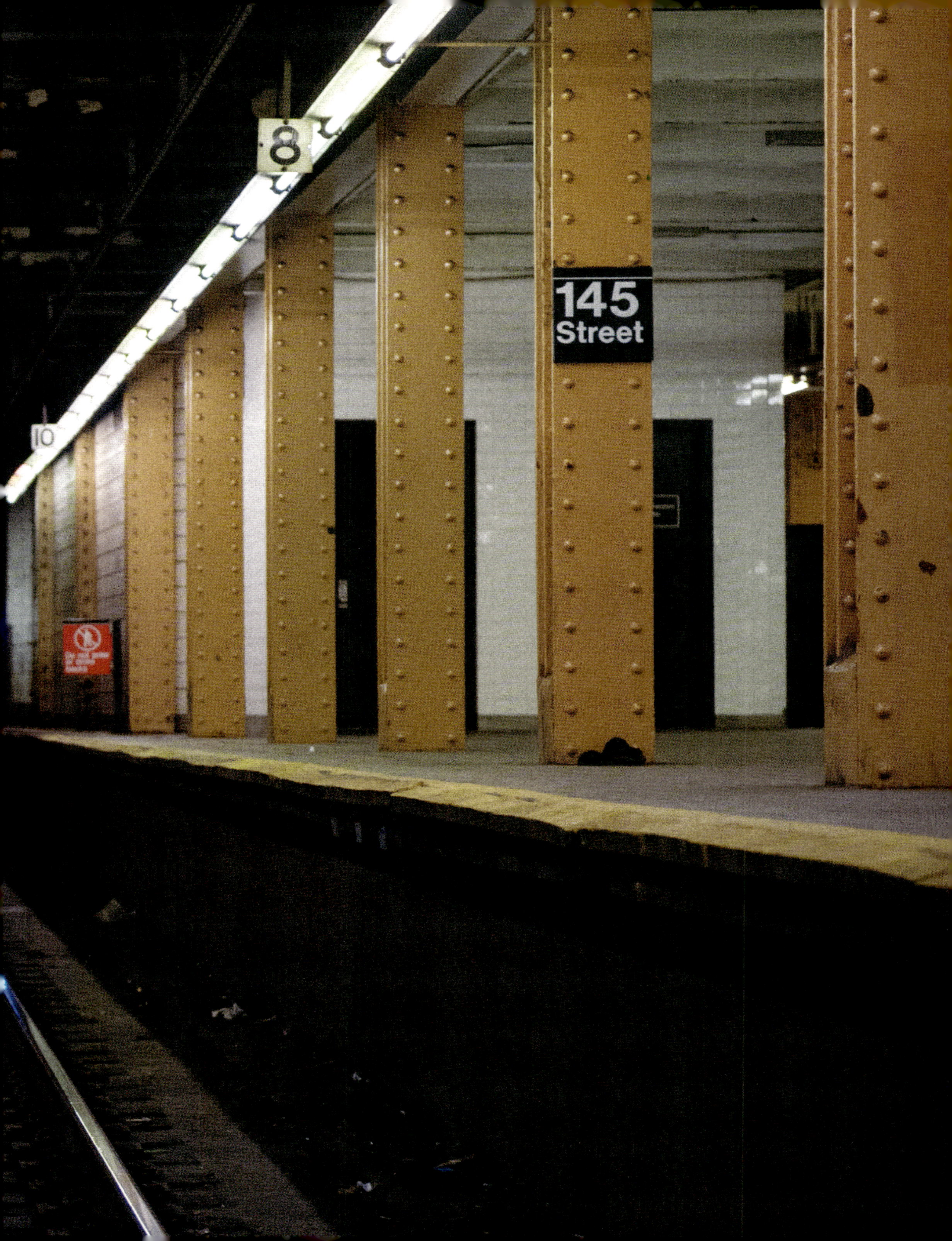
8
145
Street
10

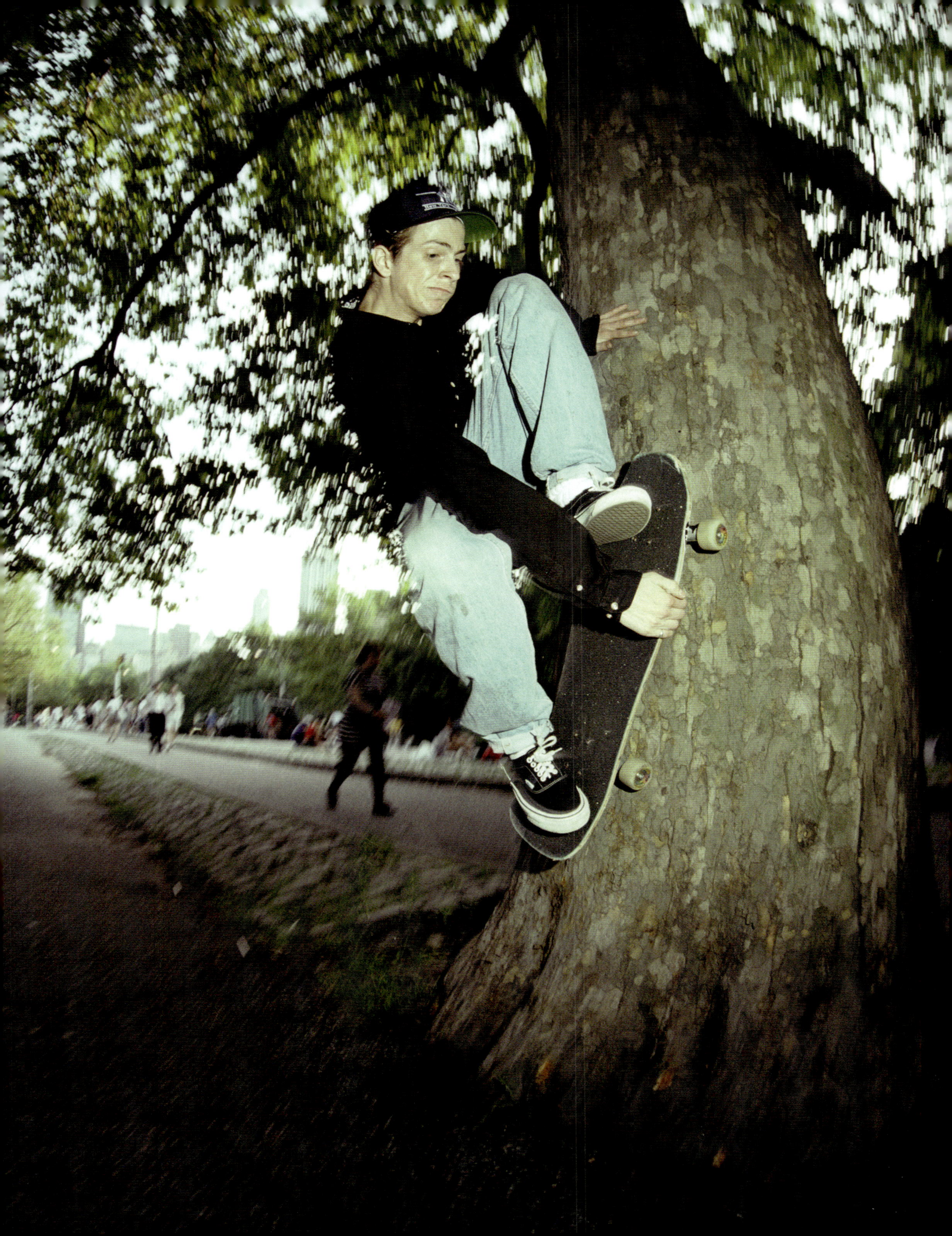

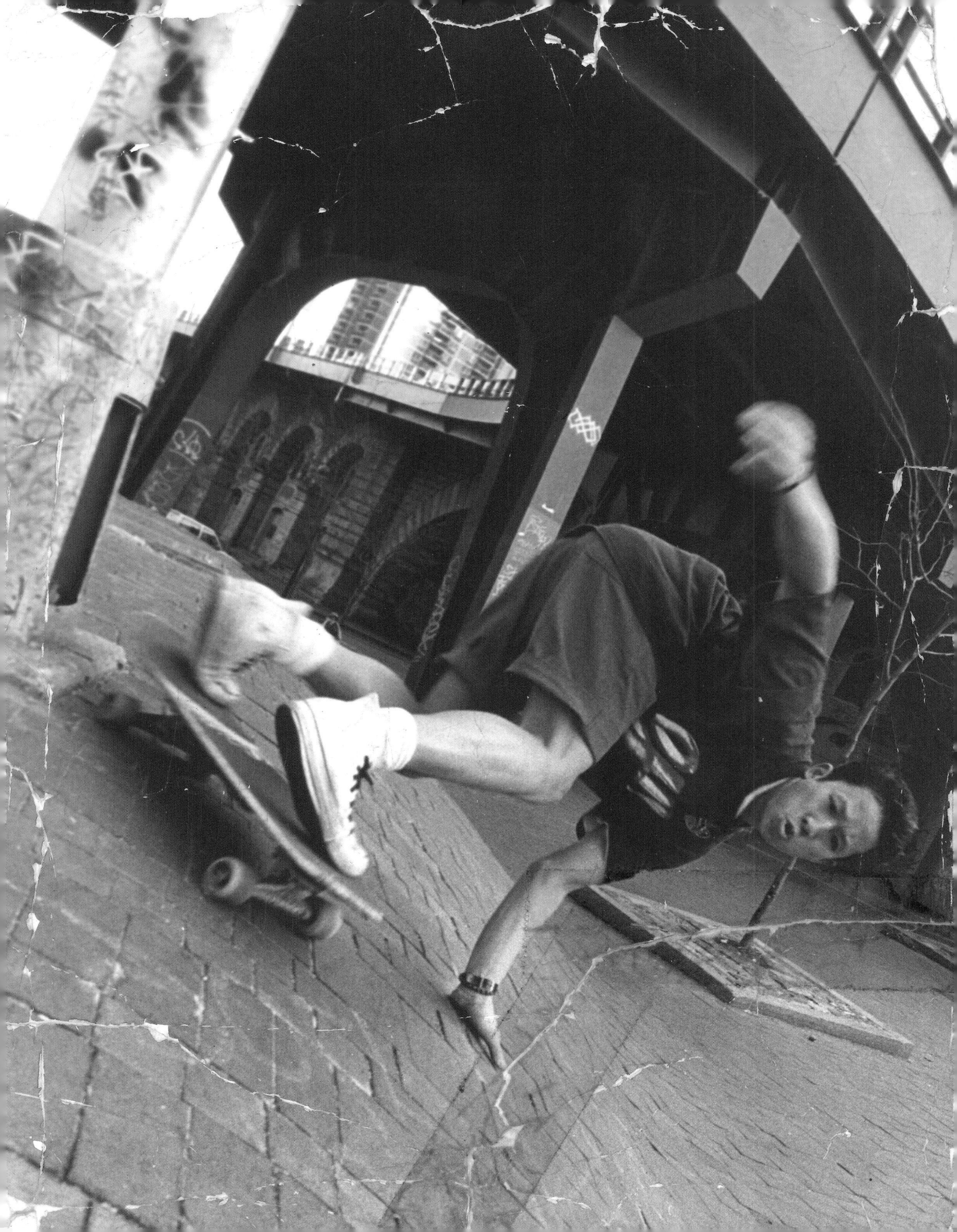

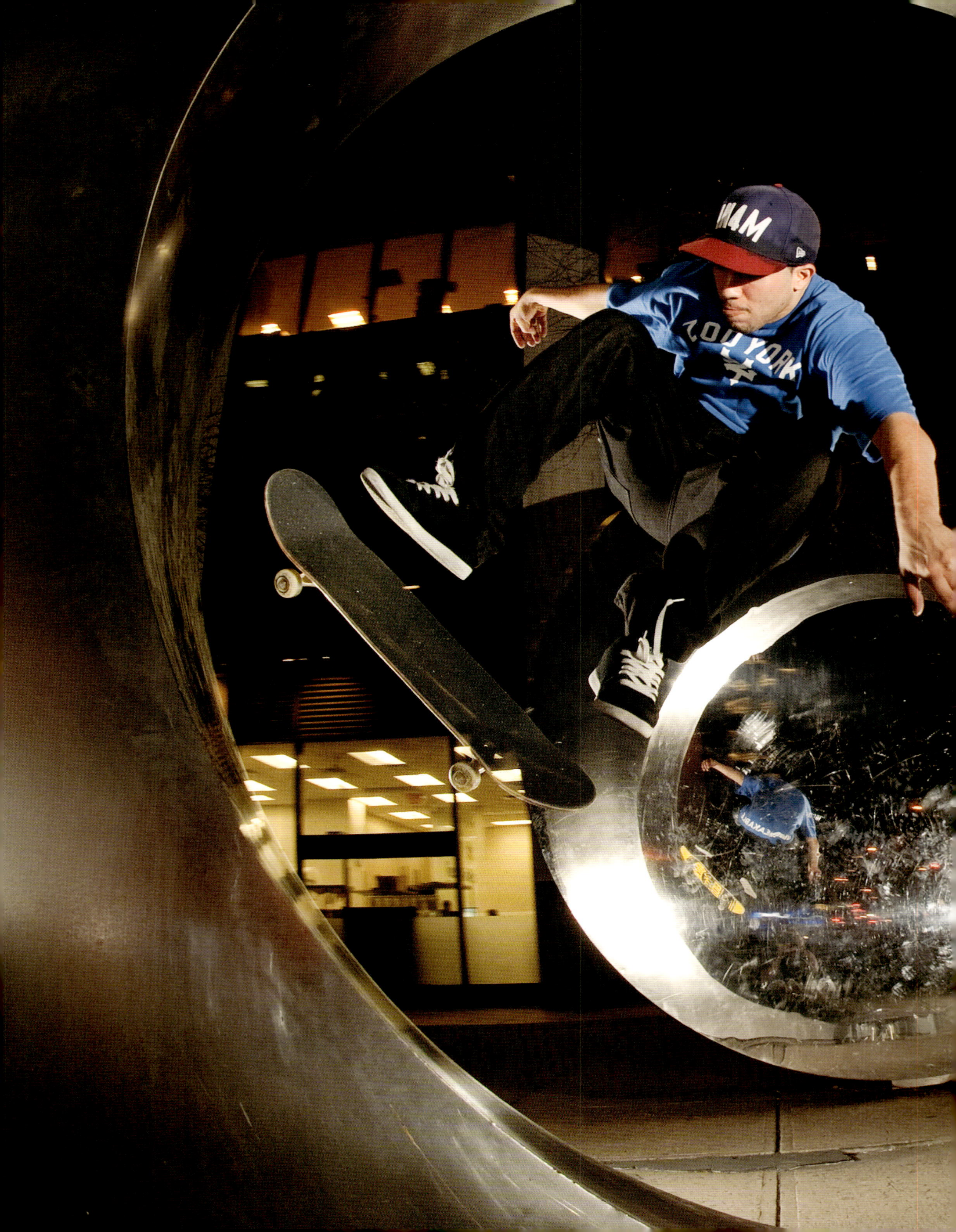

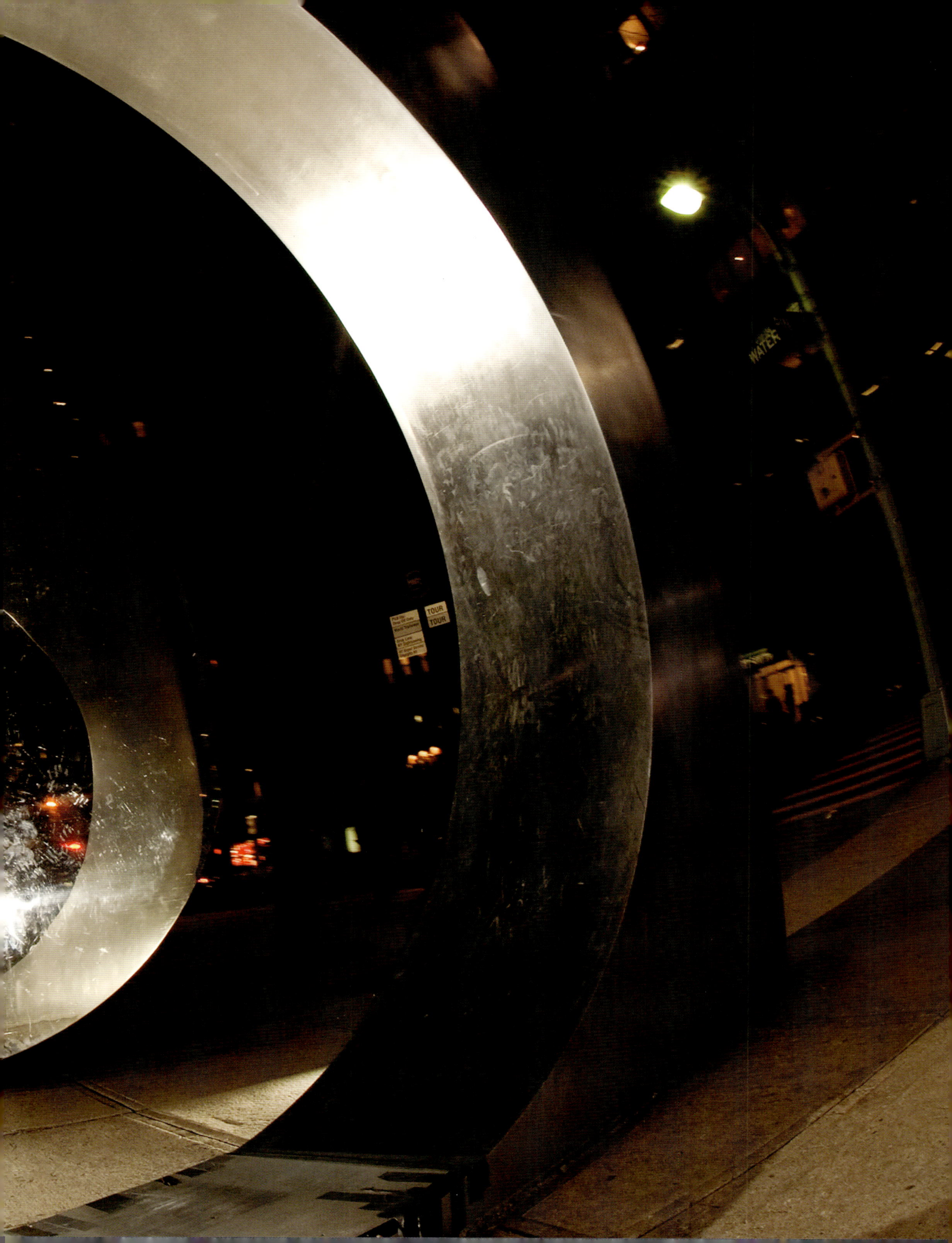
TOUR
TOUR
WATER

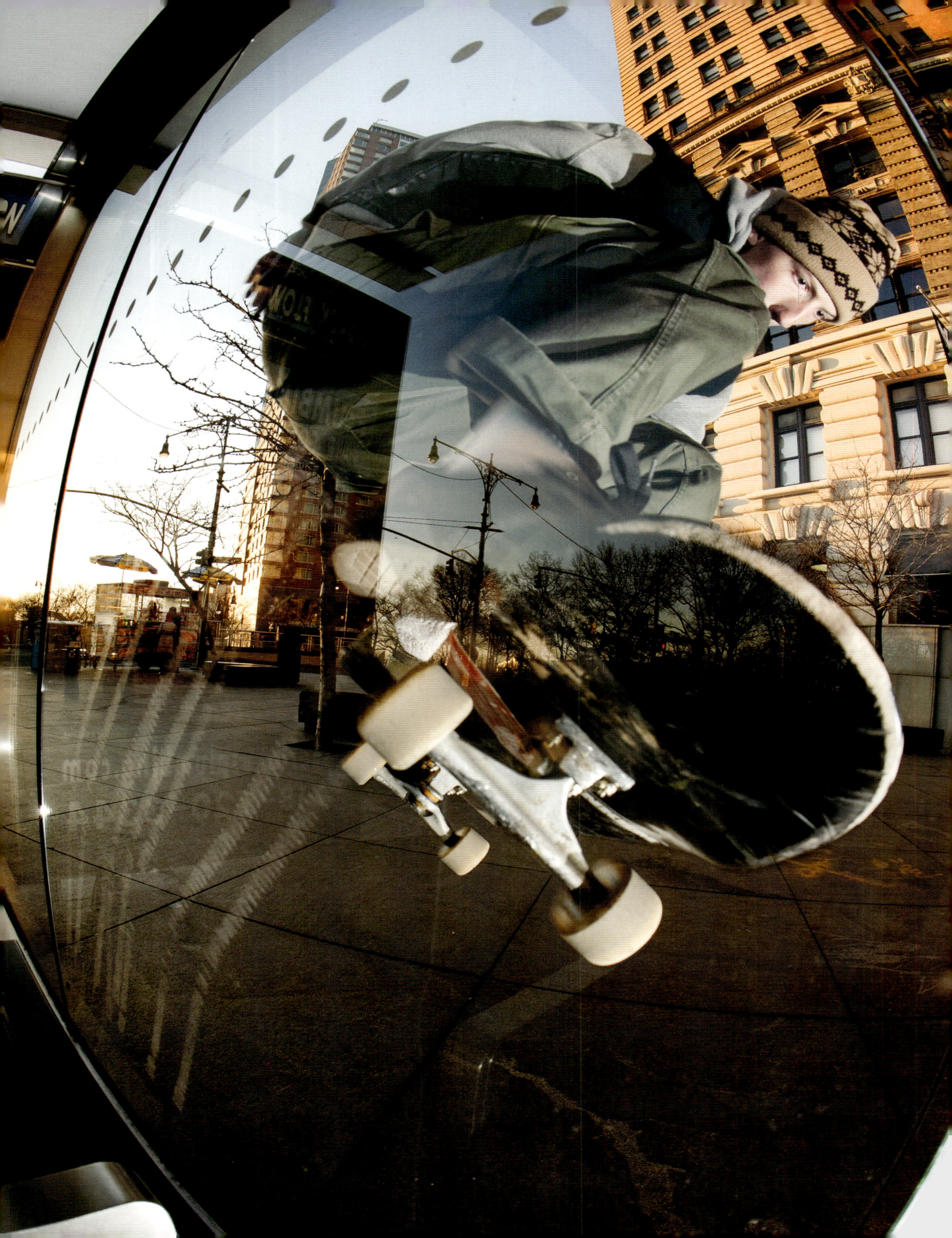

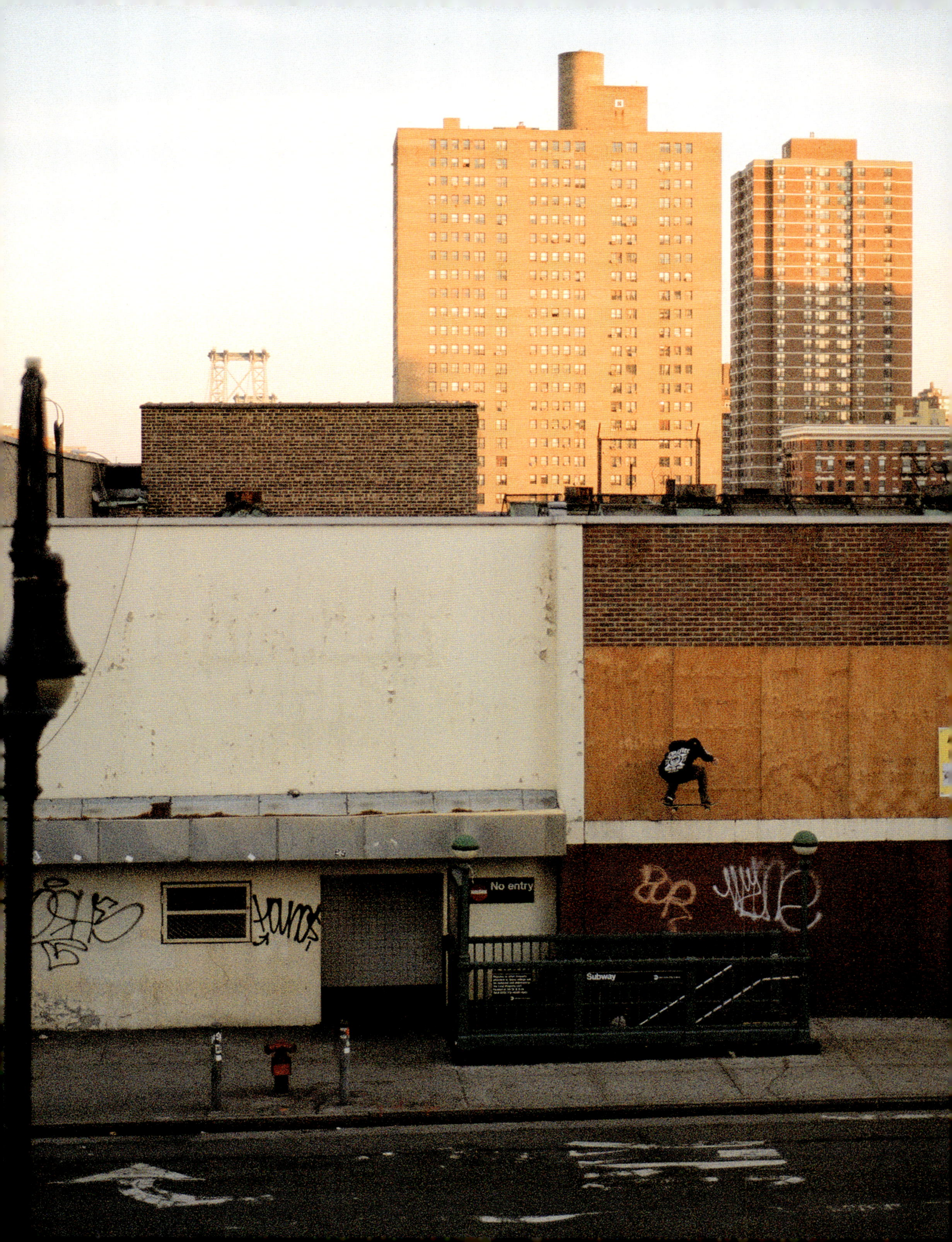
No entry
Subway

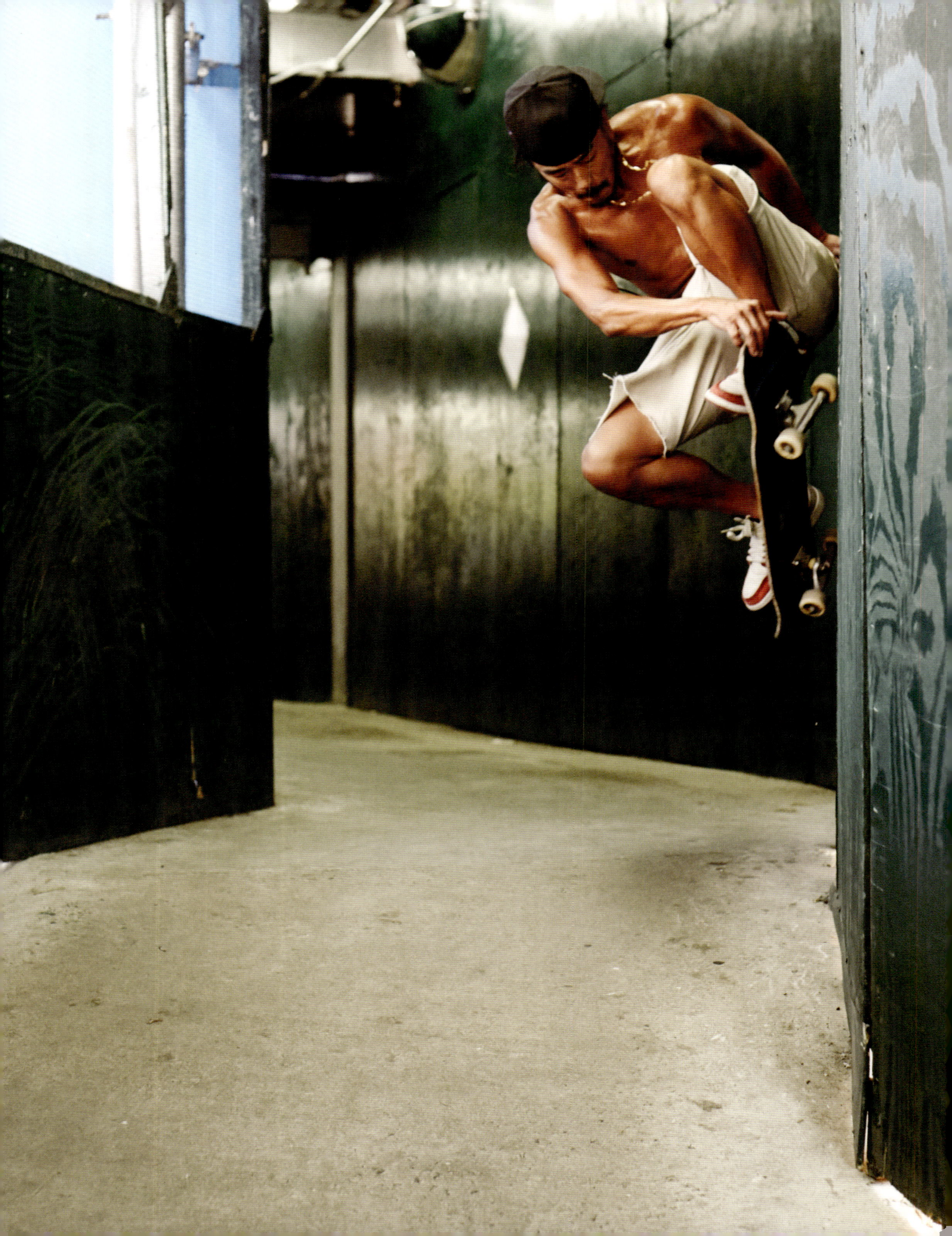

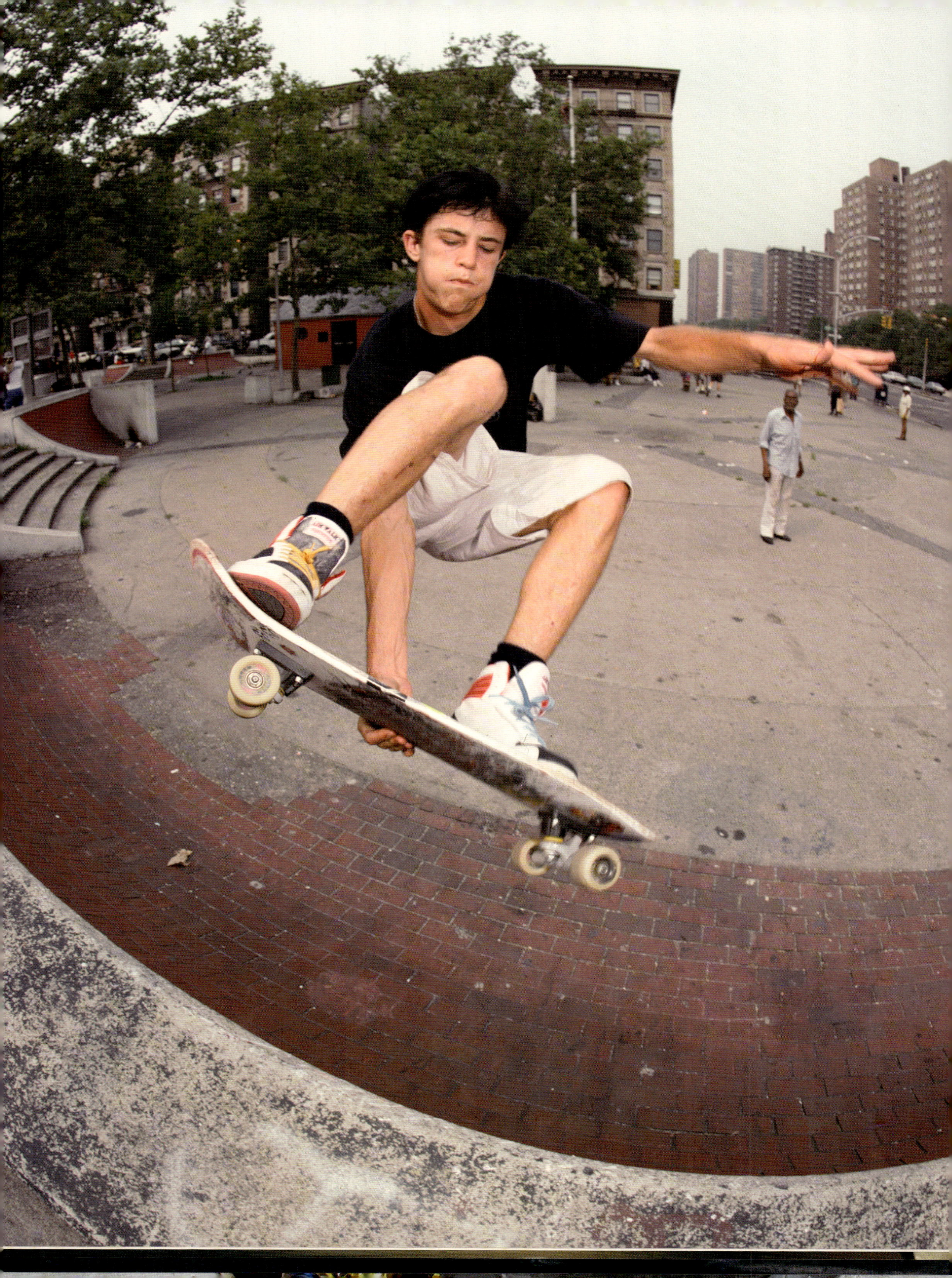

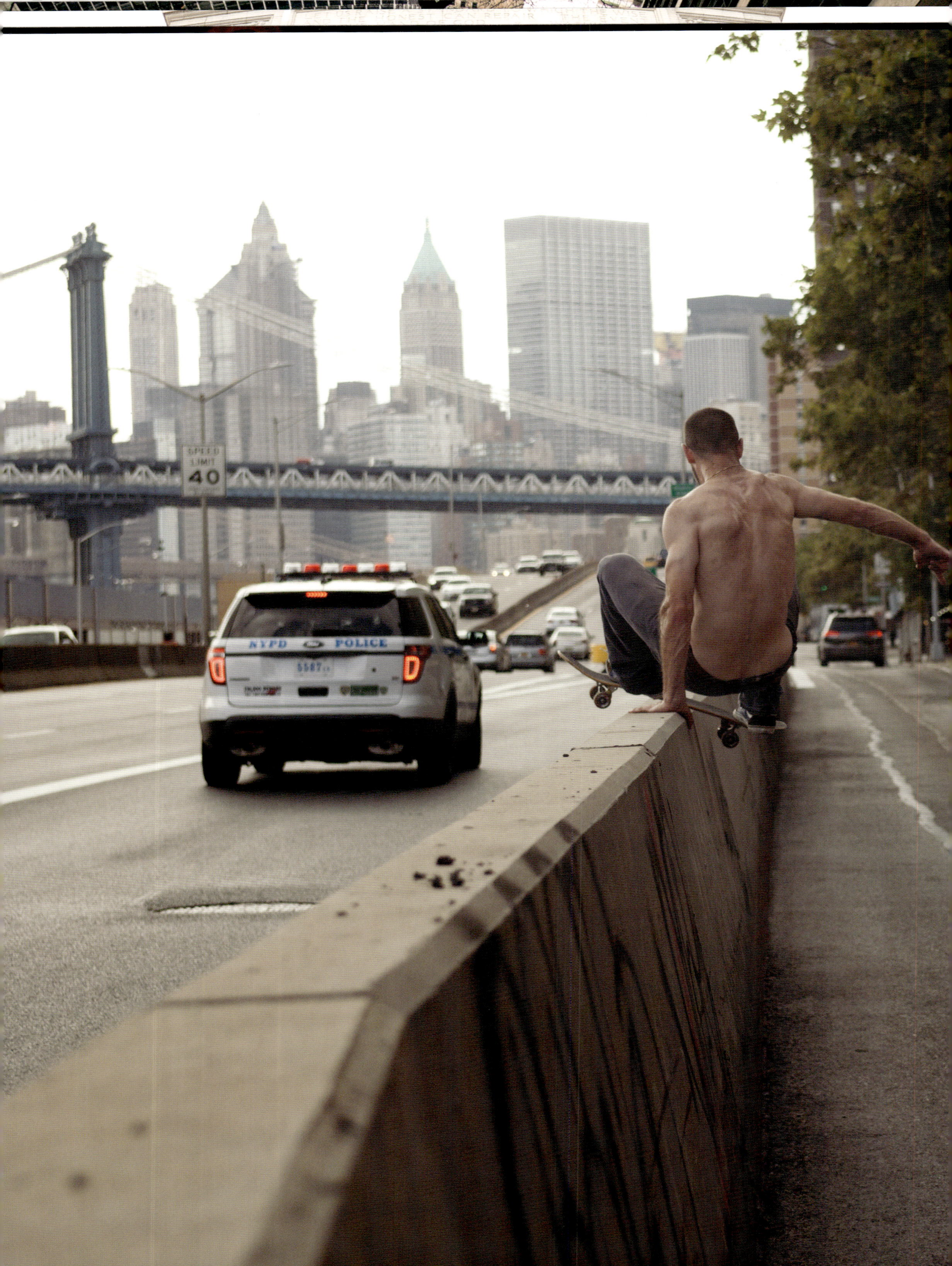
SPEED
LIMIT
40
NYPD
POLICE

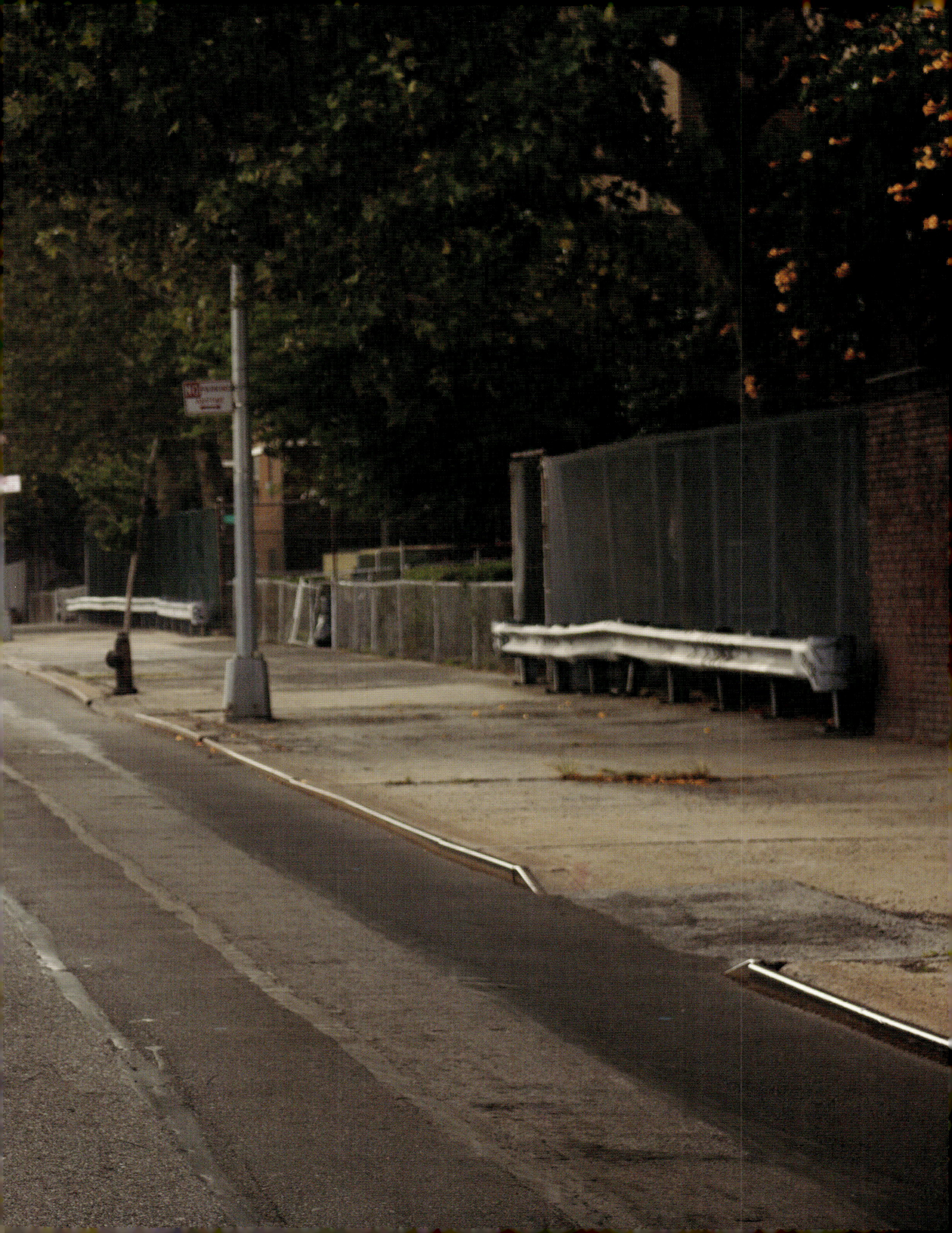

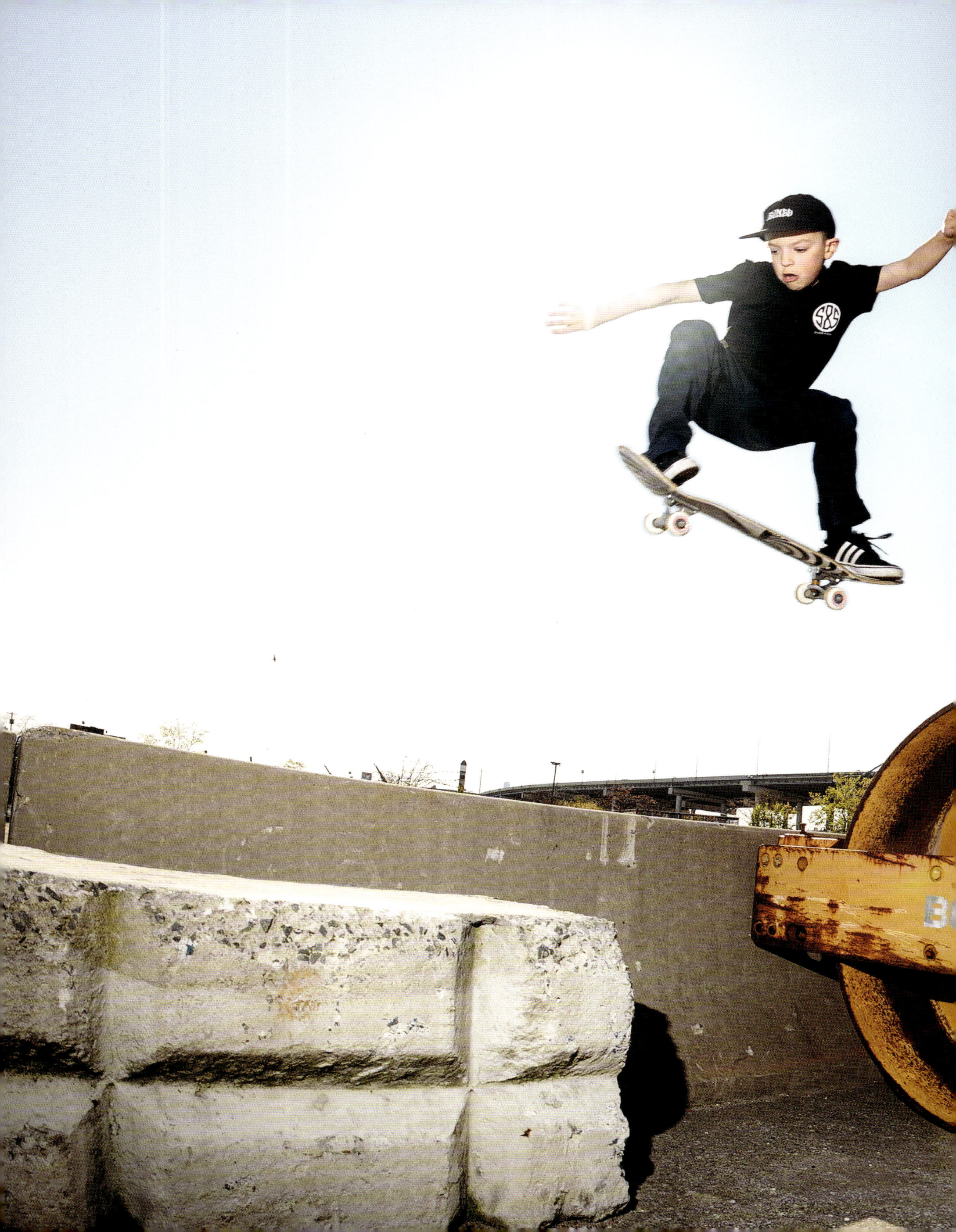

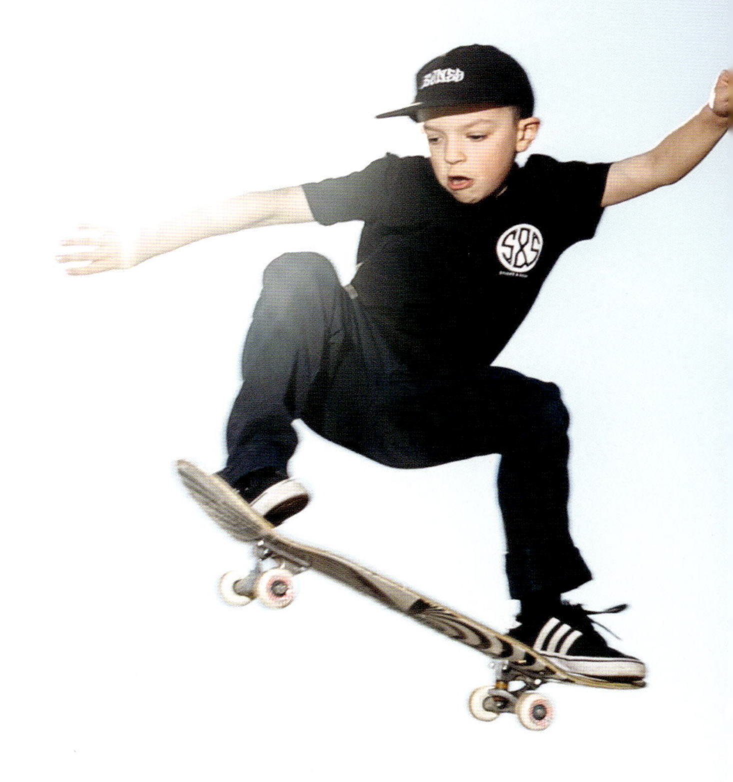

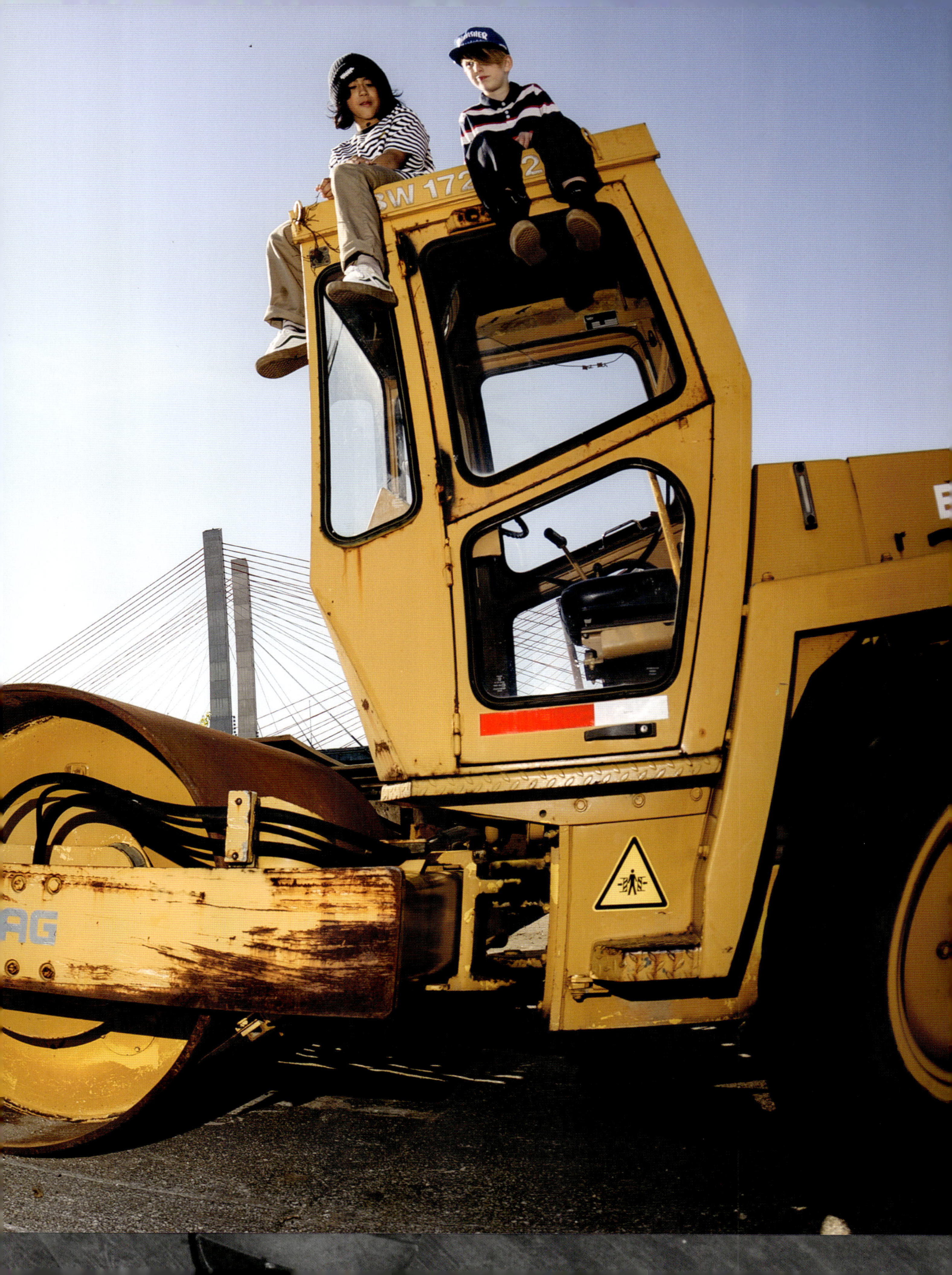

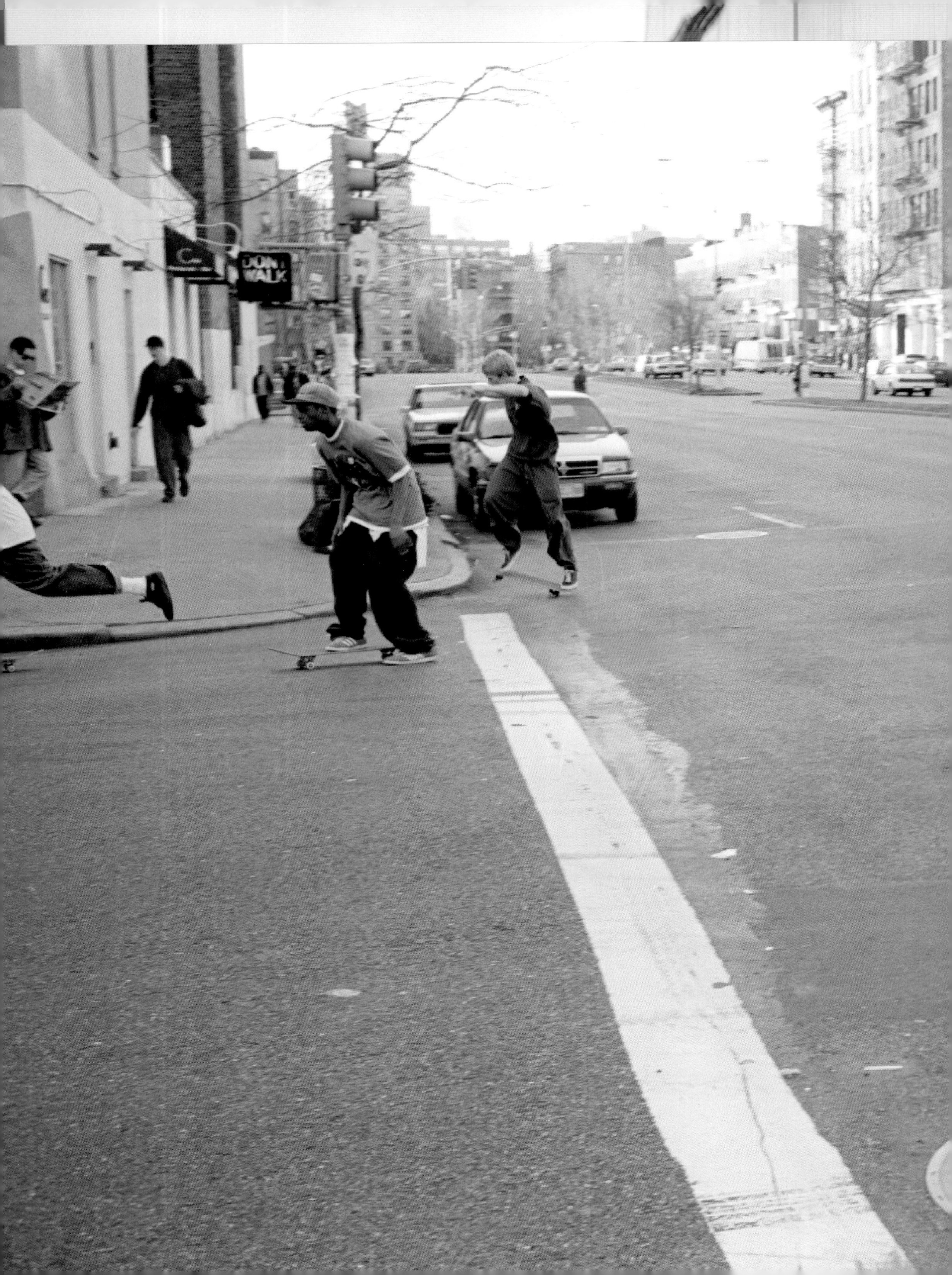
DON'T
WALK

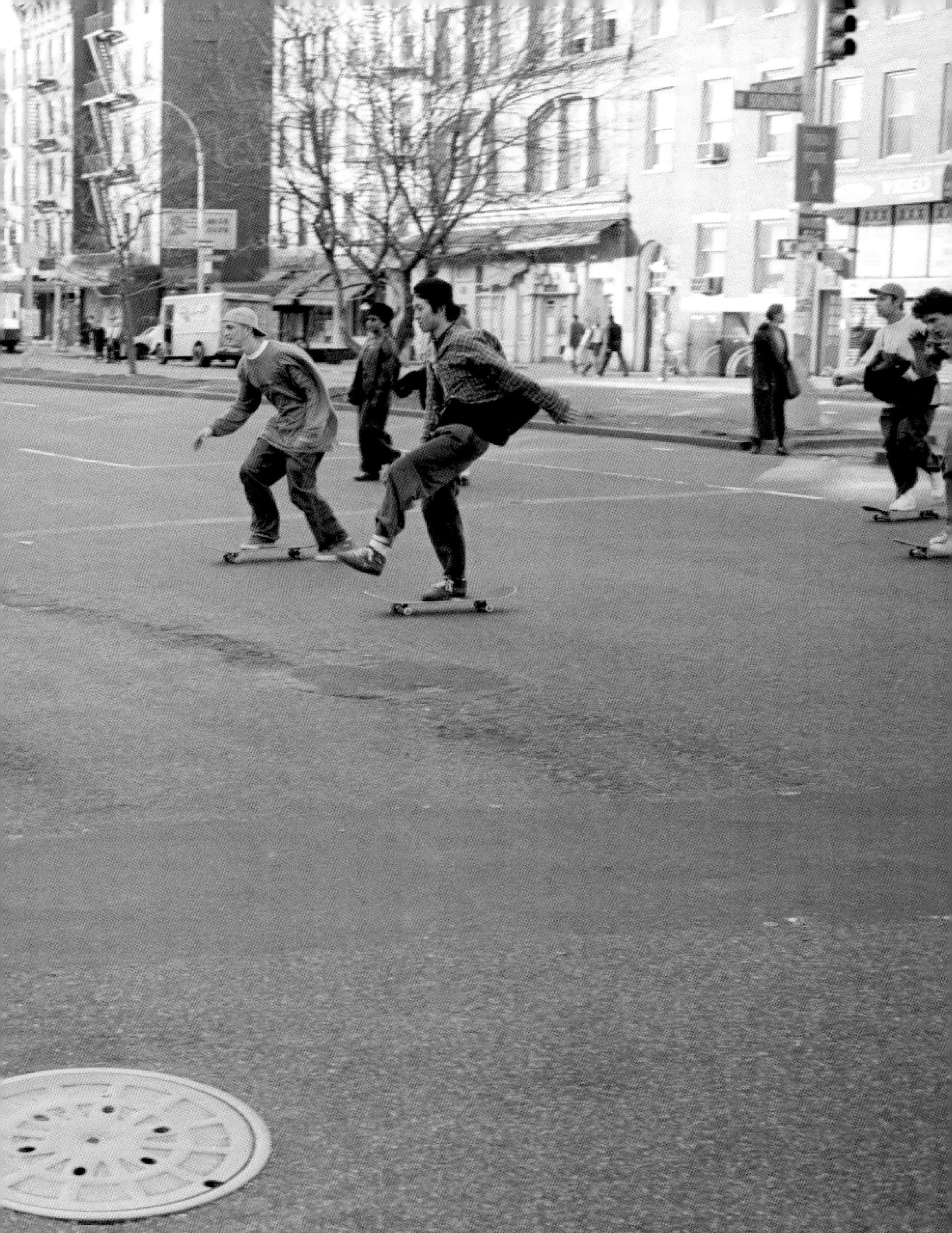

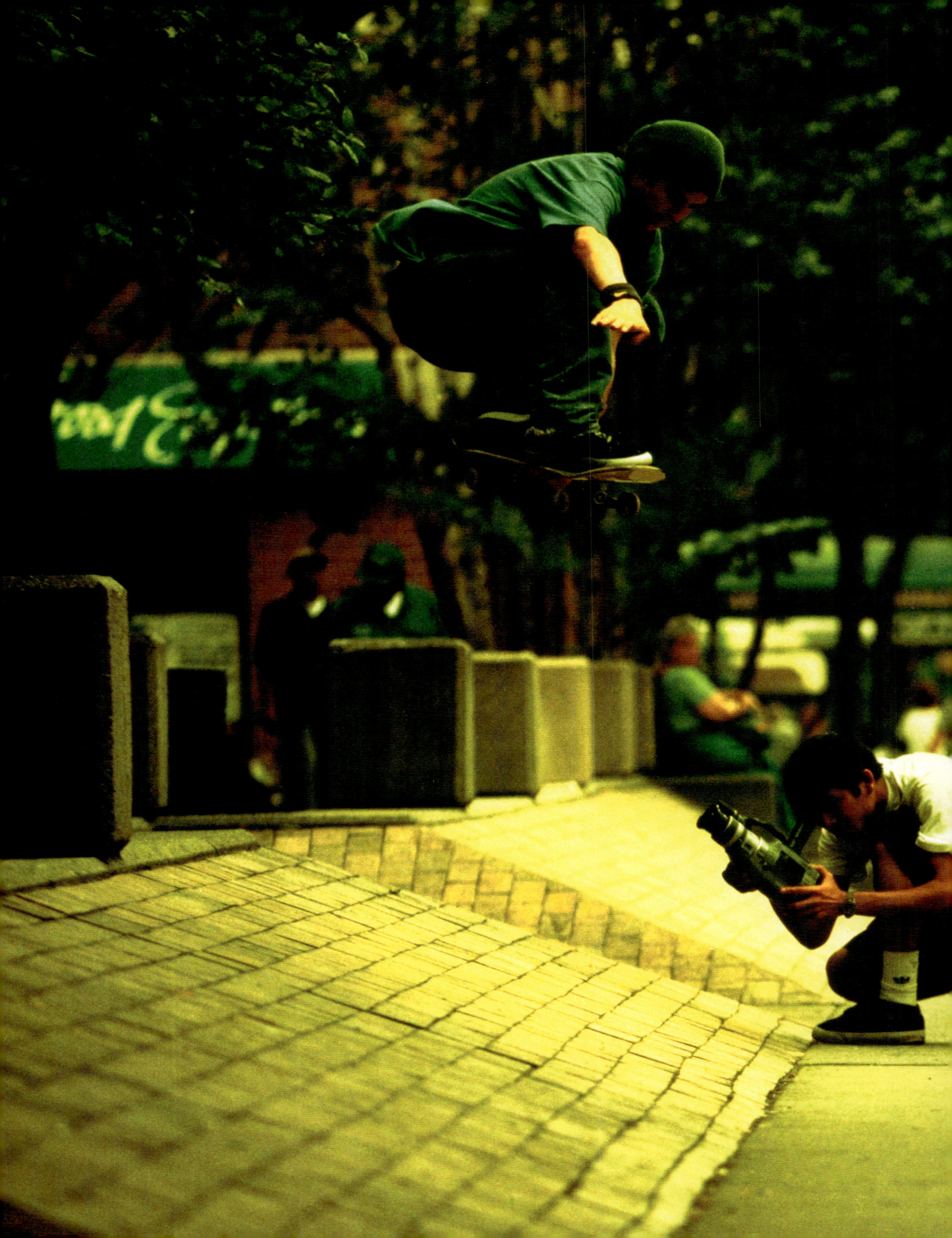

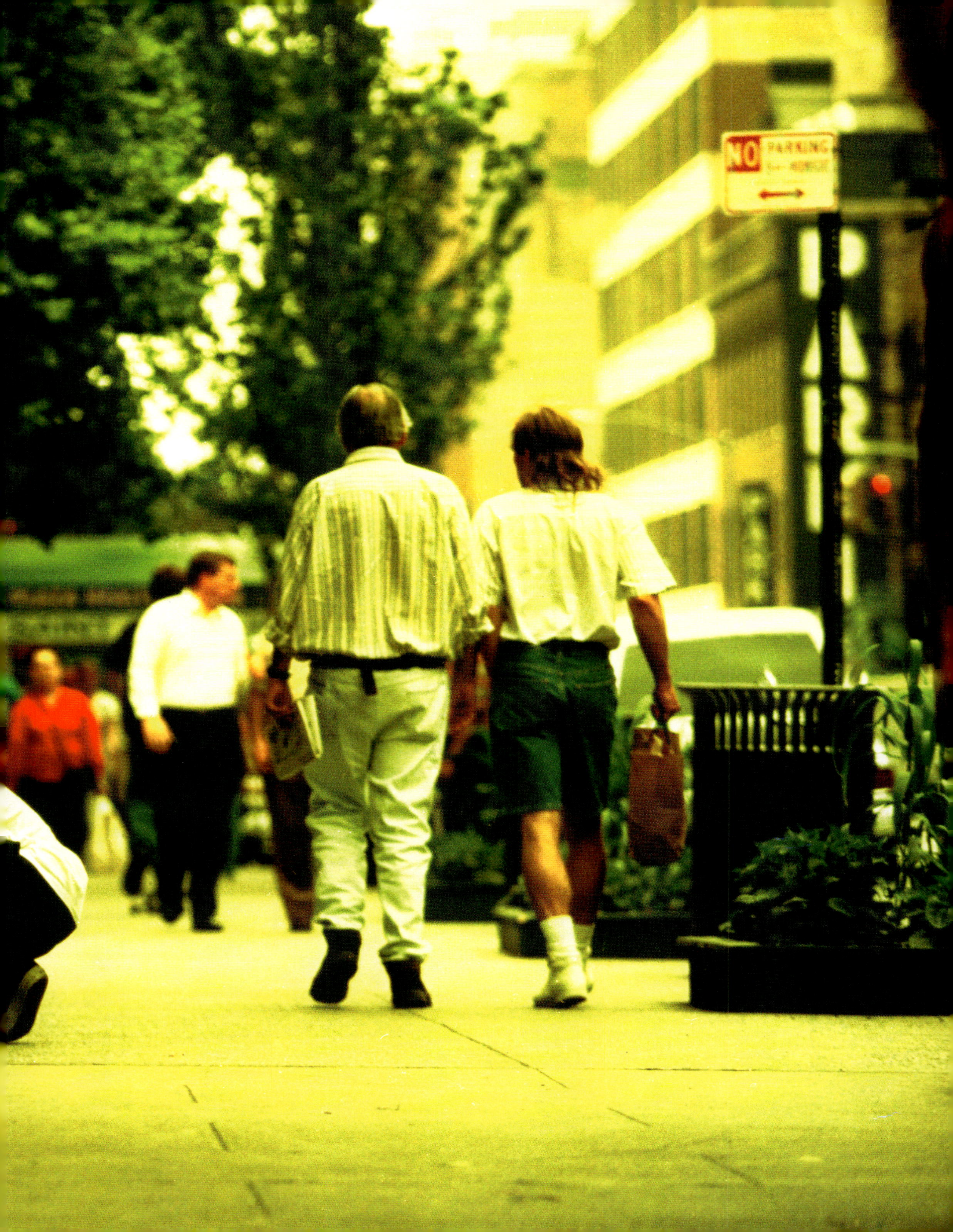
NO PARKING

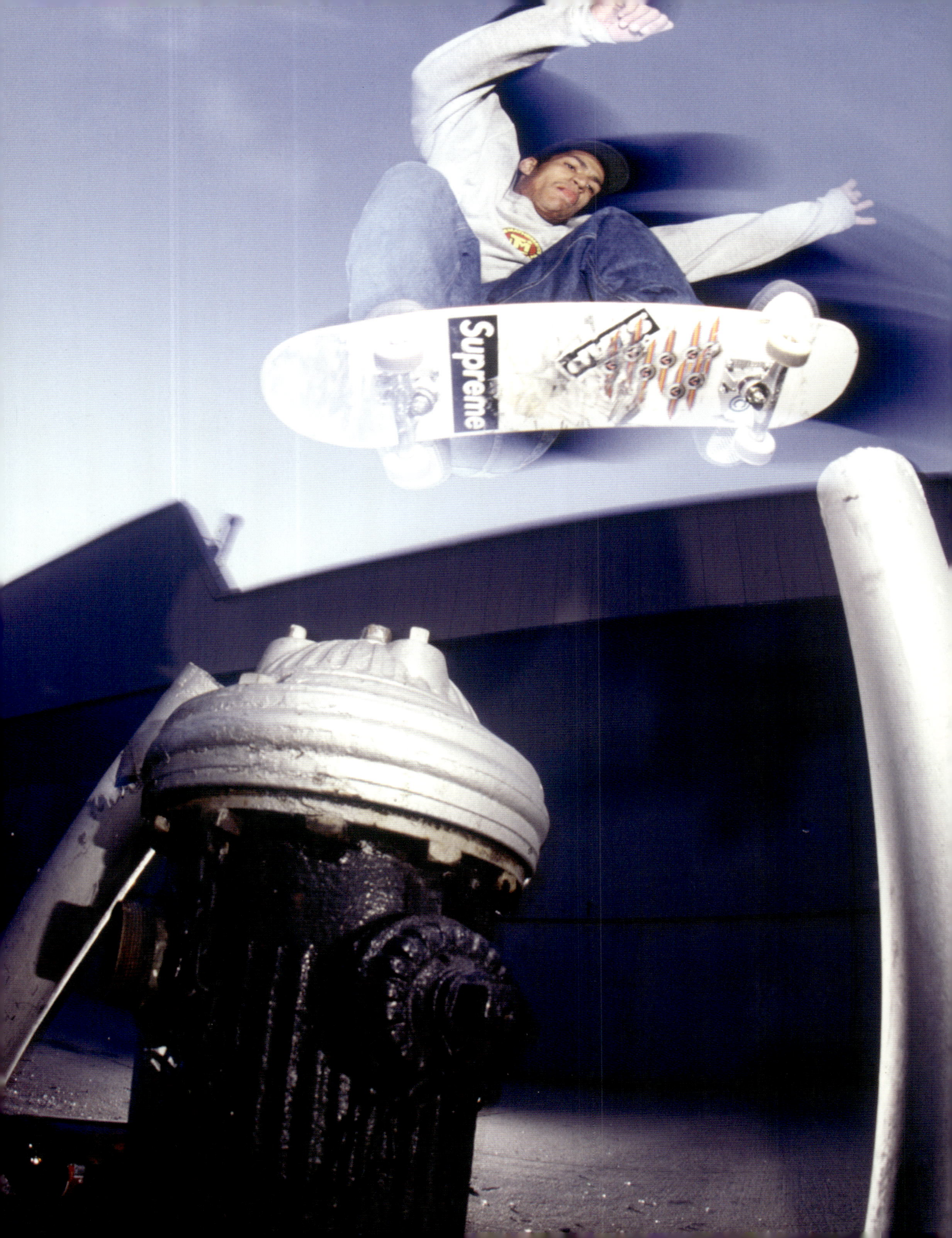
Supreme

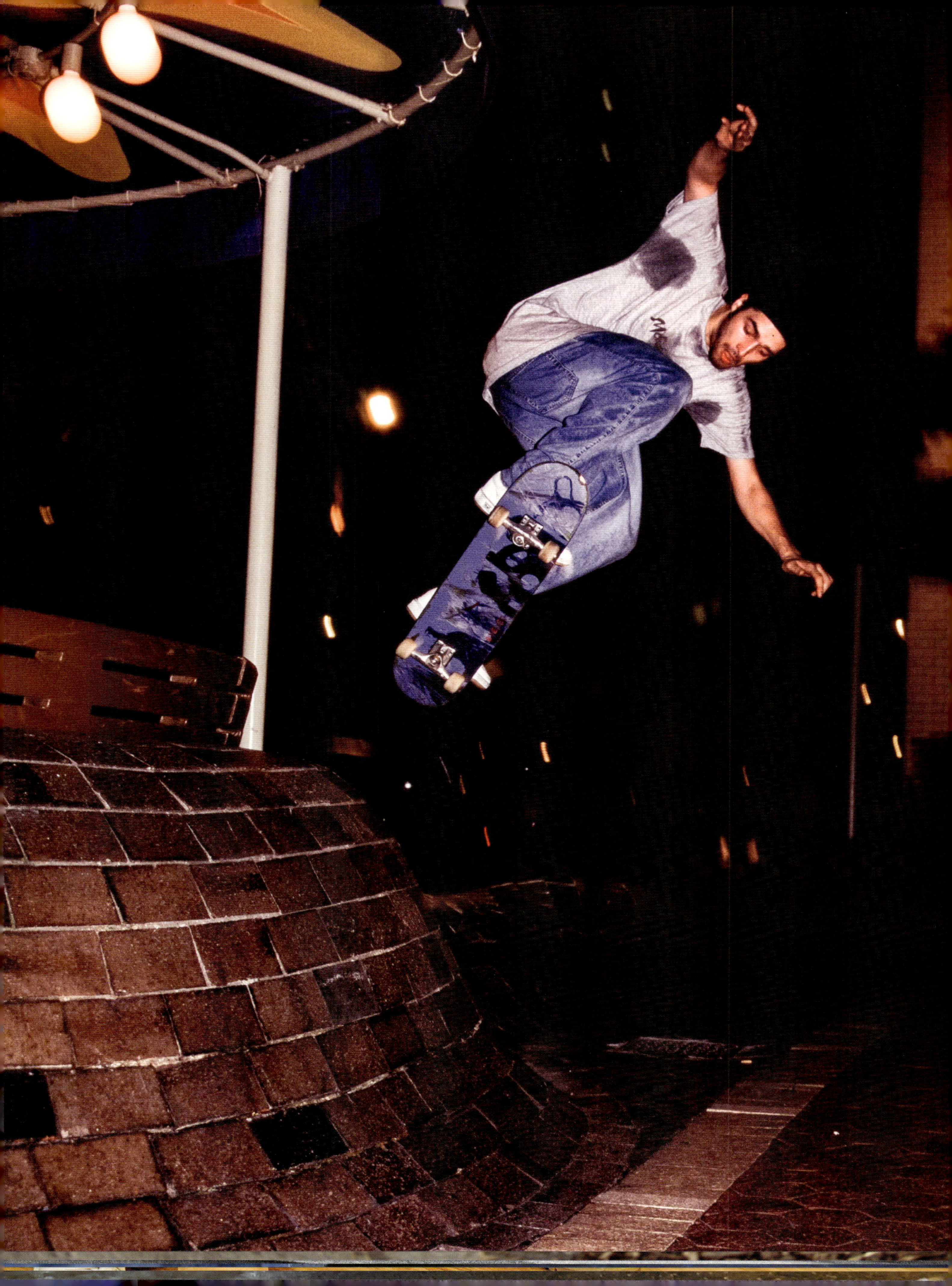

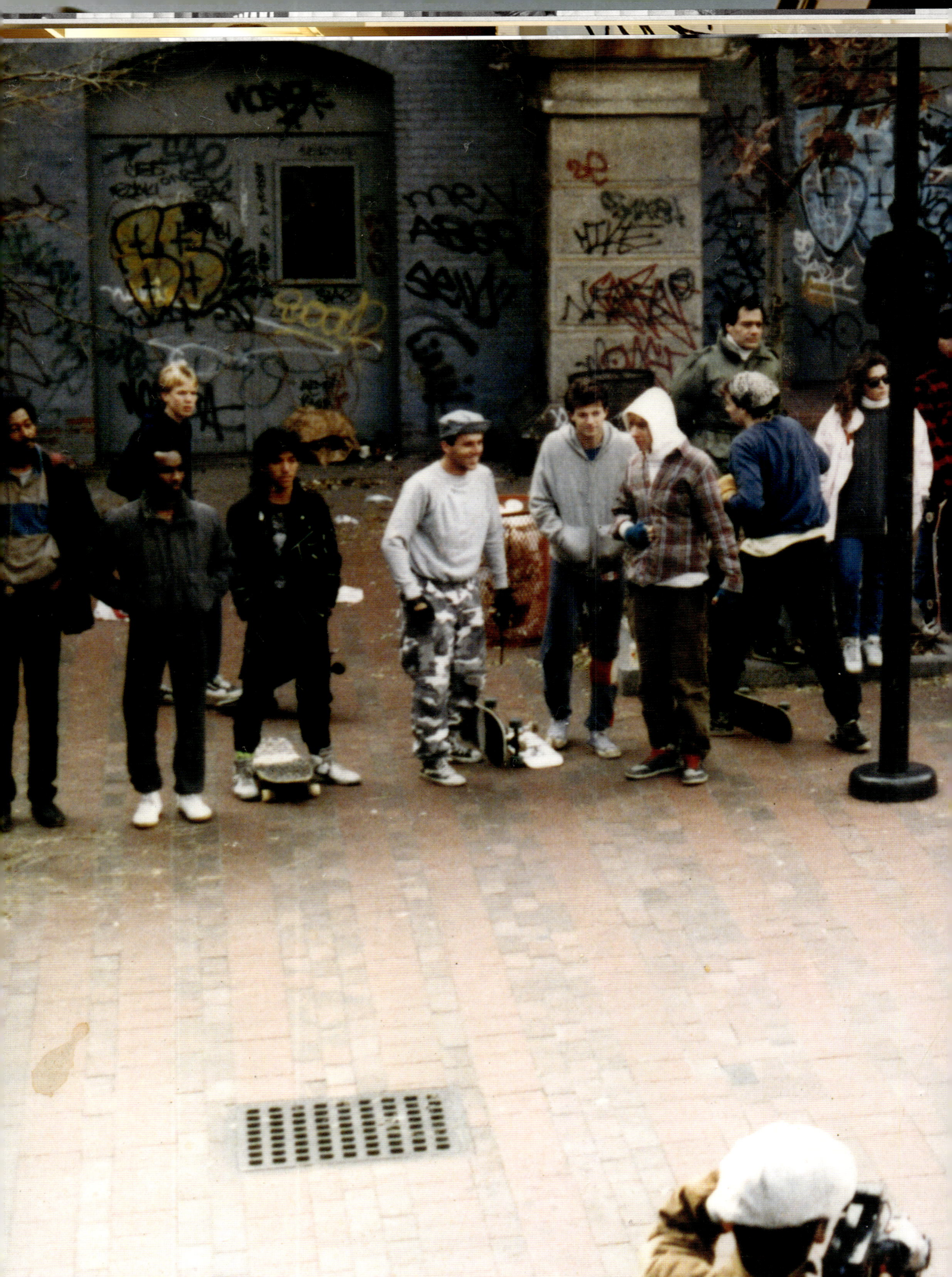

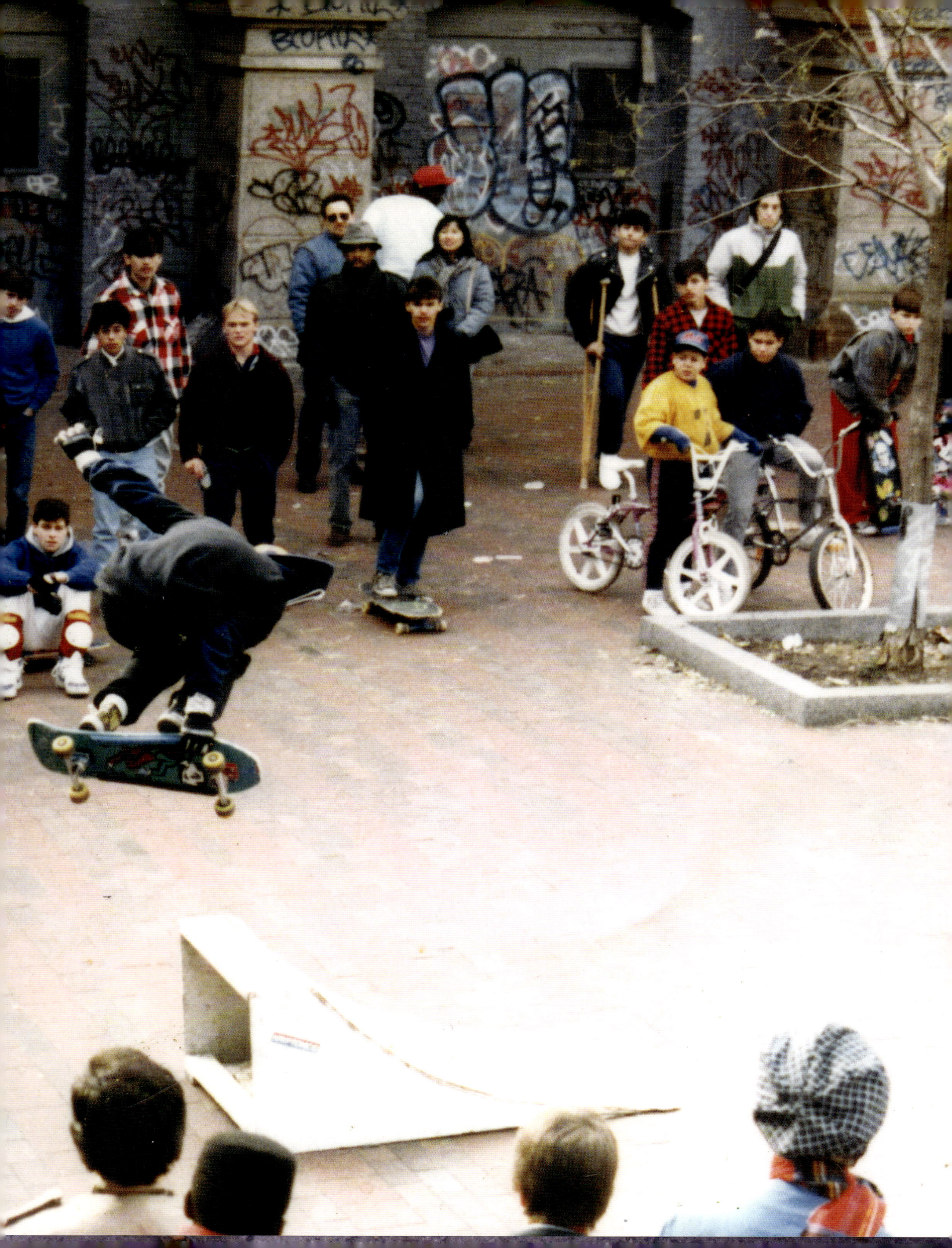

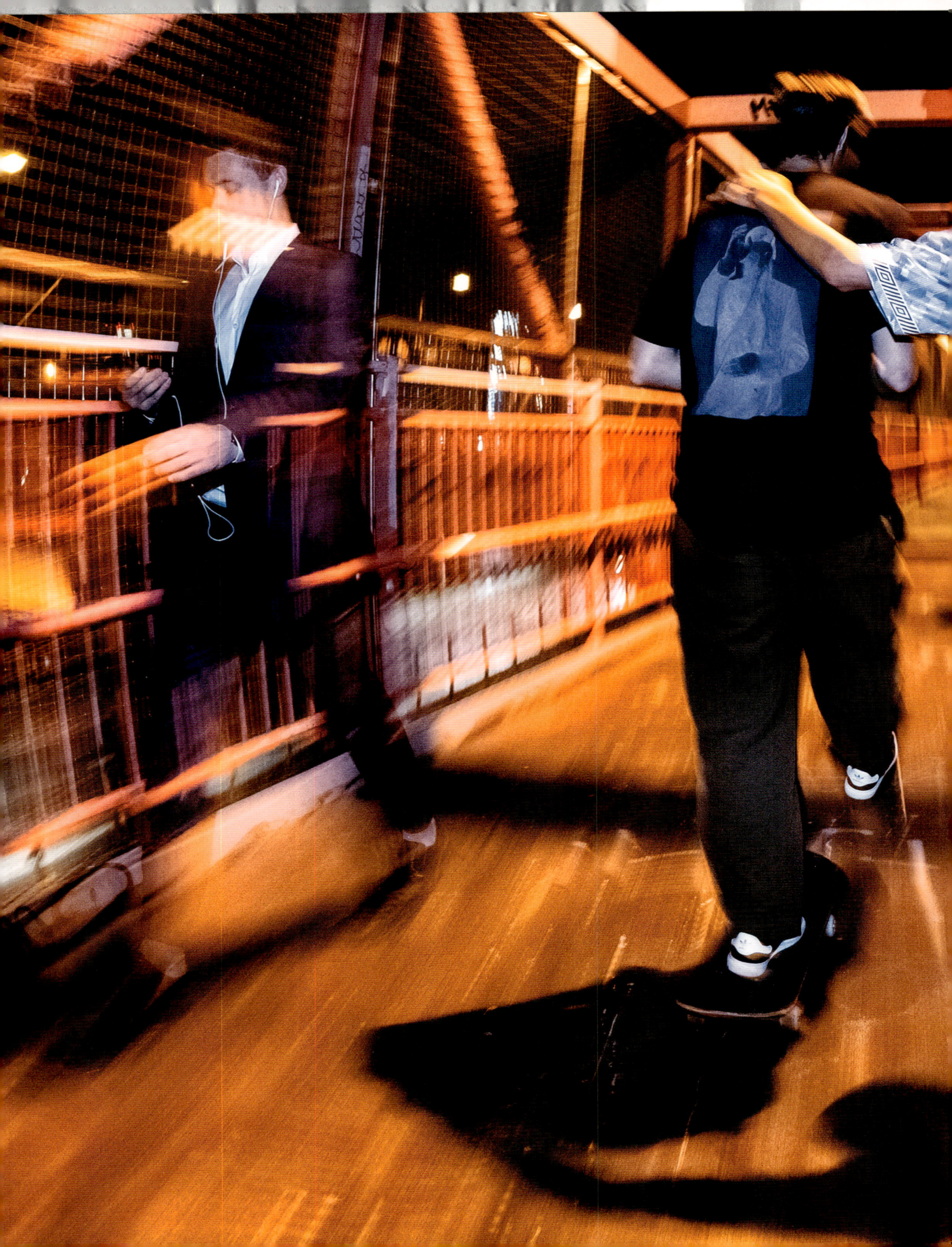

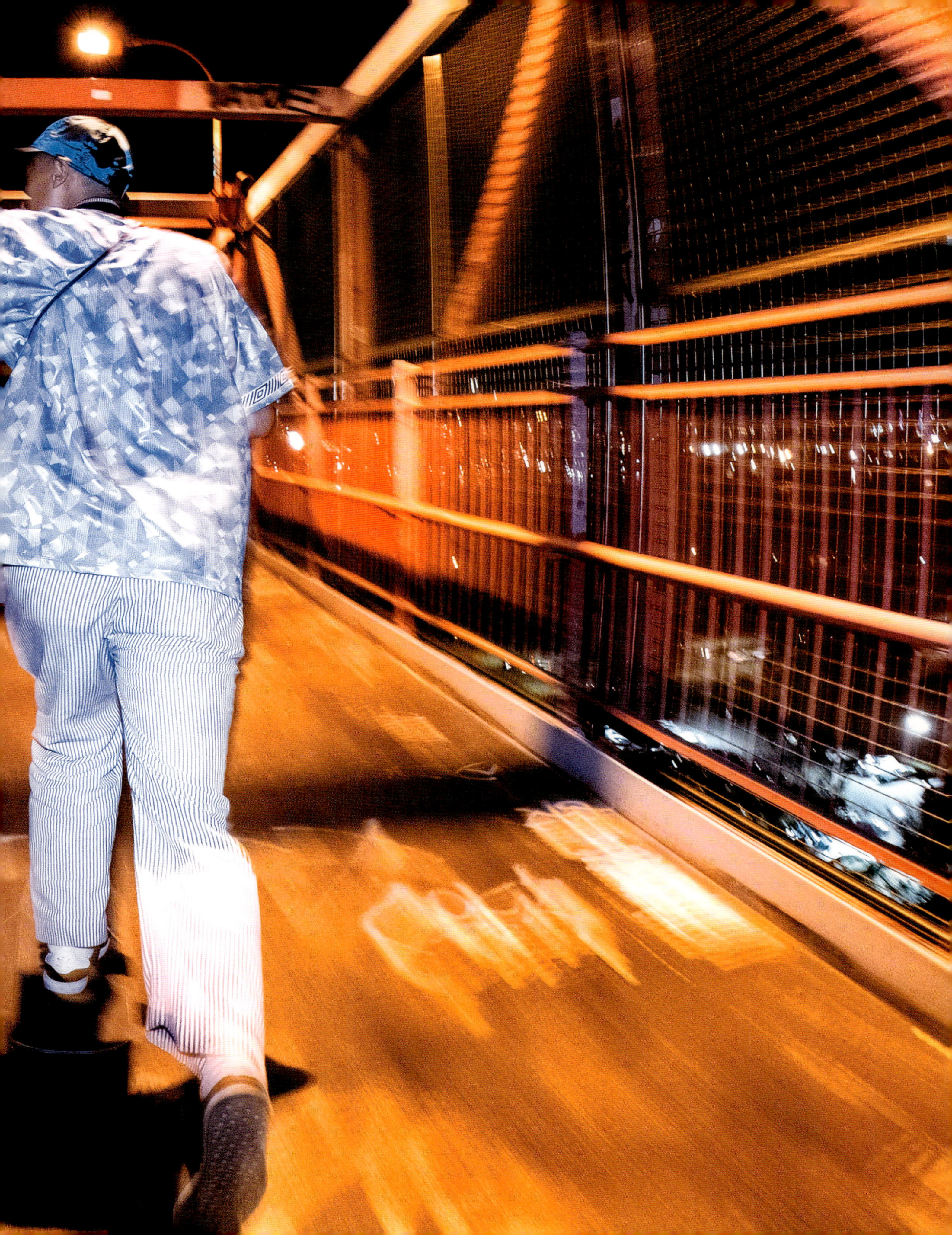

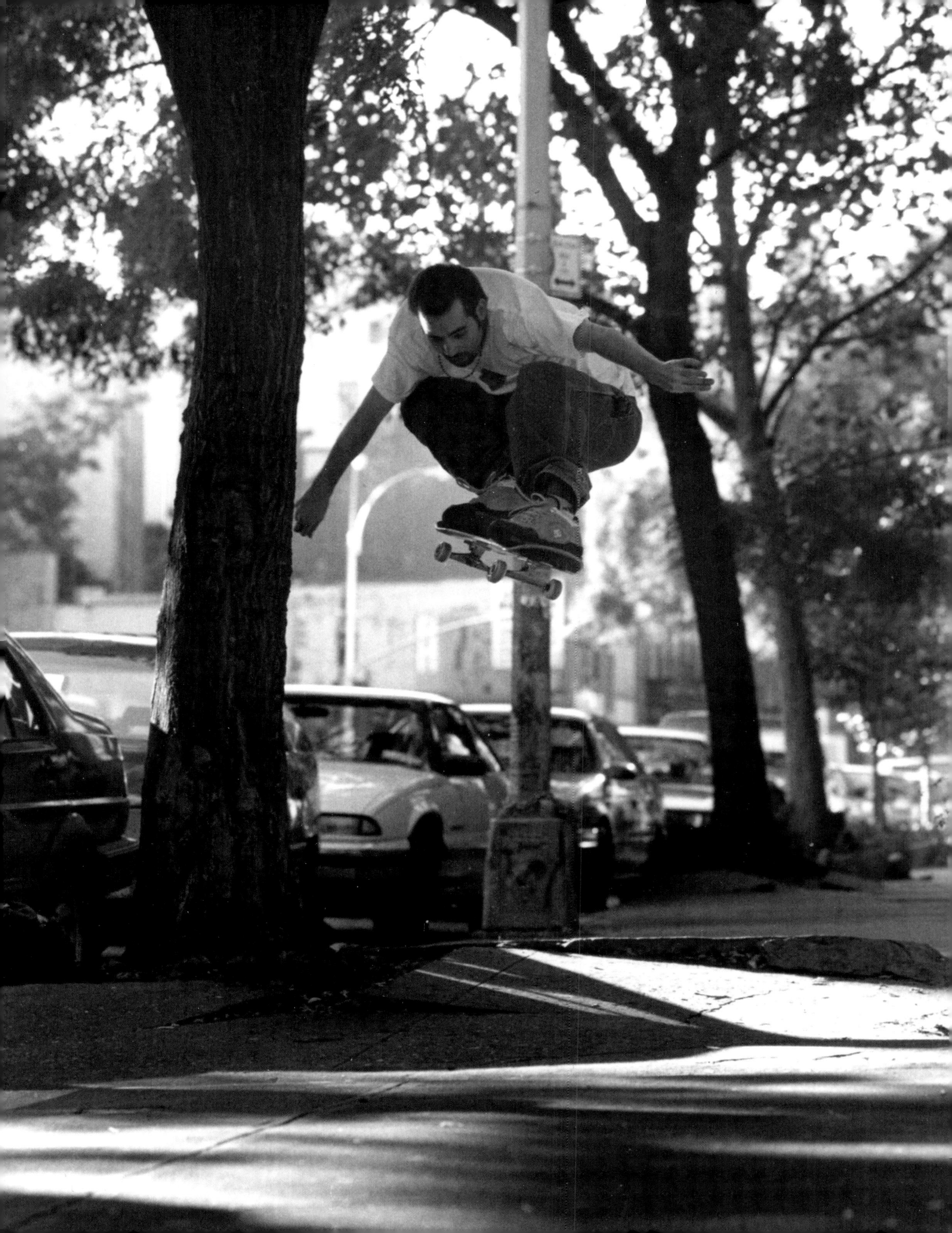

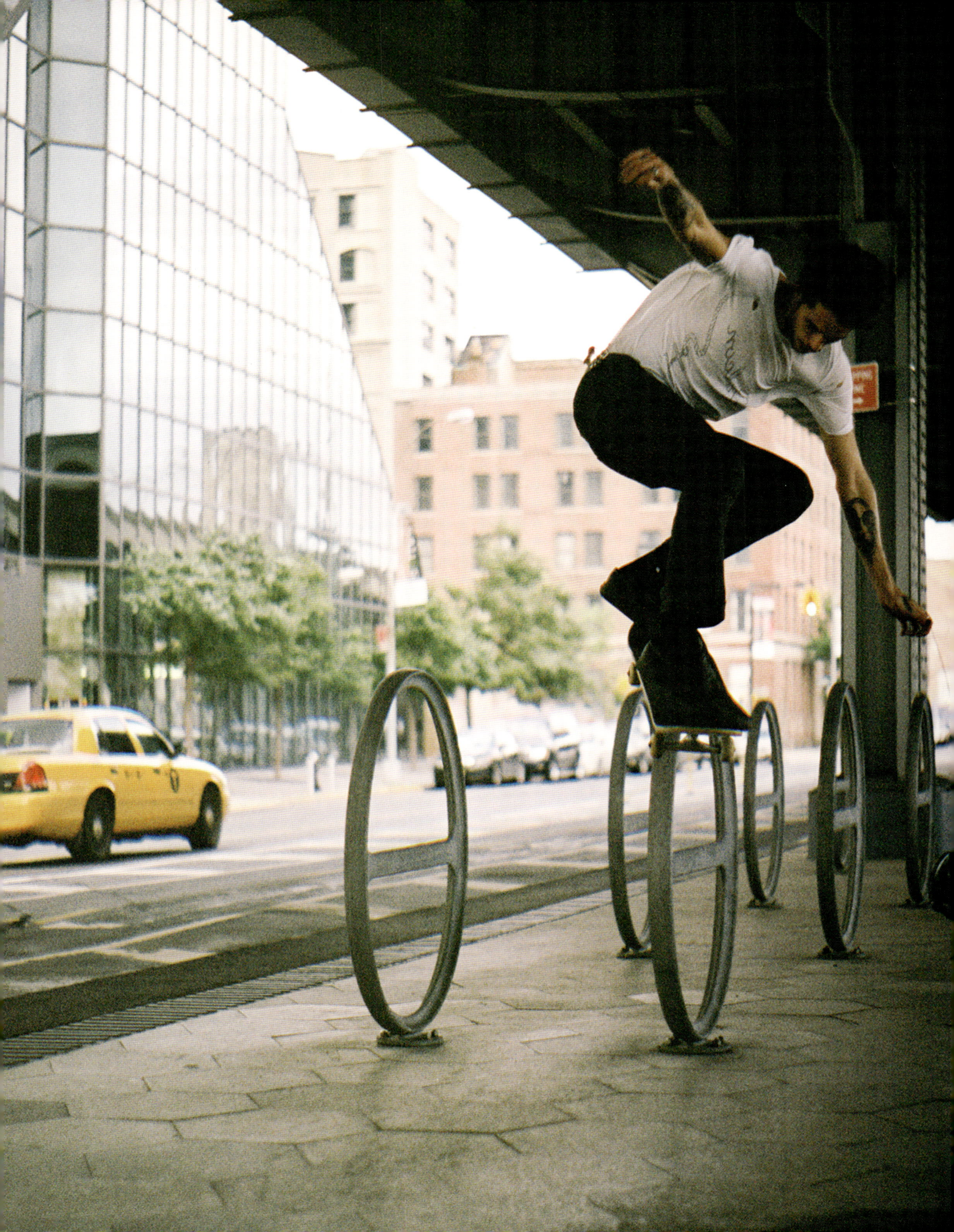

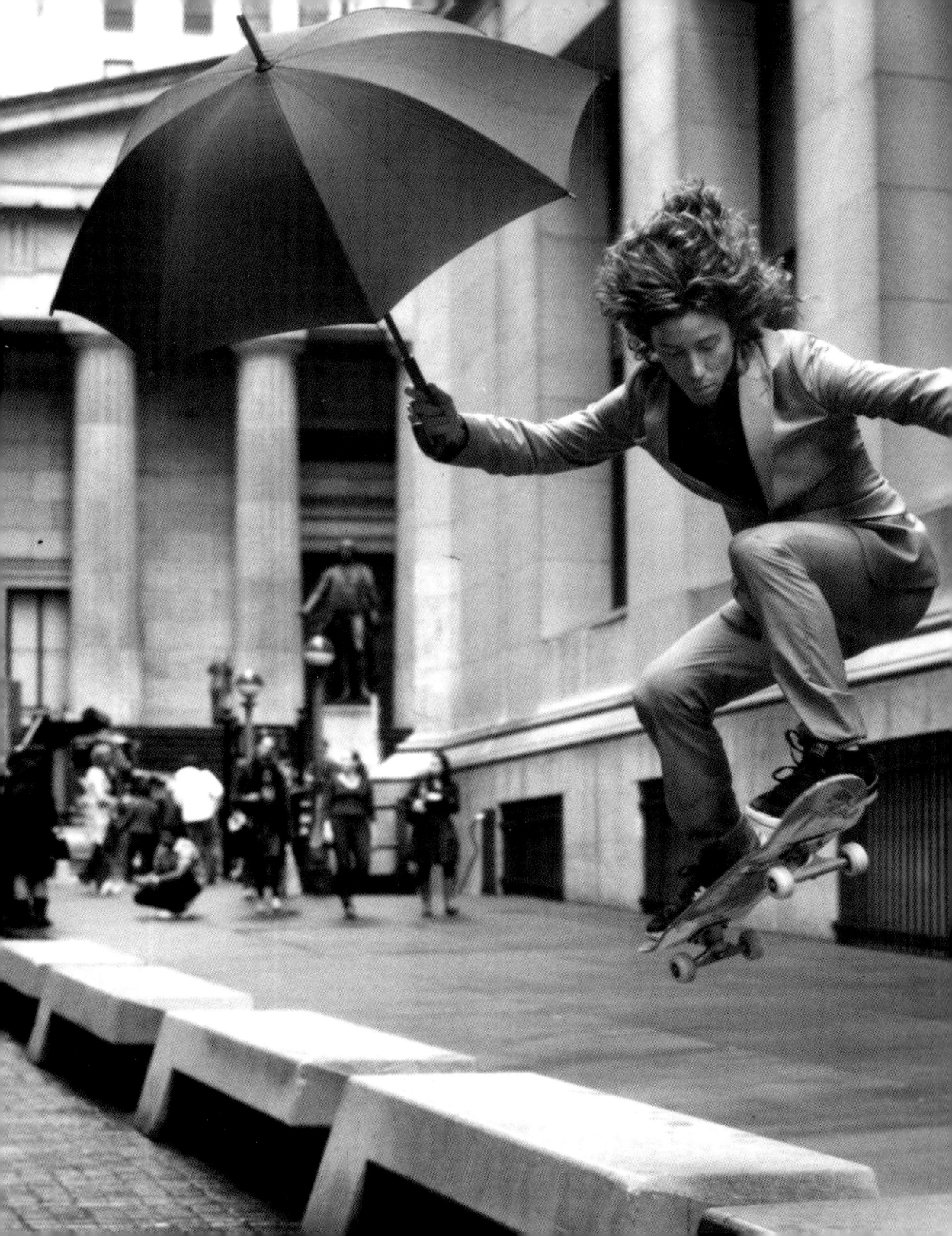

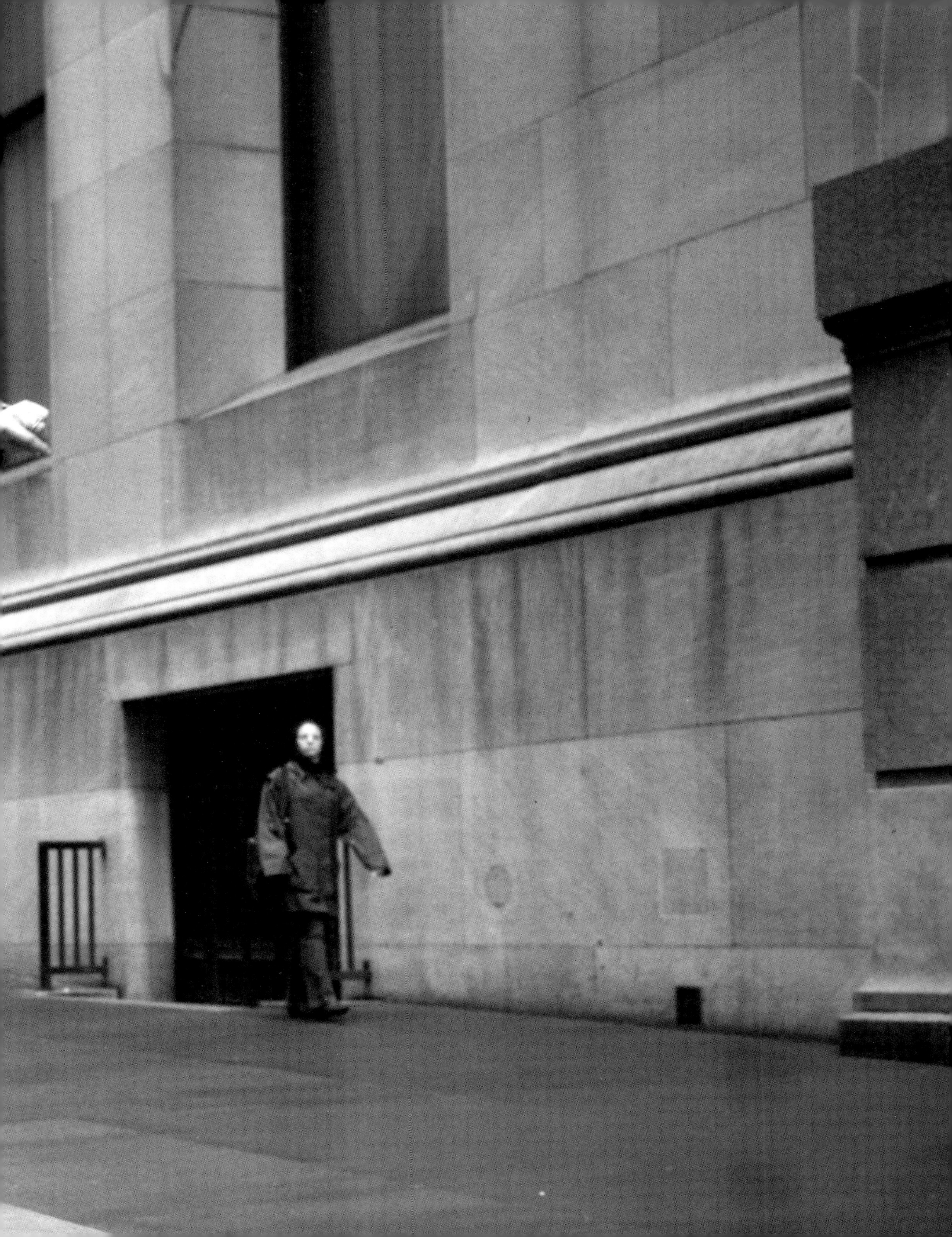

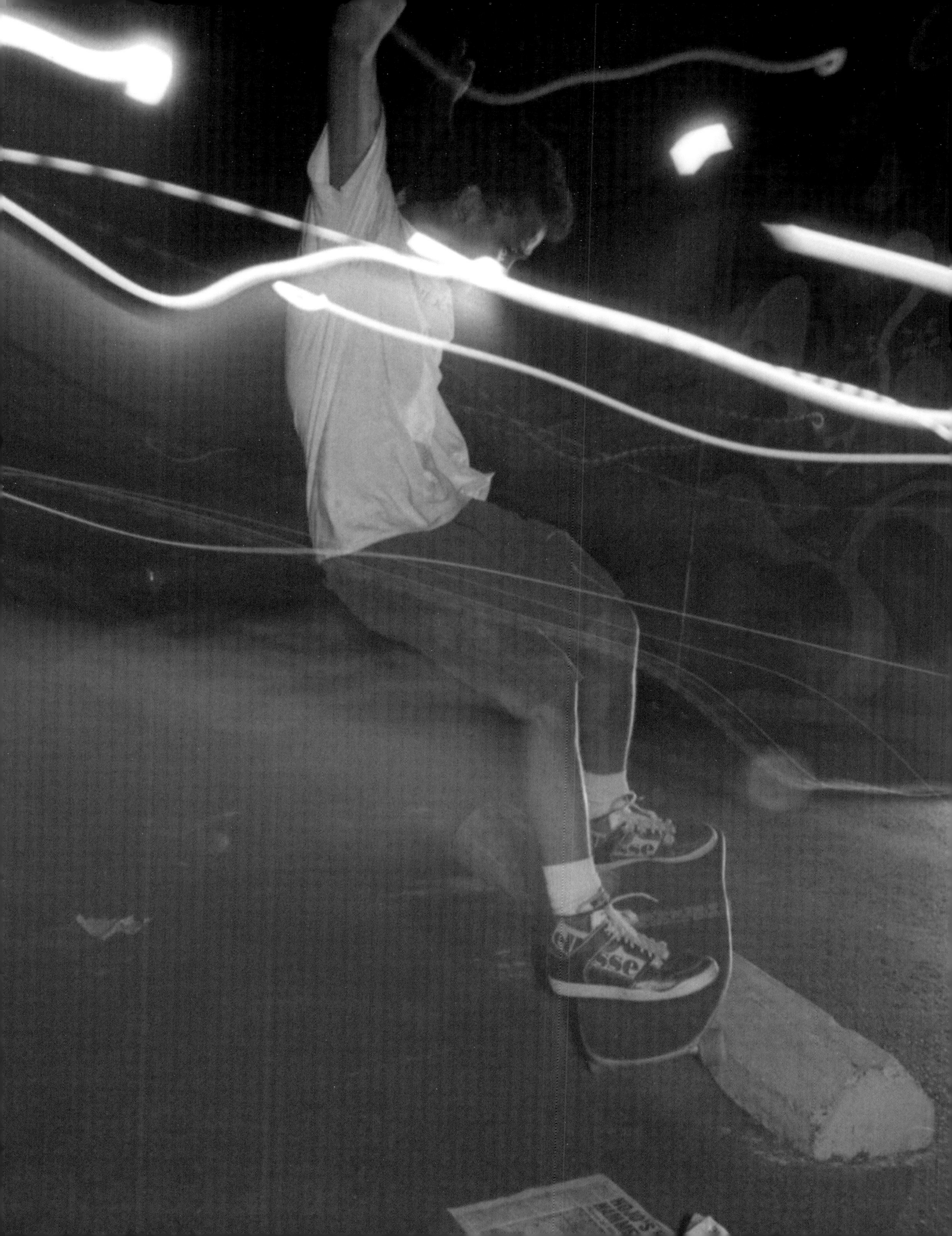

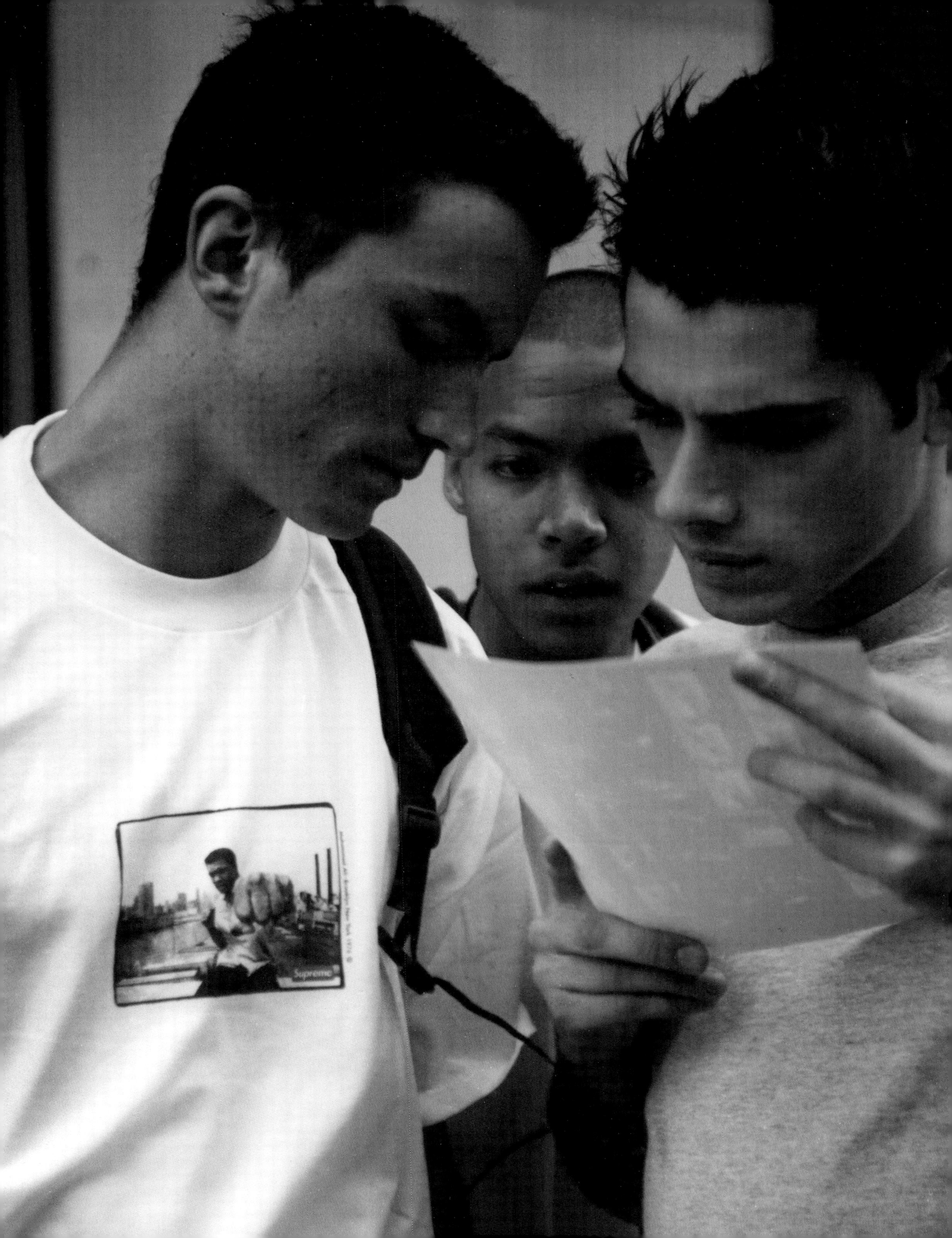

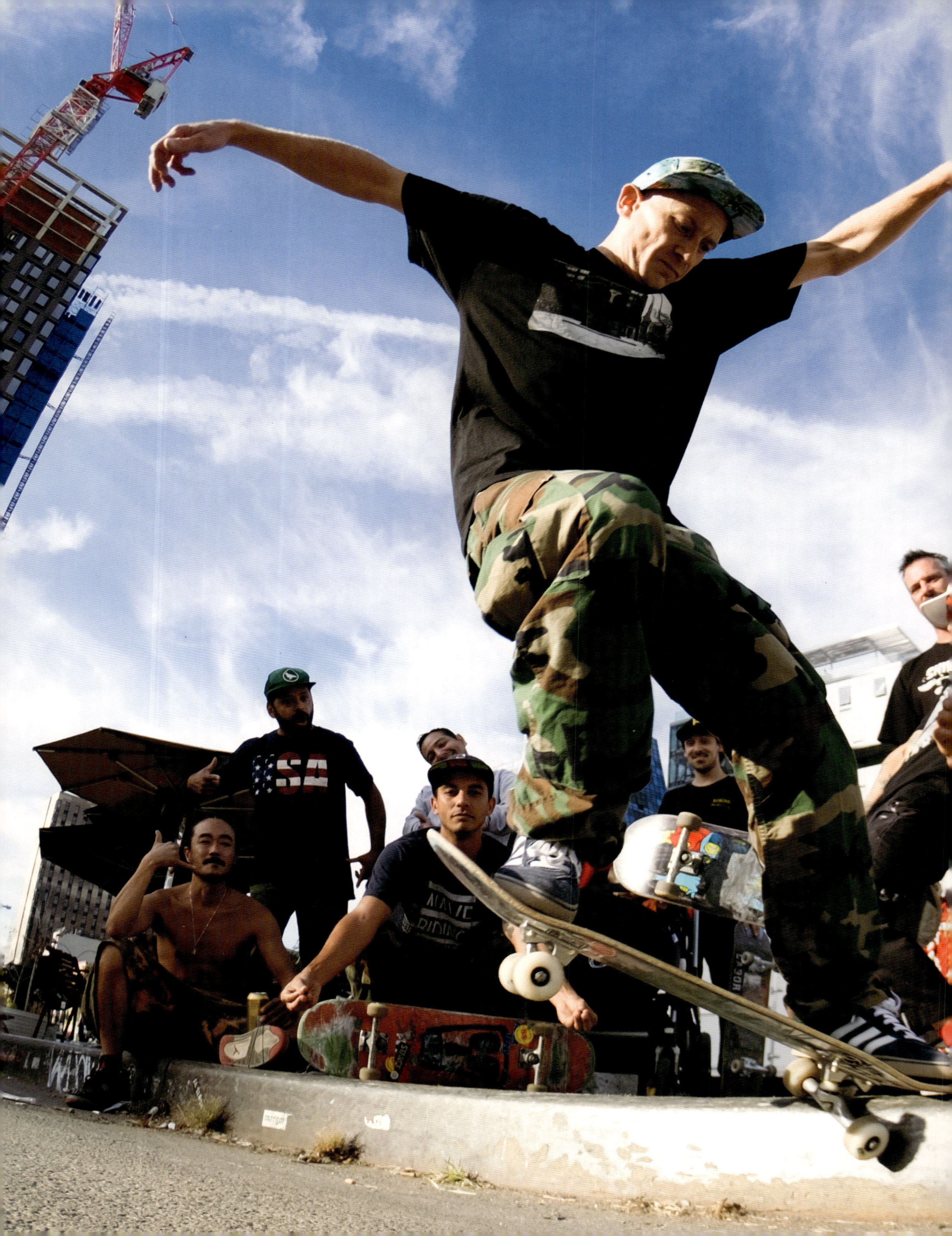

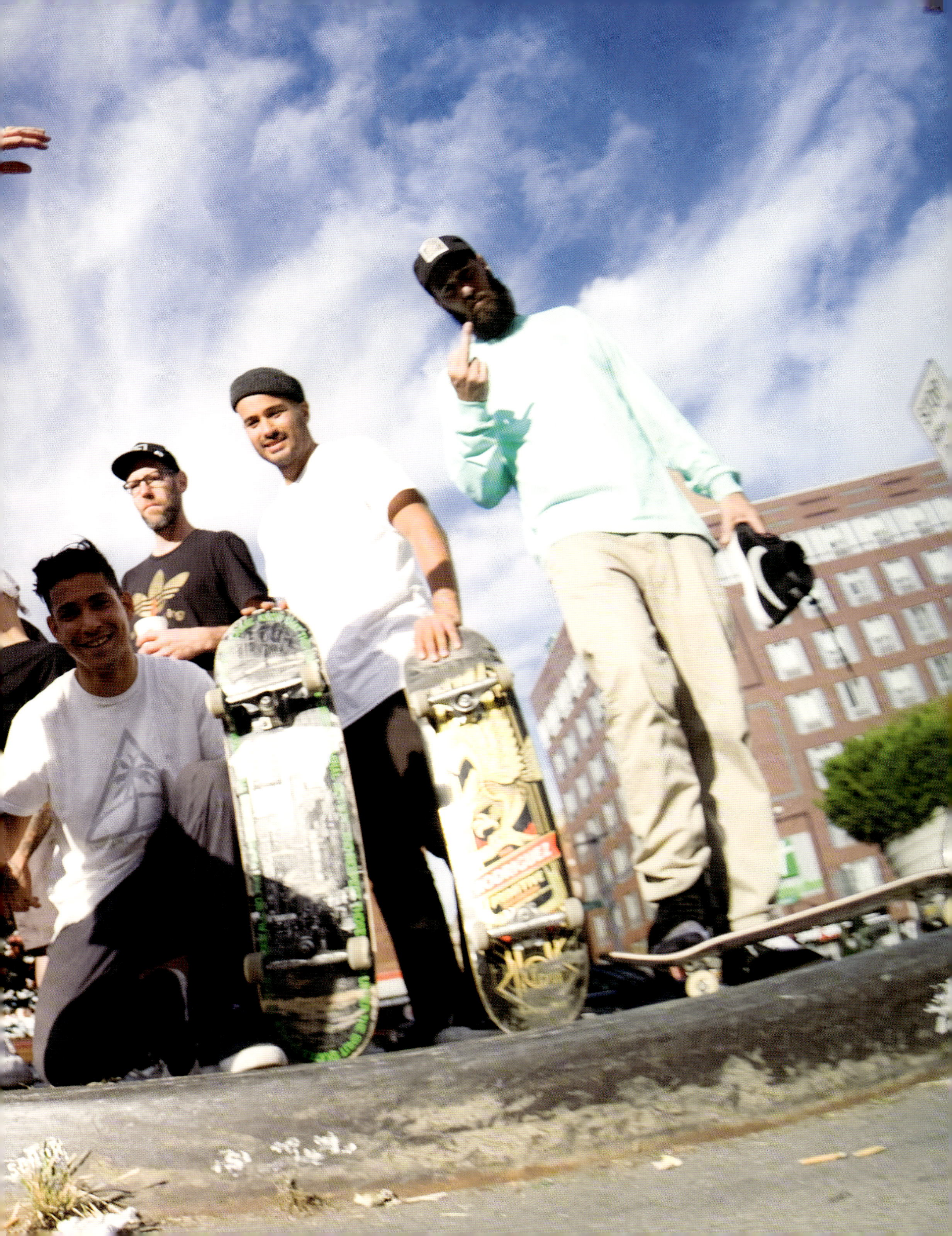

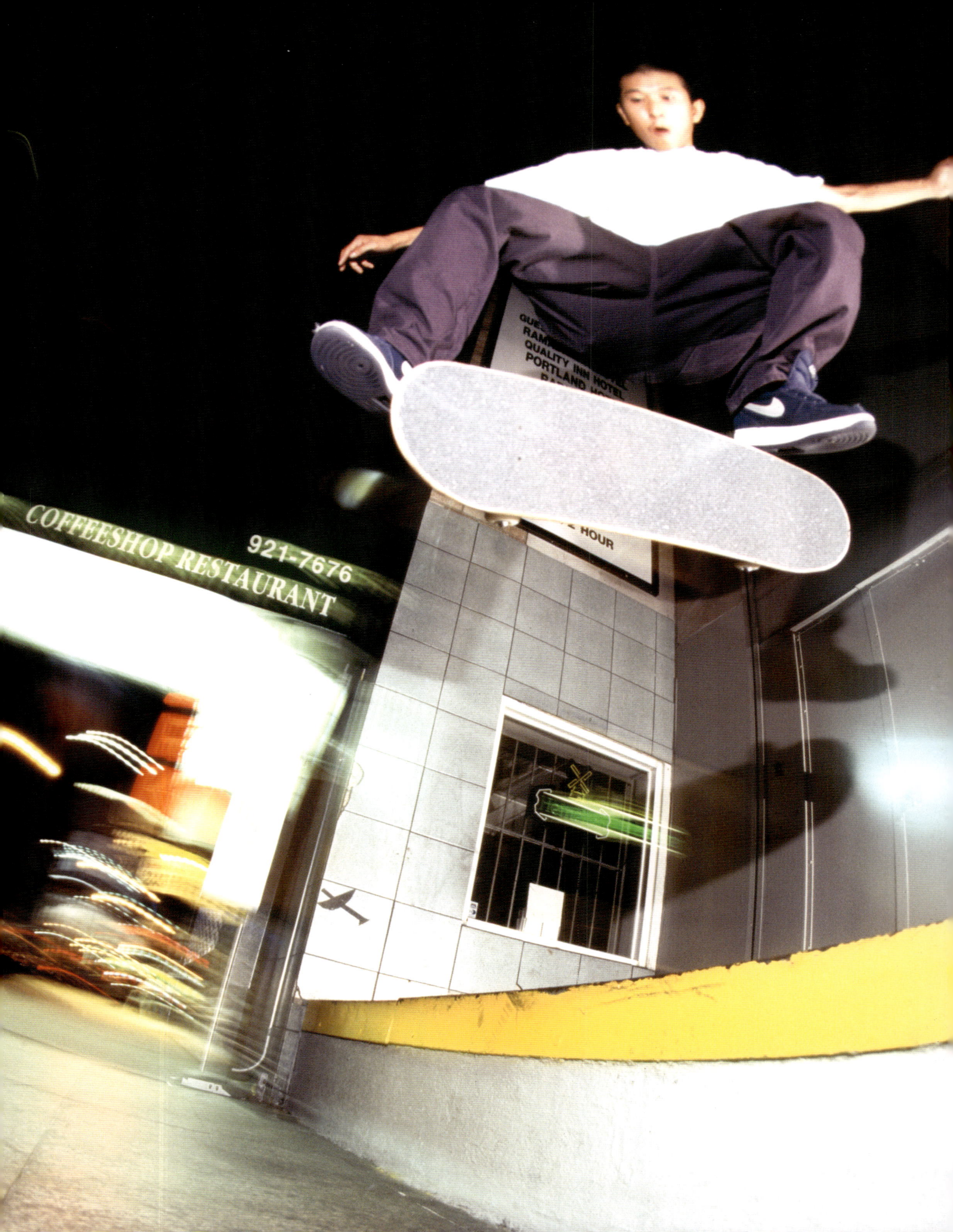
COFFEESHOP RESTAURANT
921-7676
QUALITY INN HOTEL
HOUR

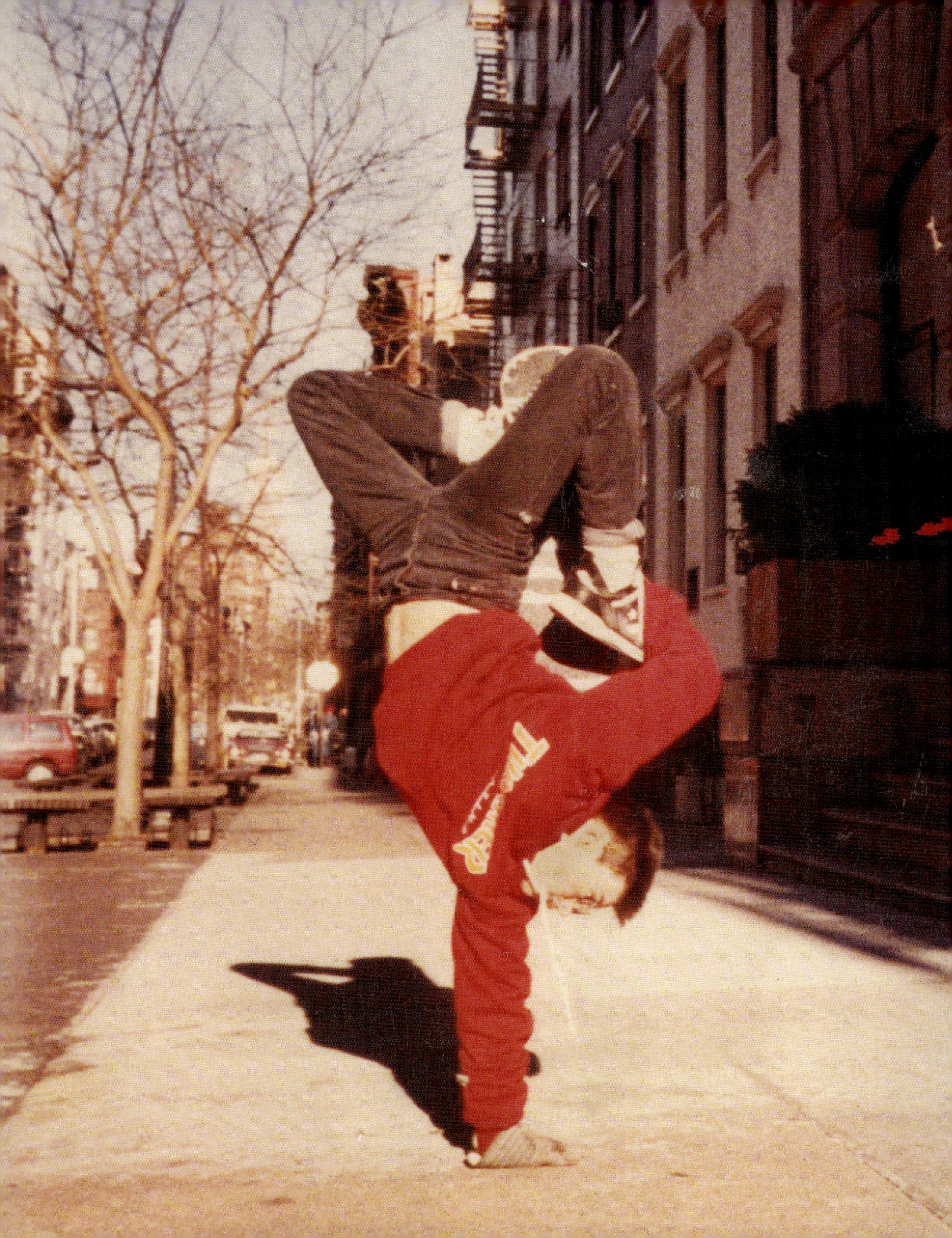

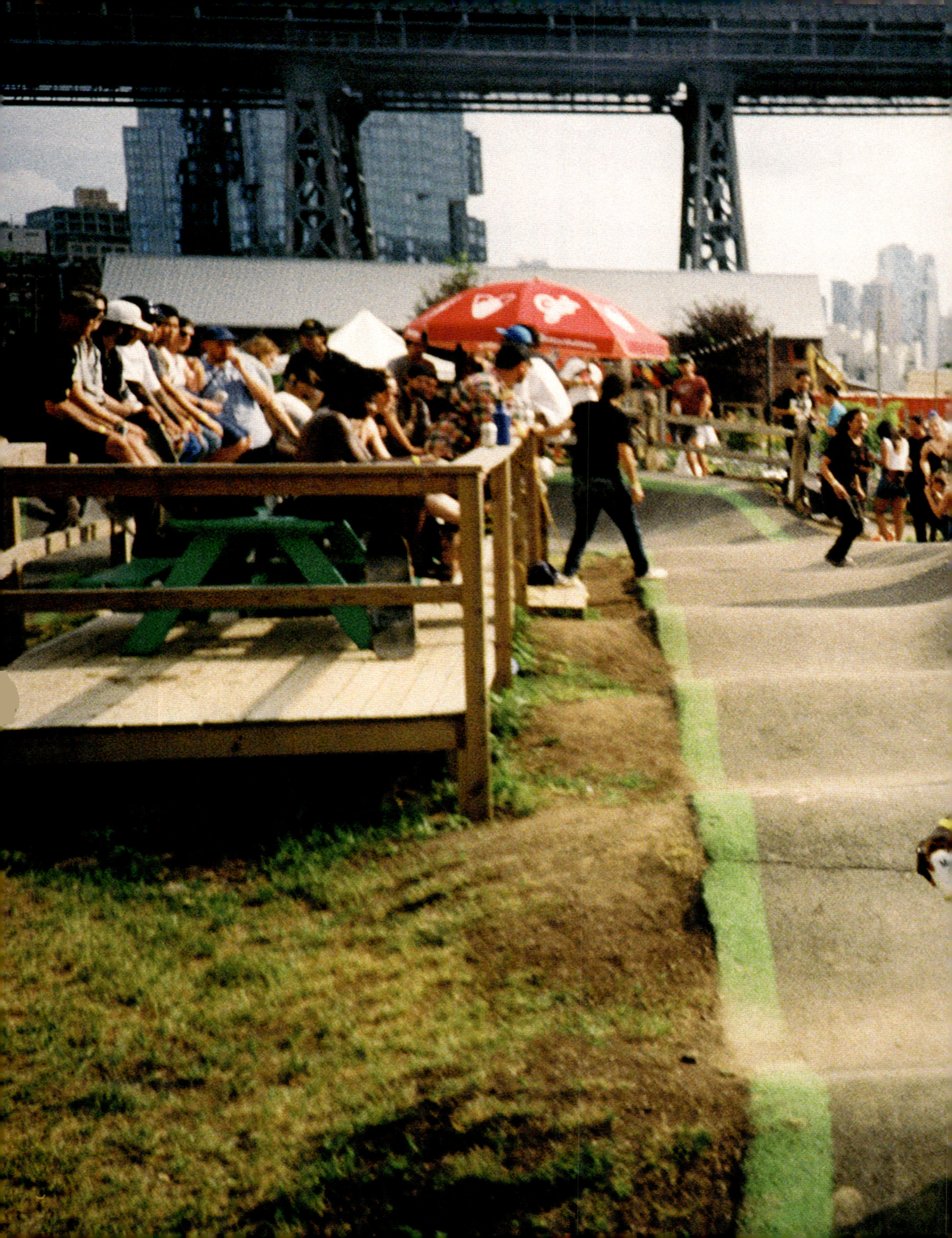

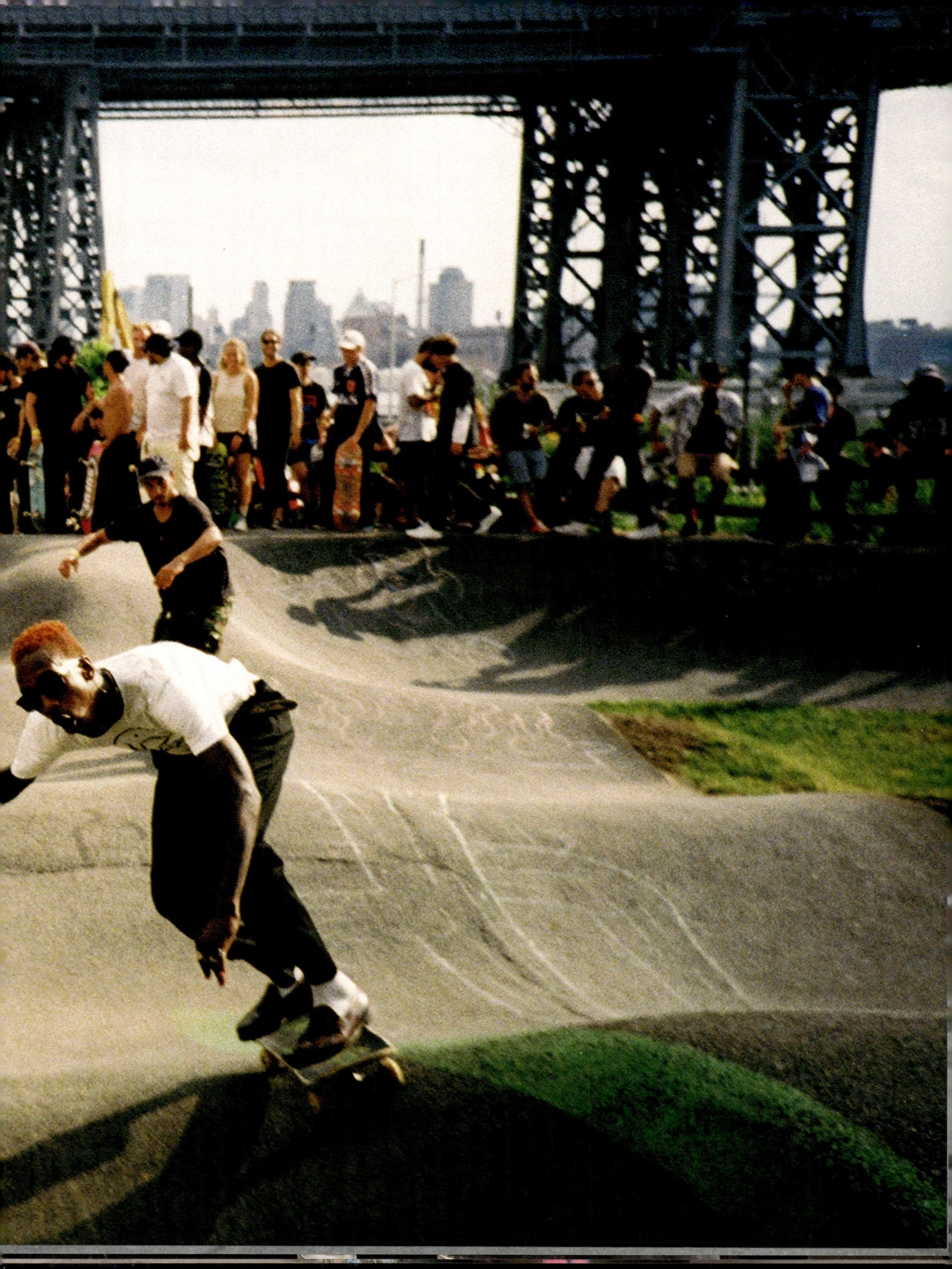

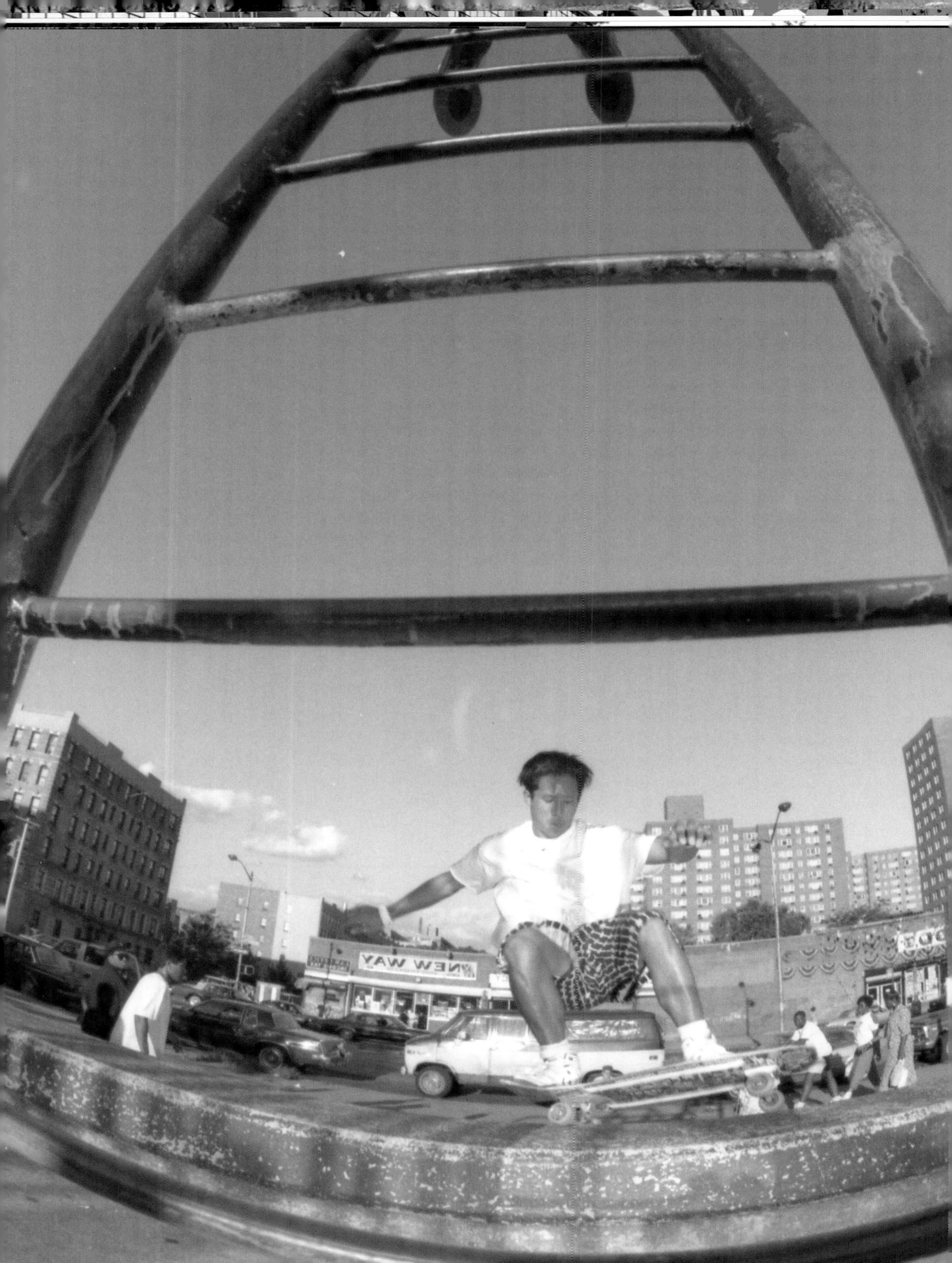
NEW WAY

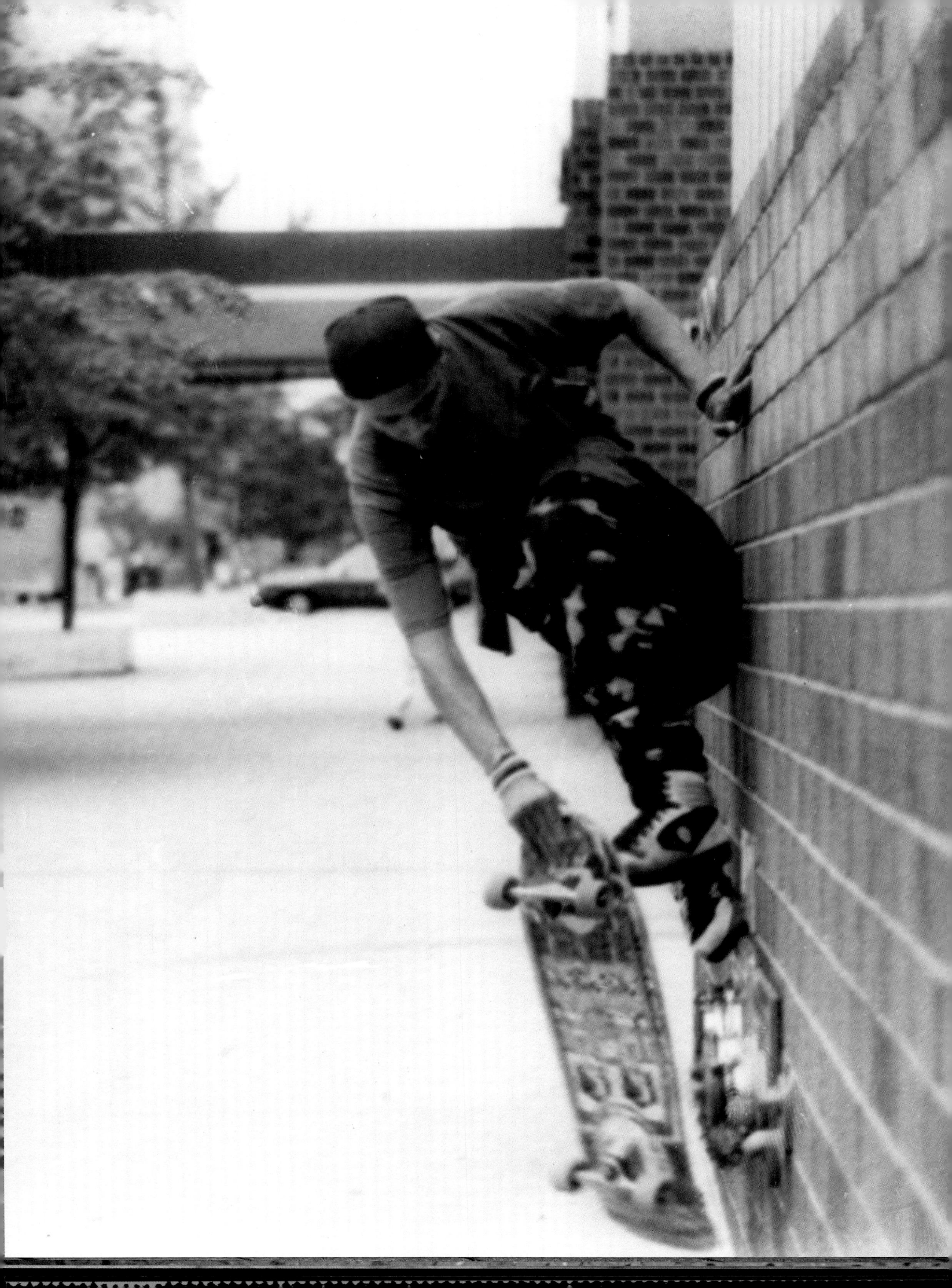

Edited and compiled by Alex Corporan, Andre Razo, and Ivory Serra
Creative Direction and Layout: Andre Razo
Assistant Photo Editor: Athena Currey, Dan Dobransky

This Tenth Anniversary Edition first published in 2021 by Salamander Street Ltd, 272 Bath Street, Glasgow, G2 4JR, United Kingdom (info@salamanderstreet.com).

ISBN: 9781914228223

10 9 8 7 6 5 4 3 2

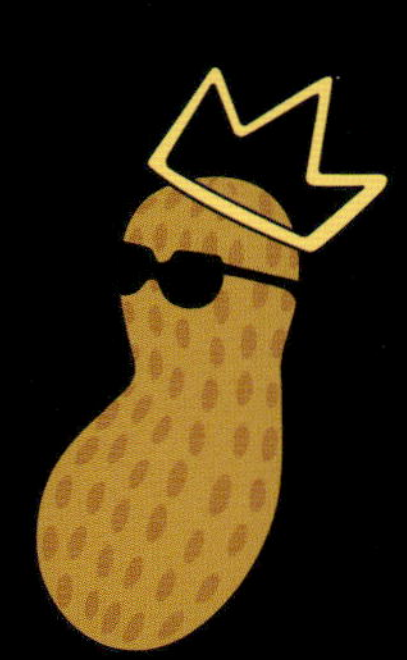